On Humane Governance

On Humane Governance

Toward a New Global Politics

**The World Order Models Project Report of the
Global Civilization Initiative**

RICHARD FALK

The Pennsylvania State University Press
University Park, Pennsylvania

Copyright © World Order Models Project 1995

Published in 1995 in the United States of America and Canada by
The Pennsylvania State University Press, University Park, PA 16802-1003

First published in 1995 by Polity Press
in association with Blackwell Publishers Ltd

Library of Congress Cataloging-in-Publication Data

Falk, Richard A.
    On humane governance : toward a new global politics / Richard Falk.
        p.   cm.
    Includes bibliographical references and index.
    ISBN 0-271-01511-X (cloth)
    ISBN 0-271-01512-8 (paper)
    1. International organization.   2. International cooperation.
    3. International relations   I. Title.
    JX 1954.F249   1995
    320.1'2 — dc20   95–9338
                                                                        CIP

Typeset in 10 on 12 pt Times by CentraCet, Cambridge
Printed in Great Britain by TJ Press Ltd, Padstow, Cornwall

It is the policy of The Pennsylvania State University Press to use acid-free
paper for the first printing of all clothbound books. Publications on uncoated
stock satisfy minimum requirements of American National Standard for
Information Sciences — Permanence of Paper for Printed Library Materials,
ANSI Z39.48–1992.

Contents

PREFACE *by Saul Mendlovitz*   vii

ACKNOWLEDGMENTS   xv

INTRODUCTION   1

1   From Geopolitics to Humane Governance:
A Necessary Journey   9

2   A Triple Indictment of Inhumane Governance   47

3   Sovereignty: A Twisting Path from Modernism   79

4   The Democratizing Imperative   104

5   Security for Humane Governance   134

6   The Struggle against Globalization from Above   172

7   In Pursuit of Humane Governance: Building Hope in the
Coming Era of Geogovernance   207

8   The Essential Vision: A Normative Project to Achieve
Humane Governance   241

NOTES   256

SELECT BIBLIOGRAPHY   275

INDEX   278

Preface

In the fall of 1986, Georgi Shakhnazarov, former President (then Vice President) of the International Political Association and a special assistant to Mikhail Gorbachev, paid a visit to the World Order Models Project (WOMP) to discuss what he termed matters of "common concern." Discerning the changes which were about to take place in the Soviet Union and elsewhere, and possessing an impressive familiarity with WOMP materials, he felt that recent events were vindicating many WOMP policy objectives while obligating many in the global community to revisit the security doctrines which had authorized Cold War hostilities. In response to those conversations and the ensuing dialogue, WOMP initiated a program called The Global Civilization: Challenges for Democracy, Sovereignty and Security Project (GCP). The overriding purpose of the GCP was and is to contest conventional notions of international relations – notions which stress the pre-eminence of the states system and the inevitability of war as a means of resolving international disputes. Throughout its work, the GCP and its global consortium of institutional affiliates have maintained the need for alternative policies which promote the "world order values" of peace, economic well-being, social justice, ecological balance, and positive human identity.

A Steering Committee was organized, composed of individuals from the major regions of the globe and representing scholarly, diplomatic, mass media, and religious concerns. Two meetings of the Steering Committee were held in mid-1987 and the Spring of 1988 (Nyon, Switzerland) for the purposes of articulating the concept of humane governance and establishing a research agenda. Under its direction five workshops devoted to the principal domains of the project were held over a five-year period: The Coming Global Civilization: What Kind of Sovereignty? (Moscow, 1988); Deepening and Globalizing Democracy (Yokohama, 1990); Global Political Economy: Trends and Preferences (Cairo, 1990); Shaping Global Polity (South Bend, 1991); Toward a Just World Order for the Twenty-First Century (Harare, 1993).

Results from these workshops were promoted in part through a public education and dissemination program, but more especially through a wide range of WOMP-inspired publications. From the Moscow workshop came the volume: *Contending Sovereignties: Rethinking Political Community* (ed. Mendlovitz and Walker). Selected papers from the Yokohama workshop were published in Japanese under the editorship of Yoshikazu Sakamoto. Other papers from Moscow and Yokohama have been published in *Alternatives: Social Transformation and Humane Governance*, especially in the Spring 1991 issue; and two papers were published as Occasional Papers of the Center of International Studies, Princeton University. Another special issue of *Alternatives* (Spring 1994) was devoted to the Harare workshop. In addition, *The Post-bipolar World: North–South Autonomies* (New York: WOMP; Belgrade; Mrljes, 1995) is a report written by Radmila Nakarada on the basis of the meeting between GCP participants and African social scientists in Zimbabwe.

After five years of intensive work, it became clear that the richness and complexity of the issues which the GCP sought to investigate defied a group product. Thus, with the cooperation of the GCP Steering Committee and the other workshop participants, GCP Rapporteur Richard Falk was asked to arrange and compose a volume of GCP insights, but in his own voice. In response, Falk has written a provocative and seminal work of relevance to scholars, activists, government leaders and policy advisors.

On Humane Governance: Toward a New Global Politics crystallizes a variety of enduring concerns of WOMP and the GCP, especially the belief that the centrality of statist forms of world is eroding; that geopolitics is being replaced by geogovernance. In the "Introduction and Rationale" to WOMP's UN Study Group, a program which has been heavily influenced by the contents of this book, it is noted that while the state remains focal for many purposes, "non-state actors, non-territorial social and economic forces, and globally-organized media and communications networks are exerting a defining influence on the shaping of large-scale social behavior." Clearly, the structures which organize the peoples of the earth are moving in more integrative directions. "Geogovernance" is the term which we use to speak of this emergence.

However, this book is more than a description of global trends. In the spirit of WOMP, it represents a profound effort at integrating analytical and normative elements. The question for the GCP is not whether the world is moving toward geogovernance, but the extent to which that governance can be made more *humane*, more people-oriented, more focused on human rights and global demilitarization. The use of "humane governance" implies the use of human security as a normative premise and a frame of reference within which "world order values" can be vigorously pursued. In this pursuit, it is necessary to enter into dialogue with diplomats and academics; but also to be directly involved with the building and mobilizing of transnational social forces which will work to ensure human rights, democracy, economic reform, demilitarization and environmental care.

The world as we know it is facing critical challenges and uncertainties. Forces of global capital remain largely unaccountable to human needs. The violent rhetoric of the Cold War has given way to antagonisms of ethnic and religious origins. The spread of "conventional" war weapons continues unabated. Population demands continue to put great pressure on ecological systems. There is a need, now more than ever, for analysis which can clarify difficult situations and provide normative parameters for needed changes.

Richard Falk's book is not only an accounting of years of activity under WOMP and GCP auspices. It is not only a sophisticated investigation of current global trends. It is also a clarion call for persons at all levels of governance, including the transnational social movements, to seize the current moment of opportunity and work to make emerging forms of global governance more just, more humane, more secure for all the peoples of the world.

Saul Mendlovitz
Co-Director, World Order Models Project

AMONG THE PARTICIPATING INSTITUTES IN THE GCP PROCESS

Center for International Studies, Princeton University, Princeton, New Jersey, USA.
Center for the Study of Developing Societies, New Delhi, India.
Department of Peace and Conflict Research, Uppsala University, Uppsala, Sweden.
Instituto Latinoamericano de Estudios Transnacionales, Santiago, Chile.
International Foundation for Development Alternatives, Nyon, Switzerland.

International Peace Research Institute Meigaku (PRIME), Yokohama, Japan. Soviet Political Science Association, Moscow, Russia.

GCP STEERING COMMITTEE

Elise Boulding, USA; Professor (Emeritus) Dartmouth College; Former Secretary General, International Peace Research Association.

Richard Falk, USA; Albert G. Milbank Professor of International Law and Practice, Princeton University; Editorial Board, *American Journal of International Law*; Project Rapporteur.

Elisabeth Gerle, Sweden; Pastor; Co-Director, The Great Peace Journey; Visiting Scholar, Princeton Theological Seminary; Performing Artist.

David Held, UK; Professor, Open University; Editor, Polity Press.

Saul H. Mendlovitz, USA; Dag Hammarskjöld Professor of Peace and World Order Studies, Rutgers University Law School; Editor, *Alternatives: Social Transformation and Humane Governance*; Steering Committee Chairperson.

Radmila Nakarada, Yugoslavia; Senior Fellow, Institute for European Studies; Research Council Member, World Futures Studies Federation; Advisory Research Panel, Transnational Foundation for Peace and Future Research; Editor, *Alternatives: Social Transformation and Humane Governance*.

Marc Nerfin, Switzerland; President, International Foundation for Development Alternatives; Member, Advisory Editorial Committee, *Development Dialogue*; Associate Member, Third World Forum, Cairo.

Maria de Lourdes Pintasilgo, Portugal; Former Minister to the European Economic Council; Former Prime Minister of Portugal.

Yoshikazu Sakamoto, Japan; Professor Emeritus, University of Tokyo; Former Director, PRIME; Former Secretary General, International Peace Research Association; Editor, *Alternatives: Social Transformation and Humane Governance*.

Georgi Shakhnazarov, Commonwealth of Independent States; Director, Center for Global Programs (Gorbachev Foundation); Foundation for Social and Political Studies; President, Russian Political Science Association; Corresponding Member of the Academy of Sciences.

Dhirubhai Sheth, India; Senior Fellow, Centre for the Study of Developing Societies; Editor, *Alternatives: Social Transformation and Humane Governance*; Board Member, World Order Models Project.

Vandana Shiva, India; Coordinator, Research Foundation for Science, Technology and Natural Resource Policy, India; Consultant, United Nations University.

Mohamed Sid-Ahmed, Egypt; Author and Columnist, *Al-Ahram*.

William Smirnov, Commonwealth of Independent States; Vice President, Russian Political Science Association; Vice President, Executive Committee, International Political Science Association; Senior Fellow, Institute for State and Law.

Juan Somavia, Chile; Ambassador of Chile to the United Nations; Current
President, Economic and Social Council, United Nations; Former Director,
Instituto Latinoamericano de Estudios Transnacionales.

R.B.J. Walker, Canada; Associate Professor, Department of Political Science,
University of Victoria; Editor, *Alternatives: Social Transformation and
Humane Governance.*

Peter Wallensteen, Sweden; Director, Department of Peace and Conflict
Research, Uppsala University.

STEERING COMMITTEE COORDINATOR

Lester Edwin J. Ruiz, Philippines; Director, Transnational Academic Program,
World Order Models Project; Assistant Professor, Peace Research Institute,
International Christian University, Tokyo.

SPONSORING ORGANIZATIONS AND INSTITUTES FOR
WORKSHOPS

The World Order Models Project gratefully acknowledges the following institutional and personal sponsors for the GCP workshops:

Institute of World Economy and International Relations, Moscow: Evgeni
Primakov.

International Foundation for Development Alternatives, Nyon: Marc Nerfin.

Kanagawa (Yokohama) Prefecture: Governor Kazuji Nagasu.

Kroc Institute for International Peace Studies, Notre Dame: Robert Johansen.

Zimbabwe Foreign Ministry, Harare: Nathan Shamuyarira.

WORKSHOP PARTICIPANTS OTHER THAN THE STEERING
COMMITTEE

*The Coming Global Civilization: What Kind of Sovereignty? (October
10–16, 1988, Moscow)*

Vladimir Askenov, USSR, Soviet Peace Fund; Alexi Arbatov, USSR, Insti-
tute of World Economy and International Relations; Mary Catherine Bate-
son, USA, George Mason University; Walden Bello, Philippines/USA,
Institute for Food and Development Policy; Jagdish Bhagwati, India/USA,
Columbia University; Joseph Camilleri, Australia, Department of Politics,
La Trobe University; Padma Desai, India/USA, Columbia University; John
Dunn, UK, King's College, Cambridge University; Ivan Frolov, USSR,
Academy of Sciences of the USSR; Vladimir Iloros, USSR, Institute of
World Economy and International Relations; Gregorii Ilosin, USSR,

Department of Philosophy, Moscow State University; Jose Miguel Insulza, Chile, Instituto Latinoamericano de Estudios Transnacionales; Robert C. Johansen, USA, Institute for International Peace Studies, University of Notre Dame; Alexander Kislov, USSR, Institute of World Economy and International Relations; Victor Kuznetsov, USSR, Institute of World Economy and International Relations; Ali A. Mazrui, Kenya/USA, Center for Afroamerican and African Studies, University of Michigan; Patricia Mische, USA, Global Education Associates; Rein Mullerson, USSR, Institute of State and Law, USSR Academy of Sciences; Ashis Nandy, India, Centre for the Study of Developing Societies; Alexander Nikitin, USSR, Institute of United States and Canada; Alexander Ognev, USSR, Institute of World Economy and International Relations; Elghis Pozdhykov, USSR, Institute of World Economy and International Relations; Evgeni Primakov, USSR, Institute of World Economy and International Relations; Jan Pronk, Netherlands, Netherlands Parliament; Georgi Shakhnazarov, USSR, Soviet Political Science Association; Heinrich Siegmann, Federal Republic of Germany, Max Planck Society; Gregorii Tunkin, USSR, Soviet Association of International Law; C. G. Weeramantry, Australia, Faculty of Law, Monash University; Shang Zhi, People's Republic of China, Beijing Foreign Studies University.

Deepening and Globalizing Democracy (March 17–22, 1990, Yokohama)

Kiichi Fujiwara, Japan, Institute of Social Sciences, University of Tokyo; Osamu Fujiwara, Japan, Tokyo Ketzai University; Konstanty Gebert, Poland, *Po Protsu Weekly*; Robert C. Johansen, USA, Institute for International Peace Studies, University of Notre Dame; Jose Alvaro Moises, Brazil, Center for Contemporary Cultural Studies; Kazuo Ohgushi, Japan, Department of International Studies, International Christian University; Hitoshi Ohnishi, Japan, Faculty of Law, Tohoku University; Kwon Sang Park, South Korea, *The Sisa Journal*; Suthy Prasartset, Thailand, Faculty of Economics, Chulalongkorn University; Jomo K. Sundaram, Malaysia, Faculty of Economics and Administration, University of Malaya; Hi Jun Tak, South Korea, Korean Voluntary Arbitration Council; Keizo Yamawaki, Japan, International Peace Research Institute Meigaku.

Shaping Global Polity (April 4–8, 1991, Notre Dame)

John Attanasio, USA, Regan Director, Kroc Institute for International Peace Studies; David Cortright, USA, Kroc Institute for International Peace Studies; Randall Forsberg, USA, Executive Director, Institute for Defense and Disarmament Studies; Claire Greensfelder, USA, Greenpeace; The Most Reverend Thomas J. Gumbleton, USA, Bishop of Detroit; Robert C. Johansen, USA, Institute for International Peace Studies, University of Notre Dame; Joanne Landy, USA, Campaign for Peace and Democracy; George Lopez, USA, Kroc Institute for International Peace Studies; Robert

S. McNamara, USA; Robert Musil, USA, Director of Policy and Program, Physicians for Social Responsibility; Vladimir Petrovsky, Commonwealth of Independent States, Undersecretary General of the United Nations; Amin Saikal, USA, Center of International Studies, Princeton University; Elaine Scarry, USA, Department of English, Harvard University; Maria Stern-Pettersson, USA, World Order Models Project; Franklin Wallin, USA, Joyce Mertz-Gilmore Foundation.

Toward a Just World Order for the Twenty-First Century (January 28–February 2, 1993, Harare, Zimbabwe)

Ana Maria Alonso, USA, Department of Anthropology, University of Arizona; Thelma Awori, Zimbabwe, UNDP; Emma Chikuturudzi, Zimbabwe, Ministry of Foreign Affairs; N. T. Goche, Zimbabwe, Ministry of Foreign Affairs; Johan Galtung, France; Robert C. Johansen, USA, Institute for International Peace Studies, University of Notre Dame; Samuel Kim, USA; Ibbo Mandaza, Zimbabwe, SAPES; Ali Mazrui, USA, State University of New York at Binghamton; M. Mbeki, Zimbabwe, Ministry of Foreign Affairs; Toshiki Mogami, Japan, International Christian University; Alice Mogwe, Botswana; G. Mudenda, Zimbabwe, Ministry of Foreign Affairs; B. Muganiwa, Zimbabwe, Ministry of Foreign Affairs; E. G. Mukonoweshuro, Zimbabwe, University of Zimbabwe; M. W. Murphree, Zimbabwe, Ministry of Foreign Affairs; Paul Nyathi, Zimbabwe, Ministry of Foreign Affairs; Hasu Patel, Zimbabwe, University of Zimbabwe, G. Punnungwe, Zimbabwe, Ministry of Foreign Affairs, A. Rukobo, Zimbabwe, Director, Institute of Development Studies; Nathan Shamuyarira, Foreign Minister of Zimbabwe; Simona Sharoni, USA; Violet Siguake, Zimbabwe, Ministry of Foreign Affairs; Nyoni Sithembiso, Zimbabwe, Ministry of Foreign Affairs; Maria Stern-Pettersson, USA, World Order Models Project; Yash Tandon, Zimbabwe.

Acknowledgments

This report, more than is normally the case with scholarly enterprise, is the outcome of collaborative effort. My role, indeed, was that of "rapporteur" for the GCP Steering Committee identified in the preface. Because the issues are complex, the context dynamic, and consensus elusive, and because we shared a dislike of "committee language," it was felt by all of us that it would be better for me to have the freedom (and the responsibility) to act like an author. At the same time, acknowledgments are meant here in an organic fashion.

From the outset of the Global Civilization Project each stage was planned after consultation with other participating scholars and institutions. The meetings in Moscow (on sovereignty), Yokohama (on democracy), South Bend/Notre Dame (on security), and Kodama, Zimbabwe (on WOMP in general) were formative. Chapter drafts were discussed at various stages by a writing committee composed of members of the Steering Committee. Saul Mendlovitz, in particular, was a pervasive presence with respect to all aspects of the process from inception to completion.

I owe a particular debt of gratitude to Rob (R. B. J.) Walker and Kevin Frost for their heroic editorial work on the penultimate draft, doing their very best to make the manuscript as readable as possible without sacrificing the texture of analysis, argument, and prescription. I am also thankful to David Held, both for his intellectual inspiration at various stages and for his role as enthusiastic publisher. Indeed, each member of the Steering Committee contributed in distinctive ways that helped make the long ordeal of authorship less burdensome.

I want also to thank the WOMP office, especially Robert Zuber, for valuable logistical help. As usual, I was hopelessly dependent on my gifted secretary, assistant, and friend, June Garson, who has been impressively responsive to the many unexpected challenges associated with completing this manuscript. The Center of International Studies, my home base and one of the academic sponsors of the project, has been supportive all along, and I thank especially its former Director, Henry Bienen, for his original interest and willingness to make an institutional commitment to this work. I am also most grateful to Cheryl Kim, my former research assistant, for an especially sensitive reading of an earlier draft; most of her suggestions have been adopted. In the final stages of preparation, my current research assistant Astrid Arraras has been most obligingly helpful. I am also deeply indebted to Ann Bone, whose meticulous and sensitive copy-editing has saved me from many lapses. And finally, Elisabeth Gerle has been my close companion in the entire process both professionally and personally, adding joy and love to the whole undertaking.

In addition to those already noted in the Preface and above, the scope and magnitude of the project has required and received indispensable funding from a series of sources. We are most indebted to our individual donors who over the years of WOMP have provided us with encouragement and sustained our morale, as well as generously given financial help. Several foundations, in particular the Ford Foundation, the John D. and Catherine T. MacArthur Foundation, and Joyce Mertz-Gilmore Foundation have supplied funding at crucial stages of the Global Civilization Project. Also, the government of Zimbabwe, particularly by way of the Ministry of Foreign Affairs, supported a workshop held mainly in Kodoma, but also in Harare. And above all we wish to acknowledge the generosity and commitment of Ira and Miriam Wallach. Over these years their contributions have provided a significant portion of the monies for WOMP activities, making it possible to continue our ongoing program of research, education, and policy outreach, as well as to follow through to the end with the Global Civilization Project. Their steadfastness and wise counsel have bolstered our morale throughout these decades, providing us with some of their own inspiration. It is with profound gratitude that the entire WOMP family, but especially the main leader of the effort, Saul Mendlovitz, expresses thanks on this occasion.

RICHARD FALK

Introduction

Prospects and Projects

Several features of the present historical setting shape this enquiry. The world is moving rapidly toward a more integrated economic, cultural, and political reality, a set of circumstances identified here as *geogovernance*. One consequence of this trend is to diminish the capacity of the sovereign territorial state, as a political actor, to shape the history of humanity, and thereby to dominate *geopolitics*. The main set of forces now challenging the state is associated with the operation of the global market, creating a new capital-driven geopolitics, but these forces remain largely concealed as political actors. A subsidiary set of forces, variants of the politics of identity, is causing fragmentation of many states, and is a further factor producing a declining governmental capacity at the level of the sovereign state. On this basis, the probable world of the early twenty-first century will be a variant of geogovernance that is appropriately regarded as "inhumane governance," one that maintains continuity with the most recent stages of the state system.

This inquiry relies upon several criteria to classify this probable form of geogovernance as one of inhumane governance. "Inhumane governance" is assessed in relation to the following five dimensions of international political life:

- the most disadvantaged 20 percent of the world's population are not provided with adequate food, shelter, health care, clothing, education, housing;
- the most socially and culturally vulnerable identities (for instance,

indigenous peoples, gays and lesbians, women and children) are denied full protection of human rights;
- there is no tangible, cumulative progress toward the abolition of war as a social institution;
- there is insufficient effort in relation to the protection and restoration of the environment in its various aspects, resulting in the deterioration of the health of those alive and an impairment of the life prospects of unborn generations;
- there is a failure to achieve a dramatic growth of transnational democracy for the years ahead, and little progress with respect to the extension of the primary democratic practices of respect for others, of accountability by political leaders as well as by market executives, managers, and traders, and of participation by the peoples or their freely elected representatives in critical arenas of decision.

The project to supersede inhumane governance is identified here as a commitment to establish geogovernance in the form of "humane governance," that is, a set of social, political, economic, and cultural arrangements that is committed to rapid progress along these five dimensions of assessment. The emergence of humane governance will depend on the dramatic growth of transnational democracy, and on the extension of the primary democratic practices. It will also depend on an evolving sense of allegiance to global civil society and on the plausibility of humane governance as a political priority commitment for women and men from all parts of the world. It is doubtful whether such a commitment to the establishment of humane governance will be wide and deep enough unless it engages both the political imagination of many persons of diverse cultural, ethnic, class, and gender identities, and is reinforced by supportive religious and ethical interpretations of the meaning of life.

Western Triumphalism and Human Suffering

The mood of exhilaration that accompanied the end of the Cold War and Soviet collapse now seems a dim and distant memory. It requires an effort of will to acknowledge the brief, yet vivid, glow of political expectation it created. There has been an abrupt awakening to the realities of the new era, including the harsh human costs associated with speeding the transition from state socialism to market constitutionalism and the realization that many acute causes of human distress in the world had virtually nothing to do with the East/West axis of struggle or with the sterile choice between Marxism-Leninism and globalizing capitalism.

Our point of departure must be this current historical setting, a period of transition, turmoil, acute humanitarian crises, and disillusion. As Samir Amin writes, "the historical drama of our epoch is situated precisely here, and has its roots in the failure of social consciousness to imagine positive and progressive alternatives."[1] Rajni Kothari, another leading thinker and committed activist, expresses the same dominant concern in even stronger language when he identifies the underlying torment of the moment as "a basic crisis of vision, a decline of engagement with utopias – in a sense, an end of 'alternatives' in the real and comprehensive sense of the term."[2]

This widespread sense of disillusion, some of the explanations for which will provide the themes of the first two chapters, provides the background for our struggle to fashion an alternative orientation and vision. An alternative to what? First of all, to disillusionment itself, and most substantively, to the prospect of and enthusiasm for a commercial globalism that is capital-driven, market-validated and media disseminated.

While alert to the failures of the past, this reaffirmation of a visionary politics builds on the best hopes of socialism, on various strands of green and feminist perspectives, on the great humanist premises of solidarity and decency, on the practices and discoveries of nonviolence in many distinct cultural settings, and on the more idealistic impulses associated with international law and the operation of international institutions. More specifically, it grows out of several decades of world order theorizing associated with the World Order Models Project and its belief that visions of an attainable preferred world are a necessary and practical part of a realistic politics.[3] As an expression of this rich heritage of visionary commitments, this report focuses on a quest for humane governance.

Chapters 3–7 depict the outlines of this quest in some detail. They associate hope with the empowering potentialities of transnational democratic tendencies, and their cumulative prospect of creating a global civil society capable of realizing human rights for all the peoples on the earth. This global civil society must be both respectful of and celebratory toward cultural diversity, and mindful of human solidarity and planetary unity in the struggles against cruelty, violence, exploitation, and environmental decay.

A commitment to humane governance places special emphasis on global constitutional challenges, especially to the state and the United Nations. These challenges will be shaped by political struggles between globalizing market forces and the more rooted democratic forces of transnational and local resistance. In the course of these struggles, the character and strategic modalities of democracy will themselves be a core issue (whether political parties and elections will remain the basic form of citizen participation or whether transnational affiliations and social movements will provide the main instruments for citizen participation).

There is no doubt that a new, more integrated world order will emerge in the next century. This outcome will be some form of geogovernance. But the normative status of geogovernance remains problematic and uncertain, and it is here that laments about the absence of progressive alternatives have their fullest impact. The notion of a type of humane governance to be explored in this report is an attempt to fill the normative vacuum with a positive and transformative politics, one animated by horizons that might seem utopian from the outlook of the present, yet are part of a coherent project to bring such results into being. As with the great religions, humane governance as a future for the peoples of the world is a statement of faith in human possibilities as much as it is an expression of hope.

This hope cannot be founded on any easy polarities of opposition. From civil society flow destructive and nihilistic responses as well as compassionate and reconstructive initiatives. More profoundly, civil society itself embodies many of the social and economic deformations that are then encoded in geopolitics and globalizing patterns of control and abuse. Who is free and who is not free to act democratically at the grassroots is itself a dimension of the liberating concerns of adherents of humane governance. There is no intention in this report to romanticize the politics of civil society. Regressive tendencies are also present and must be neutralized if the positive prospects of humane governance are to be realized.

As the title of this report insists, some approximation of humane governance is a real human possibility. Its plausibility will depend on the degree to which the peoples of the world are drawn toward the pursuit of higher normative horizons. The possibility of humane governance outlined here offers a sense of direction, though not a program. It focuses attention on process as much as structure. The achievement of humane governance requires commitment to an open-ended dialogue with comrades and adversaries alike. It must repudiate all efforts to associate otherness with evil, and resist tendencies to demonize particular peoples, religions, approaches, and individuals. The aspiration for humane governance must be inherently self-critical as well as critical in outlook, seeking to be constructive and reconstructive in response to world order challenges.

A decisive test of humane governance is the treatment accorded to those people who have suffered most in the past, as targets of genocide and ethnocide or objects of neglect and contempt. For this reason, in part, the fate of indigenous peoples is singled out here as a special concern. All major civilizations have in common the taint of severe abuse toward indigenous peoples.

Authority and well-being emerge from civil society as well as from the state and formal institutions. The persistence of untouchability and caste abuse in India, for example, is not primarily attributable to the failures of the state, but to deformations embodied in the culture itself, aggravated by local circumstance and traditions that make the pattern of abuse vary through time and from place to place. Vaclav Havel, President of the Czech Republic, has recently compared the liberation from Communism for the societies of Eastern Europe with a release from an extended prison term, a liberation that has had the paradoxical effect of heightening "manifestations of intolerance, xenophobia, racism and nationalism," social attitudes forbidden expression under Communism. In the spirit of humane governance, Havel calls "the gypsy problem . . . a litmus test not of democracy but of a civil society."[4] That is, the government can enact laws protective of the rights of gypsies, but it can rarely fully protect a scapegoated minority against expressions of hatred, *especially* if it is democratic! Herein lies the irony. In the Czech Republic, the skinheads, having emerged in the post-Communist era of recovered freedoms, have been responsible for the worst outbreaks of violence against gipsies. Nevertheless, the most systematic and dangerous forms of abuse directed at those scorned by society have been associated with policies of the state, as was, of course, the case with the Nazi experience after 1933.[5]

It is not only the matter of ethnic passions that raises concerns about the quality of governance in post-Communist societies. The renewed influence of patriarchal institutions and values has produced a variety of pressures on women, especially in the domain of reproductive rights. As a consequence, despite the welcome liberating impact on political life of the Communist collapse, there were and are normative costs that may lead to the deterioration of the life situation of a majority of the population.

The basic contention here is that abuse of those most vulnerable is a highly contextual matter, although its manifestations are very nearly universal. The political neglect of the homeless in many US cities reflects the latest phase of capitalism as much as anything else, a phase in which the challenge has shifted from the appeal of a more compassionate socialist alternative to an emphasis on the efficiencies needed for "competitiveness" in the world market. The state has been commandeered into the role of promoting these market priorities, thereby eroding its welfare function. But the point remains, the local and global litmus test of humane governance is the treatment accorded to those most vulnerable.

Such a test also applies interregionally. The litmus test of globalism is its approach to the least advantaged region, that is, sub-Saharan Africa. As long as the competitive geopolitics of the Cold War persisted, Africa counted; it received aid and attention. With the shift to market criteria of value, Africa and Africans have come to be seen as either irrelevant or as a millstone. Geogovernance so structured has led to *inhumane* governance.

The struggle to achieve humane governance encounters *democratic* obstacles even in states that have not been traumatized by long periods of brutal authoritarian rule. In response to violent and frightening crime, the citizenry of countries such as the United States and the United Kingdom increasingly and overwhelmingly support capital punishment. Such sentiments are morally regressive, and are correlated with an approach that stresses more and better armed police and bigger, harsher prisons as the best response to the civil challenge posed by criminality. This interplay between crime and terrorism on one side and repressive law enforcement and counterterrorism on the other side manifests inhumane governance at its worst.

The Claims of World Government and the Project of Humane Governance

A final preliminary issue concerns the relevance of world government. Some continue to believe that the only practicable form of humane governance requires the establishment of world government, either through radical reforms of the United Nations or as a result of a global constitutional convention.[6] But the feasibility of something on this order under current global conditions seems highly dubious. There are no requisite political foundations that could support either a negotiated process or lead to an imposed governmental order of global scope.

The most likely scenario by which world government would find its way on to the political agenda is through pressure brought by global market forces for a greater degree of political institutionalization to complete the work of building a viable world economy of optimum efficiency. In this regard, there are certain instructive analogies from

European regional experience, especially the emergence of capital-driven advocacy of Eurofederalism. If geogovernance moves toward a heavy, coordinated network of governmental institutions, including the centralization of control over war-making and police functions, then world government could come about, but not in a form that would qualify as "humane governance" by the criteria affirmed here.

A slightly more positive scenario that generated a mode of geogovernance that might properly be called "a world government" could result from a convergence of market influences and populist demands. If grassroots concerns about environmental harms deepen and the chaotic conditions of interethnic strife of the 1990s persist and spread, then the revisioning of world government as a project of transnational democracy is quite likely. In such a setting, the political conditions might then exist for the realistic promotion of world government in a form that would qualify as humane governance.

In all of this speculation, there is an important semantic question: on what basis do we properly attach the label of world government? The position taken here is that world government presupposes at least the following features: compulsory peaceful settlement of all disputes by third-party decision in accordance with law; general and complete disarmament at the state and regional levels; a global legislative capacity backed up by enforcement capabilities; and some form of centralized leadership. As such, world government is not necessarily responsive (or unresponsive) to democratizing ideas about consent, participation, accountability.

Adherents of humane governance should not be dogmatically opposed to world government. Nevertheless, skepticism is in order. The only elites that are likely to contemplate world government favorably in the forseeable future are those that currently seem responsible for the most acute forms of human suffering. The abstractions of world government, even if phrased with a sensitive awareness of the plight of the poor and vulnerable, are not likely to produce beneficial results unless tied to a democratic political movement that includes the establishment of world government as an integral goal.

Of course, there are many intermediate stages of institutionalization that seem to be on the path to humane governance but do not seem to add up to world government. These include the strengthening of international law in relation to the foreign policy of major states, the extension of international law to the activities of the global marketplace, the expansion of the authority of the World Court, the establishment of peace forces under UN command, and many others, some of which will be discussed in chapter 7. Finally, the view being affirmed here is that

humane governance can be achieved *without* world government, and
that this is both the more likely and more desirable course of action.
Bearing these considerations in mind, we move on to an exploration of
the case for humane governance and the depiction of the pathways
toward its realization in the decades ahead.

1

From Geopolitics to Humane Governance: A Necessary Journey

Forms of geogovernance are emerging rapidly. Although now fluid, their contours will grow more and more discernible. Many different images of the character of geogovernance have been put forward as a definitive interpretation of our future prospects, but it is unlikely that a consensus will emerge as to whether geogovernance exists and what its main features are for at least a quarter-century. However, in this process the geopolitical axis will almost certainly shift from statist concerns with balance of power, stability, self-defense, spheres of influence, and alliances to global market concerns with competitiveness, financial flows, capital sources, trade expansion, coordinating mechanisms, and labor markets.

Humane governance is a preferred form of geogovernance. It is both a process and a goal. Humane governance emphasizes the achievement of comprehensive rights for all peoples on earth. It accords priority to those most vulnerable and abused, providing an alternative source of security to that associated with geopolitics and seeking to resolve conflict and establish order with a minimum reliance on violence and through dismantling by stages the mental and material components of the war system. Humane governance also presupposes environmental quality to protect the health and well-being of those now alive and those as yet unborn. Thus humane governance is less a negation of geopolitics than an insistence on its essential irrelevance to the proper ordering of political life at all levels of social interaction.

Situating the quest for humane governance is confusing and controversial. Old habits of thought suggest a point of departure that stresses the security concerns of major states in the post–Cold War era. Fashionable adaptations to changing views of "the big picture" place emphasis on the interplay between states and the global economy, a process that is often refered to as "globalization." These perspectives usually view history as a top-down narrative in which wealth and power are the norms of value. The unit of analysis may change, as in Samuel Huntington"s recent insistence that we are at the threshold of an era of intercivilization conflict that will eclipse the statist outlook of international relations,[1] but the normative orientation remains elitist to the core.

While mindful of the significance of states and market forces, the committed position that is taken here seeks to achieve a different normative stance. Its basic criterion of value is the well-being of peoples, individuals, and groups distributed throughout the planet in radically different circumstances, animated by rich varieties of overlapping identity. Its understanding of history is based on the significance of struggle, resistance, the enactment and implementation of political, economic, social, and cultural rights, and the rediscovery of sustainable ways to collaborate at different levels of community and in relation to different types of technology for the sake of human survival and satisfaction. Much of the substance of humane governance is disclosed by a telling of the stories of human plight and aspiration.

The Scope of the Challenge

As is characteristic of periods of transition, contradictions appear in relation to all crucial contemporary trends. Thus technological innovation is a driving force in the dynamics of global integration, but it is also, by way of affordable microelectronic developments, encouraging unprecedented decentralization and cooperative and participatory structures that span the earth without relying on bureaucratic hierarchies. Keeping in mind such opposed sets of tendencies helps us to grasp the complexity and originality of the present era. These trends would have gone forward even if the Cold War had persisted for several more decades, but its ending makes them more salient.

Such trends are making the metaphor of "a global village" increasingly suggestive. Yet what sort of global village will it be? Who will exercise authority, and by what means? Will democracy prevail, and in what forms? Will the United Nations, or some successor organization, serve the global village as the central political actor and acquire over time a governmental character? And will states find a way to remain at the center of things? Or will corporate and financial actors take on a more and more direct role in the management of the world economy?

Will transnational democratic forces supportive of human rights find ways to exert influence and exercise authority in the global village? Will war remain the core of security for the status quo, or will negotiations and nonviolent practices gradually supersede war as a social institution? All of these questions, and many more, are generated by the master question: transition to what?

In very general terms, the complexity and fragility of the world, economically and ecologically, will by stages generate overarching arrangements, identified here as "geogovernance." But geogovernance, as such, is normatively neutral. It may be a vehicle for restructuring on behalf of the rich and powerful; it may be a vehicle for restructuring on behalf of the poor and dispossessed – but it is much harder to envisage how this might be brought about. What is most likely is a blending of these twin scenarios, with many variations across space and through time, and wide disagreement in the assessment of what is happening and who is getting the upper hand. The media are already inserting a partisan element into the process of perception, viewing the future overwhelmingly from the outlook of the rich and powerful. But there also exist countermedia bearing an alternative agenda. The question of the media balance to be struck is itself a contested political terrain that will not yield a single answer that holds everywhere.

Contending Images of Humane Governance

Although still predominant political actors on the world scene and in relation to the lives of most people, territorial states are being bypassed, their authority diminished, and their competence and legitimacy eroded as a result of a double historical movement: globalization beyond their reach presents one set of developments; fragmentation beyond their grasp presents another. Globalization indicates the planetary scale of emerging technologies and their implications for the world economy, for market and capital efficiency and opportunity, with an overall homogenizing impact on human experience and aspiration. Conversely, fragmentation sustains a resurgent politics of identity taking many shapes and forms, drawing both on the unspent passions of nationalism and religious belief and on the networking possibilities open to segments of civil society. This tendency toward fragmentation places a pervasive stress on particularity, and hence on the heterogeneity of the human experience. The many contexts in which this interplay of seemingly opposed tendencies becomes manifest is complex beyond easy generalization. They perhaps suggest the possibility of rediscovering the universal in the affirmation of the particular, or even the noncontradiction of opposites.

The usual Western reflex is to pose these two historical challenges in heavily evaluative terms, with a preference for globalization, and with fragmentation perceived as the threat imperiling a bright future. David Fromkin, a cultural historian, expresses this perspective as a matter of *functional* priority: "what the world economy and the world environment now require are larger rather than smaller units; regional and global regulatory bodies corresponding to the worldwide activities of businesses and utilities." Fromkin links such an interpretation to a vigorous denunciation of fragmentation as a shadow over the future. He writes that "the central question in the politics of the twenty-first century everywhere in the world will be the tension between holding together and pulling apart: between the centripetal pull of a modern world economy that requires regional and planetary organization, and the centrifugal pull of atavistic tribalisms. It is a conflict that pits rational interests against irrational feelings."[2]

The obverse of this view appeared as a lead editorial of the Islamic journal, *Al-Tawhid*:

> Does the Western world and the countries ruled by the big powers possess any remnant of spiritual and moral life to warrant hope of its recovery and survival? Will this rotten member of the ailing frame of humanity be able to recover from its petrifying gangrene? Unfortunately, there are few signs to justify any optimism . . . A "civilization" that conveniently and unscrupulously subordinates values to interests is not really worthy of being called a civilization. No matter how it may develop its material aspects, it will remain hollow at its human core, which is always moral-spiritual. The more it advances in sacrificing ideals and values to interests, the more perverse and degenerate it becomes.[3]

Typically, universalizing views tend toward polarization. The other is demonized and the self associated with a brighter future for the whole of humanity. The possibility of regarding oppositional encounters as opportunities for learning about the other and for transcending, while appreciating, difference is ignored.

The Prospect of Geogovernance

The position taken in this report affirms human solidarity as crucial, but also appreciates the integrity and fallibility of distinct civilizational voices as well as the historically crucial need to engage others by listening rather than declaiming. Such a directive is especially important for the West, dominating as it does the newly constructed superhighways of information, communication, and popular entertainment, thereby shaping the tastes and priorities of the global marketplace, beaming its messages everywhere, but hearing few echoes or responses. Terrorism and religious extremism are the primary echoes that are heard. More muted – yet widely shared – forms of backlash are rarely reported. Until events in the South erupt into violence, screams of pain are not deemed worthy of report. The revolt by Chiapas Indians in southern Mexico, for example, become a prominent story in January 1994, although the underlying conditions of poverty and resentment among the Indian population of Mexico and Central America had long pre-existed.

The sense of the impact of globalization and fragmentation upon the quality of world order in the decade or so ahead of us orients and shapes this study of the human future. The globalizing trends are moving so rapidly in integrative directions, especially with respect to economic, environmental, and cognitive[4] dimensions of reality, that it seems almost inevitable that some form of geogovernance will take shape. Prevailing tendencies suggest that geogovernance will be achieved by a coalition between leading states in the West (possibly including East and South Asia) and transnational capital as deployed by corporate managers and banking operatives. These state and market forces will, in turn, wire the world for purposes of advertising, indoctrination, and administration. The severity of environmental decay and challenges emanating from civil society and from the peripheries of world society (that is, the restive elements of fragmentation, augmented by radicalized governments arising in the subordinated portions of the world) are likely to make the impact of geogovernance on many societies and peoples coercive and interventionary. The success of geogovernance, so oriented, will be mainly assessed by its leaders in terms of growth in output and trade, and by its ability to impose their will on the entire planet with minimal resistance. There will be little sense of responsibility to the poor and marginalized, or to the life prospects of future generations. Territoriality will be subordinated, creating large pockets of embittered poverty in the affluent heartlands of technological innovation. Such a conception of geogovernance merges with the dystopic imagination, but represents at the same time a genuine historical possibility, being perhaps the most plausible scenario given current trends.

The form that geogovernance assumes will be the outcome of political struggle, and will not necessarily be successfully managed by secret protocols agreed upon by global market elites meeting in well-paneled boardrooms, possibly in collaboration with representatives of intelligence agencies. There is no doubt that discussions of such eventualities are taking place in the corridor talk during meetings of the Group of Seven (G-7)[5] and at the annual joint sessions of the boards of the International Monetary Fund (IMF)[6] and World Bank and in other global market arenas, but whether such a vision and its execution will be adopted as a plan to exert effective control over the future remains to be seen, and depends on what others do to promote contrary possibilities.

The Prospect for Humane Governance

Our hopes must continue to rest on the democratic energies of the peoples of the world, acting in all their diversity, yet conscious both of the threats that confront them and of the historic necessity to adapt emergent geogovernance to the realization of human rights. To emphasize this dual imperative, a conception of the future under the rubric of "humane governance," conceived of as the most preferable variant on the range of possibilities encompassed by the anticipation of geogovernance, must be developed. Humane governance emphasizes people-centred criteria of success, as measured by declines in poverty, violence, and pollution and by increasing adherence to human rights and constitutional practices, especially in relation to vulnerable segments of society, as well as by axiological shifts away from materialist/consumerist and patriarchal conceptions of human fulfillment.

Can humane governance become a reality, or is it merely a cry in the wilderness that is partly sentimental, partly utopian? We cannot know. What is known is that some totally unexpected turns of reality have recently confounded the "experts" whose conventional wisdom had been allowed to delimit the horizon of plausible hope. We have in recent years been passing through the zone of "the impossible": the emancipation of the countries of Central and Eastern Europe from Soviet rule, the abandonment of apartheid by the white elite in South Africa, the end of the Cold War, the handshake between the Israelis and the Palestine Liberation Organization. The impossible keeps happening, but not by accident or miracle. These generally encouraging, yet complex and contradictory happenings would not have occurred without struggle and resistance by those being victimized.[7] In this regard, advocates of humane governance have a grave responsibility to be participants in the unfolding struggle to shape and define geogovernance; their passivity will ensure the triumph of the G-7 view of the human future.

There are other grounds for hope. At the core of humane governance is the conviction that societal relations from the personal to the intercivilizational can be addressed nonviolently. Recent historical experience makes such hope rest on a solid foundation that has two complementary features: evidence of the effectiveness of nonviolence and of the frequent disutility of military approaches to conflict resolution.

Also generally encouraging is the degree to which many types of warfare have been confirmed to be on their way to obsolescence. The rational impossibility (coupled with the historical possibility) of nuclear war is the most dramatic form of obsolescence, reinforced by the colossal human costs of the two world wars fought in this century. Interventionary militarism has repeatedly failed when under the auspices of the superpowers despite their total battlefield superiority, most spectacularly in Vietnam and Afghanistan. This lesson is being extended by the catastrophic effects of UN efforts during 1992–4 at political restructuring inflicted on the people of Somalia, to the point of defaming the label "humanitarian" (which was valid to the extent it was confined to safeguarding relief activities). Enlarging the mandate of the United Nations beyond the limits specified in the UN Charter (namely, prohibiting the Organization from intervening in matters essentially within the domestic jurisdiction of sovereign states) invites frustration and defeat. Because of military dysfunction, the UN may fail even when it is primarily motivated by benevolent moral and legal goals.

Still, it is not yet the case that military force is useless in relation to political goals: Israel has demonstrated on several occasions since 1948 that military victory can be politically rewarding; the US-led coalition with minimal damage to itself did succeed in restoring Kuwaiti sovereign rights in the Gulf War. Nevertheless, the main contention about obsolescence remains persuasive: military means can destroy, but cannot create. This limitation on military power is primarily a result of the spread of nationalist forms of popular resistance and the unintended side-effects of continuing distributions of sophisticated weaponry to many countries in all regions by way of arms sales and military assistance programs.

Humane governance represents a multifaceted project of transnational and grassroots democratic forces. Its reality has to be established and transmitted in the numerous sites of struggle, ranging from the family to the various arenas of the United Nations system. Unlike the

G-7 and assorted other versions of geogovernance, it is not disposed to centralized coordination and the homogenization of planetary lifestyle, yet it acknowledges a variety of practical pressures requiring governance at regional and global levels of social and political organization. To the extent that such authority is vested in regional and global institutions, the perspectives of humane governance stress the accountability of elites and the participation by the peoples of the world and their directly elected representatives. Succeeding chapters of this book explore the meaning of humane governance in a series of conceptual and policy settings, as well as some implications of counterprojects to shape geogovernance in more beneficial ways than those resulting from global market forces.

The Mission

For several centuries the political destiny of the world has been largely shaped by the elites of the most powerful and richest states. War has been a major instrument in this process, both sustaining structures and mounting challenges. The territorial sovereign state emerged as the dominant political actor, although formal and informal multistate empires have played a large part as well.

First nuclear weaponry, then environmental overload have severely challenged the viability of this political structure, which has also been associated with an economics tied to growth. In addition, normative concerns arising out of acute poverty and various denials of human rights have also mounted challenges to the status quo.

For the sake of viability and legitimacy, the world must evolve structures of governance (not necessarily government) that offer improved prospects of achieving sustainability (that is, environmental balance enabling lifestyle to be continued at present or improving standards) and decency. Indeed, governance structures should be as decentralized and localized as possible consistent with such goals as equity, implementation of human rights, promotion of democracy, environmental protection. A global consensus appears to support this conclusion, at least as generally formulated, and it is acknowledged in the official rhetoric of statespersons. But hard adjustments on a behavioral level have not generally been forthcoming. Both state and market forces seem stuck with old ideas and outmoded means – old and outmoded to the extent that dominance is the goal and reliance on war is a principal means of sustaining a deformed status quo, though possibly new and innovative to the extent that interstate rivalry is moderated and reliance for compliance is placed on the control of information and symbolic consciousness.

Humane governance, in this usage, is as concerned with equity and human distress as it is with stability and sustainability. It is sensitive to the claims of the unborn for undiminished life prospects. Shaping the structures and practices of governance in humane directions is the core task of democratizing processes. It involves not only the deepening of democracy in state/society settings, but the outward extensions of democracy to transnational arenas fashioned by states, corporations, and banks and the inward extensions of human rights to villages, rural areas, as well as to schools, homes, the workplace. Most conceptions of geogovernance are limited to coordinating mechanisms at regional and global levels. This view of humane governance is one that links the global and regional to the national and personal. The aggregation of the various sites of governance from the local and personal to the global and bureaucratic cumulatively constitute humane governance. The inclusion of the personal within the scope of humane governance is an acknowledgement of, for example, feminist claims that the home and family are units of social control that model behavioral roles in public space. The work of women has been habitually neglected by locating its domain within the sphere of "the personal," which is excluded from assessments of governance.

Can these widely dispersed social forces be stimulated by societal initiatives? Are there creative energies of sufficient magnitude embodied in transnational social forces to exert a real legislative impact on the future? Is it justifiable to identify these sources of thought and action as comprising emergent realities here identified as "transnational democracy" and "global civil society"? Is there any available evidence to uphold conceptions of governance that downplay reliance on violence and of forms of geogovernance that simultaneously do away with war and poverty?

This book is written on the assumption that sane and intelligent persons should be giving affirmative answers to these questions. Only with such confidence can there be any genuine hope for the sort of transformative adjustments that are needed if we as a species, and as a network of distinct cultures, races, and religions, are to make this earth a benevolent habitat in the decades ahead.

This, then, is the mission. The rest of this chapter sets forth the rationale for it, grounding the vision in an assessment of global trends and tendencies. The overall political and ethical intention is to set forth a program of action that will enlist the energies and resources of women and men throughout the world. The mission is a widely participatory campaign to establish a global polity that embodies widely shared views about the human interest in ethical, ecological, cultural, political, and even spiritual sustainability. This polity would give structure and substance to humane governance within the wider historical frame of emergent geogovernance.

An Extraordinary Opportunity Wasted: Notorious Failures of Leadership and Imagination

The years leading up to the end of the Cold War gave the North an extraordinary opportunity to shift geopolitical gears: to renounce militarism in thought and action, releasing economic resources and political energies to construct better civic relations at home and to engage in the struggle for a safer, more just, and sustainable world. It is now clear that such shifts will not take place without further struggle of a sustained and militant character by those being victimized. The existing structures and mindsets of elites remain firmly entrenched in the terrain of warmaking and economic rivalry. The political imaginations of the rich and powerful are still caught up in greed and by efforts to retain short-run advantage. As a consequence, the historical opening at the end of the Cold War has been largely squandered, being treated as one more opportunity to consolidate power and wealth.

There is a curious irony in this: instead of midwifing the once heralded "new world order," the geopolitical leadership in key countries has consistently turned out to be content with their roles as steadfast guardians of entrenched interests. Such a role does involve a shift in orientation from statist geopolitics to market geopolitics, but without any more fundamental adjustments associated with equity or sustainability. In one respect the concerns of the Trilateral Commission[8] about transnational economic policy moved center-stage after the Soviet collapse. But if there is to be a more benign world order enacting a transformed politics of nonviolence and social justice, it will be brought about by struggles mounted from below based on the activities of popular movements and various coalitions. Such democratic social forces might well seek collaboration with sympathetic established leaders to the extent helpful for the realization of overall goals. Mikhail Gorbachev and F. W. de Klerk are examples of governmental leaders who pursued policies of drastic reform, and did so unexpectedly, without any prior democratic mandate, and quite possibly without themselves appreciating in advance how momentous the future course of events would be. There is no *necessary* opposition between transnational social forces and those of a statist – or even a global market – orientation.

What Western global economic leadership sought instead of change was to take advantage of the disappearance of the Soviet challenge by tightening its grip on the South. The main unstated goal was to foster further affluence and consumerism among the middle and upper classes throughout the world, vigorously insisting that the failure of command socialism demonstrated once and for all that there is no acceptable socialist alternative to the operations of the market, and that even welfare capitalism was an unneeded and inefficient encumbrance on economic growth. And capitalist ideologues, in a triumphalist mood, argue that purifying the market is the only proven route to progress even if it entails hardship along the way for those societies and persons that are not "competitive." Those cast out by market forces are better pitied, than helped; their misfortune is the inevitable, the necessary shadow side of efficiency in the use of resources, and, according to capitalist mind games, only efficiency should be valued if material progress is to be maintained in an integrated, highly competitive world economy.

Quite independently of the Soviet collapse, real power in the North over the course of the past 30 years had been shifting away from government to a variety of interlinked elites: corporate, financial, and media. These elites also built globalizing networks of collaborators in high government and business circles in the South, and penetrated various Communist societies as well, especially China. The state and its bureaucracies were in many respects being converted by stages into high-prestige collection agents and bodyguards for world capitalism, losing much of their capacity at a state level to set independent and somewhat compassionate economic policies beneficial for their citizenry and for their countries.

No wonder the quality of political leadership has seemed to be deteriorating in governmental settings throughout the North. It reflects partly the selection process that seeks pointmen for transnational capital and partly the impossibility of successful domestic governance in an increasingly globalized setting. It is evident that the constitutional side of governance pulls toward the satisfaction of territorial priorities, while the market side of governance pulls toward the realization of nonterritorial or global objectives. The political leaders caught in such a crossfire are bound to appear to be either inept (to the extent that they juggle contradictory pressures or shift with the prevailing wind) or deforming (to the extent that they lean to one side). An unpleasant aspect of the governmental role in this new configuring of power and wealth is to neutralize forces of domestic discontent by providing for internal order, controlling especially those at the margins of society who were being consigned to lives of prolonged structural (as distinct from cyclical) unemployment and acute poverty, engendering widespread crime and despair.[9] As the bloody riots of 1992 in Los Angeles disclosed, this oppressive imperative is as real for the United States as it is for, say, Iran and Egypt.

An essential international dimension of geopolitics on behalf of the global capitalist order was exposed for all who wished to see it during the Gulf War, and, by way of contrast, in relation to the long and continuing Bosnian ordeal in the former Yugoslavia and the UN/US fiasco in Somalia. These challenges of the early 1990s illuminate shortcomings of political leadership in the post-Cold War world. There are many historical differences between the perception and reality of these situations, but there is also a unifying thread. When major strategic interests of the North are engaged, a potent and unified response based on a major military commitment is likely to be made. When such interests are marginal or fragmentary, political and regional divisions are likely to block all serious efforts to fashion an effective, peace-restoring policy, and unspeakable intensities of violence and human abuse are likely to be "tolerated," especially if the costs of intervention are perceived to be high, and the geopolitical consequences of nonintervention acceptable. In foreign policy discourse, indifference is expressed by concluding that no vital national interests are at stake. Yet the specification of vital national interests is by no means a self-evident matter; rather it expresses hierarchies of power and belief within elite circles, as well as the impact of domestic pressure groups.

In the paragraphs that follow, the Gulf War will be shown to have provided a vehicle for militarist pressures, but these criticisms are mirrored by the equally disturbing willingness to "indulge" genocide in Bosnia.

The encounter with Saddam Hussein"s Iraq since 1990 has many facets. The motivation to protect favorable access to Gulf oil for reasons of both price and access was surely uppermost. Yet the demonstration to both North and South of the US will and capability to project its strategic military power in the post-Cold War world was strongly motivated, as was the closely related effort to find new justifications for force by way of the United Nations. Coalitions of governments and financial/military resources of the North required a new type of legitimation to meet challenges arising from threatening developments in the South. In this regard, the frequent assertion that proliferation of nuclear weapons in the South represented the greatest threat to the post-Cold

War world order must be understood in relation to Northern dominance. Such expressions of concern rarely emanate from the South,
which would be the most probable scene of devastation if the capabilities associated with proliferation were to be used in a combat situation.
The idea of the South attacking the North directly, with or without
nuclear weapons, seems quite far-fetched.

Also relevant during the Gulf crisis was the bureaucratic pressure in
the West to find new enemies in a world without strategic rivalry. There
was also strong pressure exerted by military-industrial elites to demonstrate the battlefield performance of a post-Vietnam generation of high-
technology weaponry under the favorable conditions of mid-intensity
warfare. A dimension generally more removed from public view was
the renewal of a struggle that has flared over the centuries between the
Christian West and the Islamic Middle East in what has been interpreted in some circles as the onset of an era of intercivilizational
warfare.[10]

Historians are likely to debate for a long time about whether these
darker designs of the suddenly challenged West were present even
before Saddam Hussein threw down his gauntlet by recklessly and
brutally invading Kuwait on August 2, 1990. There was little doubt
throughout international society at the time that such aggression could
not be allowed to succeed. Further, in UN circles the credibility of the
Organization was put on trial, especially as Iraq had crudely and cruelly
annexed Kuwait, thereby purporting to extinguish a member state for
the first time since the UN was established. Something effective had to
be done to avoid an impression of the impotence that had come to be
associated with the failures of the League of Nations during the 1930s,
especially the League's inability to respond effectively on behalf of
Ethiopia in response to Fascist Italy's aggression.

From the outset of the Gulf crisis, the United States seized the
occasion to manifest and establish its ascendent role as global leader.
At first there seemed reason to be hopeful about the character of the
response in Washington, and even to believe that the United States
government realized how important it was for the future of world order
to reverse Iraq's aggression without resort to a military solution. Such a
course would have disclosed a real willingness to initiate some "new
thinking" in Western foreign policy, partly by building up the authority
of the UN and international law in this period, and to do so in the spirit
of the UN Charter by emphasizing its central mandate "to save
succeeding generations from the scourge of war." Heeding such an
imperative could have meant, above all, searching every possible path
that would have produced a diplomatic process that reversed Iraq's

aggression without relying on war-making. A commitment to the avoidance of UN war-making would have encouraged full discussion in a collective spirit at each stage of the crisis, with consensus achieved in the Security Council as to next steps. Such a consensus would have relied upon a collective spirit and procedures, distinguishing itself from the unilateralism of the American-led North.

The Cold War was indeed over in relation to the structures and practices of bipolarity, but the old geopolitics of power politics, especially in North/South settings, was still in evidence. The refusal of the Security Council to insist on limiting military action to the minimalist mission of restoring full sovereign rights to Kuwait reinforced the impression that the UN was being used by the United States to achieve a series of additional, unauthorized objectives (destroying Iraq"s future war-making potential, especially in relation to nuclear weaponry). Somewhat paradoxically, the Security Council would have seemed more in line had it done more, undertaken an expanded conception of a UN role that accorded more genuinely with the UN Charter by accepting a maximalist mission that centered not just on repelling aggression, but additionally on the democratic restructuring of Iraq, including human rights.[11]

In this regard, the Gulf War as a military operation underscored its geopolitical character – in effect, it was partially a preventive war waged beyond its defensive mandate so as to foreclose Iraq's suspected nuclear ambitions and to achieve a new regional balance, but not extended so far as to risk a new regional imbalance by way of facilitating Iranian ascendancy. This offsetting concern provided the excuse for failing to address the roots of aggression in terms of oppressive militarism in Iraq. Instead, the United States government"s regional priorities to contain Islamic fundamentalism and limit the relative power of Iran were given precedence, confirming the judgment that the Gulf War was not a positive precedent for the future of collective security, and that the United Nations lacked the strength and integrity to uphold the spirit, if not the letter, of its own Charter. Recalling Secretary General Boutros Boutros-Ghali's now celebrated oblique reference to the deficiencies of recourse to UN mandate in the Gulf War: "There must never again be such a failure of collegiality."

Without such adherence to the spirit of the Charter on such key matters as seeking peaceful outcomes to crises, limiting recourse to military measures, maintaining some sort of supervisory relationship to military operations carried out in the name of UN collective security, and ensuring genuine collective participation by the members of the Security Council, there is a suspension of constitutionalism. The UN then inevitably becomes an instrument, for better and worse, of prevailing geopolitical tendencies.

In certain respects, this new patterning of geopolitics could become even more menacing to the human interests than was the case during the Cold War years. The North is now fundamentally united ideologically and strategically, and able to pursue its hegemonic ways without friction among strategic rivals and even without much adverse publicity. Specifically, the absence of bipolarity leaves the United States undeterred. To some extent, this removal of inhibitions is balanced by the weakening of incentives to intervene for the sake of ideological goals. It all depends on context, and the interests at stake. In some respects, the diplomacy of the Gulf War prefigured the contours of geogovernance. To receive the original blessings of the organized world community as embodied in the United Nations was an added bonus.

The progressive weakening of the nonaligned movement has been evident in recent decades. During the Gulf crisis there was little disposition by countries from the South to challenge the US-led approach, despite private misgivings of many leaders. In actuality, the sense of vulnerability felt by many goverments from Asia, Africa, and Latin America was directly associated with the weight of the debt burden on many countries, and the leverage of the North being exerted through the IMF and by way of trade relations. In the Gulf War, the North once more demonstrated its dominance by way of the superiority of its military technology, arguably more spectacularly than ever before. Although Iraqi civilian deaths and suffering were rarely evident in the managed TV presentation of the combat phases of the war, the devastating impact of the war on the civilian population, especially women and children, became evident in subsequent months. Shortly after a ceasefire in the Gulf War, an official UN report to the Secretariat described the damage as "near apocalyptic," driving Iraq back before the industrial age; to the same effect, a Harvard health survey estimated hundreds of thousands of war-induced casualties among children under the age of five by the end of 1992.[12]

In its substance, as distinct from its form, the Gulf War resembled earlier high-tech interventions by the North in the South such as occurred during the Cold War in Korea, Vietnam, and Afghanistan, but the absence of superpower rivalry and counterintervention helped ensure a battlefield victory in Iraq rather than stalemate or escalation. Disturbing, also, was the extent to which Washington's contrived image of the war as directed exclusively toward military targets by new generations of wonder weapons was uncritically conveyed to the peoples and leaders of the entire world via CNN satellite television – information, censorship, and propaganda were ingeniously blended as never before in wartime in this new and symbolically lethal type of globalism. Bullets and missiles were perceived as cool objects, prompting the frequent reaction that the early stages of the war resembled an electronic game. This portrayal of the war was definitely misleading, as subsequent reports by visiting delegations confirmed. Iraq's infrastructure was devastated in such a way as to cause countless civilian deaths, especially from the deliberate destruction of the centralized water purification facilities of virtually the entire country.

Perhaps most distressing of all was the extent to which the one-sidedness of the military outcome was enthusiastically celebrated by the citizenry of the United States and the United Kingdom, suggesting the extent to which militarist, racist, and nationalist attitudes seem currently embodied in the political cultures of the world's most durable democracies. It is now evident that democracy, at least as constituted in liberal democratic societies, is not by itself a sufficient precondition for a peaceful and just world. Democracy as an operative political form seems quite compatible with certain types of militarism and racism, perhaps resting in turn on patriarchal practices and hidden assumptions. The main problem is that the underlying political culture does not sufficiently embody such values as empathy and nonviolence. Whether this concern is expressed as a need to overcome the deficiencies of democracy or as a matter of emphasizing the cultural preconditions for democracy by way of a new pedagogy for citizens, the character of the problem is centered on the mix of socialization and operative societal values.

All along, the Cold War had been a costly and dangerous process for the peoples of the world, especially those in the South. Intervention from the North was a recurrent and frequent phenomenon, intensifying and extending the violence of indigenous patterns of conflict, and manipulating and magnifying the turbulence that was an inevitable sequel to oppressive decades of colonial rule. Even more harmful was the diversion of attention from a political agenda responsive to the aspirations, needs, and circumstances of all the peoples of the world – avoidance of war and militarism, promotion of economic policies that seriously addressed poverty, realization of human rights in the face of political and social oppression, and the shaping of development strategies that reconciled growth with environmental quality.

This reformist agenda had acquired an urgency resulting from the incidence of devastating warfare fought with ever more sophisticated weaponry, from the scale of human suffering resulting from the spread of poverty amid rapid increases in population size, and from the variety of signals that environmental deterioration was reaching points of no return in several sectors vital for human health and well-being and even survival.

Although an activated public opinion induced leaders of states and officials in international institutions to acknowledge these challenges to varying degrees, the main attention of leading states during the period from 1945 to 1989 was devoted to the ideological and geopolitical battlefields generated by the East/West struggle and by materialist ambitions to increase as rapidly as possible the gross national products of the two titans that dominated the world political scene. The Cold War served as excuse and pretext for cynical deployments of power and influence by both superpowers. It carried on the main enterprise of international relations in modern times: by means of trade, investment and force of arms, keeping the rich and powerful, rich and powerful; exploiting the weak and poor to the extent possible and suppressing them to the extent necessary. This period resulted in several benefits for the South. Decolonization occurred, and the rivalry of East and West caused competition for hearts and minds in the South that released additional resources for developmental purposes. Each side in the Cold War was trying to demonstrate the superiority of its approach to development, and wanted their acolytes in the South to succeed. And these countries in the South, or some of them, did benefit materially from the overall mix of policies in place.

Perhaps sub-Saharan Africa and the Middle East are most affected by the disappearance of East/West bidders for political influence and allegiance. There are no geopolitical bidders these days. From the perspective of autonomy and development this seems desirable. Yet for countries facing deep structural problems in relation to globalization, and burdened by heavy indebtedness, the loss of geopolitical subsidies may be a threshold disaster that goes beyond the capacity of the leadership to fashion a policy of adaptation. As a result, strife, extremism, despair abound, and external stabilizing influences are no longer able to exert control. The result is a new world *disorder*.

Focusing on the United Nations

The United Nations reflects to a considerable degree the contradictory political tensions that exist at a state level in international life, and the Organization is itself an arena of struggle that reflects relative power and ideological perspectives.[13] In this light, it is not surprising that the Security Council was stalemated during the Cold War, or for that matter that the General Assembly had a period of prominence, expressing the grievances of the South in the early stages of postcolonial history, reaching a strident pitch in the 1970s as global obstacles to development and independence began to loom large. Nor is it surprising that the North should use its financial leverage and political influence to rein in the Assembly and to hold down those facets of UN activities that could be viewed as oriented toward the priorities of the South (that is, the United Nations Conference on Trade and Development (UNCTAD), the United Nations Development Program (UNDP), the United Nations Educational, Scientific and Cultural Organization (UNESCO), and most especially the United Nations Center on Transnational Corporations). This reaction by the North was intensified by the emergence in key member countries of ardently market-oriented governments that perceived the demands of the South as essentially "socialistic." But to some extent the UN also reflected the shifting character of transnational societal concerns, especially through the mechanism of consciousness-raising conferences under UN auspices on such topics as environment, development, population, food, women, and human rights. The 1992 Earth Summit has been the most recent climax of this aspect of UN activities, perceived as a triumph by those seeking to stress the magnitude of the consciousness-raising effects of the event, and as a disappointment by those hoping to translate environmental concerns into a tight treaty framework of behavioral constraints, moving in the direction of environmental governance for the planet.

The UN has over the decades played an indispensable role in standard-setting in the human rights and environmental domains, creating a normative framework that can be invoked as authoritative by transnational social forces, especially by citizens' associations, as well as by conventional domestic oppositional politics. However, in the 1990s a backlash has developed in the South to the UN role, especially regarding the human rights area, based on the claim that alleged violations were being used as a pretext for a new cycle of Northern-led interventionary diplomacy. China has emerged as the informal leader of this movement of resistance, which was expressed in the Bangkok Declaration subscribed to by 59 countries in the months preceding the UN Conference held in Vienna in June 1993, and insisting that alleged human rights violations never justify intervention even of a nonmilitary character (for instance, conditionalities attached to economic relationships). As an actor, however, the weakness of the UN has been especially evident with respect to peace and security issues in the context of implementation. In this regard, the post-Cold War structure of international relations exerts influence and creates opportunities for the UN, removing the problem of paralysis, but risking the deformation of the Organization to the extent that its most prominent activities come to be controlled by and for the sake of the United States and its allies in the North, and increasingly for the benefit of global capital formation, both by its acts of commission (in Iraq) and of omission (in relation to Serbia and Bosnia).

Demystifying the UN is meant to be constructive. Despite criticism and concern, it remains important to acknowledge the contributions that the UN has made and is making, and to call attention to its unrealized potential in relation to the mission of humane governance. The UN remains the rock upon which to build the most encompassing structures of governance, and its global reach is indispensable. But such a dependence needs to be coupled with active appreciation of the reality that the UN is not above the fray. The UN consists of an intensely political series of arenas where different versions of potential geogovernance after the Cold War are contending for influence; some of these versions are to varying degrees militarist and tied closely to the interests of transnational business and capital, and others are seeking to turn away from militarism and address the vast human suffering throughout the world. It is important that transnational social forces regard the UN Charter as part of the basic law of global civil society and enter actively into the struggle to make the organs of the Organization more responsive to the needs and concerns of peoples throughout the world. The UN had already in the late 1980s convincingly shown its potential usefulness for the cause of peace during the final phases of the Cold War, especially as a result of the altered mood arising from the Western-oriented leadership in Moscow. Such regional conflicts as Iran/Iraq, Kampuchea, Afghanistan, and Namibia benefited directly and dramatically from this new UN capacity to play a mediating and peace-restoring role in situations previously off-limits for Cold War reasons. That is, the last phase of the Cold War displayed East/West cooperation that may, paradoxically, have been more constructive from the perspective of world order values than the circumstances of geopolitical unity that has existed since 1989. The Soviet Union under Gorbachev was more oriented toward humane governance, at least in external arenas, than has been Russia under Boris Yeltsin.

But the UN and the world geopolitical leadership is being tested in another domain, that of developmental policy and the structure of North/South relations. The South mounted a major drive in the 1970s to achieve a New International Economic Order, aiming at a partial restructuring of the global trading and investment system in directions helpful to the South, demanding a framework less tilted in favor of the rich and technologically advanced countries in the North. Even without resistance from the centers of capital in the North, there were problems with this essentially statist vision of global economic reform. Many of the states in the South, including several of those spearheading the drive for a New International Economic Order (NIEO), were themselves under the yoke of oppressive and corrupt governments – moves at a global level that strengthened the governing structures of such states hardly seemed a helpful way to assist the poor and oppressed in the world, and indeed, efforts aimed in this direction uniformly caused disillusionment, tending to stabilize inhumane governance at the state level.

Degrees of democratization are an important precondition for ensuring that useful and necessary reforms of the world economy along North/South lines will actually benefit those who are currently being most victimized. Although the drive in the 1970s to establish a NIEO may not have added up to much in the end, it did for a time clarify and focus concern on international economic disparities. It also mobilized the South and achieved a high degree of solidarity that gave an encouraging, if temporary, salience to issues of poverty, equity, and the future of North/South relations.

Instead of a NIEO emerging out of this ferment of the 1970s, the South was effectively slapped down in the 1980s. Large transnational capitalist interests, at the initiative of David Rockefeller, founded the Trilateral Commission to serve as a policy-forming and coordinating transnational pressure group operating in the trilateral domains of North America, Europe, and Japan on behalf of "enlightened" economic policies. It is a measure of the success of the Trilateral Commission that its views are now embodied in official policies. Its distinct existence has been marginalized by success, not failure! In the meantime, the South lost much of its unity. The oil producers were not able to agree and a split in the ranks of the Organization of Petroleum-Exporting Countries occurred on issues of price and production quotas, aggravated by eight years of Iran/Iraq warfare. Several East Asian countries found ways to grow rapidly enough to lose most of their southern identity, and more recently, additional countries have joined this rapid growth group in South Asia. These so-called Newly Industrializing Countries (or NICs) were welcomed as junior participants in the capitalist world economy, and remain the most dynamic participants in the world economy during the 1990s.

Most important of all, the recycling of petrodollar surpluses in the mid-1970s, together with falling commodity prices and rising interest rates, imposed a burden of indebtedness that has trapped many countries of the South, causing as much vulnerability to and abuse by outside pressures in several instances as had been characteristic of the colonial era. The combination of IMF Strategic Adjustment Programs (SAPs) and policies of conditionality to sustain fiscal solvency, reinforced by coercive trade policies and periodic military interventions to discipline governments pursuing a more confrontational approach, has both subordinated the South in the 1980s and the early 1990s, and made it virtually impossible for even highminded governments in the South to design social policies to reduce poverty and unemployment. The disappointing record of Corazon Aquino in the Philippines between 1986 and 1992 is illustrative of the frustrations that paralyzed a government that came to power on the basis of a powerful mandate for social and economic reform, and in a setting of massive poverty. This disappointment was to some extent predictable, given Ms Aquino's elite ties, persisting US influence, the difficulties associated with a legislature dominated by vested interests, as well as the inherited problems of debt, corruption, and a faction-ridden military.

After the Cold War

This new Northern ascendancy is no longer hidden behind the slogans and competing claims of Cold War rhetoric. The South has ceased to be a strategic zone of competition between superpowers and their rival ideologies. What rivalry exists among the dominant states in the North, and it could grow nastier in the 1990s, involves market access and shares. If world trade revives its expansionist ways, then this rivalry is likely to be muted, but if bad times persist, then the pressure to shift the burdens of hardship could take on an ugly character. The South's worst agonies and troubles are largely ignored, as evidenced most vividly by the neglect of sub-Saharan Africa. They no longer seem to count nearly so often in the calculations of the rich and powerful that comprise geopolitics. Also, the countries of the South are no longer buoyed by the excitement of decolonization and the first fruits of political independence. The North in this era feels no pressure from a unified South. Nearly all of Africa and much of Latin America have experienced sharp declines in real standards of living over the course of the last decade, although there are several partial success stories in Bolivia, Chile, and Mexico, and many countries in the Pacific Basin continue to grow rapidly.

Of course, considered globally, the ending of the Cold War and the mutation of the Soviet Union into a loosely confederated series of independent republics has produced some important benefits in relation to the quality of world order. On the global level, the menace of strategic nuclear war has definitely receded – the fate of the earth no longer seems destined to be resolved by nuclear catastrophe.[14] It was also beneficial that the great transformations in Eastern Europe and the Soviet Union were achieved without great violence, disclosing the potency of mass popular resistance by citizens even after decades of stifling indoctrination and oppression. It is especially encouraging that the last ten years have witnessed an upsurge of impressive nonviolent challenges to established structures of oppressive state power all over the world – people power in the Philippines; prodemocracy movements in China, Burma, Korea, Nepal; the intifada in occupied Palestine; remarkable negotiated transitions away from military rule in Argentina and Chile; the repudiation of apartheid in South Africa; diplomatic resolutions of relentless civil wars in El Salvador, Angola, and Mozambique. Some of these democratizing challenges were crushed, some of the negotiated arrangements are fragile and even reversible, but the overall record is impressive and encouraging. Democracy as the basis of governance at the state and substate level has been spreading during this period, seemingly for reasons of both practicality in relation to policy and legitimacy in relation to acceptance at home and abroad.

With far more ambiguous results, the self-determination of peoples has been successfully promoted in a variety of contexts, although sometimes causing bloody struggles, bitter ethnic strife and intolerance, and leading to antidemocratic outcomes dictated by the groups that gain the upper hand. Such developments, while troublesome in their overall effects, have had great significance for particular societies and their peoples, as well as for the general move toward democratizing the struggle for change and demilitarizing governance structures at the state level. To illustrate this complexity it is only necessary to reflect once more on the opposed tragedies of Yugoslavia, experiencing the full nihilistic brunt of self-determination, and Tibet, experiencing the demoralizing burdens of thwarted self-determination and the criminal cruelties of persisting Chinese occupation.

From the viewpoint of geopolitics, the dissipation of Cold War structures and patterns left intact the basic geopolitical framework and mindset of the modern world – that is, the control of the whole resource base of the world for the sake of the richest, militarily strongest, and most technologically advanced and assertive states and elites, with the locus of control remaining with the trilateralist North. This set of relationships is underpinned by the military dominance of the North, and by its willingness to spill blood in disproportionate quantities.[15]

Ending the East/West rivalry has not disclosed a comparable willingness to encourage the demilitarization of international relations to any significant degree, astonishingly not even with respect to nuclear weaponry. Especially bewildering is why the non-nuclear states have not mounted a strong denuclearizing campaign, especially given the option of threatening a collective withdrawal from the nonproliferation regime embodied in the Non-Proliferation Treaty. Such passivity reinforces the disposition to stand pat on the part of "the wizards of Armageddon." As Robert Lifton and others have shown, the roots of nuclearism were much deeper than deterrence, and thus the end of deterrence does not imply the end of nuclearism.[16]

It is true that a seemingly dramatic quantitative reduction of US/Russian nuclear arsenals has been tentatively agreed on in 1991, but the residual stockpile, should all current agreements be fully carried out, which is uncertain, continues to number 3,000 or more sophisticated warheads in the megaton range. Until a concerted grassroots effort in 1993, the United States insisted on continuing to test weapons and to develop new systems; even now it has merely assented to a conditional moratorium on testing, and even this was agreed upon only after a great deal of popular pressure. So far, the US government has refused to commit itself to a posture of no first use with regard to nuclear weapons (even a pledge restricted to non-nuclear powers), while at the same time claiming an interventionary option to prevent adversary countries in the South from acquiring weaponry of mass destruction. The nonproliferation regime (beyond the treaty) reflects a geopolitical consensus interpreted and enforced primarily by the United States against "pariah" states (including Libya, Iraq, Iran, North Korea, and to an extent Pakistan). The problem of double standards is presented here in the most extreme of all forms – the odious idea that certain political elites shall be allowed to possess, develop, threaten, and conceivably use apocalyptic weaponry into the indefinite future while other political elites are forbidden to do so. It is evident that the Islamic world lives under a shadow of interventionary threat vis-à-vis nuclear weapons capabilities, whereas Israel's nuclearism has been quietly tolerated, despite acquisition and continuing development.

To construct regimes incorporating such double standards is to deny the equality of rights enjoyed by sovereign states and to reject democratically grounded law in the peace and security field – the most basic idea of law (as linked to ethics and democracy) is the notion of treating equals equally. The geopolitical leadership, then, in relation to the global extension of the rule of law reveals itself as beholden to the contrary ethos of dominance by the strongest, and of treating equals unequally.

It is not states with a distaste for war, but the most persistent bullies that insist on the retention of nuclear weaponry. Instead of proceeding urgently in the direction of denuclearization, the surviving superpower consistently signals its allegiance to a two-tier structure of world order – discretionary development and possession of the weaponry of mass destruction for the global overlords and denial at the pain of devastating military intervention of such acquisition by the pariah states among the underlings. By and large, Israel excepted, the rest of the South is acquiescent, neither endorsing the two-tier nuclear weapons hierarchy, nor challenging it. Some states, such as India, Mexico, Zimbabwe and others, have supported moves to prohibit nuclear weaponry altogether, and continue to consider recourse to the World Court for a declaration of illegality.

One major aspect of the pressure to have a military solution in Iraq in 1991 was to establish the geopolitical "right" to pre-empt Saddam Hussein's efforts to acquire nuclear weaponry, and thereby also to deter other undesirables in the South from moving across the nuclear threshold; a diplomatically coerced Iraqi withdrawal from Kuwait would not have accomplished this result. Even the targeting of all known facilities connected with a nuclear weapons program was deemed insufficient. The post-ceasefire inspection claims under UN auspices have been a continuous source of tension ever since the spring of 1991. The result has been to justify the maintenance of extensive sanctions imposing hardship on the Iraqi people without discernibly weakening Saddam Hussein's rule.

Similarly, the geopolitical leadership of the world is not meeting the environmental challenge in a responsible fashion. There is a reluctance by the rich countries in the North to accept the financial burdens of adjustment in the South, to encroach upon their own environmentally dangerous consumerist lifestyle, or to agree to regulatory guidelines that could diminish growth prospects. As George Bush made clear prior to the 1992 Earth Summit, "the American standard of living is non-negotiable." The implication is, of course, that human survival or the poverty of the South is negotiable! Whether Bush was environmentally regressive as a leader or spoke as agent for wider global market interests that would exert an effective influence on *any* mainstream American leader remains to be seen. The evidence so far seems to suggest that it doesn't matter which political party is in power. In effect, the world order framework remains committed to maximal economic growth without a sufficiently serious regard for sustainability of resources in the years and decades ahead, thereby reinforcing the tendencies that are producing environmental decay at an alarming rate and are especially damaging to the global commons (that is, seas, atmosphere, space – those domains of the earth's ecosystem lying beyond the territorial reach of states). The unwillingness of several rich states in the North to back the main directions of substantive effort to increase global capacities to regulate environmentally harmful activities revealed vividly this refusal of the wealthy to acknowledge the urgency of environmental priorities or to join sufficiently in the campaign to redirect human aspirations in light of mounting evidence of the need for a more dedicated and intrusive effort on the part of governments and international institutions.

The picture that emerges is depressingly coherent when one considers the problems of life on the planet. An assertive United States, more or less backed by the countries of the North that were allied during the Cold War (most notably Germany, Japan, United Kingdom, France) and now augmented, often ardently, by the states that made up the former Soviet bloc and by the successor states to the Soviet Union, especially Russia – this tacit alliance has acted consistently to sustain control over a reconfigured geopolitics. This control extends to the most important international institutions, including most arenas in the United Nations and the international financial agencies.

The independence of the World Court, the judicial arm of the UN, was signaled by its 1986 decision finding the US government guilty of several serious violations of international law arising out of its anti-Sandinista policies in Nicaragua, but so also was the Court's impotence in the face of US defiance. The Security Council did not make any concerted attempt at enforcement, even aside from being thwarted by the US veto, and there was no display of any strong political will to confront the US on grounds of the integrity of the global judicial process. Such an assessment should not be understood as a dismissal of the decision as useless. In fact, it helped the Sandinista government to maintain economic support, especially in Europe, and it strengthened oppositional tendencies in the United States.

The end of the Cold War has not initiated any serious move from above in the direction of global reform, as distinct from the atmospherics of global management. It is a seldom noted irony that Gorbachev's decline and fall, and the related Soviet implosion, removed from the intergovernmental scene the most significant visionary voice on behalf of the sort of world order future that is needed. Vaclev Havel and Gro Harlem Brundtland also have made major visionary contributions in this period, yet neither of their voices was fully sustained or truly comprehensive. Even Gorbachev never extended his global concerns to the priorities of the South, thereby worrying progressives in Africa, Asia, and Latin America that the United States was being given a blank check to act in the South at the end of the 1980s by policy-makers in the Kremlin. One expression of this Soviet withdrawal was its abandonment of the Cuban/Central American arena, highlighted by the US military intervention in Panama at the end of 1989 that produced heavy civilian casualties, abducted the head of state, installed a new leader, defied regional opposition, violated international law, and encountered almost no serious criticism on a global level.

The post-Soviet Russian presence in the world is so far completely, and perhaps unavoidably, preoccupied with domestic and regional challenges, and is highlighted by a revival of nationalist sentiments of a regional and traditional character. These include pro-Serbian sympathies in the Bosnian setting, various efforts to reconsolidate Moscow's control over several former Soviet republics, and even a Russian effort to discourage the inclusion of East European countries in an expanded NATO. Acquiescence by the West in this attempt by Russia to flex its regional muscles has been ironically, and perhaps hyperbolically, referred to as "Yalta II".

Toward Hope

The peoples of the world have not been well served by this shortsightedness on the part of leading states. The best hope for a brighter human future lies in mounting a variety of democratizing challenges to this reestablishment and recreation of geopolitical normalcy. It is of special importance at this time to develop effective regulatory control over international banking, financial, and corporate activity. These challenges to the prevailing order must aim at discrediting double standards and the resultant two-tier structure of rights and privileges across the whole spectrum of global concerns. Closely connected, these challenges must expose the gross unfairness of the current structure of the world economy, especially to the poorest and most disadvantaged societies, and the dangerous consequences of existing levels of environmental disregard. Part of this campaign involves presenting in feasible form an array of viable normative projects, based on alternative thinking, ranging from debt cancellation to disarmament.

Containing the new geopolitics may require strengthening the sovereign state, at least in the short run, and even accepting a rise in economic nationalism. At this stage, only states pushed hard by their citizenry would have the political possibility of constraining global market forces, and even then the effort might be self-destructive and short-lived unless coordinated on a regional or transnational basis. Shaping global economic policy on behalf of human interests (rather than on behalf of private capital or national interests) would require a much stronger global civil society than currently exists. The realization of economic and social rights for all peoples, the materialist side of humane governance, presupposes such an orientation for the world economy.

This prospect of challenging a regressive transition to geogovernance is beset by the complexities of the world, being both facilitated and obstructed in distinct respects by several closely interrelated developments:

- the strength and effectiveness of transnational citizens' associations in areas such as human rights, environment, and peace;
- the historical move on the part of transformative political visions toward an ethos of democratization and nonviolence, rejecting armed struggle as a tactic of challenge and discrediting militarist modes of governance;[17]
- the difficulties of states and international institutions in maintaining popularity and legitimacy in light of the deepening problems of world order and the encroachment on the relative autonomy of state/society relations by global market forces;
- the globalization of business, finance, and popular culture, eroding the capabilities and resolve of the state as problem-solver and as guardian of territorial autonomy and independence.[18]

Such cumulative developments are facilitating the birth and growth of global civil society at this time. They carry the possibility of an extension of the movement for democratization beyond state/society relations to all arenas of power and authority, including international institutions, corporations and banks, and of moving, under feminist influences beyond those traditionally associated with organized labor, to encompass workplaces and, going further, extending to homes and personal relationships as well. It is not a matter of insisting upon a confrontation with the geopolitical leadership, but of expressing an overriding commitment to join the struggle to shape emergent geogovernance structures in more satisfying directions and orienting normative order at all levels of social interaction by reference to the goals of humane governance. An additional dimension of humane governance is to make those in positions of governmental and financial responsibility and authority progressively more accountable for compliance with human rights standards and more prepared to adopt and develop a human-centred ecological and economic world-view that seeks to uphold the life prospects of future generations while devoting "peace dividends" to the reduction of avoidable suffering throughout the world, with special attention to alleviating the condition of those most victimized. Of course, not all human suffering is a consequence of governance. Much distress arises from unresolved tensions *within* civil society. The effort by humane governance to stress the need for bottom-up reconstruction of personal relations, especially intergender roles and attitudes, does acknowledge that many inhumane modes of governance are supported by societal norms and practices, rather than being imposed from *above* or *without*. Cultural attitudes are also crucial, including the sense of life's purpose. Without the rise and spread of a new spiritual/religious consciousness oriented around human solidarity and humanity/nature co-evolution, it is highly dubious that global market forces can be successfully challenged or regressive forms of geogovernance avoided.

Still, positive change is possible. Its likelihood depends on the continuing growth, capability, and orientation of transnational democratic forces. These forces need not aspire to become the new ruling elites of the world, but rather to influence and constrain the existing geopolitical leadership sufficiently so that dominance/exploitation patterns can be supplanted over time by equitable, participatory, accountable, life-sustaining alternatives. It is partly a matter of neutralizing the generally baleful effects of globalization from above which take the form of cultural homogenization, franchise capitalism, and a centrally guided media. But such resistance is not enough. Negation induces despair and inaction unless connected with a set of credible affirmative, alternative responses that embody human solidarity and that arise out of transnationalizing democratic tendencies. These expressions of globalization from below can be contrasted with a geopolitical approach to geogovernance, and amount to a multifaceted struggle to achieve a new equilibrium that reorients market and state to an extent that is nurturing toward both nature and its human inhabitants. Such a reorientation embodies the spirit and substance of humane governance.

It does not, however, predicate *structure*. The structural bias of humane governance can be expressed abstractly: as much decentralism as possible, with as much centralism as necessary. What is generated concretely will depend on the outcome of the three-cornered complex and interactive struggle to control the transition to geogovernance being waged by statist, global market, and transnational democratic forces.[19] Theoretically, a wide range of structural alternatives are compatible with humane governance, including varieties of world government and of communitarian socialism (in the tradition of philosophical anarchism). Historically and functionally, this assessment suggests the attractiveness of intermediate conceptions of structure, combining greater central guidance and institutional presence for regulatory purposes in relation to the global interdependence agenda, and more delegation and reliance on socialization for the domain now covered by state/ society relations.

Realism, Reality, and the Normative Opportunity

While deeply disconcerting, the failure of entrenched elites to respond either on the basis of necessity (the environmental/equity imperatives) or on the basis of opportunity (the geopolitical opening after the Cold War) should not come as a surprise. Elite attitudes on global policy among leaders in the North has converged in recent decades around an ideological and epistemological approach to the political behavior of states known as "political realism," an orientation that is not frequently contested in the domain of governmental authority, especially with respect to foreign policy. There are many versions of political realism, and the academic discussion of realist perspectives is often carried on in a sophisticated political language. The realist mindset, operating from the assumptions of its own "morality," forecloses the political imagination in several respects: it dismisses moral and legal criteria of policy as irrelevant for purposes of explanation, prediction, and prescription; it grounds speculation on an assessment of relative power as perceived by rational, even ultrarational, actors, essentially states, and is therefore unable to take account of passion, irrationality, and altruistic motivations as political forces, or of the impacts of nonstate actors.

What concerns us here is "the realist consensus," a simplified account of which will be presented to convey the essence of the position. To begin with, each actor at whatever level of social organization is assumed to act in such a way as to maximize self-interest by a rational calculative process that is not swayed by moral or legal considerations, and is not sensitive to long-term implications. Realists convert such selfishness on behalf of collective interests into a virtual moral duty when it comes to representing the behavior of sovereign states in the world. If a government were to act unselfishly or in response to the claims of human, rather than state or national, interests, its behavior would be scorned as naive and self-destructive or even criticized as dangerous, inviting aggressiveness elsewhere. Prevailing views about the importance of economic growth based on the play of unimpeded market forces reinforce this realist disposition in political settings. Yet it also casts doubt on the focus on states as rational actors in view of deference to global market forces.

It is generally incorrect to regard realist approaches as amoral, much less as immoral. The morality of realism is, however, of a special kind. It is based on the belief that in a societal space that lacks community sentiment and the agencies of government the only appropriate morality is the pursuit of self-interest of statist scope. That there is no room for civic virtue and comity is a rigorous realist doctrine. Similarly, for economics. Adam Smith's "invisible hand" relieves the rich of any special duty toward the poor except to continue their own pursuit of wealth by way of economic growth carried on as efficiently, hence as profitably, as possible. Each actor, at whatever level of social organiz-ation, acts to maximize its interests. In a society with government this competitive dynamic is regulated by a framework of law, although the central idea is one of rewarding efficiency. Market logic reinforces in economic settings the psychological insights of this realist approach.

Part of the credibility and influence of the realist outlook reflects the rise of science and an image of scientific rationality as indifferent to ethical concerns or human aspiration. The political realist conceives of the world as a force field, and accepts the interplay of actors as a scientific datum. With such an orientation, law and morality as substan-tive traditions are exercises in wishful thinking, and to the extent that they are taken seriously are treated as diversions from "reality." the "morality" of realism is procedural, acting in a calculative, rational, self-interested fashion.

The predominance of this hard-core realist mindset in elite circles is a long, tangled story. There are degrees of realist affirmation; some elites are more unrelentingly realist than others, and some elites are situated amid power and wealth while others are aspiring, but deficient. Also, there are cycles of thought within the realist consensus, reflecting the varying impact of societal concerns and political pressures. It was a predominantly realist idea at the end of the nineteenth and beginning of the twentieth century to accommodate the demands of industrial labor by way of allowing strikes, labor unions, and through institution-alizing welfare policies to varying degrees. That is, realists can be pragmatic about grievances formulated in terms of morality and equity, equating concessions with acknowledgments of relative power. Indeed, the liberal end of the realist spectrum seeks to combine protection of the individual against abuse with a flourishing framework of private economic initiative based on market principles.

The emergence of the realist consensus as the basis of diplomacy is both an old and a new story. There is a distinguished realist lineage that is often regarded as anchored in Thucydides, is reinforced by references to Machiavelli and Hobbes, is applied in military settings by Clausewitz, and given lucid contemporary expression in the work of Hans Morgenthau and George Kennan. In this regard, it is possible to argue that "realism" has been, and continues to be, the orientation of statecraft since ancient times, and that any other view of international relations relies on substituting wishful thinking for the hard facts of power politics.

Such a realist critique of more idealistic views of human nature and world politics has been an important part of the post-1945 narrative. This realist critique has been especially directed at American diplomatic thought and practice, allegedly because of earlier lapses castigated as "moralist" and "legalist."

The main adversary for realists is Woodrow Wilson and his crusade to overcome balance of power approaches to international peace and security in the aftermath of World War I. Of course, Wilson's brand of normative internationalism was never endorsed even by his own country, being defeated at home mainly as a result of isolationist thinking, the American tradition of remaining uninvolved with the Eurocentric tensions. But the carnage of World War I, and the sense of futility that large segments of European public opinion felt, did produce a variety of moves in the 1920s toward a less war-prone approach: disarmament treaties, the establishment of the League of Nations, the outlawing of war, the emergence of a pacifist mood. The effort to punish Germany for its alleged responsibility for starting World War I in the form of punitive reparations and humiliating encroachments on German sovereignty contributed, in the setting of a severe global depression, to the rise of Hitler and to a kind of militarist backlash in other countries that felt dissatisfied about their place in the world order of the 1920s, especially Japan and Italy. The Western European democracies looked away, relying on the infamous policies of "appeasement" to meet the aggressive threats posed. This dominant "reading" of the failure of statecraft to avoid World War II was frequently and influentially invoked after 1945 as a means to avoid a repetition of such mistakes. This reading of history led to the celebrated "Lesson of Munich."

Along with Winston Churchill, George Kennan and Dean Acheson were crucial realist thinkers of this period, architects of the Cold War world. They were concerned that the US, emerging ascendant from World War II, would again squander its leadership opportunities by a

reversion to isolationism or by promoting a revival of idealistic undertakings, thereby shifting attention away from the unavoidable dependence of a stable world order on balance of power geopolitics. The UN
has been viewed by leading realists in the 1940s as a marginal actor, at
best, one that could produce misguided confidence if taken seriously as
an autonomous actor not responsive to geopolitical priorities. The
realists, worried about the Soviet Union and the challenge of Communism, anxious about a drift toward a third world war, worked hard to
forge a consensus around ideas of "containment" and "deterrence."
Their views carried the day in the West, and have been, for many,
vindicated – a third world war was avoided, Soviet power was contained, and the collapse of the Soviet empire occurred without war. It
is hardly surprising that the realist world-view persists until now, despite
the altered circumstances.

The practice of realism tends to be two-faced about normative
dimensions. It seeks to preserve *all options* for itself and friends, but to
hold its adversaries strictly accountable to the constraints of international law and morality. The Gulf War is paradigmatic – the censure
of and response to Iraq was explicitly premised on the illegality of Iraq's
aggression and the criminality of Saddam Hussein's behavior in relation
to foreigners seized as hostages and to Kuwaitis abused by their
conquerors. Such a rationale would not have had much mobilizing force
unless Iraq was perceived as a strategic enemy, either because of oil,
potential nuclear status, security of Israel, or regional balance. It is the
incoherent dualism that is especially disturbing – the attempt to seize
the normative high ground despite an analysis that argues against the
relevance of morality and law. Incoherent this may be, but it is
expedient and even indispensable for sustaining the legitimacy of
concentrations of power and wealth.

What is at issue, of course, is the normative consciousness of society.
How can society be mobilized to forgo material advantage and accept
financial and human sacrifice? By spiritual dedication. By fear, if the
homeland of a person and way of life are directly threatened by
outsiders. Beyond this, by traditional realist manipulations of public
attitudes – demonizing "the other," while celebrating "the self." Such
an ideational landscape was characteristic of the Cold War period, and
offers sufficient reason for doubting the coherence of realist assumptions about human nature.

There is a further realist source of confidence: namely, the failure of
the Marxist-Leninist utopian vision as a historical undertaking embodied in the Soviet experience. In essence, the Marxist-Leninists promised
emancipation, but delivered oppression. A common argument on the

left concerns whether Marx (and in some accounts Lenin) was perverted by his revolutionary heirs, and therefore improperly discredited by the failure of the Soviet approach. Realists contend that this failure of the Soviet project demonstrates conclusively that both efficiency in relation to production and freedom with respect to the political order is best protected by markets, constitutional government based on checks and balances, and a readiness for war in relation to potential adversary states.

This realist reading of recent history is, of course, highly selective, largely uncritical, and insensitive to the situation of the poor and victimized whether conceived in class or regional terms. Also, the historical knowledge that moralism and legalism failed to deter the aggressions of Hitler and Mussolini is not equivalent to the contention that law and morality are irrelevant to the rigors of political life. The moralism and legalism of the 1930s was partial, without deep cultural roots, tainted by vindictive policies toward Germany, and unavoidably intertwined with a colonial order that rested on dominance by the strong, rich, and white. It is not necessary to repudiate realism altogether in order to look elsewhere for change and hope about the human future.

The realist mindset is most strongly present among elites. In civil society, ideas about truth, decency, and destiny have always held sway. The social landscape of politics moves in mysterious ways that express underlying religious sentiments as well as spiritual and ethical ideals. Not all of these normative energies in civil society are congenial with the promotion of human rights and democratic values. There are populist tendencies that are frighteningly destructive, regarding "others" as enemies to be destroyed; there are many varieties of ethnic hatreds, local prejudices, patriarchal outlooks, religiously sanctioned cruelties, and deeply entrenched populist resentments (Nietzsche's diatribes against herd mentality) that should make us exceedingly wary about celebrating the particular and condemning the general, or about romanticizing the traditional and uncritically affirming the precepts of cultural practice.

The Politics of Bounded Conviction

Realism is a normative choice that can be defended by political and moral arguments, and can be explained, in part, as a reflection of modernist faith in reason as well as a reaction to the perceived failure of "appeasement" to stem the challenge of fascism to the established world order system of the 1930s. The realist outlook has also been validated, according to its adherents, by the experience of the Cold War, containing Soviet expansionism while avoiding strategic warfare. Such a validation acquires added force when contrasted with the failures of idealism and accommodation to stem either the expansionism of the Axis powers or to avoid World War II. Nevertheless, the realist consensus rests on claims of knowledge and objectivity that are deceptive.

To some extent, debates about realism – its virtues and defects – are a US phenomenon. Elsewhere, a more opportunistic, less coherent, and possibly less democratic approach towards global security is often taken. In Europe, a modified kind of realism as the basis of foreign policy is taken for granted, since warfare and its imminence have been a constant feature of modern European history, at least up to 1989. In Japan, the preoccupation has been with reducing vulnerability to attack, erasing the failures of Japanese militarism, and above all, avoiding its revival. In the South, by way of overgeneralization, the security concern has been regional and defensive in relation to the global level.

The record of realism is mixed. The realist emphasis on "peace" through preparations for war deserves some credit for avoiding a third world war in the face of the Soviet-led Communist challenge, but it is a provisional claim in at least two senses. We can never know what would have happened if a more peace-oriented approach had been adopted by the West. We need to take account of the failures of the realist approach to stem violence in the South, to build more effective international institutions, and to advance the rule of law in relations among states.

But realism was never altogether convincing, even as a basis for the foreign policy of leading governments. In the post-Cold War world, realism seems especially ill-adapted as a framework for problem-solving and human betterment. The erosion of territoriality by way of complex interdependence, the integration of capital, the scale of environmental decay, and the burdens of poverty places an unprecedented emphasis on cooperation and solidarity. The deficiencies of realism in the present era are ironically being dramatized by realist recourse to antirealist political language to describe and justify security policy – a provisional reference to the salience of the humanitarian agenda, including an emphasis on the role of the UN and the desirability of mandating "humanitarian intervention" in the face of gross violations of human rights. Both the humanitarian rationalization of policy and the reliance on an augmented UN role are at fundamental variance with the realist stance, but seem like a short-lived phase in light of UN failures in the early 1990s.[20]

Since we do not know enough to explain or predict political behavior, reliance on interpretation of historical circumstances is unavoidable, as is choice with respect to normative direction. In this regard, the case for adoption of a desirable program of global reform seems overwhelming, even if current realist constraints make such a program seem unlikely of adoption at the present time. That is, the horizons of politics are self-fulfilling: if the main agents of political action are confirmed realists, then a realist landscape results. If the visionary convictions of dedicated exponents of global civil society hold sway, then a more humanistic landscape results.

This turn to a politics of *bounded* conviction[21] is encouraged by several additional factors:

- the collapse of Communism in Eastern Europe and the Soviet Union by nonviolent means seemed highly unlikely from a *realist* viewpoint as recently as a decade ago, confirming both the severe limits on a realist capacity to *know* what is possible (being extremely discrediting to the social science claims of realism with its pretensions of explanation and prediction) and the validity of establishing political horizons on the basis of what is *desirable*;
- the current regime of double standards works against achieving such minimal goals of world order as avoiding ecological collapse and exerting degrees of control over the dynamics of global capital;
- scientific advances in a number of domains, including chaos theory, suggest the extent to which small changes (or inputs) can and do generate large effects (or outcomes); in the setting of world order systems we cannot begin to know what might be possible given their complexity and the volume and velocity of change at virtually every entry point. This does not confirm an optimistic reading of historical prospects, since what is unexpected may also be negative, but it certainly undermines the sort of gloomy and generally deterministic Kissingerian reading of history that is embedded in the realist outlook. Neither optimism, nor pessimism about the future can be convincingly validated, and neither seems appropriate, as compared to acting on the basis of bounded convictions and personal engagement in political struggle to overcome concrete circumstances of cruelty and deprivation;
- such engagement, however, needs to be tempered by humility, including respect for restraining norms on process and goals as embodied in international law. The discredited utopias of this century, especially those associated with Marxist-Leninist claims of scientific certainty, left behind a trail of blood and a vast gulag as a testament, suggesting the dangers of being convinced that history and

ideology warrant recourse to violence against opponents and the stifling of critics and opposition, using an overarching invocation of the slogan "the end justifies the means." Experience with claims of religious and political certainty – whether in earlier periods or currently – strongly reinforces these cautionary comments on a politics of conviction. A politics of conviction as advocated here, against the background of recent historical events, is strongly biased against recourse to armed forms of struggle and emphasizes tolerance, mandating respect for nonviolent critics and opponents, but it stops well short of a Weberian embrace of rationality and moderation as the guide to political action;

– because the scale of global reform is so large, a broad scanning of normative horizons is appropriate; alternative thinking and forms are emerging. It is a matter of naming these developments, identifying those that appear positive, encouraging confidence in popular iniatives, while remaining open to criticism and dialogue. In this spirit, an emphasis is placed on positing the reality of "global civil society" and of accenting transnational extensions of democratic and nonviolent forms of governance. As earlier projects for reform called primarily for disarmament or world government, the call here is for "global constitutionalism" within a political atmosphere that could follow upon a successful movement to strengthen transnational democracy.

It is the goal of this book to articulate a politics of bounded conviction conceived along these lines.

Reinforcing the Politics of Conviction: A Macrohistorical Reading of the Transitional Ferment

The conventional tendency is to perceive the present global circumstance from a media-dominated perspective on current events, one that stresses the collapse of bipolarity as the essential casual influence on the forward motion of history. Social activists in various settings generally have a different take on the historical situation, stressing either the continuity of human suffering on the ground (the unchanging local circumstance) or the deteriorating agenda of human concerns, ranging from poverty, through patriarchy to environmental decay. For both of these perspectives the ending of the Cold War is tangential, aggravating the situation in some respects, alleviating it in others, but essentially irrelevant to the challenges of democratizing the sites of human encounter and of the need for a variety of normative and structural innovations.

Both sets of interpretations draw our attention usefully to aspects of the emergent setting of politics. The focus on geogovernance intends also to proclaim a macrohistorical interpretation of the changing scene: the depth and magnitude of the transitional context can only be compared to the agricultural and industrial revolutions. Such depth of transforming possibilities arising out of new technologies creates an opening for advocates of humane governance. Nothing less than the adoption of a new axiological posture toward human destiny will suffice: dismantling global apartheid in favor of a one-world community premised on nonviolence, human rights, democracy, respect for international law, environmental balance, planetary unity. Whether or not ecofeminism or some as yet unimagined coalition of societal and spiritual energies is the agency of transformation, the outcome must be a democratic and benevolent form of geogovernance, the realization of the project to establish humane governance. Such an outcome is a positive alternative at this macrohistorical crossroads to the regressive year-by-year slide toward the eventual embodiment of an eco-authoritarian variant (that is, authoritarian methods to contain or suppress evidence of environmental damage and to shift its main burdens to subordinate classes, races, and regions) of global apartheid.

To be clear, the integrative tendencies at the level of culture, economy, environment (together with disintegrative tensions) will inevitably generate during the decades to come some variant of geogovernance, but its form and human impact will depend on the outcome of struggle. Specifically, it will depend on the degree of success achieved by a politics of bounded conviction rooted in the quest for humane governance, a quest primarily associated with the construction of a global civil society as a successor to a world of states dependent on patterns of geopolitical conflict and domination, and as an alternative to a tightly centralized system of geogovernance preoccupied with the expansion of the world economy within existing frameworks of privilege and hierarchy, implying the suppression of challenges from below by whatever means necessary.

From Geopolitics to Geogovernance with Humane Governance as the Goal

In giving substantive content to this politics of bounded conviction, emphasis is placed on the possibility, desirability, and necessity of superseding geopolitics, either as it has been understood and practiced in the era of the state system or as it is being refashioned to accommodate the rising ascendancy of global market forces. The content of humane governance will become evident in succeeding chapters, but since this orientation is so central, a few salient characteristics can be set forth here by way of preparation.

First of all, the focus on humane governance emphasizes the importance of governance for the entire planet and its peoples. As such, it relies on global constitutionalism both to overcome the negative features of geopolitics as currently operational and to construct a positive form of world order. The stress on global constitutionalism encompasses both the democratizing agenda of bringing law and popular participation to bear upon policies that control the exercise of economic and political power, and the extension of regional and global institutional capabilities to address functional problems of environment and equity.

Secondly, the language of humane governance is intended as a deliberate contrast to the behavioral patterns associated with geopolitics, whether statist or market-driven, and generative in the past, present, and future of various modes of "inhumane governance." A summary of the general structures of such negativity is set out in chapter 2.

Thirdly, the pursuit, attainment, and continuous refinement of humane governance is the principal project of emergent global civil society, engaging both powers of reason and analysis, but also summoning the energies of imagination associated with hope, desire, and fantasy.

2
A Triple Indictment of Inhumane Governance

The failures of geopolitical leadership in the aftermath of the Cold War have been evidenced both by the militarist approach taken to the Gulf War and by the missed opportunities to reconstruct global society along more durable lines. At the substrategic level, warfare and anarchy are features of "the new world order." The persistence of the realist mindset still constrains the political imagination of elites dominating statist, market, and media operations. The political imagination of adherents of humane governance has also failed to challenge conventional wisdom very effectively during this period of fluidity and transition.

This chapter extends the argument of the previous chapter in two principal directions. It stresses the strong tendency of capitalism to operate in particularly cruel ways, especially given current global conditions, reinforcing structures of inequity, misappropriation of resources, and neglect of those most impoverished. It depicts, illustratively, the resulting human ordeal, and the numbing accompanying pattern of response. Although globalization creates a general frame for market activities, capitalist roots remain primarily territorial, thereby making comparisons between Japan, Europe, and the United States highly relevant in terms of style, market penetration, and the approach taken to unemployment and welfare systems. In this regard, the degrees of cruelty vary considerably, being perhaps far more pronounced in the United States than elsewhere. At the same time, even the best safety nets, as in northern Europe, do not overcome the human damage inflicted by chronic unemployment, and a feeling of worthlessness.

Although capitalism has historically operated in accordance with a certain coherent dynamics, classically analyzed by Marx and many followers, the specific human consequences of capitalism have been notoriously uneven through time and across space. This unevenness can be expressed in terms of more or less compassion for those segments of society that are most impoverished and in relation to the disparities in global terms between rich and poor countries, regions, peoples, and races.

The current phase of capitalism is especially polarizing with respect to both class relations and center/periphery patterns.[1] That is, capitalism is in the midst of an especially cruel phase (as contrasted with, say, 1955–75) for the following reasons:

- Capitalism is essentially uncontested ideologically, and capitalist dominance is accepted globally as a fact of life, with socialist, and even strong welfare alternatives, being discredited, at least temporarily;
- industrial and postindustrial restructuring of the world economy, introducing a new technological cycle, has created a period of economic stagnation for most affluent countries, generating domestic pressures to improve conditions at home and to discourage a commitment to the alleviation of poverty elsewhere; such a trend is reinforced by the weakening of organized labor as a political factor either within leading states or internationally;
- restructuring sharpens intracapitalist rivalries and places a premium on efficiency, growth, and "competitiveness" – an emphasis that inhibits welfare approaches in state/society and North/South contexts;
- this emphasis is aggravated by an increasing tendency to rely on capital rather than labor for increases in productivity, making labor a smaller part of the value-added component of production and creating a large surplus of excess labor at all skill levels, resulting in a deepening crisis of unemployment in Europe and North America; these effects accompany a shift in the technological frontier from industry to electronics;
- the efforts of the countries of Eastern Europe and the former Soviet Union to make a successful transition to market-oriented constitutionalism has been treated mainly as a geopolitical opportunity to solidify the victory of the West in the Cold War, including an enlargement of market opportunities, and has diverted both normative commitments and resources from societal distress in the South;
- the globalization of financial markets, fiscal policies, and trade relations has reduced the experimental space available to smaller states to pursue more compassionate orientations toward political economy and development; this tendency is strongly reinforced by the influence of the IMF, especially in relation to the more heavily

indebted countries in the South, through the medium of Structural Adjustment Programs that place strong restraints on governmental efforts to assist the poor by subsidized food prices and credit facilities;
– disillusionment with foreign assistance, both at the giving and receiving ends, as well as the rising costs of environmental protection further weaken compassionate impulses;
– and in addition, the collapse of bipolarity has undercut the pragmatic rationale for foreign assistance, which was always important in the domestic debate.

These factors constitute the backdrop against which to develop a critique of the mode and manner by which the dynamics of the world political economy impact upon human lives, including unborn generations. Only generalized patterns are explored here. There are many specific variations, and the patterns should be adjusted accordingly in each specific setting.

The First Indictment: Global Apartheid

The Westphalian conception of international society – so-named because of the Peace of Westphalia in 1648, treated as the origin point of the modern state system with its stress on territorial supremacy as a juridical right – is based on the equality of sovereign states. A traditional geopolitical perspective provides a focus on the statist hierarchies that dominate international life, reflecting inequalities among states, and especially reflecting the influence on the history of peoples exerted by the most powerful states. In the period between 1945 and 1989 this geopolitical perspective has emphasized the roles of the two superpowers, thereby highlighting the hegemonic implications of military superiority and understating the importance of economic criteria of power.

With the collapse of bipolarity, two geopolitical tendencies have become evident. The first, relating to statist geopolitics, accentuates US ascendancy as "the sole surviving superpower," producing a so-called "unipolar moment."[2] The second post–Cold War viewpoint is more attuned to capital-driven geopolitics, and is oriented around the relative economic decline of the United States, coupled with the rise of Japan and Germany, or in some formulations Japan and Europe, producing a kind of multipolar or tripolar pattern of geopolitics.

Conventional geopolitics views only the top of the pyramid of power; it neglects the bottom. The leading geopolitical actors do not even purport to represent the great majority of women and men on the planet. Moreover such states represent only the dominant class, gender, and race within their own territorial space. The orientation of this book is the opposite, to take a careful look at the negative consequences of inequality for the poor and weak, and for those especially vulnerable, and to conceive of international relations from the perspective of the global interest, and its bearing on the well-being of peoples. Such an orientation is partly based on according normative priority to the circumstances of the most disadvantaged, giving the highest place to those ethnic and civilizational units threatened with extinction or confronted by genocidal tendencies. Such a calculus helps account for the great attention given to the situation and voices of indigenous peoples. The emphasis on "peoples" also draws on democratic notions of equality, above all the recognition that 80 percent of the world's population lives in the South, excluded from such geopolitical arenas of interaction and decision as the annual economic summits of the G-7 and permanent membership of the UN Security Council.

The South Commission in its report *The Challenge to the South* exemplifies this basic concern with the dynamics of inequality:

> Were all humanity a single nation-state, the present North/South divide would make it an unviable, semi-feudal entity, split by internal conflicts. Its small part is advanced, prosperous, powerful; its much bigger part is underdeveloped, poor, powerless. A nation so divided within itself would be recognized as inherently unstable. A world so divided should likewise be recognized as inherently unstable. And the position is worsening, not improving.[3]

One should add class, gender, and race dimensions: within the North, as well, there are growing problems of impoverishment that are having a disproportionately harmful effect on women and on peoples of color, while within the South there are rich elites, characteristically operating in patriarchal modes.

For heuristic purposes, this world structure is characterized as a system aptly described by the metaphor "global apartheid." The term global apartheid was initially introduced by Gernot Kohler in the course of WOMP discussions of the early 1970s. Kohler reasoned as follows: "the apartheid structure of the global society has important similarities with that of South Africa. Indeed, the global society is a mirror reflection of South African society. One can go a step further and say that global apartheid is even more severe than South African apartheid."[4] Kohler reinforced his provocative analysis with various indicators of inequality and poverty that remain structurally revealing despite the fact that the assessment was made 20 years ago. Indeed, Kohler's demonstrations of race-correlated inequalities have been accentuated in the intervening years by most economic trends, although rapid growth in parts of Asia requires a more differentiated model of global apartheid than a mere North/South or white/nonwhite conception.

There was a reluctance to adopt such a harsh metaphor of inequality until recently, but the growing sense that the North was managing global economic policy with scant attention to the claims and needs of the peoples of the South has stimulated the spread of reliance on "global apartheid" as a descriptive term. In the preface of an important book by Arjun Makhijani one finds this sentence: "The principal conclusion here is that the structure of the world economy is in most essential ways like that of apartheid in South Africa – a kind of global apartheid."[5]

Undoubtedly the most intriguing adoption of this comparison between South Africa (with apartheid) and the world is to be found in a recent essay by Thomas Schelling, a conservative thinker, famed for his earlier work on conflict theory that laid the groundwork for the sorts of graduated escalation policies relied upon by the US government at the height of its involvement in the Vietnam War. Schelling's speculations are particularly relevant because he conceives of global structure in relation to plausible prospects for geogovernance. It seems worth quoting him at length:

> If we were to think about a "new world order" that might embark on the gradual development of some constitutional framework within which the peoples of the globe would eventually share collective responsibility and reciprocal obligations, somewhat analogous to what we expect in a traditional nation state, and if we were to think about the political mechanisms that might be developed, what actual nation, existing now or in the past, might such an incipient world state resemble? If we were to contemplate gradually relinquishing some measure of sovereignty in order to form not a more perfect union, but a more effective world legal structure, what familiar political entity might be our basis for comparison?
>
> I find my own answer stunning and embarrassing: South Africa.

Schelling continues by explaining the fit:

> We live in a world that is one-fifth rich and four-fifths poor; the rich are segregated into the rich countries and the poor into poor countries; the rich are predominantly lighter skinned and the poor darker skinned; most of the poor live in "homelands" that are physically remote, often separated by oceans and great distances from the rich.

Migration on any great scale is impermissible. There is no systematic redistribution of income. While there is ethnic strife among the well-to-do, the strife is more vicious and destructive among the poor.[6]

This stress on the similarity between South Africa under apartheid and the global order serves two purposes. A strong and global moral consensus exists that apartheid was and remains an unacceptable and even criminal system of governance. One would suppose that what has been repudiated as unacceptable at the level of the state must certainly be rejected at the level of the world.[7] The second purpose of the metaphor is mobilizing, to insist that a high priority be accorded to global economic reform by those transnational forces dedicated to fostering the transition to geogovernance in the form of humane governance, and that the shape and substance of this reform must come to grips with racist implications of present global structures of authority, wealth, and prestige.

Unlike South African apartheid during the period of Afrikaaner rule, global apartheid contradicts the policy edicts and rhetoric of geopolitics. Global apartheid in this sense indicates the hidden racist and classist structure of geopolitics. On the surface of policy, there are commitments to reform, compassion, sovereign and racial equality, human rights, and democracy. These commitments have several consequences aside from the diversionary and propagandistic ones of obscuring the illegitimate underpinnings of geopolitics. Firstly, there is a sense of reformist obligation that can be reinforced by pressures of various sorts. For instance, the publication of an annual Human Development Index by the UN Development Program is an attempt to actualize these obligations by depicting the degree and locus of suffering, as well as progress toward its mitigation. Secondly, the nascent influences of global civil society can press for reformist measures (without necessarily directly challenging geopolitical underpinnings).

The gap between reformist promises and performance is immense, and has grown wider in the last several decades as a result of the evolution of a normative order, especially in the setting of human rights. A few examples may demonstrate the point. Article 6 of the International Covenant on Economic, Social and Cultural Rights (1966) obliges states to "recognize the right to work, which includes the right of everyone to the opportunity to gain his living by work which he [sic] freely chooses or accepts" and commits states to "take appropriate steps to safeguard this right." Similarly Article 11 of the same Covenant recognizes "the right of everyone to an adequate standard of living for himself and his family, including adequate food, clothing and housing, and to the continuous improvement of living conditions" and obliges states to take steps to realize this right. The most comprehensive of all welfare promises is contained in the Universal Declaration of Human Rights (1948), in Article 28: "Everyone is entitled to a social order and international order in which the rights and freedoms set forth in this Declaration can be fully realized."

If we ponder these reformist promises we might wonder why they were ever made. Surely their conscientious implementation would lead to the dismantling of global apartheid. It is necessary to assume that the governments that have generated and formalized these commitments regarded them merely as aspirations, not to be acted upon in the serious domain of politics. But is it necessary for the governments of the South to regard them as politically irrelevant?

Such commitments might have been regarded as "soft" law, that is, undertaken without serious expectation of implementation and on the assumption that no efforts at enforcement would be made. But "soft" can become "hard" if the political climate generates pressures for implementation and enforcement. The role of transnational social forces is highly relevant. One could imagine, for instance, strong efforts in the years ahead to insist that the right to meaningful employment is legally protected and should be upheld through the enactment of plans for full employment.

Recall, for example, the experience with the obligations of the Helsinki Accords to promote human rights in Europe. Back in 1975 these provisions were looked upon as scant repayment by Moscow for the West's acknowledgment of post-1945 European boundaries, including the division of Germany. The Helsinki Accords were viewed at the time of negotiations as principally concerned with European boundaries, stabilizing *de facto* circumstances and thereby relinquishing revisionist claims associated with Western challenges to "the Yalta system," a system seen as unwarranted deference to Soviet geopolitical ambitions. The insistence on human rights commitments as part of the bargain was regarded as giving the outcome some semblance of reciprocity, thereby weakening reactionary critiques of the agreement as one-sided. But the whole assessment of totalitarian rule as irreversible made it seem futile to mount objections. The rise of democratic forces in Eastern Europe was especially ignored by conservatives, being an excluded possibility by their own pessimistic analysis. In contrast, peace groups in the West, most notably European Nuclear Disarmament (END), were far more receptive to social developments in Eastern Europe, taking them seriously from the outset. What happened in the late 1980s, and to some degree earlier, particularly in Poland and

Czechoslovakia, was that resistance movements were inspired by these promises of human rights. The oppressive governments were thrown on the defensive; their sense of legitimacy was eroded, which led to a dissipation of the will to rule.[8]

In relation to global apartheid, the most immediate challenge is to demonstrate the extent of the gap in actual conditions between what has been promised by the normative order of geopolitics and what is being done. It can be seen, then, that even acute suffering is increasingly tolerated, and not just in the South, but in the most affluent cities in the countries in the North.

One expression of this tolerance is the gradual acceptance of homelessness as a fact of life in American cities. This has become so ingrained that even the Democratic Party, despite its historic connections with the socially disadvantaged, ignores the issue, as was evident during the 1992 presidential election campaign, and subsequently in the early years of the Clinton presidency. Another recent expression is the absence of concern about acute distress in several countries in sub-Saharan Africa. Such indifference toward suffering also disclosed the ideological tensions and priorities that are characteristic of global apartheid: normative promises arising from needs and rights are subordinated to the quite contrary logic of capitalism. Capitalism functions best during its restructuring phases (that is, when one technological era is replacing another) by rewarding marginal increases in efficiency and by addressing inefficiencies ruthlessly as occasions for restructuring.

The impact of these periodic restructurings are themselves exceedingly uneven, generally falling most heavily on those societies and social sectors that are least competitive and that are most dedicated to overcoming the specter of economic decline. This is especially the case if, as in the United States, a highly individualistic ethos is read as the capitalist way, with rewards and punishments distributed according to "merit" by the market (perceived as neutral and objective). Where social cohesion is more highly valued as part of competitiveness, as in Japan and parts of Europe, then restructuring may be less painful for the poor, but even in these model societies the pendulum is swinging toward market-guided appraisals of human worth. Overall, the burdens of restructuring are borne disproportionally by the most disadvantaged sectors of society, but there are significant exceptions in this recent period. For instance, cutbacks in aerospace demands have caused hardships for high-tech salaried employees since the mid-1980s.

The evidence discloses patterns of a widespread refusal by the rich and powerful to overcome avoidable suffering despite their normative promises to the contrary and in the face of strong indications that relatively small inputs of resources could have highly beneficial effects.

It is not suggested that a sadistic element is lurking in the background, namely, a kind of satisfaction gleaned from witnessing the suffering endured elsewhere. Such an emotional deformation cannot be totally dismissed, but it is not fundamental. The neglect of avoidable suffering is mainly associated with the implicit workings of an investment model, what output is likely to be forthcoming over what time period, and the conviction that the globally marginalized people, even if their suffering is alleviated, are unlikely to be significant consumers or producers in the global marketplace for the foreseeable future. An exception to this attitude concerns Russia; this is viewed as a gamble, and as a source of trouble if it fails.

The Second Indictment: Avoidable Harm

The first indictment implicates structure, the second indictment relates to policy failure in relation to matters of normative concern. This indictment insists that policies being pursued by those in authority, whether as officials or agents of civic initiatives, are causing harm to humanity. The quantum of such harm is impossible to measure, and criteria of interpretation of what is harm are somewhat subjective, although they can be linked to standards that enjoy virtually universal support. The current dynamics of world order generate many varieties of avoidable harm. The project of humane governance, rooted in the concrete responses of the here and now, is dedicated to its reduction, and its possible elimination. In every social and political setting the commitment to humane governance implies intolerance toward all forms of avoidable harm. This will be illustrated by a discussion of several representative concerns.

The second indictment begins with the existence, and spread, of absolute poverty. It judges the hardship and anguish that arise from repression and exclusion, and the whole range of circumstances of oppression at various levels of social reality. Arising from this is the sense of avoidable harm that results from the misery and waste generated by militarism and warfare.

The intent here is to depict and illustrate some of these concerns by selected reference to statistical assessments and through several impressionistic reminders of the sorts of suffering that exist that could be overcome if the political will to do so existed. No claim is being made here to be original, systematic, or comprehensive. There are better sources to obtain a fuller picture, including the annual Human Development Report of UNDP, the reports of the World Bank and IMF and specialized agencies dealing with food, health, environment, as well as the analyses issued by many nongovernmental organizations (NGOs) disseminating information and assessments that pertain to their areas of particular interest. Also valuable as tools of comprehension and interpretation are the films, novels, poems, and songs that are responding intuitively to the congeries of local and global circumstances. Cultural artifacts, at their best, have an extraordinary capacity to empower and expose, and should never be regarded as alien to the methods or outlook of the social sciences, especially in an undertaking of this sort.

Some headline items provide a backdrop of normative challenges against which to fashion proposals and offer interpretations that are intended to strike responsive chords among those engaged in strengthening global civil society by overcoming patterns of inhumane governance. The aim is twofold: to underscore the severity of human suffering, and to show that ample capabilities exist to move by degrees toward humane governance. In the most basic sense, the challenges are *political* and *ethical*, and possibly *psychological*, but do not arise from any absolute *scarcity* or from an absence of *resources* and *technical capabilities*.

Children   According to the UNICEF report, "Development Goals and Strategies for Children: Priorities for UNICEF Action in the 1990s": "Critical poverty affects about 45 percent of children under five years old in developing countries (excluding China), or about 155 million. About 40 million of them live in urban areas and about 115 million live in rural areas."[9] Additionally, "at the end of the 1980s, some 14 million children under the age of five years died every year in developing countries" (p. 8). Sub-Saharan Africa is proportionately hit the hardest.

The issue of maternal well-being is also crucial, touching upon the condition of women as well as the life prospects of children. This same UN report says that "about 500,000 women die each year from causes related to pregnancy and childbirth, leaving over 1 million children motherless; and less than half the married women of child-bearing age have the necessary knowledge to enable them to space child births and to prevent unwanted pregnancy" (p. 8).

Further, as the report states, "It is the greatest condemnation of our times that more than a quarter of a million small children should still be dying *every week* of easily preventable illness and malnutrition. *Every day*, measles, whooping cough and tetanus, all of which can be prevented by an inexpensive course of vaccines, kill almost 8,000 children. *Every day* diarrhoeal dehydration, which can be prevented at almost no cost, still kills almost, 7,000 children. *Every day* pneumonia, which can be treated with low-cost antibiotics, kills more than 6,000 children . . . Death on this scale is simply no longer necessary; it is therefore no longer acceptable" (p. 3).

In some respects, the challenge to keep young children alive is the easy part. According to UNICEF figures, an additional $2–3 billion per year would do the job within a decade. The more difficult challenge is to provide food, health, education, and employment opportunities to meet the material conditions for a satisfying life from start to finish.

Poverty   The alleviation of poverty as a blight upon the planet is also within easy fiscal reach. It would require "real progress . . . in reducing the outflow of debt and interest payments and increasing the inflow of investments to the developing world." If this could occur, "it can be estimated that an additional $50 billion a year would be required, throughout the 1990s, to move forward towards the great human goals of adequate food, water, health care and education for every man, woman and child on earth. The approximate price tag for moving convincingly in this direction is therefore less than half of one percent of the world's gross international product or about 5 percent of present military spending." If half of this amount came from the North it would still represent a very small-scale increase in aid – "it would mean increasing today's aid levels by approximately 50 percent so that, for example, the Western industrialized nations would be giving an average of 0.5 percent of their GNP's instead of today's 0.35 percent. The aid target agreed in the 1960s was 0.7 percent."[10]

The persistence and concentration of poverty in the South is well documented. During the 1980s, average incomes fell by 10 percent in Latin America and by over 20 percent in sub-Saharan Africa, the poorest region by far, where the great majority of the people must spend three quarters of their incomes on food. According to the *Human Development Report 1991* there are about 1.3 billion poor people in the South, a figure that is expected to increase by 100 million by the year 2000, and a further 200 million by 2010. Again, the situation of Africa is particularly grave: "if African leaders and the international community do not take action now, more than half of the continent's population will be below the poverty line at the end of the decade."[11]

The division between North and South is widening, but so is the distance between rich and poor countries and classes. At the present time 23 percent of the world population lives in the North and appropriates 85 percent of the world's income, while the other 77

−10%	−3%	+4%	+9%	+34%
Bottom fifth	Next lowest fifth	Middle fifth	Second highest fifth	Top fifth

Figure 2.1   Changes in income distribution in the US between 1977 and 1988 (*Source*: *International Herald Tribune*, July 25, 1991)

percent lives in the South on the remaining 15 percent. It is not surprising that the report of the South Commission should stress the North/South disparity as the central fact of current world order. It is also worth noting that democratization on a global scale is not tenable given the double whammy of widening disparities and the geographic concentration of poverty in the South. Indeed, if reliance on militarized conceptions of regional and global security persist, including intervention as an instrument of geopolitics, democratization faces a triple whammy.

The unbridling of capitalism during the 1980s, combining the decline of social democracy and organized labor, as well as the Western victory in the East–West rivalry, has introduced a new hardness into class relations everywhere in the world. From China to the United States leaders are justifying the neglect of the poor by reference to their utter devotion to the play of market forces, reinforced by a preoccupation with the avoidance of inflation, the encouragement of profitability and savings, and the attraction of investment. It is expressive of this pattern, and an ironic comment on the decline of ideological politics, to note that the free market sectors of the Chinese economy, which for several years have been growing at spectacular rates, are ultracapitalist in their neglect of human consequences, and rely on the exploitation of women and children, made to work for absurdly low wages in often unsafe conditions.

Recent figures on income distribution in the United States confirm this trend toward polarization in the North and a widening gap between rich and poor. According to figures released by the Center on Budget and Policy Priorities, the income of the top 1 percent of US households increased from $203,000 per household in 1977 to $451,000 in 1988, an increase measured in current dollars that was a dramatic 122 percent; the top 5 percent did only slightly less well, experiencing an average increase over the same period of 60 percent. Figure 2.1 shows how the distribution of income was dramatically tilted against the already deprived bottom fifth in the same period.

There are several points to make here. The figures leave no doubt about the monetary distribution of rewards at this stage of capitalism – the rich are getting much richer and the poor are growing significantly poorer. Such trends may be accentuated or moderated, depending on the orientation of the political party or faction in control of government, but the basic impact of capitalist restructuring is an upward redistribution of income shares.

According to the US trends, 60 percent of the population is improving its circumstances, but for many other less affluent societies, with smaller middle classes, the proportion for whom life circumstances are improving is a tiny percent of the whole. Further, even in the rich countries, being poor can mean living under conditions of severe deprivation – no shelter, health care, and scarcely any food. As privatization of social services proceeds during this period, a decline of family income and real wages causes even greater hardships than in the past. A further factor in weakening the political leverage of the poorer half of society is the marked decline of labor union influence almost everywhere, with a consequent loss of leverage by organized working people in general. This decline, in turn, encourages political alienation, resulting in rising levels of nonparticipation by the poor in electoral politics, making politicians in constitutional democracies less worried about supporting policies that favor the rich and giving them almost no incentive to address the problems of those most marginalized.

Of course, social disruption, especially if not contained, does challenge political complacency about deprived social classes. The Los Angeles riots of May 1992 provided a temporary wake-up call for US politicians and for American society, but the restoration of order quickly dissipated concerns without relieving the misery that caused the eruption. A film like *Menace II Society*, set in South Central Los Angeles, vividly portrays both the despairs of entrapment among black inner city youth and the dangers to larger social wholes arising from neglecting this pent-up fury.

The way democratic politics is financed by private wealth and special interests further reinforces the trends and patterns. And finally, behind such patterns of income redistribution lie deeply ingrained racist features, such that nonwhite minorities are heavily overrepresented in the lower reaches and underrepresented in the upper reaches of the overall income profile. Beyond this, of course, is the tendency of those who escape from poverty to turn their backs on their communities of origin. This is especially pronounced, in some settings, where the escape has racial overtones leaving behind the identity of racial victim and identifying with the dominant race.

What is particularly noteworthy and discouraging about this new consensus that the heaviest burdens associated with the stimulus of economic expansion should be borne by the poor is the absence of alternative strategies and of notable mainstream opposition. It is part of the wider process of decline of political parties as instruments of policy challenge and ideological debate. Whether it is the socialism of France or Spain, the new economics of Brazil or Mexico, the attempted entry into the world market by the Soviet Union or the countries of East Europe, the same orthodoxy prevails, at least for now. Even so, this deterioration of politics at the center creates unprecedented opportunities for the rise of new and progressive political movements out of the turmoil and distress of civil society, bearing new visions of economic and social priorities.

But such opportunities will not be acted upon until coherent, progressive options are depicted, especially with respect to economic policy. It is here that the failure of the Soviet approach has exerted its strongest influence, disparaging any scheme that purports to rest on a role accorded to the state in promoting social justice. Of course, the conceptual situation is confused, as the Japanese "miracle" is partly attributed to bringing the state into the market as facilitating partner. It is true that the Japanese impulse was paternalistic rather than socialistic, but an active governmental role was deemed the most effective way to build up corporate capacity to gain access to overseas markets and to maintain control over the domestic market.

It is necessary to add a caveat here about unevenness of perception, situation, and policy consequences. Although the rise of capitalist orthodoxy is a near-universal trend, crucial differences of response continue. Scandinavian countries are searching for ways to restore profitability to investment these days, but they are doing so in a manner that interferes only at the margins with their provision of social services. But in a country such as Sweden, long an inspiration to democratizing tendencies in the South, political forces espousing the unbridling of capitalism are growing in strength and even the Swedish Social Democratic Party is trying hard to bolster its support by claiming to possess impeccable capitalist credentials. Much of the debate in Sweden during the early 1990s centers around which political party has the most credibility to lead the country into the capital-driven arenas of the European Community, which is regarded as the path to a more beneficial participation in the overall tendency toward economic regionalization and globalization on the basis of market forces. There is an ebb and flow in domestic public opinion on these issues in Sweden and elsewhere. The globally and regionally oriented elites have not done such a successful selling job, and various constituencies are now more sophisticated about calculating specific gains and losses. The dynamics of this process in the North are best revealed by the debates that have emerged in Europe and North America *after* (and only after) the negotiation of the treaties of Maastricht and the North Atlantic Free Trade Area (NAFTA).

The view taken here is that this ascendancy of capitalist orthodoxy is a temporary phenomenon. It is temporary because it runs counter to what arguably has been a stronger trend over the last century toward the protection of human rights and the growth of democracy, and the insistence by countries of the South on safeguarding their sovereign rights. It is temporary, also, because unregulated economic growth severely aggravates tendencies toward ecological collapse. In effect, this report contends that such unbridled capitalism is not sustainable on a planet that is crowded and impoverished. It is not ecologically, politically, or normatively sustainable. Because the present framework is not sustainable does not ensure that the sequel will be beneficial. It could easily be followed by a set of arrangements that yield even worse human consequences. The pressures on the environment could induce a variety of North/South and intraregional and intranational adjustments that move in eco-imperialist and eco-authoritarian directions, restabilizing through renewed reliance on statist modes of coercion.

There are a number of troublesome trends in the North suggesting political swings to the far right. Disillusionment with the center in the absence of a coherent and vibrant left stimulates such a rightward swing. In Germany, for instance, this reality has been reinforced by chauvinistic responses to a growing presence of foreigners and increasing flows of refugees and asylum-seekers. In the United States, a resurgent right wing has inflicted a crushing defeat on liberal political prospects by its overwhelming victory in the midterm Congressional elections of 1994, partly a continuing middle class revolt against taxes and government and partly a reflection of the failure of the Clinton presidency to inspire respect. Whether this rightest reorientation will dominate the near future of American political life remains uncertain.

Imposing capitalist discipline on the South has been entrusted in many settings to the IMF, using the leverage it gains from global indebtedness and the quest for developmental capital. When the IMF prevails it creates new forms of dependence and an erosion of political independence, as well as imposing added burdens on the poor by restricting wage levels, cutting government subsidies on food and energy, and reducing credit available to those with low income. One should not assume that the political leadership of a country in the South necessarily resists IMF controls. In many instances, especially where the economic policy of a government seeks to increase investments and exports, IMF controls are welcomed and an IMF bill of health is seen as an indispensable precondition for economic success. But not always: in a contrary instance of such pressure, an IMF official, José Faigenbaum, insisted in 1991 that Brazil reform its constitution so as to implement structural adjustments. The Brazilian President, Fernando Collor de Mello, although himself an ardent capitalist, reacted so angrily on nationalist grounds that the IMF dropped its demand, and replaced Faigenbaum "with a better-qualified person."

In the 1990s there is a revival of Malthusian pessimism, a sense that demographic trends associated with population growth and urbanization are overwhelming either governing capacities or carrying capacities (that is, environmental overload).[12] At the same time, there is a reluctance by governments to take on the tasks directly of demographic management. The issue is sensitive, also, because of its relationship to debates about the proper religious and ethical limits of reproductive rights. Finally, demographic adjustment in the North is especially important in relation to environmental challenges even when it is not associated with governmental capacities. Such demographic adjustments could be made, at least in part, by technological means (energy efficiency, conservation) and by lifestyle adjustments (mass transport, low-intensity light bulbs), but moves in this direction have so far been disappointingly trivial.

The demographic adjustments attempted by India and China are suggestive. During the so-called Emergency of (1975–77), the Indian government under Indira Gandhi instituted a clumsy policy of enforced birth control and sterilization at the village level, convinced that continuing population growth would become disastrous for the future of the country. In strictly managerial terms, the Indian attempt was understandable, especially since the softer methods of persuasion previously relied on were not having much of an impact. But the implementation was draconian and frightening, antagonizing the most vulnerable sectors of society and inducing an upsurge of militant popular opposition. India was democratic enough to repudiate these policies at the ballot box and through massive grassroots resistance. When Mrs Gandhi was voted back into power in 1980, it was with her assurance that no further attempt would be made to regulate compulsorily the expansion of the Indian population. The results have been disturbing, a steady deepening of India's economic plight amid a further swelling of population, especially among the legions of the poor, accompanied by an alarming spread of communal and regional violence.

India is now expected to have the world's largest population, surpassing China no later than the second decade of the next century, climbing to the alarming figure of over 1.5 billion.

The Chinese experience with the same challenge is also instructive. Starting in the mid-1970s, China established a one-child family norm that was enforced with rigor. The results were impressive in terms of reducing the fertility and growth rates. Abuses and hardships were widely reported, especially the revival in the countryside of female infanticide or neglect of ill female children to ensure that the one surviving child was male, capable of carrying on the family line and providing old age social security. China's authoritarian manner was criticized. It is impossible to tell whether China's relative success, as compared to India, is to be primarily attributed to the cultural differences between Confucianism and Hinduism or is more of a reflection of the contrast between China's authoritarian rule and India's constitutionalism. The view taken here is to regard both factors as intertwined, and hence relevant to interpreting these differences. The failure to approach sustainability of resources by the way of democratic dynamics of adjustment induces antidemocratic patterns of adjustment that are likely to be unpleasant if successful (China) and ineffectual if democratic resistance is mounted (India).

Parallel difficulties exist in relation to North/South adjustments to sustainability. Either the global commons deteriorates beyond restoration, or the burdens of adjustment are shifted southwards. Brazil is pressured to save the tropical rainforests of Amazonia for the sake of absorbing greenhouse gasses, but North America, Europe, and Japan mindlessly continue to encourage production of cars that rely on the internal combustion engine and to induce consumer dependence on private transport.

Oppression There are many varieties of oppression that arise from intolerance and the abuse of power and authority. Oppressive violence can emanate from the state or its enemies in civil society, or from prejudiced elements embedded in civil society. The existence of oppression illustrates a type of avoidable harm that is the essence of inhumane governance. The project to establish humane governance must therefore respond to the many varieties of oppressive behavior, and not restrict its attention to the abuse of state power. Here, the particular concern is with the prevention of violence deliberately directed at those who are innocent or vulnerable.

The latest Amnesty report indicates that more than one hundred governments practice torture and abuse political prisoners in a variety of other ways. For all the excitement connected with the spread of democracy in the 1980s and early 1990s, there persists widespread continuing state violence against the person, as well as relapses into outright autocratic and military rule. Burma and Nigeria, as well as China, have regressed, imposing harsh punishments on individuals or groups suspected of oppositional activity.

But there are nonstate forms of oppression as well, that often escaped notice in the past. It is necessary to call attention to the suffering that is produced by religious and cultural practices that seem to enjoy continuing support within civil society, especially in the setting of the village and countryside. In the past, our own statism has blinded us to societal and grassroots modes of local and "invisible" oppression that account for a very large proportion of the suffering experienced by people subjected to coercive abuse. In this regard, abuse of women within marriage (marital rape) would qualify in many settings as an instance of inhumane governance to be overcome.

As with the phenomenon of poverty, it is a racist mistake to restrict concern to non-Western cultural circumstances. For instance, the rise of homophobic behavior in the North, so-called "gay-bashing," appears to be a response to both gay liberation and to the alleged role of gays as vehicles for the spread of AIDS. Japan, despite its economic miracle and constitutionalism, continues to persecute its own version of "untouchability" (the *burukamen*) at the societal level, and persists after several decades in treating its Korean resident community, largely a legacy from World War II, as inferior outsiders. In Germany over the last several years, neo-Nazi groups have been responsible for numerous violent incidents directed against "foreigners," especially targeting Turkish residents who have often been in Germany for more than a generation.

Ajoy Bose reported from New Delhi in 1991 on a grotesque instance of cruelty at the local level arising from the persistence of caste norms in India despite the existence of governmental norms to the contrary for several decades. In the village of Mehrana in Uttar Pradesh two young lovers eloped; the boy, Brijayendra, was from a lower caste and the girl, Roshni, aged 15, was the daughter of an upper caste landlord; their elopement was evidently facilitated by a third youth, a lower caste male friend, Ram Kishan. The three were captured, brought before a village tribunal, and promptly sentenced to death by hanging. As a further example to others in the village, the fathers of the condemned youths were given the task of carrying out the sentence, and when they hesitated, a local mob kicked and beat them until the noose had been tightened. According to the report, two of the fathers fainted. After a government investigation some arrests were made but "most villagers are refusing to cooperate with the police."[13]

This incident is important to reflect upon, suggesting more general concerns. It challenges an uncritical reliance on democracy at the local level. It questions whether deference to tradition and cultural diversity is appropriate under all conditions. It suggests that non-Western cultural traditions, as well as Western traditions, can be oppressive.[14] It points to the difficult predicament raised by a need for metacultural norms, and it encourages all of us to engage in interrogations of our own cultural heritage and to engage in intercultural dialogues.[15] Cultural reality is no more univocal than political reality, and one must resist the temptation, often inflamed by ethnic and racial prejudice, to reduce an alien culture to its most violent and literalistic traditions. Such a tendency is especially pronounced, at present, in the stereotyping of Islam in the West, and of the West in Islam. There are also Hindu/Muslim tensions evident on the Indian subcontinent, both in Indo-Pakistan relations, the conflict relating to Kashmir, and most of all, in the rise of Hindu extremism within India, with its strong anti-Muslim orientation.

The Salman Rushdie affair illuminates many of these issues in an alarming intercultural clash of perceptions and priorities at a point of extreme civilizational difference. When his novel *The Satanic Verses* was published a few years ago there occurred a widespread, adverse reaction in the Muslim world weeks before Ayatollah Khomeini issued his infamous fatwa that decreed death to Rushdie for blasphemy against the Prophet. This was subsequently followed by a huge monetary award of several million dollars promised by the Government of Iran to any person who committed this murder, as well as assurances of martyrdom as a further incentive to such a "holy" act. Since that time, Rushdie has been forced underground, surrounded by security guards, deprived of his public existence, a hunted man.[16] The credibility of the threat posed was revealed in July 1991 when in separate incidents Rushdie's Italian publisher and Japanese translator were both victims of violent attack, the latter one being fatal. More recent violent incidents have also occurred.

There are many concerns raised. One should note that many moderate Muslims felt deeply offended both by Rushdie's novel and by Khomeini's death sentence. Many favored banning of the book or restricting distribution for the sake of community cohesion and sensitivity, yet opposed any attempt to hold Rushdie criminally accountable, much less to incite his assassination or violence directed at those associated with its publication. In a similar vein, Rushdie is widely criticized in some moderate Muslim circles for failing to be more sensitive. His provocative treatment of sacred material is even held morally accountable for the riots that arose in India and Pakistan, taking several lives; Rushdie's critics argue that these responses should have been anticipated, especially in light of religious violence connected with earlier books, especially the novel *Shame*.

From another angle, those with a fundamentalist attachment of their own to Western secular ideas about free expression regard all wrong-doing as falling on the Muslim side. Fay Weldon, the British writer, perceives the issue in one-dimensional terms: "Something monstrous and peculiar is going on. Monstrous that a foreign power should pay terrorist gangs to kill a British writer for writing the novel he wants to write."[17] Ms Weldon also finds it "monstrous" that the English government would even consider normalizing relations with Iran so long as Tehran does not repudiate Khomeini's fatwa, and she concludes her diatribe by wondering aloud whether some sort of concealed racism makes it easier to ignore the intrusion on Rushdie's life. "I cannot but conclude that if Salman Rushdie's name was something un-foreign and he looked like Prince Charles, the British reaction to his plight would be less equivocal, and less peculiar."

What can we learn here? As Ali Mazrui has pointed out over the years, the preconceptions of cultural penetration flowing inevitably from North to South can be reversed, and when it is, the North will scream, but still not appreciate the agony it has caused in the South for several centuries in non-Western settings by its massive, often crude, and quite deliberate programs of cultural penetration. Ayatollah Khomeini demonstrated that in a world of dispersed cultures the North is no longer immune from efforts by the South to hit back, sometimes with ferocity, causing tragic results for the individuals concerned. The statist capacity to provide security within territory is shown to be quite limited, vulnerable to the point of not being able to provide Rushdie with reliable prospects of safety if he should choose to live a normal life in Britain.

The Cold War is not the only ideological form of warfare in our world. As Kalim Siddiqui, head of the Muslim Institute in London, observes: "*The Satanic Verses* is viewed by Muslims throughout the world as part of a global war declared on Islam by the West. If we had not stopped Rushdie and his collaborators, there would by now have been a spate of films, videos, novels, poems, stage-shows and so on, 'exploring' the 'themes' pioneered by *The Satanic Verses*. Islam is a global culture and civilisation. As such it has a duty to defend itself."[18] This report acknowledges that there is, at minimum, a dangerously inflamed relationship between Islam and the West, producing political violence, tension, hostility, and enemy imaging.

The upsurge of anti-Western terrorism of Islamic origins in 1993 has further aggravated intercivilizational relations. Egyptian secular rule is one target, with the West, especially the United States, being viewed as responsible by extremist Islamic elements, resulting in such practices as attacks on visiting tourists and lethal explosions in public buildings in the United States. The most spectacular of these was the 1993 bomb detonated in the Trade Center in New York City killing six and injuring up to 1,000, as well as doing considerable physical – and even greater psychological – damage. These occurrences need also to be understood in relation to the failure of the West to respond sufficiently to anti-Muslim Serbian aggression and war crimes in Bosnia, or to express serious concern about anti-Muslim riots in India. Intercivilizational peacemaking is a world order challenge that is only beginning to be treated with the seriousness it deserves.[19]

There is at the core of the Rushdie encounter a tension between sovereignty as territorially based and sovereignty as culturally or religiously based. Ayatollah Khomeini insisted that the revolution he was leading was an "Islamic revolution" rather than, as the media presented it, an "Iranian revolution." By Muslim law, Rushdie could not relinquish his Islamic identity without committing the crime of apostasy, as serious as that of blasphemy, for those who adhere to Islamic law. He could not, in theory, go beyond the reach of Islam no matter what his own convictions or location in political space, and this perception in rigid Islamic circles was not affected by Rushdie's apologies or willingness to affirm his Muslim identity while being hunted.

But even if Rushdie had lived in Iran, and never left the country, a fundamental issue of human rights would have been posed by the suppression of his book, and the imposition of a criminal punishment, especially if Rushdie had been executed for the crime of blasphemy. The issue posed here has to do with limits on territorial sovereignty imposed by international human rights standards. Indirectly present as well are questions of implementation and enforcement, but also matters of legitimacy. Are the standards products of Western law-generating procedures or universal? How can we judge cultural and civilizational infractions of human rights? Implicit in this challenge directed at Rushdie and at the publication of his book is a radical denial of the individualism that underpins the Western understanding and experience of human rights. But is this understanding and experience sufficiently embodied in international law to override the communal or collective orientations of other civilizations?

Standing in contrast, of course, is the territorial notion of the modern state system. Such overlapping conceptions of sovereignty would not pose serious problems if their underlying ethos was shared. The problems in this setting arise because the West regards freedom of artistic expression as almost an absolute right of the individual, even if the results prove offensive to the community or parts of it and even if the work in question is deemed of little artistic content. Debate rages in the West, fueled recently by feminist concerns with the commodification of women, about the dividing line between artistic work and pornography, and whether and to what extent pornography should be protected as free expression. There is little doubt that Rushdie was working well within contemporary Western conceptions of law and morality when he decided to publish *The Satanic Verses*, although there are some laws on the books, yet never enforced in recent decades, in Britain and elsewhere in the West that make blasphemy directed at Christian beliefs a crime. Whether, given his undoubted awareness of Muslim sensitivities, he was acting prudently or empathetically is another matter.

In the emerging nonterritorial reality of global consciousness, a fundamental issue is raised by the inability of international law to generate metacultural norms in relation to some sensitive questions. As matters now stand, international law generally reflects the secular world-view of the West, which many non-Western elites accept, at least as providing a shared and authoritative normative framework. Perhaps Khomeini posed an exceptional challenge by his refusal to accept some sort of compromise between religiously based sovereign authority and secularly based sovereign authority. The compromise would involve accepting censorship in Muslim countries and free dissemination in the West, but it is a jagged compromise. What does it mean to call some countries "Muslim"? What about the Muslim overseas communities? What about artists in Muslim countries seeking to exercise creative freedom in the sense embodied in the international law of human rights? What about the rights of non-Muslims in Muslim countries?

One dimension of these issues is the status of secularism in the sense of protecting plural belief systems against claims of religious truth. If secularism can be put aside by a political leadership that accepts religious traditions as the only true basis of belief and practice in the name of self-determination of a people or nation, then the foundations of a normative consensus based on tolerance are shatterd. Of course, a religious state may claim to possess secular credentials, as is the case with Zionist Israel, but here, too, the position of non-Jews is made precarious and explicitly subordinate.

We must also be concerned with the human suffering that arises from intense collisions of values within a particular cultural space. Recently an alliance of groups representing gays in Great Britain announced a campaign to expose closet homosexuals occupying positions of prominence in British society while concealing their sexual identities. The claim of this group is that prejudice against gays would be mitigated by the wider public realization that many respected public figures in all spheres of life are gay. The issue raised, of course, is whether such unilateral and nonconsensual exposures of identity violate rights of privacy and whether, given the continuing prejudicial effects attached to gay identity, there is an ethical and legal issue of defamation present. While the importance of viewing the private as political in addressing a range of social issues is here endorsed, it is also apparent that specific forms of privacy ought to remain protected.

How is it possible to mediate, in this instance, between the attempt of the group to overcome its oppressive circumstances and the rights of an individual to conceal some aspects of his or her identity? Such questions may appear frivolous in a world struggling against racism, collective violence, sexism, acute poverty, militarism, but not in this discussion. Here it is a primary concern to specify the contours of humane governance in order to contain the prospects for shaping an identity for women and men that is at once rooted in the specifics of time, place, and preference and, as well, sufficiently transcendent to facilitate feelings of solidarity with the human species as a whole. Sexual identity is critical to this constituting process, and has been too long excluded from serious political thought. Only by reconstructing intimate relations on a humane basis can the world move toward the wider public and collective realities of human community. This reconstruction, starting in the home, is a critical precondition for the emergence of the sort of global polity that could inspire trust and have a reasonable prospect of providing humane governance for a democratically constituted global civil society.

In essence, this stress on the personal, even the intimate, is valuable for its own sake to the extent it reduces anguish and pain arising from repressive traditions and practices, but the wider world order claim is that if humane standards do not prevail in the personal domain, inhumane practices will re-emerge as ascendent in any effort at global restructuring, no matter how idealistic its motivation. The pattern of revolutionary betrayal in this century involves the betrayal by revolutionary movements of their fundamental commitment to improve the quality of justice in a given society. Instead of a new, more just social order the evils of the prior social and political forms are reproduced, and often on a grander scale. The Soviet story from the original revolutionary triumph onward is paradigmatic for these observations, and needs to be studied with care to learn some lessons for the future.

Militarism   The war system is alive and well. It is throughly embedded in geopolitics despite some generally encouraging moderating trends. Fundamental assumptions about the essential character of security remain tied to statist control over war-making, which remains the remnant of statist geopolitics during this period of ascending market-oriented geopolitics. These older patterns of geopolitics were preoccupied with the shaping of collective state action through alliances, interventions, and the so-called "management of power" (balances, deterrent stability, spheres of influence, security zones). The altered status of these traditional concerns will be discussed more concretely in chapter 5. The emphasis here is on the persistence of militarism during the transition to geogovernance, inducing skepticism about the outcome. The intent is to challenge the euphoria that initially gripped the North during the aftermath of the Cold War.

In this book it is of less interest to attempt to moderate the manifestations of the arms race (numbers of warheads, levels of spending, size of research and development) than to consider qualitative steps that might eliminate destructive practices and that could contribute to the demilitarization of the political imagination. There has been little evidence of a cultural disposition to take such steps. Indeed, the jingoistic reactions to battlefield victory in the Gulf War, especially in the United States and Great Britain, suggests that war-making retains deep and vibrant populist roots in the political culture of the West, and can continue to be exploited by political leaders to build their popularity.

The aftermath of the Gulf War, with its vindictive anti-Iraqi policies, has reinforced militarist impressions. These were further validated by President Clinton's recourse to a cruise missile attack in retaliation for an alleged plot to assassinate former president George Bush during his unofficial 1993 trip to Kuwait. The emphasis here is on prospects for global security anchored in an ethos of nonviolence, not necessarily dogmatically pacifist, but viewing recourse to collective violence as a failure of "security," not as its embodiment.[20]

"The Cold War is dead, long live the Cold War." The reality of a post–Cold War set of circumstances in international life did not produce the range of downward adjustment in militarist posture that would seem to correspond with abatement of East–West conflict. At first the two superpowers of old formed a de facto "global partnership," with the

Soviet Union accepting, almost gratefully, its new role as a junior partner with only a muffled voice in the corridors of decision. Such was the case, most obviously, in the deliberations of the UN Security Council during the period 1989–91, as well as in such key diplomatic settings as the Middle East peace process of the last several years. Of course, with the Soviet collapse and virtual withdrawal from geopolitical activity, the partnership dissolved, not because of a change in political will but because Russia no longer possessed the capacity to be even a junior partner in this latest phase of statist geopolitics. In 1994 this withdrawal has been somewhat reversed, with Russia reasserting its interests more actively, especially in the Balkans and "near abroad," partly in response to the domestic challenge of ultranationalists.

There was the welcomed conclusion in 1991 of the complex START (Strategic Arms Reduction Treaty) treaty after nine years of negotiations, resulting in approximately 30 percent reductions in warhead arsenals. But what has been achieved, even assuming full implementation, which is by no means assured? The Soviet stockpile will be reduced over a seven-year period to 7,000 warheads from the present total of about 11,000, while the US stockpile will diminish to 9,000 from its present total of 12,000. By the strangest of symmetries, these reductions will reduce the respective arsenals to *almost* their size in 1982 when the START negotiations commenced! What is more, sophisticated commentary gives the impression that this agreement is the end of the road when it comes to arms reductions. The prospect for going further with START, as is formally implied by the commitment to engage in START II negotiations, is dismissed by virtually all establishment voices as chimerical.[21] Perhaps even more disquieting is the uncontested view that some continued efforts will be made to improve nuclear weaponry and to extend military capabilities to space-based systems.

In real security, Europe in particular has benefited from the short-run change in political atmosphere. The tensed readiness for diabolical war that had persisted for decades has definitely been superseded by an era of calm and confidence when it comes to strategic conflict. This development has been made possible and is sustained by the emancipation of East Europe and its precarious embrace of the dynamics of democratization. But even in Europe the balance of benefits and burdens remains unclear, especially given the various consequences of the breaking up of Yugoslavia. It can be doubted whether Yugoslavia would have collapsed had the Cold War persisted. Surely outsiders would have viewed such a collapse with alarm rather than with equanimity, let alone as a desirable development. The disclosure of the concealed diplomacy of Germany and other European states during the period immediately preceding the breakdown in 1991 would clarify these matters of speculation. Western mainstream analysts now seem to agree on the bizarre designation of the Cold War era as "the long peace," and view the period of superpower bipolarity with a tinge of nostalgia.[22]

The removal of the blocs has generated new tensions in state/society relations which were long suppressed by brutal, authoritarian rule. Ironically and tragically, it is Yugoslavia, the European state which had earliest made a geopolitical escape from Cold War structures to proclaim a neutralist, nonaligned stance, which has experienced the sharpest tensions between statist unity and ethnic separatism in its aftermath. Self-determination of peoples is a fundamental human right that is being claimed on all sides. But what is the unit and dynamics of self-determination? The proposed new state or government born of such encounters seems likely to be governed by reactionary forces that are themselves abusive of the rights of minorities. The struggles in former Yugoslavia raise all of these questions in an agonizing form.[23] Similar fissures are evident elsewhere in Europe, ranging from Northern Ireland to the former Czechoslovakia to several of the major successor states in the Soviet Union, although moves toward reconciliation are also evident. These conflicts are capable of producing major collective violence, either through terrorism/counterterrorism (Algeria since 1991) or recourse to civil war (as in movements for independence in several former Soviet republics).

There is, finally, the issue of shifting demilitarization from a process based on mutuality and consent to one based on hegemony and coercion. Was it worth fighting a preventive war to deny Iraq a nuclear weapons capability? Was such a cause a legitimate part of the UN mandate to restore Kuwaiti sovereignty? Before the crisis was resolved by a diplomatic bargain, there were American threats in 1994 to extend the Iraqi precedent to North Korea if the latter does not convincingly abandon those aspects of its nuclear program that are allegedly dedicated to weapons acquisition. At the same time several countries in the North are retaining abundant numbers of nuclear weapons (despite reduced arsenals) and continue to spend billions to refine potential military applications of nuclear weapons, refusing even to renounce first use options, or to accept the constraints of a permanent comprehensive test ban. The US participation in the extension of the conditional moratorium on underground nuclear testing was obtained in 1993 only after a huge Congressional and lobbying effort. Similarly, there is often well-intentioned advocacy of restrictions on arms sales in

North/South settings, but no suggestion at all of restricting North/North sales. If arms sales are perceived to have serious adverse strategic consequences then it becomes a matter of real policy concern, as with pressures by the United States on China not to sell missile technology to countries such as Pakistan and Iran. This is, in part, an extension of the pariah state problematic.

There are some proposals to scale back arms sales – likely to run into obstacles, given the importance of the arms industry in generating jobs and exports for key countries – but few dare to mention corresponding and complementary restrictions on the production of arms. It is essential to develop a consistent position against all forms of militarism and its underpinnings. It is appropriate to be suspicious of one-sided perspectives on demilitarization that tend to locate the danger to the world in the heartland of the weak and victimized, and to regard demilitarization for the strong and rich to be beyond the pale of practical politics. There is no reason to subscribe to the two-level logic of hegemonically guided demilitarization, with its grant of discretion to the strong and its attempt at rigid constraint in relation to weak states.

We ought to be deeply concerned with the roots of war in cultures that continue to glorify war and seem both fearful of and infatuated with violence and its technologies. The electronic games children play seem so often to model the wars, real and imaginary, that their elders contemplate and execute. The media, oriented toward Western sensibilities, helps portray the non-Western "other" as the main source of evil in the world, raising this process to intense levels during times of actual encounter, as with the handling of the terrorist issue in the 1980s and of Saddam Hussein in the early 1990s. The evil "other" provides the forces of good with a clear mandate to wage cleansing warfare with little regard for the consequences to the civilian populations that inhabit the target areas.

It is necessary to conceive of social violence, that which Johan Galtung long ago labeled "structural violence," as falling within the wider sway of militarized politics. When the life expectancies of different regions, races, and classes are so widely disparate, there is systemic disorder present of a very fundamental sort, but one that is correctable, at least in principle. When blacks in the inner cities of the United States face a greater risk of violent death before attaining adulthood than blacks in South African townships during the turbulent late 1980s or Palestinians in the Occupied Territories during the *intifada* there is present "a war zone," no matter how concealed and distorted the reality, presented by mainstream media exclusively in terms of the "criminality" of the victims and the "victimization" of the perpetrators belonging to the dominant class, race or ethnic group. Here the real moral equation of suffering and social responsibility is inverted, presented in distorted form to justify "enforcement" rather than the quest for "emancipation."

This diverse material presented under the second indictment shares one salient feature: the suffering being generated is "inhumane," and could be eliminated if the political will existed to do so. The prospect of such a political will arising out of the new geopolitics seems remote to the point of fancy. If "humane governance" is to address the array of practices and social institutions responsible for widespread human suffering, then it will depend on a bottom-up dynamic of transformation that encompasses the personal domains of sexual preference and of gender relations in family settings. Without eliminating violence at home, the prospects of eliminating war and other forms of large-scale political violence are illusory. Overcoming avoidable suffering requires patience, a clear agenda, and the further strengthening of global civil society.

The Third Indictment: Drifting Toward Eco-imperialism

The formation of geopolitics accompanying the rise of the modern state occurred long prior to the realization that the continuation and extension of industrial civilization in the context of an expanding world population was causing levels of environmental damage dangerous to health and well-being, threatening human survival. In contrast, the perspectives of global civil society that underpin the groping toward humane governance have been formed with a vivid awareness of ecological constraints on human activities, so much so that it is common for citizen pilgrims to emphasize their loyalty to the earth as strongly as their membership in a global community that can be glimpsed at the horizons of human aspiration.

In line with the structural analysis set forth in this chapter, a further pattern that could be anticipated is that the North would try to shift as much of the burden of blame and adjustment in relation to environmental policy as possible to the South. One notes the parallel here with the apportionment of blame by affluent states for the social discontents of severe urban blight. Who defines "the crime"? Where is the locus of violence?

In this regard, the environmental challenge adds a dangerous new dimension to the already painful realities of global apartheid and to the complex policy matrix of avoidable suffering. This pattern has emerged in a variety of settings, ranging from the use of the supposedly "remote" islands of the Pacific for lethal nuclear weapons tests to the dumping of toxic wastes and even garbage in the South. It includes shocking disclosures that both the Soviet Union and the United States deliberately inflicted on thousands of their own more marginalized citizens large doses of radiation to assess effects, using innocent persons as guinea pigs without their consent or knowledge. The Rio Earth Summit of 1992 confirmed the impression that many governments in the North are unwilling to question the viability of extravagant consumerist lifestyles or prepared to devote sufficient resources to arresting environmental decay beyond their borders, while still insisting that the South agree to constrain development policy so as to preserve tropical rainforests.

The third indictment involves the political consequence of two interactive processes: the worsening of environmental conditions and the persistence of dominant growth-oriented economic priorities. What is foreseen is a series of efforts to shift responsibility for environmental adjustment to the South, and move over time toward coercive implementation in the South of policies designed to prevent some forms of environmental collapse. Thus the South will be expected to rein in development without being assisted in any substantial way to overcome poverty. It is unlikely that such a North/South relationship can be managed without continuing recourse to military intervention, which is proving to be a costly, and often ineffective, method of control.

The third indictment also concerns the failure to assess the environmental challenge and encourage a variety of timely adjustments. The overall situation could be greatly improved by rapidly shifting significant resources from military to environmental priorities,[24] by social pressures to cut waste, luxury consumption, and energy inefficiencies in the North, and by further reductions in population growth through birth control, late marriages, female education, and other means.

Without such lines of improvement the pressures will grow to premise geogovernance on dominance of the South by the North, sustained by coercion: an extension, and intensification, of inhumane governance. If the patterns of dominance prompt reliance on high-tech military intervention, then the emergent reality is likely to result in a kind of eco-imperialism, signs of which are already present.

Let us consider first of all the cognitive refusal to confront the failures of anticipation in the 1980s or the specific urgencies of the 1990s. From an ecological standpoint there are two kinds of dangerous response: a value-free globalism and a reconstructed realism.[25] In the former the search for a global framework for inquiry is emphasized, while in the latter the search is for a way to reproduce the Cold War modalities of stability (deterrence, military balance) in the altered circumstances of the 1990s. Neither emphasis acknowledges the claims of the South in an era of ecological challenge. Indeed, what redeployment of resources and energy has occurred seems to be equally neglectful of the South and of the environmental agenda.

One such redeployment of normative energy is the shift of concern about economic deprivation from the South to the East. It is understandable that there should be both an empathetic response by the West to those societies that have finally emancipated themselves from the iron grip of the Soviet empire, providing urgent help so that these governments can improve their prospects of making a smooth transition to market-oriented economies and constitutionally grounded politics. In fact, the scale of assistance is surprisingly small as compared say to what was done for Western Europe after World War II through the Marshall Plan, but nevertheless this preoccupation with former Communist states has had the effect of diminishing further attention devoted to economic distress in the South, especially in Africa. Indeed, even this reduced attention is alleged by the media to have induced a public mood of "disaster fatigue" in response to the numerous accounts of famine and the many other reports of humanitarian emergency in the South. Such a numbing mood is undoubtedly reinforced by the continued economic recession in the North and by the widespread belief that past efforts to provide foreign economic assistance have generally not been productively used, but have encouraged corruption and inefficiency in the recipient countries. The affluent sectors of the world are averting their gaze from the South, preferring for now to lend help to and emphasize the plight of these former Communist countries in the North that share racial, geographical, and cultural affinities.

There are already definite signs that the South is being made to bear the burden of adjusting to the rigors of the new agenda of geopolitics. Such a shifting of the burden to the South could be discerned in relation to the so-called "war on drugs," involving paramilitary encroachments by the North on countries in the South that are supply sources, while little effort is made to control the dynamics of demand. Such efforts also overlook the jobs and economic benefits associated with the drug trade, and the consequent further social harm that can result from disruption of supply sources. With respect to terrorism, the locus of global concern is mainly restricted to Islamic countries, with no corresponding willingness to address the terrorism of "covert operations" in the North, or to address the social causes of terrorism to the extent that recourse to such forms of political violence rests on injustices. This same dynamic is evident in relation to human migrations and refugees. Most extraordinarily, Africa, Asia, and Latin America are being increasingly blamed for contributing to environmental decay either by way of population increase or as a result of environmentally destructive societal practices and developmental plans.

A revealing expression of this new mood, partly shaped by market logic and by the realization that there is no longer any serious geopolitical competition for influence in the South, was a leaked policy memo apparently written by the then Chief Economist of the World Bank, now a prominent US government advisor on foreign economic policy. The memo begins by posing a rhetorical question, conveying its tone and imparting its message: "Just between you and me, shouldn't the World Bank be encouraging *more* migration of the dirty industries to the LDCs?" The language used is as extraordinary as the policies being proposed. The memo actually contains such words as "I think the economic logic behind dumping a load of toxic waste in the lowest-wage country is impeccable and we should face up to that," "I've always thought that underpopulated countries in Africa are vastly *under-polluted*," and "The demand for a clean environment for aesthetic and health reasons is likely to have very high income-elasticity. The concern over an agent that causes a one-in-a-million change in the odds of prostrate cancer is obviously going to be higher in a country where the people survive to get prostrate cancer than in a country where the under-five mortality is 200 per thousand."[26]

There were several lines of reaction to the publication of this memo that found their way into public discussion: shock in the face of such acute moral insensitivity from an individual placed so high in an international institution that is part of the UN family; vindication of critical assessments of the World Bank by this stark confirmation of more intuitive condemnations that have been directed at characteristic policies of the international financial institutions, especially those directed toward economic operations in the South; reflection on the human and social implications of market logic when its reasoning is observed in such a crude free-fall state, especially in its striking absence of human solidarity and compassion.

Both the geopolitical logic that underlies the rationale for the Gulf War, the failures to act in Bosnia, and the coercive approach to nonproliferation, as well as the economistic logic that diminishes concern for the well-being of the South are on the rise in managerial circles, especially within the United States government, which has assumed the virtually uncontested mantle of global leadership in this early post–Cold War period.[27] Most states in the South are so befuddled by the new global setting and/or regard their positions as so weak that they have either assented to this ascendancy or become entirely passive. Given these conditions of inhumane governance, alternative lines of response, if they are to be forthcoming, depend on the creativity and communicative capacities of democratic social forces expressing the visions and aspirations of global civil society. This will not require a countermanagerial logic of its own, but rather the fashioning of many specific, normatively grounded responses forged in struggles against oppressive conditions, animated by the possibilities of achieving humane governance both in immediate circumstances and in relation to more remote goals. The challenge is now directed as much to our minds (the need for cognitive renewals) as it is in the domain of policy and practice.

The triple indictment implies a program for global reform to avoid a type of geogovernance that is inhumane in tangible respects. To become a reality, humane governance will have to address the economic and environmental policy agenda by adopting appropriate procedures and establishing institutions of a magnitude capable of overcoming global apartheid. Only then will it be possible to focus on the various forms of avoidable human suffering, arrest environmental decay, and ensure that the patterns of environmental adjustment do not produce eco-imperialist North/South outcomes. Critical to this process of instituting humane governance is a rethinking of sovereignty, democracy, and development, the subject-matter of the next three chapters, and essential features of whatever type of global civilization becomes established in the decades ahead. The central goal of such rethinking is to consider these salient frames of reference for the peoples of the world in a manner that interprets and promotes their struggle for humane governance.

3

Sovereignty: A Twisting Path from Modernism

The Transition to Geogovernance: Challenges to the Sovereign State

The essential feature of the transition to geogovernance is the process by which the territorial state is displaced from its dominant role in the era of geopolitics. The position argued here is that the form of displacement has profound implications for human well-being and environmental sustainability. On the basis of preceding chapters the orientation toward transition emerges:

- the state (and states system) is being gradually displaced, and this process can proceed most constructively through political effort by stages in a manner that is mindful of and guided by the contours of humane governance;
- from a normative perspective this politics of displacement should be centrally dedicated to overcoming the triple indictment of the present world economy, providing, in hopeful contrast, the means by which to dissolve apartheid structures, to overcome avoidable human suffering, and to minimize the waste and misappropriation of resources;
- additionally, the positive potential of displacing the state as central actor on the world political stage implies a far less militarized and more globally institutionalized set of approaches.

For these reasons, the chapter focuses on sovereignty as the normative hinge that separates the still prevailing geopolitics from the new circumstances of geogovernance. The realist view underpinning geopolitics accords *internal* supremacy and *external* status (access, membership rights) and discretion (self-help, security rights) to states. Realism also confers special hegemonic roles on dominant states that are at once the key actors in conflict patterns and the creators of extraterritorial ordering principles. World order during the era of statist predominance reflects the structure of geopolitical rivalry, whether unipolar, bipolar, or multi-polar, and has been preoccupied with dominion over and the defense of territory. As a result, war and militarism remain salient features.

Sovereignty – secularized and anchored in the state – provides both an explanation of such a world order and a subtle camouflage that obscures the actuality of inequality and exploitative relations, as well as the violent epicenter of geopolitics. The legal/political notion of the sovereign equality of states is in dynamic tension with the empirical expressions of hegemonic rivalry. The abstractions of sovereignty also serve to insulate patriarchal assumptions from exposure and criticism. It becomes evident that the idea of supremacy over "domestic society" and the doctrine of "nonintervention in domestic affairs' is a way of ordering the world in accordance with patriarchal prerogatives, includ-ing discretionary recourse to violence by a patriarch in domestic space. The domestic sphere as the place where women are traditionally confined and ruled, thereby constraining their dis-ordering impact, is the implicit basis of all patriarchal constructions of political order.[1]

Despite these oppressive roles, sovereignty and statehood remain a normative horizon for most peoples in the world, especially for those who are victimized, and provides the outer limit for the most collective of rights, the self-determination of peoples. The persisting vitality of sovereignty as a normative ideal reflects the power of nationalism as the decisive basis of political community. This power is expressed through patriotic fervor, ranging from victory in sports organized as competition among countries, to participation in war for the defense of the home-land. Sovereignty embodies the moral, legal, and political claims of nationalism at the state level, establishing its strong symbolic and substantive presence in world order thought and practice, while provid-ing the decisive link between "self" and "other" in international political life.[2] Unless the transfer of sovereignty, as a willed act, is accompanied by the refocusing of political identity, it may be strongly resisted at the grassroots. In one sense, the ideals of an Islamic revolution attempt such a redirection of identity more potently than do the secular ideals of Europe, primarily a base for more effective economic growth, but both movements to supersede the state and enlarge the concept of primary political community bear witness to nationalism as a continuing obstacle, and to the related difficulty of relocating sovereignty in more inclusive political actors than the state.

Sovereignty for captive nations (those currently imprisoned within alien state boundaries) remains a dream. In favorable circumstances it takes the form of a difficult political project, while for those in discouraging circumstances it can often be little more than a cherished fantasy. The displacement of the state is, and will continue to be, uneven and incomplete, leaving the quest for community and identity linked to the acquisition of sovereignty, with the fundamental political bond remaining that of nation and state.

Sovereignty is a status claimed from *within*, conferred from *without*: it is linked to issues of autonomy, military capabilities, territorial delimitation, and mutual acknowledgment. A tiny territorial community such as Liechtenstein, enjoying full membership in the United Nations yet lacking even its own currency or security forces, suggests that the concept of sovereignty can be stretched far beyond textbook definitions. At the other end of the statist spectrum is the multination empire held together by brute force, splitting asunder as soon as popular sentiments associated with nationalist identities are allowed political expression. The former Soviet Union and Yugoslavia are recent examples of violent fission, confirming the explosive energies of nationalisms long repressed beneath the forms and coercive capabilities of state sovereignty, while the 1992 fission of Czechoslovakia exemplified the possibility of a negotiated and peaceful mutual acknowledgment of distinct nationalist claims.

What most concerns us in this chapter is to *situate* sovereignty in the ongoing and unfolding struggles to achieve humane governance. What does this mean? It suggests relating the discourse of sovereignty to the concrete aspirations and projects of transnational democracy to construct a benevolent global civil society. It also supposes selective resistance to global market forces. Resistance to economic globalism may even justify a temporary strengthening of the hold of state sovereignty in certain settings, while weakening it in others.

The struggles involving the establishment of regional and global frameworks for the expansion of trade and opportunities for capital investment are illustrative of the *defensive* roles of sovereignty. To what extent should the dynamics of the global market be allowed to override the well-being of territorial communities? To what extent are the interests of people, especially those who are most vulnerable, being protected on this path to globalization? One notes the inclusions and exclusions in typical arenas of emergent geogoverning authority: the entire South, including even the newly rich, are excluded from *any* participation in the annual G-7 economic summits; the Asia-Pacific Economic Cooperation framework is evolving on the basis of direct collaboration between business representation and the 18 participating states. The 1993 consultations in Seattle led to the formation of nine committees to develop proposals, procedures, and policies for regional cooperation in the Pacific in which business, but not labor or consumer, representatives would participate along with governmental officials. In this regard APEC may be more of a window on the future than the European Community. The significance of these developments will be considered in more detail when it comes to the consideration of democracy and emergent geogovernance. To anticipate, without participation by all sectors of global civil society there is a democracy deficit in the transition period that will necessarily deform the successor structures of geogovernance. Here, the main contention is that sovereignty as a territorially delimited frame for political community can be selectively helpful in slowing down the rush toward regressive forms of geogovernance.

As a fragment, sovereignty *as bonded with statism* breaks up the potentiality for perspectives based on the well-being of the whole, as distinct from the part. Realism, with its moral commitment to the pursuit of the national interest – or state interest as defined by political leaders – treated as an unconditional goal of political leadership, leads to the validation of warfare, the marginalization of international law and morality, the privileging of the logic of economic growth at the expense of ecological sustainability, and the uncritical acceptance of the patriarchal heritage. By contrast, humane governance asserts the priority of the human interest, the central authority of international law and morality, gives precedence to the logic of ecological sustainability at the expense of economic growth, makes explicit a critique of patriarchal patterns, and seeks new postpatriarchal forms of order, authority, and justice.

This chapter manifests an ambivalence to sovereignty, both as inherited doctrine and in the practice of geopolitics given current world conditions. The first section seeks to address the complexity of sovereignty with respect to discourses on geopolitics and geogovernance. This is followed by a discussion of how a partial critique of sovereignty influences the revitalization of the related idea of citizenship, connecting the citizen with the construction of global civil society, as well as with allegiance to a given territorial community. The third section argues that sovereignty cannot be abandoned despite its misuse and partially anachronistic character, but that its practices can be evaluated by reference to the project of humane governance. Finally, a short concluding section makes proposals for the realignment of sovereignty, and anticipates the further development of these themes in successive chapters.

Locating Sovereignty

During the 1992 Olympics there appeared in several prominent news-papers an imaginative ad covering two full pages, arranged in such a manner that after reading the first page it was necessary to turn the page to see the second part. On the first page was a map of Europe without boundaries, no delimitation except between land and sea, the entire expanse empty except for a single dot with the designation "Barcelona" just about where you would expect to find it. Underneath the map was a caption in bold capitals:

IN WHICH COUNTRY WOULD YOU PLACE THIS POINT?

Turning the page you see the same map reproduced, but showing the land contours of Europe, and the following caption:

IN CATALONIA, OF COURSE

The "of course" softens the assault on conventional sensibility, makes the assertion charming, rather than polemical. But the basic point is not lost. Where we locate "sovereignty" is not self-evident, and always reflects viewpoint, history, legal doctrine, power relations, institutional arrangements, and political will. The difference between the caption "In Catalonia, of course," and a caption "In Spain, of course" is profound. The latter would be self-evident to the point that its assertion would raise a question where there had been none, while the former definitely problematizes our notion of "Spain," at least for a moment. The degree of problematization would reflect both an assessment of how serious and benevolent is the Catalan project of self-determination, and an attitude toward whether Spain as a polity is oppressive or inclusive in its approach to distinct ethnic and nationalist identities that subsist within its boundaries.

Such detachment is not possible in other settings where the delimita-tion of sovereign borders is currently a matter of life and death, and the struggle an occasion for both courageous martyrdom and hideous crimes against humanity. The several bloody encounters over the future shape and substance of previously nonsovereign subdivisions of Yugoslavia is an anguishing reminder of sovereignty as a life-and-death issue because it is so closely linked to beliefs about identity, community, security, and prosperity. In years prior to 1991, the borders of Croatia, Slovenia, Bosnia and Herzegovina were indicated on maps, if at all, as constituent republics in the federated state of Yugoslavia. What these republics lacked was sovereign status, including the right of their governing elites to maintain armies and to ignore the legal authority of Belgrade as the governing center of their polity. Yet the human costs of tearing the fragile entity "Yugoslavia" asunder have turned out to be immense, and have also borne witness to the cynical geopolitics of Europe as a region. Without assessing the merits of contending geopolitical stands of the various European states, it is evident that Germany has promoted Croatian interests, France and Russia have been reluctant to oppose Serbian interests, and the United Kingdom has not wanted to help either Muslim or German interests. Such is the geopolitical backdrop to the failure to fashion any serious, coherent response to "ethnic cleansing" in Bosnia, for which atrocities the Serb leadership within both Bosnia and Serbia bears overwhelming, although not exclusive, responsibility.

Respect for the "sovereignty" of Yugoslavia might have averted tragedy, especially if combined with diplomatic pressure to redefine the social contract among the republics and the center. There definitely exists a complex set of tensions and dilemmas that associate claims of self-determination with an overriding commitment to humane governance. These claims need not be state-shattering, but when empires dissolve the emergence of new states is likely, often accompanied by quite traumatic behavior. Identities long repressed or contained assert themselves aggressively, thereby threatening others and creating new acute vulnerabilities. The resulting situation can generate intense strife that is the very epitome of inhumane governance. Relating to transition, it seems crucial to reconcile claims of self-determination with respect for and protection of human rights.

The symbols of sovereignty can often be retained but its substance abridged to varying degrees. Normally, federated states affirm the internal sovereignty of the constituent units so that flags can be flown, songs affirming statehood sung, holidays associated with the republic or province celebrated, but on an international level the central government represents the federal whole.[3] In discussions about the future of Europe there is frequent reference to "the pooling of sovereignty" as a lesser degree of integration than "supranationality," presumably the extinction of sovereignty.

In the context of military defeat, the defeated state sometimes retains the symbols of sovereignty but relinquishes important substantive powers, as was the case with Germany and Japan after World War II. A similar pattern emerged during the Cold War in the form of opposed blocs each headed by a superpower with the effective authority and capability to commit its subordinate allies to catastrophic warfare without their approval, or even without consultation; such subordinated states were fully "sovereign" in the eyes of law and diplomacy, yet the most important expression of political independence – the power of decision over war and peace – had been given up.

There are no abstractions that give guidance. All is context and interpretation. The entire tangled narrative history of the doctrine and practice of sovereignty needs to be approached in this spirit. There is no question that sovereignty has been a central coordinate in the modern political sensibility in which the world is politically organized around entities delimited in territorial terms with governments mutually empowered to accord "recognition" and enter into full diplomatic relations with other such entities; these entities have been known as "sovereign states" and their interactive reality has often been designated as "the state (or states) system." Statehood was bound up with sovereignty and provided the foundation of full legal and diplomatic membership in the formal arenas of international society. No other actors possessed this status to a comparable degree. Such an assertion is confirmed by the rules of membership and full participation associated with international institutions and by limitations on rights of access to the World Court. Geopolitics is grounded upon statism; statism rests upon sovereignty. In this period of transition to geogovernance, no matter how uneven and contradictory the tendencies, their cumulative impact is to supersede the role of states and diminish the significance of sovereignty. Note that the stress is on superseding, not extinguishing, on diminishing, not eliminating. Sovereignty will remain relevant, even decisive in many settings, but the rights, status, and role of states will be distributed in a more complex and confusing, and less territorial, manner. Henceforth the clarity and significance of sovereignty will be reduced.

In the first chapter the position taken was that geopolitics engrafted upon statism has produced a world political arrangement that is based on the dominance of the few, producing a very unequal sharing of benefits and burdens. This logic of dominance both remains and is under increasing challenge as a result of global market developments and the rise of transnational democratic forces. Two historical conditions in the post–Cold War years give further definition to the transition process: first, the removal of any pattern of strategic antagonism in the North, leaving the North, as provisionally led by the United States, in substantial control of global power/resources management and as the source of ideological cohesion; and secondly, as one expression of this ascendancy, the seeming appropriation by the US government of the United Nations, especially the Security Council, as an instrument of geopolitical legitimation and public mobilization, at least in some situations. Such moves involve a reshaping of geopolitics, but also define a path toward geogovernance.

It has also been contended that the normative effects of this restructuring of geopolitics, while desirable in many respects relating to the dangers of large-scale warfare, are unacceptable with regard to other dimensions of the war/peace agenda, with respect to the global political economy, and in relation to the increasing problem of the impacts of human activity on nature. Further, it is being argued that globalization from above is integrating the economic and social bases of human existence to an unprecedented degree, and with them the life of the mind (especially by means of the spread of popular culture by way of music and media and through the growth of franchise capitalism – licensing products, opening branches, using logos, operating in an essentially borderless world). This trajectory implies geogovernance in some form within several decades (suggesting that a world order collapse into a condition of pervasive social chaos and strife would be the only other currently plausible alternative). Such geogovernance involves the emergence of relatively stable mechanisms of global scope designed to sustain the distortions described by the triple indictment, including the effective suppression of resistance activities.

To the extent that such conceptions accurately anticipate the future, world order thinking can be truly dubbed "the new dismal science." Fortunately, offsetting this prospect is a countervision of the future arising from a different interpretation of historical possibilities, stressing an evolving normative project based on the strengthening of democracy, human rights, international law, and international institutions. These perspectives encourage the strengthening of wider identities than those associated with a given territorial, national, or ethnic experience, and diminish, indirectly, the role of sovereignty. This project, with its roots in the Hague peace conferences of 1899 and 1907, can be understood as a global constitutional process culminating in a progressive form of geogovernance, that is, geogovernance as a normatively enhancing displacement and reversal of geopolitics, not as something static, once and for all, but as a continuous unfolding, leading to what is being called here "humane governance."

Subsequent chapters on democracy, security, development, and governance elaborate on this positive image of the future. The stress is on the vertical deepening of democratic social forces in relation to state and market and the horizontal expansion of democracy beyond state/society relations through the agency of transnational social movements and citizens' associations, facilitating the growth of global civil society. This countervision presupposes the possibility of globalization from below to establish new identities and communities, reclaiming the instrumentalities of law and global institutions to promote the goals of nonviolence, social justice, and ecological balance.

In this chapter sovereignty serves as the bridge between the analytical presentations of the opening chapters and the more prescriptive material in the subsequent chapters. Sovereignty is here associated with the concentration of formal authority to act and command loyalty, a complex, constantly changing, and mixed political, legal, and moral conception, part theory, part practice, part aspiration and ideology, part myth, and part sheer fiction. Sovereignty has been significantly connected with the centrality of the state in most types of world order thinking, almost to the point that the common phrase "the sovereign state" strikes most of us as a redundancy. Sovereignty is associated with bounded territorial units that also continue to demarcate the effective *outer* limits of identity, community, and citizenship for most peoples in the world, but not necessarily the *inner* limits. The identification of sovereignty with the territorial state has been powerfully reinforced over a period of centuries by nationalism as a political creed, initially fabricated to sustain loyalty to the state, more recently providing the political energy that demands a state to complete its search for security and dignity. Historically, then, statism preceded nationalism in the early modern period, whereas nationalism often precedes statism in the late modern period, but in both settings the two are confusingly intertwined in diverse ways.

There is also an often forgotten historical dimension to the sovereignty debate: the initial European preoccupation with sovereignty as doctrine and practice was weighted toward the build-up of the ideological and functional case for the *internal* consolidation of authority and capabilities, and must be understood against the dystopic background of crime and local violence in the late Middle Ages. The function of sovereignty was to help overcome often severe civic disorder and an endless round of feudalistic struggles and many overlapping claims to exercise local control that made it impossible to construct commerical markets of sufficient scale and efficiency. Secondarily, the attractiveness of sovereignty for secularizing, territorial leaders in the early modern period of European history was definitely associated with finding an effective justification for opposing the universalistic and intrusive claims put forward on behalf of the Holy Roman Empire and the Papacy. Only later, and in a much less salient manner, did post-Westphalian jurists, most notably the eighteenth-century Swiss international law writer Emmerich de Vattel, rely on sovereignty to deny that a state could be bound in any reliable way to other states, although the theoretical bases for such secular and territorial absolutism in external relations can certainly be found in the writings of Machiavelli, Hobbes, and Bodin. It is, however, this theoretical tradition, culminating in the writing of Hegel on the state as the highest possible expression of moral and political consciousness, that grounded the sense of "we" in the community of citizens owing allegiance to the state, and "they" as those legally and physically located outside these territorial boundaries. Such spatial coordinates were undoubtedly in part an extension of the siege mentality associated with the walled cities of medieval Europe, and encouraged the polarization of political identity between those *within* and those *without*, thereby providing the justifying ethos of war, both dying and killing.

The idea of sovereignty was borrowed from theological accounts of the dominance of God in relation to earthly affairs, a view of sovereignty that is totalistic with respect to time, space, authority. There is no "other" to challenge the divine sovereign, and thus no contrast between the community *within* and the anarchy *without*. In this crucial regard, the secularization of sovereignty involved a deformation of its essence. To some extent, the transition historically by way of kings, with their claims of absolutism and divine right to rule, created a superficial link to the earlier religious idea of a single, perpetual ruler of the universe. Hobbes expressed the spirit of this idea, referring to the king as a "Mortall God" in *Leviathan*. Yet, more closely examined, such an assertion borders on blasphemy: the king is one among several such kings, and as such a denial of the monotheism that made the Judeo-Christian-Islamic claim of a unified divinity so distinctive. What remains relevant here is that the idea of sovereignty is so useful and fundamental that theorists can manipulate its meaning to serve quite antagonistic purposes as the structure of power and authority undergoes historical shifts. In this regard, the survival of "sovereignty" in this era of an emergent globalism needs to be watched carefully to identify what has been retained, what has been abandoned, and above all what has been reconstituted. Such a critical perspective is needed to consider the extent to which sovereignty can be adapted to the specific requirements of humane governance, and the extent to which it poses an obstacle to its realization in various settings.

Globalization from above undermines the postulates of sovereignty, but without truly extending the sense of community.[4] World citizenship of a mechanical sort emerges for the globalizing elites, based on the market/media global nexus of commonalities: speaking English, traveling, phoning, faxing, sleeping in hotel chains, listening to CNN, renting cars from Hertz and Avis. But there are no bonds with the peoples of the world and their various ordeals; in fact, a globalist of this informatics variety lives in a homogenized, electronically serviced milieu that makes home as a distinct place disappear altogether. A connectedness of a new sort takes the primary form of class and symbol consciousness: the nonterritorial and online mindset of the globalists that manage the financial markets and the electronically administered political economy. In this process of geogovernance, the sense of rootedness and community is diluted, even lost, rather than being enlarged. As shall become clear in subsequent sections, globalization from below extends the sense of community, loosening the ties between sovereignty and community but building a stronger feeling of identity with the sufferings and aspirings of peoples, a wider "we," as well as a series of narrower identities arising from the interplay of local/global identity chains. A democratizing globalism encourages identification with natural ethnic and bioregional communities, whatever their contours, but gives existential force to the experience of humanity, of the species as sharing a destiny for better or worse. In this regard, the territorializing of community that historically connected sovereignty to the state seems anachronistic and often artificial, depreciating the validity of species and ecological dimensions of identity, of transnational associations of individuals with compelling political agendas, and the dynamics of transnational bonding based on shared characteristics of race, gender, class, and even profession.

Despite the erosions of territoriality as a consequence of globalization, it is definitely premature to cast traditional notions of sovereignty aside. Sovereignty retains a critical importance in contemporary thinking about world order, especially because of its instrumental connections with nationalism, still the most robust mobilizing ideology on the planet. Several dimensions of this importance can be identified:

- our image of the world is still mainly derived from maps that divide the earth up into sovereign states; this basic territorial division of space is reinforced by international organizations that only accept such states as full members, from competitive sporting events such as the Olympics that associate the identity of participating athletes with their state, and from state flags and anthems that remain primary symbols of difference and community on the global level;
- this statist image, resting on the formal status of sovereignty, is a fundamental principle of international law and is enshrined in the United Nations Charter, the closest thing to an organic law for the world community: Article 1(1) of the Charter lists "sovereign equal-

ity" among members as the first principle of the UN; Article 2(7) prohibits intervention by the UN in matters within "domestic jurisdiction," thereby affirming the idea of territorial supremacy of the sovereign state; and Articles 3 and 4 restrict membership in the UN to states, that is, political entities entitled to claim the status of territorial sovereignty;

– the sense of sovereignty is valued by all states in a variety of settings, but it is especially important for strong states with global and regional ambitions, providing a rationale for the pursuit of vital interests as self-defined and without accountability to international law or to any external procedure of accountability, such as a court; in this regard, sovereignty in diplomatic practice remains closely linked to the realist world-view, but critically considered, such linkages are a contested interpretation of the appropriate role of sovereignty;

– sovereignty as status is also of great relevance to weak states seeking to insulate their territorial domain against warranted and unwarranted forms of external intrusion. To disenfranchised and captive nations that lack a state of their own and associate their victimization with this absence, the acquisition of a recognized state is regarded as "a solution" to the agonies of vulnerability – both as an ideal and a program, as in the historically prominent instance of the Jewish people, and more recently of the Palestinians.

This enumeration of the persisting relevance of sovereignty on the levels of political doctrine and practice has attempted to ignore normative effects. It is also necessary to distinguish among various invocations of sovereignty as positive, anachronistic, and regressive. From a WOMP perspective, always taking account of context, reliance on sovereignty by a weak state to inhibit geopolitical pressures, including interventionary claims, operates in a generally positive manner: for instance, the efforts by the Sandinista government in Nicaragua during the 1980s to seek respect by the United States for their sovereign rights by reference to international law as set forth by the International Court of Justice. But a qualification needs to be made, as the government asserting its sovereign rights may be guilty of repressive policies toward its own people. A normative tradeoff results, but account also needs to be taken of the likely aftermath of intervention, which so often leaves bloodshed and humiliation and fails to enhance the well-being of the society whose protection supposedly induced the intervention.

Sovereignty may also be anachronistic, as when a government claims a sovereign right to construct nuclear energy facilities that pose high safety risks or to destroy tropical rainforests in a manner that jeopardizes biodiversity. Sovereignty may be regressive as when strong states rely on "realist" orientations to justify their disregard of international law. This occurred when the US government defied the World Court decision in 1986 that held US support for the Contra war against the government of Nicaragua to be illegal, and more generally, refused to accept accountability under international law in relation to contested uses of force.

Despite the vitality of sovereignty in the practice of states, some of its anachronistic and regressive features are becoming ever more apparent. Sovereignty was above all an apt expression of the modernist achievement in Europe which rested on the unity of state, market, and nation. This unity accorded priority to the claims of the citizen as opposed to the person, establishing community as a matter of territorial sovereignty, replacing medieval religious ideas about a Christian universalism centered in Rome with a more secular tolerance of religious diversity. This fusing of idea and function helped the state claim for itself the energies of political loyalty and patriotism, with the corresponding right to stigmatize disloyalty and punish treason, and regard those beyond borders as evil others. Globalizing tendencies from without and fragmenting developments from within weaken these claims – the state is losing its capacity to exert authority effectively within territorial boundaries, thereby allowing other forms of association and identity to make stronger claims on loyalty and affection. These threats to the relationship between state and political identity are provoking various backlashes aimed at coercing those that enter a state to conform to its *cultural* norms.

Sovereignty, then, embodies contradictory features and induces ambivalence as to its role in the transition to geogovernance:

- sovereignty remains an essential concept, yet its reality is being steadily and inevitably subverted;
- sovereignty can not be relinquished, but its invocation by strong states to justify disregard for international legal restraints on the use of force can be challenged;
- sovereignty, state, and territorial community remain a powerful, if variable and uneven, nexus of identity expressive of the old world order based on geopolitics; at the same time, sovereignty, peoples, and global civil society are emerging as an overlapping, alternative, and future-oriented secondary nexus of identity that is engaged in promoting the possibility of humane governance.

There seems, then, to be no way to escape the ambiguity of sovereignty as concept and organizing principle in this period of transition. It represents both an expression of self-determination and human rights and an instrument of geopolitics. Abandoning sovereignty prior to overcoming the regressive sides of geopolitics would remove, especially in certain settings, one of the few means of protection available to weak and vulnerable states. It is not too soon at all, however, to condemn regressive reliance on sovereignty to justify nonaccountability by governments to international law or to expose anachronistic uses of sovereignty to avoid the implications and responsibilities of interdependence. To the extent that the transition to geogovernance proceeds, territorial sovereignty is being inevitably displaced and transcended by new modes of authority. Inquiry about contested behavior shifts away from sovereignty to issues of accountability, participation, and sustainable development, the sinews of democracy, not just in state/society settings, but increasingly in all settings and sites of collective influence and action, including family, neighborhood, workplace. A process of decentering authority occurs that also reflects the changing nature of democracy, to be considered in the next chapter. The state remains a primary actor, but is losing its exemption from scrutiny, whether the perspective of assessment is personal and local or public and global, as well as gradations in between; moral accountability and legal accountability are being extended, in this normative restructuring, to *all* actors that shape lives and well-being.

State/society relations are, by comparison, more democratically constituted than are regional and global arenas. In Europe, linked by the most participatory of regional structures, the significance of the Brussels institutions far outweighs those in Strasbourg (where human rights activities and the directly elected European Parliament are located). Most global arenas of decision, especially the most influential, are dominated by rich and powerful states (UN Security Council, IMF/World Bank, and the annual economic summits that bring together the heads of state of the seven leading industrial states of the North to set global economic policy). The significance of the internationalized state is related to its control over those external arenas, although ultimate influence is shifting to global market forces. Mercantilist logic is being inverted, the state is becoming the agent, the market the principal.

Sovereignty in origin and practice is a quintessential expression of patriarchal notions of authority – men and machismo continue to dominate statist practice within structures of hierarchy. Ideas of exclusive control *at home* and anarchy *abroad* are expressive of a patriarchal view of order and chaos. Whether the transition to geogovernance retains this patriarchal character depends on the outcome of many struggles to define the future. The increased, yet still marginal, participation of women in structures of power and wealth and nondiscrimination against women could be substantially achieved within a patriarchal framework of values, behavior, and outlook. A decisive test of the capacity to erode patriarchy during transition may be the extent to which feminist orientations toward non-hierarchical networks of relationship supplant the more masculine stress on organizational hierarchies. As Ann Tickner persuasively argues, the patriarchal basis of international relations is so deeply embedded that women with a feminist consciousness find the domain of international relations alien and their interpretations of evolving political reality disregarded as irrelevant.[5] Her point here is reinforced by the male domination of professional literature. An article by a woman in a leading journal on international issues remains a rarity. Most "serious" media discussions of global policy are still carried on among men, and this remains true even when the organizers "make the effort" to include "qualified" women.

Sovereignty and Citizenship

Geopolitics cannot be wished away at this stage, but neither are its capabilities comparable to what they were during the height of the modernist era, that is roughly from the Peace of Westphalia in the seventeenth century to the eve of World War I. Attentiveness to the contemporary conditions of peoples requires sensitivity to context and to the importance of interpretation. These considerations underpin this reinterpretation of citizenship as a category of affiliation and loyalty.[6]

To associate citizenship with humane governance, that is, geogovernance on behalf of the peoples of the world, would provisionally shift the location of political identity away from territorially delimited states in many, but not all situations, and further undermine the hold of sovereignty on the political imagination. Such shifts are currently in process and they are beneficial if the dynamics of interpretation conclude that *in context* statist identity is either anachronistic or regressive, as compared to other genuine alternatives. Given this transition setting, the weakening of statist bonds seems like a positive step in relation to the world order for those in a secure class, gender, and race setting, so long as it is associated with an emphasis on accountability to international law, the wider claims of conscience (taking suffering of others seriously), as well as the governance requirements associated with environmental protection and market regulation.

Economic globalism, as the Maastricht and NAFTA struggles suggest, can intensify a deterioration in the relative circumstances of peoples, and push transitional processes toward a regressive type of geogovernance. It is regressive because it further marginalizes the more vulnerable elements in society, as already witnessed by high unemployment as a permanent feature of most affluent societies even when their economy is in a robust phase of rapid growth. Given this *internal* unevenness, a rejection of globalism, so structured, may be the alternative in the present political climate which supports the least of a range of evils. Rejectionism is not enough to offset the force of integrative pressures. A more benign alternative to globalism needs to be imagined and pursued – one that lifts employment and environmental standards and prospects – rather than privileges capital. There is encouraging evidence that transnational networks are emerging under such labels as North American Worker-to-Worker Network, People's Plan 21 (Asia-Pacific region), Third World Network (Malaysia), and they have produced valuable orienting and action documents such as "From Global Pillage to Global Village" and "Toward a New North–South Economic Dialogue." These initiatives will be considered more fully in the next chapter in assessing the reinvention of democracy during transition to geogovernance.

For those who are acutely deprived, the strengthening of statist bonds in some situations may be beneficial as a means to establish sufficient autonomy and overcome a heritage of abuse and exploitation from without, especially if combined with an affirmation of accountability to democratic procedures of constitutionalism and respect for human rights of all those living within territorial boundaries. The relevance of traditional sovereignty to the promotion of humane prospects depends on context. For instance, the Kurdish struggle in the Middle East would seem to be assisted by a weakening of state sovereignty in such countries as Turkey, Iraq, Iran, and Syria. In different circumstances, weakening Canadian sovereignty by way of the secession of Quebec would seem to further deteriorate the prospects of the Algonquin and Cree nations by dividing their communities between separate states, or incorporating them against their will into a new sovereign entity that is particularly insensitive to the priorities and values of indigenous peoples.

The strength and weakness of sovereignty as a protective shield for identity and community depends on many situational factors, including the immediate, perceived effects of associating nationalist, ethnic, class, and gender interests with an existing state structure. As such, creating a national community based on tolerance and respect for ethnic, religious, gender, and class difference may be the most meaningful short-run approach to specifying the content of citizenship. One thinks of Lebanon or Cambodia or Somalia or Sudan as extreme instances in which healing the wounds within the scope of territorial reality remains of prime importance regardless of globalist tendencies. The 1992 Los Angeles riots (the largest instance of bloodshed within the United States since the American Civil War) and the growing violence against foreigners in several European countries confirm that even powerful, ascendant states are not in a position to ignore the internal urgencies of territorial community-building.

Several conclusions can be drawn:

- neither the global citizenship of the emerging business/financial/media elite, nor the sentimental global citizenship of those who are under the illusion that a community of all persons is present or embodied in the United Nations can be considered positive developments, although there are positive aspects, such as the weakening of the bonds that tie elites to militarist forms of nationalism;
- neither a chauvinistic citizenship of strong/rich countries that exempts geopolitics from accountability, nor the denial of national bonds in deeply divided polities in the throes of bloody civil strife offer a positive image of citizenship during transition;
- only time-sensitive and context-determined citizenship that aspires to democratically conditioned forms of geogovernance can be affirmed. Such an identification by individuals is called here "citizen pilgrim" to emphasize a commitment to an imagined human community of the future that embodies nonviolence, social justice, ecological balance, and participatory democracy in all arenas of policy and decision, and embodies these perspectives in current modes of feeling, thought, and action. The citizen pilgrim prefigures humane governance in both imaginative and political modes of being.

Sovereignty and citizenship are caught up in a multifaceted relationship. Adherents of the global market path to geogovernance seek to keep the powerful states as guardians of strategic interests during this period of transition, sustaining militarism but shifting loyalties and priorities in globalist and market-oriented directions. Others threatened by this type of transition resist in various ways; this includes seeking to strengthen territorial bonds with a nationalist priority, and drawing on the state to give continuing emphasis to those bonded by ethnic, nationalist, and traditional linkages. Those embarked on the transition to humane governance are generally drawn to nonterritorial conceptions of identity and community, regarding the links between sovereignty and the state as mainly a relic of the past, yet acknowledging its occasional utility. This latter utility resembles reliance on a crude weapon to defend one's home against intrusion – it may deter even if it is not very effective in actual combat. Even here there are some exceptions or qualifications. The states of northern Europe – adherents of welfare capitalism – continue to be the most effective agents in the world for the realization of economic and social rights, providing housing, health, food, and education for *all* inhabitants. The state is in these settings an effective agency of human governance for the territorial population, although whether such a role is sustainable in light of global market pressures is dubious. There are signs that the drive to be competitive is eroding the exemplary Scandinavian welfare system, with similar pressures limiting the regional commitment in Europe to humane governance. Market-oriented criticism already complains that high labor/welfare costs are pricing Europe out of the world market, and must be cut.

Why Sovereignty?

The current geopolitical map of the world consists essentially of power and influence grids that are complex, overlapping, deceptive, and varying over time and space, as well as from issue to issue. When the US government proclaims "a new world order" as the sequel to the Cold War, the call is accurately heard in many places as a revised project for global hegemony, with its normative pretensions about fostering an era of an enhanced role for international law and the United Nations being dismissed as diversionary. Or worse: it is interpreted as an indication of an intention by the US government to appropriate the instrumentalities of the global community for selfish geopolitical ends. In security matters, ascendant states continue to dominate the political scene, whereas in other domains of policy even the most powerful states are caught in a crossfire of global market and ethnoreligious pressures.

The map that hangs on most walls conveys the Westphalian image of global political reality. What seems to count are territorial states enjoying sovereign rights. These states enjoy a special status as members of international society, virtually without regard to size, wealth, behavior, capabilities. The formalities of statism remain the defining criterion of participation in many global settings.

And it is more than a matter of formalities. The state remains the principal vehicle and guardian of the most powerful mobilizing ideas and destructive capabilities in political life: patriotism and nationalism. Paradoxically, because of the multinational, multiethnic, and multireligious composition of many states, the state is also the prime oppressive agent with respect to the politics of identity. The state and its sovereign attributes play a dual role in relation to identity claims. Peoples without states are perceived as especially victimized and exceptionally vulnerable, as are both encapsulated nations trapped within states whose governing elites are hostile to specific group claims of identity, and desperate individuals who have abandoned their statist affiliations, as in the case of "boat people." Those fleeing from oppressive circumstances and hardship in such countries as Vietnam and Haiti are illustrative of what it means to abandon statist identity without access to a substitute. The continually expanding refugee population of the world is a vivid reminder that a right of access on the basis of citizenship remains the most reliable source of protection for most of the world's people. Genocide is, of course, the most acute expression of human displacement, expressing the highest form of vulnerability of a people to an antagonistic state. In Cambodia between 1975 and 1978 the Khmer Rouge carried out a genocidal program of rule directed at the Cambodian people, causing the label autogenocide to be introduced.

There are many other settings where the idea and actuality of sovereignty exert a significant policy impact. The setting of civil violence has been acutely problematic in recent years, given salience by the tragic reality confronting the civilian populations in such countries as Sudan, Somalia, former Yugoslavia, Rwanda, and several of the former Soviet republics. To what extent should humanitarian relief operations be subject to the approval of the government that represents the state? Suppose, as seems the case in relation to several of the instances named, the internationally recognized governing authority of a state seems responsible for inflicting abuses on portions of its own population, amounting to crimes against humanity? Should the traditional locus of sovereignty, with its unconditional authority over access to territory, be subordinated in favor of norms that support the rights of peoples to receive humanitarian assistance? Can such norms be implemented in actual conflict situations without taking sides in ongoing civil strife? Is impartiality a duty if one side in civil strife is guilty of fundamental abuse of human rights and the laws of war? Who decides such questions? Where are the political will and logistical capabilities to intervene effectively? The record of intervention that seeks the political restructuring of the target society has been uniformly unsuccessful unless the intervening side has been prepared to pay the costs of prolonged occupation (the Allied Powers after World War II, Vietnam in Cambodia).

Sovereignty is conceptually and historically intertwined with this statist/geopolitical heritage. The transition to geogovernance will alter the manner in which sovereignty is interpreted in theory and practice. As matters now stand, the governments of most states continue to insist on their capacity to uphold the well-being of their citizenry, deny such capacity to any other actors, and even impose a homogeneous national identity on a culturally diverse population. Recently the French government, as represented by several high officials, has denied Muslim female students the right to cover their heads with scarves in schools, declaring that Muslim religious practices are not "French," and that multiculturalism would be "the end of France."

Such an insistence on territorial supremacy has been grossly misleading; since the inception of the modern state and as a result of inequality among states and the extraterritorial character of geopolitics, there have been consistent patterns of interventionary diplomacy and a variety of hegemonic arrangements: empires, protectorates, spheres of influence. Under contemporary conditions of globalization the insistence on locating sovereignty exclusively in the governing institutions of territorial states is a pompous and dangerous pretension, even if conditioned by a democratic, populist notion that sovereignty resides ultimately in the citizenry, and by a record of respect for cultural diversity and human rights. Given the porousness of boundaries and various interdependencies, even the most powerful states are unable to safeguard the autonomy of territorial space. This erosion of statist capabilities exists in all arenas of concern, whether understood in terms of security from external attack, or in political terms as competence to handle the foreign policy agenda, or in economic terms as capacity to set economic policy at home without regard to external factors, or in cultural terms as the nurturing of societal values and identity that draw upon shared memories and distinctive experiences.

Many states lacked the basic attributes of sovereignty even during the early modern period after 1600 when the sovereign character of the state was being established in Western Europe, but then the dominant states seemed "sovereign" and secondary states exercised substantial, uncontested, internal control over the basic life of their own territorial community. As Bodin and Hobbes emphasized, the original priority of the state was the consolidation of internal control and the establishment of domestic peace. Such achievements did not necessarily depend on the scale of the state, and gave to notions of sovereign equality of states a measure of plausibility. It is notable that in the early postmodern era (1980s and onwards) there has been a decline in the internal capabilities of the state as well, expressed via the outbreak of ethnic and religious strife and the rise of crime to epidemic levels.

Despite these tendencies, it is inopportune to relinquish the doctrine of sovereignty at this stage. Small, weak states often acquire a degree of protection against intervention, either by other states or by the United Nations and other international institutions. It is important to realize that deliberate intrusion upon territorial authority by external actors remains exclusively a prerogative of the strong, that is generally the North, deciding on the conditions for intervention in the affairs of the weak, that is the South. On a regional level in the South, interventions also occur, as in the case of Egypt in Yemen, Libya in Chad, India in Sri Lanka, Iraq in Kuwait. Despite recent claims to the contrary, it would be perverse to construe the history of interventionary diplomacy as either motivated by humanitarian considerations or as having benefited in any consistent manner the peoples of the countries that are the sites of intervention. Thus, to create humanitarian exceptions to sovereign rights implies an unwarranted confidence that in the present global setting such efforts will not be stalking horses for geopolitical ambition, or not much better, token efforts to challenge abusive internal behavior. The early 1990s confirms such skepticism even when the interventionary auspices are the UN and the alleged justification is based on compassion for a people caught in the throes of disaster.

In fact, a cruel dilemma exists: to tolerate gross crimes against humanity as committed by Serbian forces in Bosnia during 1992 by deferring to territorial sovereignty, or to intervene to frustrate the establishment of ethnically cleansed mini-states. Closely connected with this set of concerns are the practical difficulties of carrying out effectively a plan of humanitarian intervention. Often the effects of a failed intervention are the magnification of violence and the increased suffering of the very people whose relief provided the justification in the first instance.

Sovereignty then, is, and always has been, bound up with state-centrism. It operates internationally as both a blindfold (denying the contradictory practices of geopolitics) and a blinker (rendering conceptually invisible the transnational initiatives of civil society). The state, with an important recent assist from the media, manipulates our understanding of sovereignty, encouraging a dualist image of the world as constituted by the self and the alien other, basically postulating a condition of anarchy and continuous conflict between sovereign states. There is nothing inherently objectionable about the word sovereignty. It is the various extrapolations and applications that have impaired our capacity for and distrust of human solidarity, endorsing webs of identity and community within territorial space and denigrating those without, a potent dichotomy when fortified by the concentration of war-making capabilities at the level of the state. As a result, the linking of violence and territorial security has become the dominant mode of diplomatic discourse, carried to an extreme during the Cold War, sanitized by technicians who debated and rationalized the features of species-threatening mutual deterrence in a dynamic technological setting. Yet beneath the abstractions was the deadly serious omnicidal threat to destroy all life on earth if necessary to safeguard "the national interest," that is, to uphold the sovereign pretensions of a particular state or group of states.

Sovereignty is formalized in relation to the equality of states in the academic discipline of international relations and international law, but the political significance of sovereignty in complex interrlationship with geopolitics exerts a detrimental influence on the quality of world order, resulting in "the three indictments" discussed in the prior chapter. Sovereignty gridlocks the political imagination, provides the realist mindset with an ideational heritage that extends beyond the domain of naked force, and to the extent that the promotion of state sovereignty is a success on a popular level, both provides a democratic base for a militarist foreign policy and impedes a more appropriate historical appreciation of transnational threats to human well-being, of local and global origin.

It is not the intention here to demonize or romanticize the idea of sovereignty or the role of the state, but rather to advocate its re-evaluation in light of changing global and human circumstances. Undoubtedly, the persisting attempt to sustain the marriage of sover-eignty and state is responsible for destructive practices and attitudes, yet an abrupt divorce would seem premature given the geopolitical control of international institutions. If we are to ground global civil society effectively, then it will be crucial to recast our understanding of sovereignty in light of the shifting and multidimensional character of identity and community. At stake is whether territorial coordinates continue to correlate sufficiently with the notion of "we." The bound-aries and perspectives of global civil society do not coincide with the boundaries of states or civilizations but are delimited by shared beliefs and commitments, and by participation in specific struggles. As such, preferred forms of geogovernance will be free of those geopolitical deformations that entrap peoples in artificial sovereign entities, and will uphold human rights, including a broad right of self-determination, in a manner that disregards the obstacles to implementation now associated with claims of sovereignty. As such, the modernist stress on territorial sovereignty as the exclusive basis for political community and identity would be displaced both by more local and distinct groupings and by association with the reality of a global civil society without boundaries.

Especially since the French and American revolutions, there has been a counterdiscourse on sovereignty, arguing the case for "popular sovereignty," associating the authority of the government (and the state as actor) with the delegation to government of their powers by and for the people of a country, and subject to revocation. So conceived, sovereignty has a radical democratic connotation, especially in state/ society relations and policy-making. Usually, however, even those who endorse the idea that sovereignty resides in civil society and with the citizenry conceive of such thinking as a matter of constitutionalism confined to territory, still expecting the manifold of a world of sovereign states to follow the logic of geopolitics. Even this perspective tends, then, to grant foreign policy and national security issues an exemption from popular control – as there is no community "out there" beyond borders. Political anarchy is accepted as descriptive of the structure of international society. National interests prevail. Strong states provide systemic order, being the most influential locus of authority, not answerable to any external authority, especially if vital matters are in issue. Weaker states tend to adapt to the prevailing geopolitical order, usually by aligning their interests with a powerful actor, thereby confining their role to an enjoyment of the formalities of *external* sovereign rights, while the substance of global policy is shaped by ascendant geopolitical actors. As argued, increasingly these actors are not always states, suggesting that to describe world order as "statist" is doubly misleading, implying participation by weak states and ignoring the unacknowledged participation of various categories of nonstate actors, especially corporations and banks, with even citizens associations playing influential roles in some settings peripheral to military and market concerns.

In either event, adjusting sovereignty seems conceptually and behaviorally crucial in relation to a critique of geopolitics and the specification of an alternative in the form of transition to a normatively acceptable form of geogovernance. Global civil society treated as the hopeful source of political agency needs to free the minds of persons from an acceptance of state/sovereignty identity, and rethink the contours of community, loyalty, and citizenship.

A Few Policy Conclusions

Despite the contextuality of sovereignty and given the role of the territorial state as political actors, a number of policy conclusions emerge from the analysis.

1 The attribute of sovereignty provides no exemption from the obligations of international law, and these obligations are to be ascertained as impartially as possible by observers and participants in official positions, especially in relation to uses of military force outside of territory.

2 International procedures, particularly those associated with the United Nations, would seem to provide the most reliable guidance as to the character of these obligations, provided certain conditions are met: that the Organization achieves greater autonomy in relation to geopolitics, especially in relation to peace and security matters; that equals are treated equally, with the strong being generally as inclined to be obedient to its will as the weak, and the weak not being the only ones subjected to its coercive moves. The authority and legitimacy of the United Nations and its various organs will depend on the perceptions and reality of autonomy. An important means by which to strengthen autonomy is to keep UN operations, especially in the war/peace context, within the constitutional framework embodied in the UN Charter. The Gulf War dramatically problematized the United Nations, especially the Security Council, by making the Organization appear to operate as a legitimizing vehicle of geopolitics, and especially by the tendency to ignore Charter guidelines in Chapter VII for collective security. For more sensitive students of the UN, the Gulf War merely made manifest tendencies that had been apparent all along. Enhancing the autonomy of the UN is a priority during this transition period and it is a gradual, uneven process, a matter of degree, a wavering line that will be seen differently at different stages by the various actors in international life. The gradual emancipation of the UN from the grip of geopolitics will help ensure that transition to geogovernance improves the quality of global security and fosters the emergence of humane governance.

3 In the absence of an autonomous United Nations, other actors have a greater responsibility to provide impartial guidance as to the obligations of international law, including citizens' associations and regional institutions and procedures; the important role of the Conference of Security and Cooperation in Europe (CSCE) during the 1980s in implementing the human rights sections of the Helsinki Accords has been acknowledged by those who led the emancipatory movements in East Europe in 1989. Human rights, including the democratizing imperative in relation to state/society relations, provide one wedge by which to challenge the arbitrary claims of internal sovereignty according territorial rulers an absolute mandate.

4 Sovereignty can provide only limited protection; complementary

efforts require subordinating geopolitics to the procedures of international law and the associated Nuremberg Principles that impose individual responsibility on leaders and citizens, on the basis of the legal framework relied upon after World War II to prosecute the surviving German political and military leaders. Also crucial is a concerted grassroots, transnational effort to extend the rule of law, accountability, and the precepts of democracy to control the operation of global market forces. To the extent that such democratizing initiatives succeed, the idea of sovereignty as discretionary action by the state will decline in significance through effective constraint by law, or be made irrelevant through the bypassing of the state.

5 The role of sovereignty in the imagined reality of humane governance is likely to be nominal as the state will no longer be privileged to engage in violence as it has been during the era of geopolitics. But the erosion and virtual disappearance of sovereignty as a guiding doctrine is not by itself necessarily a sign that the emergence of geogovernance will be conducive to the human interest. One can imagine or postulate forms of geogovernance involving the ascendancy of market forces (reinforced by state power and media control) that would reinforce the conditions producing the triple indictment. Thus the displacement of sovereignty, which is an incident of transition, needs to be assessed by reference to the successes or failures of transnational democracy.

4

The Democratizing Imperative

Democracy and Humane Governance

If the world is interpreted in light of macro-tendencies toward integration at the global level, it is possible to explain why traditional democracy is no longer able to provide humane governance. To the extent that the world is organized into territorial units, political leaders, almost regardless of ideological orientation, are squeezed by various pressures to promote competitiveness at the expense of welfare and environmental protection. Such pressures in the South have been especially associated with the structural adjustment programs imposed by the IMF and World Bank as conditions for debt relief and the receipt of additional loans. Similar pressures are harshly exerted, too, in those countries in Eastern Europe and the former Soviet Union which have embarked on a rapid transition to a market economy.

But richer countries in the North are feeling the pressures of competitiveness as well. The symptoms of this pressure are pockets of deep poverty, even homelessness, as well as persisting unemployment at a level that would have been treated as intolerable two decades ago, but is now accepted as normal. The societal distress in the North seems structural rather than cyclical, and is necessarily producing political realignments. Migratory flows of distressed peoples, displaced from their homeland, are both an expression of acute deprivation in the place where they came from, and a source of tension and regression in the country of destination. The refugee population of the world has been steadily rising during recent decades, inducing a xenophobic backlash, a closing of borders, and a rise in so-called multiculturalism (which in this context refers to a priority given to distinct ethnic and religious identities over the identity associated with citizenship or with the prevailing national identity). In some countries, most notably France, there is a growing parallel tendency, inconsistent with multiculturalism, to insist that refugees must be willing to assimilate if they expect to be accepted, and this means speaking the prevailing national language, adhering in public places to the dress code, and confining their specific beliefs and practices to domestic and distinctly religious spheres. These developments threaten both domestic tranquility and the upholding of the cultural aspect of human rights, rights which are at the core of humane governance.

There is also a fundamentalist or extremist backlash that repudiates globalization from above in the name of religion, but also jeopardizes the most precious secular achievements of modernity, namely, the protection of the individual and tolerance for diversity as an essential dimension of freedom. It is a serious mistake to generalize about these tendencies, or even to regard them as an unconditional assault on democracy and democratic values. In North Africa, for instance, grassroots support for Islamic orientations toward politics arose out of disenchantment with secular government, its corruption and indifference to the plight of the poor. Islamic groups often delivered social services in local communities of the poor, thereby winning support of many people and fulfilling, to some extent, the mandate to promote social and economic rights, especially the provision of the basic necessities of life. We cannot grasp the success of fundamentalist politics if we do not also appreciate the failures of secular politics. In addition, we need to assess the fundamentalist challenge in relation to the actual circumstances of peoples. There is an irony here: whereby market-oriented elites that rely on authoritarian practices will be forgiven their transgressions on political and civil rights, identity-oriented elites will not be credited with their achievements with regard to economic and social rights.

Yet, allowing for this complexity, there are grounds for concern. Democratic procedures and structures are at risk, whether the fundamentalist challenge is centered in society or embodied in state power. Conditions in Iran, India, Egypt, Algeria, Sudan, Bosnia, and Georgia suggest the range of problems that challenge the most minimal conceptions of humane governance: religious warfare is actively promoted; ethnic cleansing is pursued with genocidal ferocity; official decrees, as in relation to Salman Rushdie, impose death sentences for activity legally protected in a foreign country; and in certain instances, religious groups threaten and carry out terror campaigns against *any* foreign presence, and against any secularized member of society, putting intellectuals especially at risk, as in Algeria. Identity politics – that is, associating a given polity with one and only one ethnic or religious identity – cannot be reconciled with the intermingling of peoples in the world or with the technological realities of a necessarily plural and electronically wired global village.

Democracy at all levels presupposes tolerance of and respect for difference. Any claim of unconditional virtue or truth on behalf of a given people or religion is a prescription, in the last analysis, for genocide, and it moves inevitably in that direction, as the Bosnian ordeal of 1991–4 has made manifest. The initial priority of humane governance is to reaffirm the wisdom of secularism in relation to all structures of authority. Such wisdom should not itself, however, become fundamentalist! The rediscovery of our spiritual roots may be indispensable to the realization of humane governance and to the fulfillment of the overall potential of the human species. To the extent that the rise of secularism (and the modern idea of governance) was associated with the ascendancy of an antireligious mode of "scientific" thought, there is a need for rethinking and reconciliation. Indeed, humane governance may depend on the curbing of secular absolutisms (including consumerism) as much as it does on the deterrence and control of religious and ethnic extremisms. The challenge to democratic thought and practice at this stage of human history is to find the institutional and ideational forms that allow difference to flourish, yet to ground the affirmation of unity and an appreciation of shared destiny for the human species on a spiritual foundation.

These adverse conditions are accompanied by some encouraging developments. There is a definite trend toward equating political legitimacy of a state with its commitment to traditional democracy (periodic fair elections, multiple parties, free media, the rule of law, constitutionalism, and the protection of civil and political rights). All over the South, the trend has been away from military rule and in the direction of civilian governance. Furthermore, the transnational initiatives of citizens associations, globalization from below, are beginning to fashion a vision of geogovernance that accords with humane governance. These initiatives are beginning to give priority to resisting the adverse human and environmental impacts of global market forces, and to the consequent urgency of enlarging and refocusing the agenda of democratic practices.

David Held and others have been encouraging a reconceptualization of democracy through a focus on "cosmopolitan democracy," a systematic call for democratizing the global arenas of decision that are now dominated by state and market forces.[1] Traditional democracy remains necessary, but it is no longer sufficient to achieve humane governance. And as argued above, traditional democracy becomes marginalized and formalized insofar as authority over an integrated world economy and information order is shaped by extraterritorial forces. Indeed in some situations the popular notion of "market democracy" is an oxymoron with Orwellian overtones. When Yeltsin's Russia dissolves its parliament and uses tanks to dislodge dissident legislators from government buildings "in the name of democracy" it is an occasion for wonderment. And when the countries of Europe, along with the United States, greet these developments with reassuring gestures of unconditional support, affirming even the alleged need to abandon the Russian constitution in order to save democracy, then we know we are in a world where language no longer signifies what we supposed it did. The phrase "market democracy" denotes for political leaders the primacy of the market regardless of its impact on even the most minimal ingredients of democracy. As Fujimora's Peru has shown in the early 1990s, political legitimacy derives from market performance, not constitutional priorities. China is at the cusp of new and the end of the old, being an illegitimate survivor from the good old bipolar days, yet a superperformer in the new framework of economic growth and of trade and investment opportunities. As such, China tests the coherence of "the new world order." The challenge has produced confused and ambivalent responses. The prevailing view in the West is to reconcile the contradictory concerns about democracy and trade through the belief that economic growth will itself open up the society, weakening the hold of the state on its critics and dissenters.

The argument in the chapter has several links: first, that traditional democracy in state/society relations is essential to protect individuals and groups against abuse by the state and to allow some measure of participation by the citizenry in the selection of its leaders; second, that such democracy may be accompanied by varying degrees of social regression as a result of the impact of capital-driven geogovernance; thirdly, that the wider horizons of democratic theory and practice are challenging these trends beneath the banner of cosmopolitan democracy; fourthly, that mounting such a challenge effectively will involve both the growth of transnational democracy and the emergence of a variety of coalitions between grassroots groups and governments that find themselves beleaguered in the global village; and fifthly, that the reworking of the theory and practice of democracy under these altered conditions is at the center of the struggle to achieve humane governance of global proportions.

Tracking Traditional Democracy

The focus of traditional democracy is upon state/society relations within a world order structure of territorial states enjoying equal sovereign rights. The democratizing imperative has been to achieve humane governance on a state-by-state basis, including the distribution of authority between different levels of social organization. It is only as a consequence of the transition to geogovernance that the evolution of democratic thought has started in a serious way to attach significance to political arenas *external* to the state. Acknowledging this crucial extension should not, however, lead to an abandonment of earlier concerns about the quality of political life *internal* to the state, which has always been tainted by exclusions, perhaps most notably the refusal to grant the right of self-determination to indigenous peoples and nations encompassed within existing states.

In passing, it should be noted that human rights have provided a bridge, obliging the state to act in prescribed ways, empowered both by the citizenry and the international community in the expectation of such behavior. The content of these expectations are set forth in political, civil, social, economic, and cultural rights as specified in the great international law texts on the subject, each drafted and adopted under UN auspices: the Universal Declaration of Human Rights (1948), the International Covenant on Economic, Social and Cultural Rights (1966), and the International Covenant on Civil and Political Rights (1966). The implementation of these standards, on the other hand, is uneven and incomplete even with regard to the states with the best records. The international law framework for economic, social, and cultural rights remains controversial, and largely aspirational in relation to the obligations of the state. Still, the anti-apartheid campaign and the Helsinki process brought to bear on East Europe are indicative of transnational and global community pressures on behalf of human rights, and as such, enlarge the political terrain on which struggles for territorial democracy are being waged.

It is important, then, to include this standard agenda of traditional democracy, namely, periodic and fair elections, multiparty competition, rule of law, and the separation of powers. These common elements of democracy are each complex in practice and can vary greatly in application depending on cultural and ideological preferences. It is the *formal* endorsement of traditional democracy that has spread around the world, but not necessarily its *substantive* enactment.

How then does traditional democracy relate to the quest for humane governance during this era of transition to geogovernance? First of all, traditional democracy, as reinforced by minimum adherence to human rights, continues to provide the main arena in which advances and setbacks in the quality of governance are registered. Secondly, traditional democracy is losing the capability to perform effectively in the social and economic domains of policy, especially in relation to the most vulnerable portions of society. The global market explicitly constrains socially progressive impulses of government at the state level in many countries of the South by way of structural adjustment mechanisms. Thirdly, giving market factors priority in the foreign policy of leading states may have the paradoxical effect of encouraging antidemocratic practices in the name of democracy (for instance, Yeltsin's Russia, Fujimora's Peru). Fourthly, intervention by military means to promote human rights and democracy rarely, if ever, succeeds, and often conceals strategic motivations (that is, control over the political life and economic resources of the target society). Fifthly, as East and South Asian experience suggests, well-admininstered authoritarian governments may outperform neoliberal democracies even with respect to welfare criteria: basic needs, income equality, land reform (for instance, South Korea, Taiwan, Singapore). Thus a traditional democratic governance pattern that fails to overcome mass poverty and archaic land tenure arrangements (as in India) may do worse from the perspective of humane governance than some authoritarian regimes. This is not an argument for authoritarian rule, but an acknowledgment that the pragmatic economistic case for democracy is not persuasive. True, authoritarian rule can be corrupt and alienating (as in Iran under the Shah, the Philippines under Marcos), and highly inefficient (the military dictatorships of the 1960s and 1970s in Latin America), but this is not a necessary outcome. Sixth, and of utmost importance, traditional democracy is under simultaneous attack, with different weightings and impacts, from without by way of market globalism and from within by way of various kinds of regressive and intolerant social forces associated with the imposition of rigid constraints on human freedoms in the name of religion, tradition, or culture. Safeguarding traditional democracy, then, requires a state strong enough to resist antidemocratic globalizing impacts and to protect the human rights of the entire citizenry. Although international cooperative regimes are needed for many functional reasons, the sovereign state remains indispensable to the achievement of positive social, economic, and cultural rights for the foreseeable future, as well as to secure the protection of civil and political rights against internal social forces.

The virtually universal endorsement of democracy is at once encouraging and troublesome. It is encouraging because it acknowledges the role of popular participation and consent in *any* legitimate arrangement of governance. It is troublesome because geopolitical forces have attempted to insist on a model of democracy that incorporates unrestricted capitalism and settles for formalistic modes of political participation unresponsive to the specific realities of a given country. The "winners' in the Cold War are promoting a version of democracy that allegedly embodies purist market approaches to development: privatization, deregulation, free trade, unlimited wealth, unconditional property rights, low taxes, and limited protection of the poor. In practice, exceptions and contradictions abound; subsidies for French agriculture, protection for vulnerable American industrial sectors, and "welfare capitalism" for the defense industry. Also, these views of democracy may accept governmental arrangements that are coercive toward their own populations, and regard them as democratic simply because periodic elections are held and some opposition political parties are permitted to operate. A critical view is taken here of such variants of democracy and the contours of alternative conceptions are set forth. Free and fair elections are an important achievement in some settings, and multiparty opposition usually represents an advance on one-party rule, but such democratizing features may coexist with extreme authoritarian practices of an oppressive state, especially in circumstances under which the military is not held accountable and justifies its internal and external behavior by relying on national security claims.[2]

The democratization of political behavior in all arenas is an essential and pervasive normative commitment of this report. Without appropriate democratization any transition to geogovernance is certain to remain subject to the manipulations of geopolitics and market forces of the sort characterized by "the triple indictment," that is, hegemonic in structure, exploitative in human effect, and wasteful of resources.

Democratization is a process. It is a matter of degree and context, and its responsiveness to changed societal priorities through the reflexive dynamics of citizens' dialogue is itself a vital element in the democratic process. Democratization will ebb and flow even in the eventuality that geogovernance of the sort advocated here is never fully realized. History never ends, nor does human creativity. Indeed, in a very real sense the end of history would imply the end of democracy, as the democratic vocation is to shape continuously the means and ends of historical reality. As new structures are embodied, new normative horizons will by necessity become a stimulus for new cycles of criticism, innovation, and reform. Democracy, as long as it persists, implies democratization, that is, renewal of the forms of participation and reformulations of the role of government in relation to human well-being.

Democratization is not itself an assurance of decency or moderation, but can be both abusive and abused. The quality of a given democracy depends on the direction and orientation of civic life. This direction and orientation can be vulnerable to manipulation by militarist and market forces, as well as by pressures generated in relation to globalization from above. Traditional populist, and provincial, influences can also be oppressive to those who no longer adhere or never adhered to traditional precepts and practices. An early account of some dangers associated with democracy, which still pertains to conditions in our world, is to be found in the later books of Thucydides' *The Peloponnesian War* in which the popular passions of the citizenry, democratically expressed within the frame of classical democracy, drove Athens to embark on a disastrous war against distant Sicily in spite of the advice of more prudent, aristocratic leaders. This experience led many thoughtful Athenians at the time to distrust democracy more than certain other forms of government. Democratization over time had become debased in Athens, and had become an empty vessel for ultrapatriotic fervor and overseas militarism.

It would be erroneous to draw anthropological lessons from such historic failures of democracy and claim human nature to be flawed, or inevitably aggressive. Rather one may draw constitutional and sociopolitical lessons that acknowledge that concentrations of power are normatively unwieldy, regardless of political orientation, and tend to be highly susceptible to various kinds of decay and manipulation. To take some account of these potential failings of democracy it is necessary to qualify an affirmation of democracy with an insistence on unconditional respect for human rights and for the rule of law, including especially respect for international law in relation to uses of military force. The republican view of democracy requires an elaborate and integral constitutional framework of checks and balances built into the procedures and institutions of governance so as to protect minorities from "tyrannies of the majority" and to protect the majority itself from the likely adverse consequences of its own passions. The discussion of democracy presented here should also be read in light of the approach to sovereignty taken in the prior chapter.

This conception of democracy is anchored in the conventional view that democratization pertains to state/society relations within the world order framework of territorial sovereignty, but it extends this view to address the political quality of market and state-to-state interactions as subject to progressive stages of democratization. Democratization is definitely conditioned in its effective practices by the dynamics of geopolitics, by the robustness of global civil society, by the closely related interplay of globalization from above and globalization from below, and by traditional beliefs and practices embodied in religious and cultural life. Replacing the cult of modernization, as a universalizing ideology spread by merchants and warriors, with a cult of democratization spread by financiers, media moguls, and warriors poses difficult and contradictory' challenges. What is not needed at present is yet another *false universalism*, however rechristened. Thus the specific reality of democracy and democratization is a matter for contextual interpretation by societal forces variously situated and dedicated to the promotion of dignity and decency. The renunciation of violence as means and end seems crucial for the deepening of democracy at this stage of social development. The 1980s were notable for the diversity of nonviolent challenges mounted against oppressive governing structures. Unfortunately, as the very different instances of Iran (1979) and the Philippines (1986) disclose, a commitment to nonviolent struggle is no assurance that the successor governments will be democratic or will respect human rights.

Because democratization has become such a defining feature of the historical moment, its content and application is bound to be sharply contested, especially by a wide and diverse range of the opposed forces already mentioned, invoking democracy for contradictory missions – each their own purposes as understood by their particular outlook. The bias adopted here is strongly in favor of democratization as interpreted by progressive transnational social forces and applied in light of local diversities of conditions and perceptions that are being embodied in global civil society, but these forces must contend with contrary interpretations of democratization, including those associated with geopolitics, with global apartheid, and with several versions of religious and secular fundamentalism. Among the most powerful types of fundamentalism, at present, is an unconditional dedication to market dynamics without regard to human consequences. The misery that is caused leads to astonishing political surprises, such as the democratic recovery of previously discredited Communists in East Europe and the former Soviet Union. In fact, a new role of electoral politics is to resist the imposition of overly harsh "shock therapy" as the means to move from the failure of the planned command economy to a more open market economy.

These latter market-driven interpretations tend to reduce democratization to empty forms of state/society constitutionalism in contexts of enthusiasm by prevailing elites for the unbridled logic of capitalism. In contrast, models of democratization associated with the positive normative outlook of global civil society are dedicated to greater participation, accountability, responsibility, legality, ecological sustainability, human rights (including economic and social rights), progressive leadership, and nonviolent conflict resolution. These are not universal normative imperatives uniformly applicable regardless of local circumstances, but are rather contextually construed by reference to the needs, actual circumstances and cultural outlook of the people, while according particular attention to those who are most vulnerable and deprived.

Democratization is concrete, not abstract. It must begin from where a particular historical process is located in time, space, and consciousness. The arrangement of priorities for traditional democracy expresses a commitment to concreteness in the setting of extremely uneven circumstances that pertain in particular states, particular regions, as well as in particular arenas. Setting a democratization agenda for Kenya is different than setting one for Japan, different again in Spain than in El Salvador, and so on, around the world. What is being asserted is that despite these radical differences in stages of development, relations to the global economy, degrees of political autonomy, sizes of population and territory, historical legacies, resource endowments, and ethnic and religious compositions, the imperatives of traditional democracy are relevant in each and every setting. Such relevance accentuates the importance of the identity of interpreter and the content of interpretation. A key issue for democratization on a state/society scale is how to democratize the process of interpretation, both with regard to participation in reaching a decision and reflection upon its purported application, as well as considerations of authority and its exercise, including effective capacity and appropriate procedures of accountability. Such attentiveness needs to be especially sensitive to groupings that are traditionally excluded, even from consciousness, as used to be the case in most societies with respect to indigenous peoples, gays and lesbians, and various ethnic and religious minorities.

As this chapter highlights, the meaning of democracy must be clarified in light of these contending forces. This is not at all simple, much less self-evident. Two lines of questioning become central:

- *whose* democracy? The locus of authority in class, gender, ethnic terms;
- democracy *for whom*? The distribution of benefits in class, gender, and ethnic terms.

In this regard, the overriding challenge within the sphere of traditional democracy is to move toward equality of participatory and substantive rights on both an individual and group basis. This sense of a normative goal needs also to acknowledge internal claims for varying degrees of autonomy, as in relation to indigenous peoples and regionally concentrated ethnic minorities seeking to uphold a certain cultural ethos. Humane governance within the structure of the states system of world order can thus be assessed by degrees of realization of individual and group rights across the spectrum of economic, social, cultural, civil, and political concerns. This formulation seeks to acknowledge the rise of the politics of identity, but also to refuse a privileged status for civil and political rights in the discourse on democracy.

Democracy after the Cold War

A remarkable feature of the early aftermath of the Cold War has been the surge of support for democratization in many distinct cultural and political circumstances, and in widely disparate geographical settings. Not all is progress, especially given a quite partial view of democracy; as well, there are also setbacks, reversals, and regressive tendencies. But overall the historical moment remains one of dramatic support for an insistence on constitutional democracy as the foundation of political legitimacy at the level of the territorial state. In this regard, countries in the North have contended that sovereignty no longer includes the right to adopt antidemocratic forms of governance in the context of state/society relations. What they mainly mean by this in practice is that the repudiation of market forces is not acceptable. Adherence to human rights is secondary, although not irrelevant. Whether the peoples of the world will be more insulated from oppression by political elites and in a better position to participate in selecting leaders responsive to their values is not yet assured, especially if the emphasis is on jobs and social welfare rather than economic growth and profits. Even neoliberal achievements with respect to constitutionalism are precarious in a number of respects: prospects for democratization are subject to abrupt reversals as in the notable instances of China and Peru; the extent of democratization is often superficial to the point of being cosmetic. The appearance of electoral freedom and human rights is belied by suppression of radical parties and by extralegal military and paramilitary security practices, as in Turkey and Egypt; the social and economic face of democracy is often severely darkened by antidemocratic pressures released by globalization from above, illustrated by indebtedness as managed by the IMF/World Bank and the complex rigors of competitiveness.

There are other problems, too, arising out of the promotion of neoliberal democratization. The United States in the 1980s linked its alleged championship of democratization with the diplomacy of military intervention in a series of North/South encounters: Grenada (1983), Nicaragua (1980s), Panama (1989), Angola and Mozambique (1980s); the Reagan Doctrine, committing the United States to support movements of resistance against allegedly Marxist-Leninist governments, was invoked to support democracy, but was actually used for strategic purposes in the latter stages of the Cold War to legitimize covert and overt forms of large-scale military intervention. Implementing the Reagan Doctrine with weapons and money often involved giving support to extreme antidemocratic political forces. In Nicaragua such a pattern was carried to absurd lengths of ideological deception when Reagan described the Samoçista Contras as "freedom fighters'" comparable to those who struggled for US independence against British colonialism. In Angola and Mozambique dubious political factions, hardly distinguishable from criminal elements, were supported in the name of democracy for the purpose of destabilizing Marxist political regimes.[3]

There are three overlapping concerns here:

1 Democracy has in the last decade or so provided a new line of justification for military intervention as an instrument of geopolitics in post–Cold War North/South relations that is always selectively (that is, not uniformly) and often arbitrarily targeted (directed at states that are relatively more democratic – as measured by observance of human rights and standards of legality – than their immediate neighbors); Cuba is targeted on behalf of the extremely antidemocratic Castro exiles, but Guatemala and Honduras are not challenged at all despite their antidemocratic regimes.

2 This geopolitical appropriation of "democracy" has to some extent confused political discourse, rendering the positive content of democracy unduly suspect in many countries, and giving repressive governments in the South a pretext for claiming that sovereign rights are at stake whenever the North promotes human rights and democracy. The result is to blur or even render invisible the boundary between support for democracy as a valued end and proactive geopolitics as a disvalued means.

3 This espousal of support for democratization of the political side of state/society relations is sometimes deliberately and sometimes innocently extended to insist that democratization necessarily implies the adoption of market economics and a capitalist ethos on such matters as private property, profits, and consumerism, thereby polemically using

the embrace of democracy to deprive poor countries of economic self-determination. This conflating of democracy and capitalism has two main dimensions. It reflects the ideological triumph of the West and the end of the Cold War, and it is part of the end-game being played with socialism. In addition, the inevitability of the subordination of public policy on economic and social issues is a structural consequence of the globalization of capital. As argued earlier, even governments in affluent welfare states seem unable to sustain social gains, given the priority attached to achieving "competitiveness" in the global marketplace. In this regard, emergent forms of capital-driven geogovernance deform democratization and problematize the relationship between democracy and humane governance.

It is crucial, then, to distinguish between the good and the bad news about the recent seemingly spectacular surge of support for democratization. The good news, expressed as simply as possible, is the widespread acknowledgment of the claims of human rights as a restraint on the discretion of political elites to wield power in state/society relations and the complementary acceptance of the rights and responsibilities of the citizenry to participate in the selection of leaders by way of free, periodic elections on the basis of interparty rivalry and within a protective constitutional framework and the rule of law. The bad news is the entanglement of the rhetoric of democratization with militarist modes of geopolitics and with the ideological insistence that capitalism with minimum regulation is an indispensable ingredient of real democracy. The challenge directed at the social forces associated with the movement to strengthen global civil society is to draw this distinction between good and bad news equally sharply in practice with respect to the specific circumstances under which interpretation takes on historical meaning in the lives of people. Part of drawing this distinction in a manner useful to people's lives and democratic choices is to break down polarizing ways of presenting choices.

For instance, is it not so much a matter of choosing or rejecting the market or the existence of a private economic sector as it is of relating the operations of the market and private enterprise to other social concerns, including the abolition of poverty and the maintenance of environmental quality. It is a matter of discerning the extent to which those most vulnerable are made to bear adjustment costs by way of unemployment, reduced social protection, falling wages and standard of living. The record of some capitalist societies on social issues is far better than others. There is no built-in need to tolerate high rates of unemployment or low wages in a capitalist society, although that need may be perceived to exist if corruption and incompetence makes the productive process relatively noncompetitive, or if wages are kept artificially repressed elsewhere. In these regards it might be instructive to compare Japan, Germany, and the United States, three exemplary capitalist countries, in relation to unemployment and poverty rates, health insurance, pensions, and disparities between salaries of top executives and line employees. This analysis suggests two distinct observations: first, some capitalist countries handle the equity challenge better than others; secondly, the pressures from globalization to gain global market shares exerts a leveling-down effect on welfare commitments.

There are more subtle problematic sides to an uncritical and unconditional affirmation of democracy. Democratization under current conditions often incorporates and intensifies cultural distortions, and can even encourage extremely regressive policies. These concerns relate to the cultural underpinnings of governance, and orient the approach of leaders to problem-solving and conflict resolution:

1 A militarist culture will often tend to use *democratic* procedures to validate reliance on organized violence to address social and political problems. As a consequence, leaders in constitutional democracies may find their popularity at its peak when they resort to war and score battlefield victories, or when they support harsh police and punitive policies to intimidate the most victimized segments of the citizenry. Margaret Thatcher enjoyed unprecedented popularity after the Falklands War, George Bush after the Gulf War. Public opinion in the United States now strongly favors reliance on capital punishment and extended prison terms to address serious crime, and generally favors high-tech military intervention to address Third World "terrorism."

2 A fundamentalist cultural mood will tend to validate *democratically* the removal of rights and the constriction of any future empowerment of oppositional political tendencies by invoking criteria of antimodernism, antisecularism, and anti-Westernism. The electoral success of Islamic fundamentalist movements in North Africa, especially Algeria, has revealed the contemporary character of the problem. Earlier, the overwhelming popular support given to Ayatollah Khomeini's leadership in Iran, despite the brutal suppression of oppositional politics and of women, exemplifies the point. Such concerns should not be restricted to Islam – every world religion has a fundamentalist streak that is likely to operate repressively if given political ascendancy. Catholicism in Eastern Europe has exerted "democratic" and regressive pressures on reproductive rights of women in a way that did not exist during the era of antidemocratic Communist rule; Hindu populism in India has recently exhibited intolerance toward Muslim communities, and sought

to embody this intolerance in legislation that reflects the popular will. Nor are these concerns merely a matter of destroying democracy through democracy within the territorial state. Iran and Sudan have promoted overseas terrorism directed against foreign targets. Israel's projections of military power beyond its borders, resting on claims of nonaccountable absolutism, during the period of Yitzhak Shamir's leadership resulted in direct attacks on civilians in other countries, especially in Lebanon during and after the 1982 invasion.

3 A serious disguised danger of democratization is associated with the mobilizing potency of the consumerist ethos at a time of ecological fragility, inducing political leaders to repudiate environmental regulation, especially those environmental challenges with long time horizons, serious revenue consequences, and real lifestyle adjustments. The effects of such democratic refusals to be ecologically responsible citizens are both to risk environmental and health disasters, and to hasten, and even support, the eventual displacement of democratic constitutionalism by some variant of eco-authoritarianism. If environmental decay reaches crisis proportions, ecofascism in some form is likely, especially if economic and governmental failure is widely perceived by the citizenry. Complementary concerns arise to the degree that democratic forces constrict their sense of community by territorial, ethnic, racial, gender, and class boundaries, reinforcing and extending existing structures of global apartheid.

Such problematic impacts of democratization need to be appreciated and considered carefully in relation to context. The policy implication is basically twofold. First of all, the normative effects of democratization of governmental procedures should not be taken for granted, but must be evaluated in relation to such other goals of humane governance as the minimization of collective violence and the implementation of human rights as validated by international law. Secondly, to the extent that democratization infringes upon basic normative objectives by way of militarism and consumerism, there is present a need for supervening constraints on political behavior of governments by way of international law. Such constraints require making international law effective *within* states, giving every citizen the right to a lawful foreign policy as a part of humane governance at the state level. Such expanded applications of international law need to be supplemented by cultural pedagogy and socialization practices that are oriented around the spread of an ethos of nonviolence, ecological sustainability, and human rights, that is, in effect an offset to consumerism and militarism, a reorienting of citizenship toward the priorities of global civil society.

At the same time, there are no conceptual panaceas. International law may or may not contribute to the attainment of positive forms of geogovernance, and it is likely to vary in its normative impact from context to context. Hence the need for interpretation on the basis of evaluation is a constant feature of the sort of democratic life that is here favored. There are no formulas or abstract guidelines. Globalization from below depends heavily on maintaining a critical dialogue, including a critical posture directed at identifying and challenging deformed cultural dispositions and practices that manifest themselves through militarist or environmentally irresponsible positions, and can flourish in democratic frameworks that endow leaders with a genuine popular mandate. A further danger is that "the people" may embody violent or racist or sexist dispositions. In such settings the government may interpose restraining limits on public opinion, serving as a vehicle of moderation in relation to regressive populism.

Extending the Framework of Democratization

David Held's diverse writings on democratic theory have emphasized, with compelling analysis, the embeddedness of contemporary politics in the global village. In Held's words, "What is new about the modern global system is the spread of globalization in and through new dimensions of activity – technological, organizational, administrative and legal, among others – and the chronic intensification of patterns of interconnectedness mediated by such phenomena as the modern communications industry and new information technology."[4] Globalization expands the domain of democratization correspondingly. It also weakens the argument for assessing degrees of democratic achievement in the role of the state as obstacle or vehicle.

During transition to geogovernance the loss of control by the state over the political process is a notable feature. As a result, prospects for humane governance depend on strengthening the impact of democratic procedures and human rights on arenas of decision that are not regulated by the state and yet affect the quality of human existence. Such an analysis stresses the importance of democratizing control over global market arenas and over intergovernmental arenas (including the UN family of institutions).

Expressing this goal of extending the scope of democratization beyond state/society relations (within territorial units) does not tell us much about *substance*. Although in general terms, participation, accountability, lawmaking, and agenda-setting by the peoples of the world, through their representatives, orients this inquiry, it doesn't carry us very far. It doesn't tell us whether and in what circumstances governments are representative of peoples, thereby satisfying democratic requirements, and when they are not. Nor are we informed about what modalities of regulation might be effective in regulating global market forces without wrecking the productive capacities of the world economy.

It is the bias and conviction of this report that the necessary enlargements of democratization will occur, if at all, only through pressure and struggle. Economic and political elites will not protect the general human interest on the basis of their own values or even through a commitment to enlightened self-interest. And there is little ground for confidence that at this stage of planetary crowding and ecological strain the pursuit of profit maximization or accelerated growth will safeguard the human interest. Only a transnational social movement animated by a vision of humane governance can offer any hope of extending the domain of democracy. To encourage such a mobilization of populist energies it is necessary to depict the problem in its various dimensions.

All standard discussions of democracy proceed as if state/society relations were the only important context of assessment. This sustains the historically influential, yet now anachronistic, fiction that in political life there is an inside (potential political community guided by law and morality) and an outside (anarchistic relations; the domain of power and realism).[5] Of course, state/society relations remain a crucial dimension of democratization, and in many instances continue to be *the* crucial arena. And in almost all instances state/society relations continue to require democratizing adjustments in complex and variable circumstances. Even in the most advanced constitutional democracies there is a long agenda of deficiencies to be overcome, including the implementation of economic, social, and cultural rights, the right of self-determination for indigenous peoples, and respect for diverse sexual identity. That is, even without taking account of globalization, the work of democratization is inherently incomplete, since technology and values change.

This concern with democratization as it relates to geopolitics and geogovernance leads to an emphasis on additional dimensions: first of all, democratization as meaningfully extended to transnational market forces, which centers upon regulatory effectiveness, corporate and fiscal accountability, protection for whistle-blowing, access and participation by employees and other interested categories of persons; secondly, democratization as extended to intergovernmental arenas, including the United Nations, international financial institutions, GATT, regional organizations; thirdly, democratization as extended to the operations of social forces that are acting as part of global civil society, which implies that the evolution of democratization produces transnational empowerment.

The difficulty of discussing adequately the various dimensions of democracy on the path from geopolitics to geogovernance in contextual detail leads to a reliance in this section on a schematic mode of presentation. A relatively oppressive state is depicted in figure 4.1, with the relative thickness of the arrows showing degrees of power. In this figure societal powers of resistance are unable to cope with the state.

Figure 4.1

In figure 4.2 there is a more democratic relationship. The arrows pointed rightwards display the degree of progress toward democratization through time of the institutional structures of the state and the social structures of society, while the arrows pointing leftwards depict a loss of democracy. The linearity of the portrayal is artificial, as the degree of democratization is likely to ebb and flow over time, reflecting

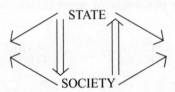

Figure 4.2

a variety of conditioning variables and a relationship to varying sites and substantive settings. Note that in figure 4.2 both state and society arenas of intraconnection are susceptible to democratization or de-democratization. More concretely, the elements of governance comprised by bureaucratic structures may become more or less democratic, as appraised by such criteria as the following: the impartial and efficient application of the rule of law; the integrity and quality of the civil

service; the independence of the judiciary and the reliance upon professional qualifications in making judicial appointments; rights of
appeal; constitutional protections of the civil liberties of those engaged
in government especially whistle-blowers; the accountability of leaders
while in positions of authority, and later. On the societal side, other
sorts of criteria are relevant to the main arenas of family, workplace,
school, social and recreational facilities: available legal remedies for the
weak and vulnerable; civil liberties; prohibitions on police violence;
participation in interpretative procedures and decisions; election of
leaders by way of fair procedures; absence of discrimination on the basis
of race, class, gender, age, ethnic background, religion, height, weight,
physical and mental capacity. Democratizing processes in social space
need to be worked out under specific conditions, involving the resolution
of creative tensions between the pull toward absolute equality in context
and the drive to achieve results as defined by the participants. That is, a
balance is sought between a democratic politics that relies on *will* and
desire and one that relies on *rights* and *legal obligations*.

To extend inquiry beyond isolated state/society constructs, each
artificially conceived in relation to a range of nonterritorial influences,
leads to the explicit acknowledgment of geopolitical and market forces.
This pattern is typical for states in the South, as in figure 4.3, subject
both to interventionary diplomacy and to severe constraints arising
from regionalized and globalized market forces. A strong state in the
North is more likely to maintain balanced relations with global market
forces and be able to maintain a high degree of autonomy in relation
to geopolitical forces as depicted in figure 4.4. The arrows to the right
and left suggest the possibility of more or less democratization over

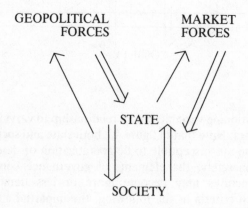

GEOPOLITICAL   MARKET
FORCES   FORCES

STATE

SOCIETY

Figure 4.3

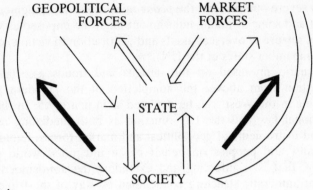

Figure 4.4

time in a manner similiar to figure 4.2. How, it might be asked, can geopolitical forces be democratized? One response would be by bringing international law to bear effectively and impartially on the foreign policies of the main geopolitical actors and their instrumentalities. How can this be done? One approach in constitutional democracies is to make citizens more inclined to demand respect for international law as a basis for paying taxes and supporting government. Another is to open up courts to challenges by officials or citizens based on allegations that a given foreign policy violates international law in certain specified respects.

The US success in manipulating the UN Security Council and constraining the diplomatic discretion of the Secretary General suggests the urgency of strengthening constitutionalism at the global level and increasing fidelity to the UN Charter and to international law in the operations of the Organization. A further means of democratizing geopolitical forces would be to impose procedures of accountability of the sort that would follow from the serious implementation of the Nuremberg Principles. Progress on this front would lead to a widely endorsed agreement among states on a code of offenses and the creation of a global commission and tribunal. There are various proposals along these lines, but leading governments have remained unresponsive. The war crimes tribunal set up by the United Nations to address war crimes allegations from Bosnia is a qualified step along this path, and one which, although belated in formation and ambivalent in implementation, could contribute by issuing a reliable report on the charges arising from such crimes as "ethnic cleansing," systematic rape, starvation, bombing of civilians. It is unfortunate that the tribunal will not allow for trials *in absentia*. Otherwise, even if the convicted perpetrators were not physically before the tribunal, and thus not subject to imprisonment or other severe punishment, the *pedagogical* value of a judgment would be great and some symbolic punishment might be imposed as well (for instance, seizure of overseas assets and distribution to victims; denial of access to member states of the UN).[6]

A scenario premised on the designs and trends associated with globalization from above, the completion of the "modern project" originating in the West, can be depicted as in figure 4.5. In this figure international law and the UN function as both mediating restraints upon and instruments of geopolitical and market forces, impinging on most states and peoples on behalf of an integrated world political economy, that is, reinforcing and extending the antidemocratic and emergent autocratic structure condemned by way of the triple indictment in chapter 2. In effect, globalization from above involves an exceedingly unhappy marriage of geopolitics and geogovernance, with the peoples of the world entrapped within states that are increasingly disempowered as autonomous actors. As a result, even if state/society relations are democratized, the state cannot exert effective control over global arenas. At present, most states in the South are in this position with respect to world order. In the North states are ambivalently situated, seeking to mediate between territorial pressures from within and global market pressures from without. Globalization has not yet received a clear electoral assent, nor has citizen opposition achieved real success or fashioned a viable alternative. There is a stalemate, as evidenced by the bitter fights over Maastricht and NAFTA, yet early outcomes favor globalizing interests, reflecting the bias of the state and mainstream media. Future developments will be shaped by the early results of these globalizing steps, and how these results are interpreted

Figure 4.5

by the media, by political and market leadership, and by peoples. A crisis for either globalization or state/society democratization, or some combination, may well be in the offing before the 1990s have concluded.

Figure 4.6 sets forth a more optimistic future in which geopolitics is marginalized in the course of establishing geogovernance through the agency of transnationalizing democratic forces operating within the forms provided by an emergent global civil society. This path to geogovernance leads toward humane governance (that is, the effective realization of human rights, including economic and social rights, and the extension of participatory mechanisms and accountability procedures to the arenas of decision in which geopolitical and global market forces are operative).

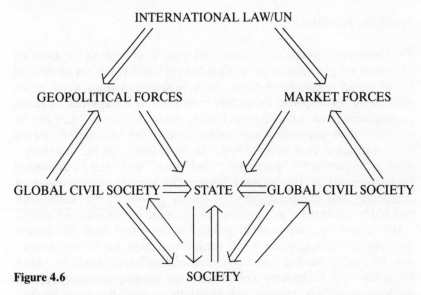

Figure 4.6

In the globalization-from-below scenario, democratization is the key to the emergence of geogovernance, which is achieved at the structural expense of geopolitics. The development and application of international law and the activities of the various organs of the United Nations are significantly democratized, which means that the agencies of global civil society balance states and market forces in the shaping of policy. The mission of normative restructuring of the political economy would receive a high priority, with the goal being a reversal of the patterns described in chapter 2 as the triple indictment. Accordingly, class, gender, and racial disparities in material circumstances would be reduced, wasteful consumption would be challenged, and the commitment of the Universal Declaration of Human Rights to establish a basic needs world would be seriously implemented. Such normative restructuring would also be sensitive to the relevance of ecological constraints. Sustainability is treated as a crucial responsibility of leadership and policy formation in all global institutional settings. That is, it is assumed that the democratic imperative is survival oriented – although the destructive energies of some expressions of fundamentalism and the consumerist inclinations of some varieties of postmodernism make us realize that such a survival orientation is part of the struggle for democratic self-identity, and cannot be merely taken for granted as a byproduct of democratization.[7]

Specifying Priorities

The contextual, localizing approach adopted in discerning the meaning of democracy provides an orientation toward inquiry, but not an assured set of policy recommendations. Such recommendations need to be worked out in response to specific conditions as interpreted by those participating in the immediate political process. Of course, they can be no more than approximations, intimations of an orientation toward democratization that stresses both the *particularity* of the situation – what is "immediate," "particular," and "local" will itself be contested by participants in the ongoing process to identify the *thereness* of democracy and democratization – and its *generality*, the wider institutional frameworks of geogovernance, centered on the United Nations.

But informing, inspirational principles associated with this understanding of democracy can be set forth which allow for the ambiguities that inevitably burden communicative and reflexive dynamics. Such principles can be broadly connected with existing circumstances of particular countries, regions, and civilizations, providing some illustrative orientations toward action, or at least suggesting opening positions in a political dialogue about what do do. The democratizing commitment is very much dependent on the dynamics of communications and conversation, especially in the face of diversity and difference. Particularly those situated in hegemonic roles, whether by occupation, class, gender, race, or religious identity, will need to listen and respond carefully to voices of opposition and resistance. Democratization implies a receptivity to difference, while constraining its manifestations within the confines of human rights and international law. But unless these confines are themselves democratized, hegemonic rule will persist. Herein lies the paradox of democratization: it cannot be realized unless it overcomes hegemonic distortion, yet the nonviolent means to control hegemony are themselves controlled hegemonically. One way out is violent revolution and armed struggle waged by those currently oppressed. Such a revolutionary perspective tends to reproduce, and often intensify, hegemony. Violence is at the core of hegemonic abuse, and needs to be repudiated as an instrument of resistance by adherents of humane governance.

Such a position is not an unconditional affirmation of nonviolence. There may be extreme circumstances of hegemonic abuse in which defensive or transformative violence is relied on to some degree without altogether tainting the undertaking. For instance, in South Africa the African National Congress relied on violence to some extent in its struggle against apartheid, as did the Palestinian makers of the *intifada*, but in both instances the provocations were great and the overwhelming weight of resistance was symbolic, moral, and nonviolent.

Against this background it is possible to consider some prominent settings of interaction between society, state, and global regimes. Part of the search here is for policies that identify the specific content of democratization in each context, and thereby link democratization to the overall quest for humane governance.

(1) Somalia in 1991 was the scene of humanitarian intervention (under joint UN/US auspices) in response to persistent clan warfare, widespread famine, and food shortages endangering the lives of 1.5 million or more civilians. In a setting of chaos and emergency, internal democratization involves the restoration of minimum order, the disarming of rival factions, and the provision of material necessities of life to the people. Democracy meant, first of all, taking seriously the survival needs of the civilian population. The Somalia operation was the most important test of the UN's capacity to act effectively since the Gulf War, but it raised again the dependence of the UN on its strongest member. It situated humanitarian intervention in an ambiguous, and possibly untenable, political zone, caught between the pressures of persisting geopolitics on one side, emergent geogovernance on the other side, and an unreliable commitment to implement governance missions not perceived as strategic imperatives by leaders and publics in leading geopolitical actors (especially the United States).

Somalia in 1993 manifested the fragility of "humanitarian" undertakings in two major respects. First, once the relief mission was extended to disarming the factions, the operation became "interventionary" in a political sense, one of restructuring government without the consent of indigenous political forces. Secondly, resistance produced casualties in the peacekeeping forces that generated domestic opposition to the commitment of young citizens, leading to strong pressures to withdraw and, in the interim, to avoid further casualties to the peacekeepers. Without strategic interests (for instance, oil; preventing a pariah state from acquiring nuclear weapons; containing a geopolitical threat to the global status quo), the political will to serve the UN is very weak, and easily broken.

(2) In Cambodia in 1993, by agreement of the contending factions within the country, the UN assumed the role of restoring indigenous governance and of promoting transition to a liberal constitutional order. The existence of indigenous consent diminished interventionary dangers, although the ambivalence of the Khmer Rouge toward the process meant that the undertaking was vulnerable to disruption. Elections held in 1993 seemed to express strong grassroots support throughout the country for the UN approach, including a willingness to defy Khmer Rouge threats and boycott. Here the UN facilitates, temporarily at least, an advance in democratization and, thereby, of humane governance, but whether the process will sufficiently withstand disruptive efforts in the years ahead remains uncertain.

(3) Burma in 1994 was under the heel of an oppressive military junta operating under the name State Law and Order Restoration Campaign (known by the acronym SLORC), and the outstanding popular leader and winner of the 1991 Nobel Peace Prize, Daw Aung San Suu Kyi, was confined in isolation under house arrest, despite some gestures of accommodation, including discussions between the military government and Ms Suu Kyi. Torture is reported to be a routine prison practice in relation to those suspected of pro-democracy activity. In these circumstances, the highest democratizing priority is the restoration of political freedom to Ms Suu Kyi, followed by the release of all political prisoners and arrangements for transition to civilian government, with important provision for federalist autonomy and group rights on behalf of Burma's minorities (135 ethnically distinct peoples live within the country's boundaries, and the most important of these minorities resist by force of arms efforts to subject them to unitary rule administered from Rangoon).

There is no argument being currently mounted for intervention by military means. Is Burma a case for sanctions directed against the current oppressive leadership? Should Burma as a state be stigmatized as South Africa was in the 1980s? Why Burma, and not a dozen other states?

(4) In South Africa in 1993, after the extraordinary strides made in the direction of democratization, the process continued to move haltingly forward, but had yet to fully challenge racist structures of economic oppression and white privileges. Creating priorities centered on the transition from apartheid to a multiracial constitutionalism has been a matter of urgency. It is particularly urgent to avoid regression and possible civil war. For the democratizing momentum in South Africa to be sustained it would seem essential, symbolically and substantively, for the main reins of political leadership to pass effectively to the African National Congress, and to bring the old internal security structures of the South African government and the rightist backlash under the effective constitutional discipline of the reconstituted state. As of early 1995, this appears to be happening.

(5) Zaire and Kenya in 1994 have both been in the grips of dictatorial and corrupt rules associated with one-party systems and dominated by single brutal rulers. It would seem essential for democratizing forces in such countries to achieve the protection of elemental human rights in the political domain and to place the governing process on firmer constitutional grounds through multiparty political competition and reliable guarantees of fair elections covering all phases, from the nomination of candidates, to campaigning, to the elections and the installation of the elected representatives in public office. Such a process presupposes the removal from the political scene of the dominating individual currently associated with deforming the state and state/society relations, and quite possibly the dismantling of the state security apparatus.

(6) Chile in 1993 was proceeding with civilianization of the governing process and reestablishing the practices of constitutionalism, as impressively illustrated by new presidential elections resulting in a strong democratizing mandate. It would seem essential for these encouraging developments in the transition from oppressive military dictatorship to go forward, and especially to build a political economy that combines growth with expanding employment opportunity, achieving dedication and results with respect to an antipoverty agenda. Given the levels of mass social distress, without progress over time on the welfare front popular disillusionment is likely to challenge a mode of democratization if it remains confined to periodic elections and submission to market logic.

(7) Germany in 1993, in spite of its great economic strength, has been challenged by the absorption of the former East Germany into an

integrated state, by a rising inflow of refugees, and by the refusal to accord citizenship to Turkish and other long-term alien residents; these forces have generated a militant ultra-rightist movement with neo-Nazi characteristics. Democratizing priorities would include special protection for those in East Germany who have been displaced in the course of this abrupt historic mutation and an approach to the bestowal of asylum and refugee status that is more sensitive to the problems presented on both sides of the debate, as well as more acknowledgment of the democratizing consensus that promises to protect foreigners, hold out prospects for citizenship, and uphold an ethos of tolerance.

(8) India in 1992 was adrift in relation to economic, demographic, religious, and regional pressures. Democratizing priorities would definitely include a new creativity and flexibility from the governmental center with respect to traditional troubled areas such as Punjab, Kashmir, Jannmu, and Assam, as well as an emphasis on ways to move toward greater demographic stability. The alleviation of the most severe forms of caste prejudice and economic deprivation is necessary. Above all, the control of religious fundamentalism and intolerance is crucial, but the most recent developments seem encouraging; it is true that the Ayodhya temple riots of December 1992 produced more than a thousand deaths and widespread Hindu/Muslim sectarian violence throughout the country, but this explosive period has been followed by the repudiation of the Hindu nationalist party in the 1993 and 1994 state elections, which discloses a dramatic ebbing of popular support for religious extremism in India, and more reassuring prospects for mutual tolerance and secularism.

(9) The United States in 1991 was a country challenged at home by increasing homelessness, crime, minority unemployment, urban decay and racial tension, and by bitter rifts concerning reproductive rights and the nature of family life, and challenged abroad by a continuing perception that the protection of its interests depended on nuclearism and militarism. Its democratizing priorities obviously include an emphasis on the alleviation of the problems of unemployment and poverty by the extension of welfare, but also by educational training designed to increase qualifications of those currently unemployable for more skilled jobs and by a humane approach to competitiveness in relation to the world economy. A shifting of resources from defense to urban renewal and infrastructure would help meet both the domestic and foreign policy challenges confronting democratizing perspectives. Also, a series of bureaucratic reforms are needed to enhance the quality of citizens'

participation and to reduce authoritarian tendencies within the national security establishment. Democratizing reforms could include the drastic reduction of official secrecy, the abolition of covert operations capabilities and the related overhaul or elimination of the Central Intelligence Agency. Perhaps the most difficult democratizing challenge in the short run is to reconcile more satisfactorily the welfare needs of the poor and the competitiveness priorities of global market forces.

These sketches illustrate various configurations in the overall global struggle for democratization in state/society relations. It should be noticed that in some instances it is a matter of curbing an abusive state that denies rights to its citizens, whereas in other instances it is a matter of empowering the state to act more effectively to constrain oppressive societal forces. With respect to democratization and humane governance the state should be perceived as helpful or harmful depending on context, and sometimes, on issue. It may be that some market democracies are protective of civil and political rights, but abusive of economic, social, and cultural rights. The state, as ever, is ambiguous in normative terms, being neither a consistent vehicle for or obstacle to democratization.

Yet, as argued throughout the chapter, state/society relationships, while remaining at the core of political life for the peoples of the world and most easily discussed, no longer suffice as a sufficient focus for those seeking to embody the values and practices of democratization.[8] The realities of globalization require that democratization efforts be extended to geopolitical and market arenas, as well as "internalized" at all levels of political organization. These extensions are more problematic to depict in situational terms than is the familiar political terrain of state/society relations, however confusing, complex, and contingent the variations of setting that have just been considered in illustrative fashion. With regard to geopolitical and market arenas it is difficult to be more than heuristic at this stage, pointing to the need and to possible directions of democratizing efforts, but being hazy about means and effects, that is, about the politics of democratization in such non-statal settings.

By geopolitical arenas are meant the treaty and institutional frameworks established by agreement among states, especially those of regional and global scope in the substantive areas of security and political economy. One indicator of deepening globalization is the extent to which prominent treaty texts seem to be relied upon to establish the framework for normal international relations (GATT, Maastricht, NAFTA), especially to stabilize the world economy on behalf of market forces. Another indicator is the extent to which nonstate institutional actors dominate conflict-related and development settings (UN, European Community, IMF, G-7). In each arena the challenge of democratization is present, but difficult to articulate, especially in relation to specific policy implications. On one level the democratic imperative in these arenas is initially to minimize the hegemonic manipulations associated with geopolitical patterns of dominance, suggesting the relevance of greater participation, more egalitarian voting rules and of more welfare-sensitive financial arrangements.

Democratizing is also essential in relation to market forces. Here a first step is to obtain relevant information, a task immensely complicated because of the varying regulatory issues that arise in different phases of market operations (ranging from trade in food and minerals to the transfer of intellectual property, financial intangibles, and such services as insurance and accountancy), as well as the difficulties of penetrating various forms of industrial and financial secrecy. Detailed studies are needed in relation to each commercial activity from the perspectives of human rights, democracy, and such social objectives as the elimination of poverty, economic waste, and environmental deterioration. Democratizing in this crucial domain also requires the scrutiny of growth orientations and media-promoted consumerism that is conditioning the peoples of the world to pursue nonsustainable development that will cause massive health problems, great risks of ecological collapse, various types of irreversible harm, and a materialist calculus of values that cannot possibly be satisfied, and if it were, would not lead to individual or collective fulfillment.

Connected, yet distinct, are efforts to democratize the UN family of institutions. Some of these efforts will be discussed in connection with global security in chapter 5. One recent promising initiative is the creation by citizens of a UN Monitor, a voluntary association assuming the task of identifying those acts and activities of the UN that are objectionable from the present and medium-term perspectives of humane governance. This initiative seeks to promote greater *transparency* in UN operations, which is one important dimension of democratization. By publishing credible reports, the hope is also to mobilize public opinion, exert influence on UN decision-making processes, and encourage the adoption of policies and programs with a demilitarizing impact and more responsive to the claims of the poor and the weak.

A Concluding Note

The democratizing challenge is both bewilderingly complex and fundamental. Meeting this challenge will determine whether the tendencies toward globalization from above can be sufficiently neutralized or redirected to spare the peoples of the world the full range of consequences flowing from what was called geopolitics in chapter 1 and from the triple indictment in chapter 2. Geogoverance that emerges without the shaping guidance of democratization in all major arenas is both dangerous to human survival prospects and oppressive in relation to the quality of life. One of the dangers of continued environmental deterioration is to engender new cycles of exploitative geopolitics (for example, the dumping of toxic materials in the South) and the menace of authoritarian forms of geogovernance. The possibility of ecofascism cannot be dismissed as a mere fantasy under these conditions. As with the chapter on sovereignty that preceded, the discussion of security that follows builds upon the normative commitment to a democratizing transition to humane governance. In this central respect, democratization as specified in this chapter is both a means to humane governance and a feature of its embodiment. Transnational initiatives in reaction to oppressive state/society and globalizing impacts have an opportunity and obligation to model humane governance in their own mindset and activities, thereby anticipating a more benevolent future for humanity as a whole. The nonviolent movements of democratization that erupted during the late 1970s and 1980s were indicative of this set of possibilities, but also of the difficulties. In general, the switch to nonviolent tactics and the negotiation of the end of protracted internal wars was an exceedingly encouraging trend, but as the Iranian revolution and the Russian experience underscores, nonviolent struggle provides no assurance that humane governance at the state level will be established. In fact, what may emerge can lead to the blatant repudiation of minimal constitutional and liberal democratic forms, and seem in retrospect to be more repressive than the original target of a democratizing movement. Such a sequence has been the story of the struggle against the Shah's Iran, and its sequel in the form of Iran's Islamic republic.

5

Security for Humane Governance

The emergence of geogovernance as trend and project poses managerial and prescriptive challenges. The mainstream market/state elites are concerned with managing the transition, adapting geopolitical methods and structures to a more integrated, efficient world. This vector of policy leads to various types of adaptation with respect to the role and character of sovereignty and to the practice of democracy. Sovereignty is deterritorialized, and subordinated to the phenomenon of globalization. Democracy is linked more tightly to the wider logic of the market, and the elites at the level of states have the task of convincing their citizens that globalization is *territorially* beneficial.

The idea of security is similarly strained by a new set of priorities. The ideological challenge of Communism seems permanently defeated, and no new ideological threat looms on the horizon. Geopolitics is being subordinated to, or else recast to satisfy, the globalizing requirements of the world economy. Challenges from the South need to be contained, or if necessary, destroyed. Iraq as regional aggressor threatening the global price structure for oil posed one kind of danger. North Korea or Pakistan, as potential nuclear weapons states, pose another type of threat.

The security challenge, as geopolitically specified, is partly political, partly logistical. The political dimension has to do with mobilizing the will to use force either against an ideological adversary, a clear strategic threat, or with a strong UN mandate. Democratic societies of leading states can mount antiwar opposition, and this concerns leaders. The impulse, then, is to base security policy on high-tech, quick-response tactics and weaponry, inflicting devastating damage at a distance without risk of losses or prolonged involvement. In effect, the geopolitical effort now centers on substituting logistics for will, and in effect severing democratic modes of constraint and accountability from decisions to use force. The United States as geopolitical leader and a main collaborator with market forces has struggled with this connection between democracy and security for several decades.[1]

The orientation associated with humane governance is at sharp variance with that adopted on the basis of a geopolitical heritage. It is ambivalent about the transition to geogovernance, regarding it as both an opportunity and posing a new range of dangers to human well-being. The opportunity is linked to an analysis of war as a social institution rooted in the dynamics of the state system and the related overall acceptance of unlimited discretion to use force at the level of the sovereign state. International law has attempted to challenge such discretion, but rather ineffectually, especially in relation to leading geopolitical actors. There is no assurance that the role of war will be diminished during the transition. This prospect will depend on which social forces define and control the mechanisms of security at a global level.

The dangers associated with the transition to geogovernance are elusive and speculative. One clear danger relates to the disabling of states as promoters of social and economic rights and as allocators of resources for the relief of mass poverty. Capital-driven geogovernance is challenging welfare-oriented public policy both by way of "competitiveness" considerations, pressures being accentuated by establishing regional and global trading regimes, and through structural adjustment programs, whether administered by the IMF or self-administered beneath the rubric of deficit reduction and fiscal balance. The state becomes drawn into a world economy that is dominated by capitalist imperatives as specified transnationally. There is no socialist alternative that induces a willingness by capitalism to be forthcoming on social issues. As a result, as is already evident, the transition to geogovernance gives rise to a cruel phase of capitalist and financial expansion that is regressive in its impacts on many of the world's people, especially those who are vulnerable.

It is difficult to assess whether the transition to geogovernance under geopolitical auspices is likely to impair efforts to safeguard the environment. Globalization brings greater awareness and administrative capacity, but also relocates authority and responsibility in ways that diminish the role of the state without ensuring substitutes. The economistic focus on growth makes investment in longer range environmental protection seem dysfunctional.

How, then, to enhance security, as perceived by adherents of humane governance during this transition to geogovernance? A first step is to clarify the mainstream tendency in terms of perspective and behavior. A second step is to locate the crisis of transition that is likely to pit populist resistance to globalization against elite support for globalization. These tensions have surfaced in debates on NAFTA and Maastricht during the early 1990s. If globalization is perceived to be responsible for the deterioration of life circumstances, it is likely to polarize politics on all levels, generating a reactionary push for "effective" geogovernance (at the expense of democratic participation) and a progressive insistence on the revival of compassionate capitalism and on more attention to environmental protection. Both political tendencies will be carried toward completion in arenas external to the state, although the struggle to control the outlook of key states will be a vital battleground: at issue will be the extent to which policies will be shaped by global forces and the extent to which they will be shaped by adherents of humane governance.

The geopolitical emphasis will lead "security" to regard "humane governance" as "utopian" or as a dangerous, irresponsible radicalism that imperils geogovernance. The humane governance emphasis will view the attainment of security as dependent on the weakening of the hold of geopolitical imagery and war on the political imagination. It is this encounter that underlies the proposals and prescriptions in this chapter. Instead of rolling back welfare, adherents of humane governance seek to roll back war and violence, and rearrange the allocation of resources by governments. Because the domains of influence are different, humane governance can be modeled at the level of the family by a deeper acceptance of gender equality and by the renunciation of such macho patriarchal practices as rape, child abuse, and violence. Such an approach to security would not immediately and in all respects challenge a top-down approach, but the criteria of success are different, as is the place accorded to violence.

Reorienting Security

Security remains the linchpin of realist thinking, and continues to dominate the practice and theory of geopolitics. So conceived, security is closely linked with political violence as challenging to stability and as providing the coercive foundation of "world order," whether "new" or "old." The ideal of geopolitical security is control from above, achieved to the extent possible by ideological consensus and conformity, supplemented by intimidation and nonmilitary modes of coercion, and where necessary, especially if vital interests are at stake, by military force. As the Cold War exemplified, this security logic knows few limits even in the nuclear age, being prepared in extremis to destroy all life on earth. Nothing inhibited such war plans, not the prospect of nuclear winter, not the expectation of one's own country in ruins, not even the death of nature or the species, nothing. By paradoxical thinking, the threat to inflict catastrophic devastation was relied upon to prevent it; nuclear weapons by this mode of thinking are given credit for avoiding a third world war, for playing a peacekeeping role. In the name of such security, a hideous, absolute right to engage in destructive violence was claimed by geopolitical leaders, and claimed for the sake of the internal and international status quo, an ensemble of structures and tendencies that has been assessed in chapter 2 by way of the triple indictment. Conceptually, such an orientation toward security achieves legitimacy through the language of abstraction: interests, balances, stability, deterrence. Risks of failure, while vaguely acknowledged, are ignored.

The ending of the Cold War has not led to any fundamental rethinking that draws into question this logic. On the contrary: without bipolarity, geopolitical logic is no longer restrained by the sort of prudence that avoided a third world war, but instead again regards war as a rational, cost-effective option in support of strategic interests as exemplified by the Desert Storm phase of the Gulf War.

The realist view of security is premised on the idea that waging war, and even more so its threat, is an instrument that can be rationally used by both the enemies and the guardians of the status quo. The ideological dream implicit in George Bush's initial call for creating "the new world order" back in 1990 was to bring the symbolic resources of international law and the United Nations to bear on behalf of the idea that *geopolitically unwelcome* challenges to the status quo were "illegal," "criminal," and "illegitimate," while wars for the enhancement or defense of the status quo were "legal" and "legitimate," and were in effect "UN wars" against disturbers of "the peace," a coded synonym for "the status quo." These categories of assessment do not deny that Iraq was guilty of aggression against Kuwait, and that the UN had a legal responsibility by way of collective security to restore its sovereign rights if at all possible. The point being made is that the prospects for *effective* response are almost totally dependent on geopolitical calculations.

For instance, a decade earlier when Iraq attacked Iran, the UN failed to respond for several years; the explanation for inaction was not the usual rationale – Cold War stalemate – but rather the *shared* interest of both superpowers at the time in weakening, if not destroying,

Khomeini's Iran. Saddam Hussein turned out to be an ideal conspirator, providing the most favorable possible normative climate in which to re-enact in a post–Cold War setting this prevailing security/war approach to world order. In a more complex setting, the disintegration of Yugoslavia during the early 1990s has also been geopolitically orchestrated, with various European powers pursuing their national and regional interests and adhering to historical, religious, and ethnic affinities. Here the impact of geopolitics, mainly of regional scope, has been to neutralize external pressures and to ratify the outcome of Serbian aggression. Note that Yugoslavia lost its strategic significance as a vital contributor to "containment" of Soviet expansion with the end of the Cold War, and for this reason there was no serious pressure mounted from a global level to prevent the dismantling of the Yugoslav state.

With the continuing globalization of economic and ideational life on the planet there is coming into being a mainstream and realist conception of geogovernance that includes as a dimension a security capability that coordinates and sustains the structures and dynamics of global apartheid. Expression of this impulse, although disguised to a certain extent by an espousal of liberal concerns with the spread of market-oriented democracies and the endorsement in words of a humanistic agenda, is evident in the emphasis on maximal economic growth combined with a minimal concern with human and environmental costs imposed by the play of market forces. On the view being proposed here, this embrace of geogovernance is part of the historical attempt by leading statist and market forces, the controllers of geopolitics, to extend their grasp on a global scale and appropriate as well the main normative instruments of the world – that is, that authority of the United Nations (and regional actors, as appropriate) and of international law.

Whether this appropriation of the formal mechanisms succeeds or not will not be decisive in the molding of geogovernance. Quite possibly the Gulf War was a special, anomalous case not likely to be repeated. Other approaches to market-driven geogovernance are possible, including reliance on one or more states which are responsive to market priorities, resorting to force as necessary but without receiving legitimating support from the organized global community. Various regional frameworks for implementing geogovernance may also turn out to be relevant. There is also a range of viewpoints as to whether human rights and democracy are integral to stability at the state level and thus high priorities of an emergent geogovernance. The strong economic performances of East Asian countries are challenging the pro-democracy position, as is the opportunistic backing of Yeltsin's Russia, Fujimora's Peru.

When critics of the failure by Europe or the United Nations to make any serious response to Serbian and Croatian "ethnic cleansing" and territorial expansion in Bosnia expressed frustration, their general explanation rang true: "The trouble is that Bosnia has no oil!" If it is not worth war by geopolitical calculations, then even genocide will be tolerated, even if not tolerable! Security policy as associated with globalization from above is preoccupied with the protection of market forces and the perceived interests of geopolitical actors, that is, strategic concerns of both global and regional scope.[2]

Participants in the projects and struggles of global civil society are fashioning many versions of security that arise out of the actualities in specific circumstances of *insecurity*, experienced as anxiety and ordeal by frightened and oppressed human beings, rather than conceiving of security as expressions of the power/wealth calculations of geopolitical and market perspectives. Avoidance of war and civil strife, relief of poverty, protection of neighborhoods against crime, control of ethnic, caste, and cultural relations, disvaluing of violence are aspects, nuanced in relation to context, of the human-centered struggle for security in the world. War itself is a profound source of acute insecurity, as evidenced by the large and rising number of refugees and internally displaced persons that result, as well as by casualty figures. The human impact is underscored by the realization that 80 per cent of the refugee population consists of women and children. Of course, working from such points of departure, the militarization of relations among states, and between North and South, is a crucial dimension of the security challenge. One aspect of this challenge is the lucrative arms trade that feeds weapons to the South, stimulating regional arms races that divert resources from social goals. Controlling the arms trade means challenging the market as well as militarization. It is instructive to compare the criminalization of the drug trade, with the supply sources being located in the South, with the legitimation of the arms trade, with the supply sources being located in the North. A telling exception is the effort to discourage proliferation of weaponry of mass destruction, the only form of arms trade that potentially challenges the geopolitical hierarchy. The approach to security taken here is one that stresses an abolitionist attitude toward both nuclearism as geopolitical practice and war as a social institution, and a demilitarizing approach to all forms of societal conflict and defense.

Transformative feminism has a special relevance for and insight into "security studies." Women have been in various culturally sanctioned ways victims of oppressive structures and practices which have been underpinned by male control over the instrumentalities of violence. In this regard, rape functions as literal and metaphorical manifestation of the one-sided male/female relationship that exists in various public settings of violence and insecurity. The prevalence of rape as a "normal" incident of war manifests this linkage. Robin Morgan's association of terrorism with the habitual fear of women in relation to men either in the intimate space of the home or in the darkness of nights haunted by strangers is paradigmatic.[3] The rootedness of this violence by men against women cannot be separated politically or culturally from the dominance of war-making and the embedded association of male identity with the capacity and willingness to engage in senseless violence, whether it be the glorification of "the cowboy" or the newer imagery of Rambo. War-making roles of men and women express the core meaning of patriarchy. And it is significant to notice that it is the USA that simultaneously gives the world geopolitical leadership, provides popular mythic imagery of male identity, and adheres most rigidly to a sense of security based on technological mastery over weaponry of mass destruction.

Even more vividly than in relation to sovereignty and democracy, this understanding of security aims at loosening and then breaking the structures of geopolitical and patriarchal bondage that currently constitute "world order." Transition to geogovernance of the sort proposed here definitely combines the extension and deepening of democracy with the reconstruction of security from the bottom up in all sites of human interaction, being sensitive to the immediacies of context that set priorities in particular settings: what "security" entails for an African township in South Africa or a Catholic neighborhood in Belfast is dramatically different than what it means for working women living in drug-saturated inner cities in the United States. And at the governmental level, the security concerns of Canada and Lebanon or Cambodia can hardly be compared.

In this chapter, as throughout the report, the attempt is to decenter and reconstruct a basic organizing idea of collective political existence, illustrating an approach and depicting an orientation that is bottom-up in spirit, but seeks to avoid romanticizing the grassroots. Cruelty and patriarchy may be embedded in popular culture and opposed by the state and the organs of regional and global community, as well as by opposed elements of civil society. Protecting innocence and vulnerability and avoiding cruelty and suffering are relied upon as universal criteria of judgment, and are not relativized. Initiatives rooted in civil society can be destructive, and need to be opposed.

An overall view of security has been eloquently stated by K Subrahmanyam: Humanity as a whole, even as it increases in numbers, will be
subjected to increasing insecurity and conflicts – unless the nations of
today, remembering their own humanity, can forget the rest and join
together in formulating a strategy aimed not only at military security but
also at other basic issues that generate insecurity for humankind. Security
is indivisible. Military security cannot be the sole focus to the neglect of
food security, ecological security, energy security and humanitarian
security. A future strategy has to be based on a vision of non-violence, a
time-bound programme towards a nuclear-free world, turning away from
conflictual to co-operative approaches among the nations of the world
and among the peoples within the nations of the world.[4]

It is particularly notable that Subrahmanyam has been India's most
influential defense analyst, respected for his work by those adhering to
a geopolitical outlook on security. This formulation could be extended
in three respects: by refusing to take for granted that "military security"
is the core sense of security; by questioning the use of "nation" as the
basic actor in international life, preferring the term state and taking
note thereby of the reality of multinational states in which "nations"
are often suppressed; by regarding the measuring rod of security to be
world order values as embedded in global civil society, bearing on the
specifics of well-being, rather than on the capacity of states to cooperate
along a broad spectrum of issues.

It is useful to recall Yoshikazu Sakamoto's insistence that security be
associated with "a maximum degree of realization . . . in terms of basic
values, such as peace, well-being, justice, eco-balance, and positive
identity."[5] Sakamoto is fully aware that this expansion of the scope of
security threatens to deprive the term of any distinct meaning, and so
encourages the secondary notion of a "minimum level" of security that
is premised on overcoming the most prevalent forms of physical
insecurity, including "war (international and/or civil), hunger, poverty,
environmental degradation, political oppression or other forms of
violence." This focus clarifies important meanings for the term security,
but one might add more: for security to exist in the hearts and minds of
peoples, there must be a positive content arising from the experiencing
of life, a sense of rootedness, belonging, and meaning, an engagement
with community and political life, with spiritual reflection and cultural
tradition, with a vision of the good, the true, and the beautiful that goes
well beyond the minimum. The Zen archer understands that she must
aim above the target to have any serious chance to hit the target.

Such a revisioning of security is crucial to the whole enterprise of
global civil society, and the shaping of global polity in accordance with

the criteria of humane governance. Subrahmanyam clearly identifies this element of necessity in the following passage:

> Either humanity unites to survive, or it is bound to face a bleak future. The strategy of a non-violent and nuclear-free world has no alternative, if future generations are to survive in conditions of sustainable development. We of this generation have a stark choice before us. Either we become saviours of our posterity or its executioners. Either we opt for life or shatter the future of mankind.[6]

This sense of urgency is here affirmed. Also to be underscored is the idea that continued democratization on a global scale depends on the establishment of a security which radically breaks with perceptions and practices that have given substance to geopolitics throughout modern history.

It is obvious that to initiate a discussion of security on this radical note is to highlight the distance separating such a position from the mainstream thought in the North and from the outlook of most governing elites in the South. And it is equally predictable that it will be dismissed thereby as "utopian." But such is the challenge of security that the perspectives of what is possible, desirable, and necessary are virtually indistinguishable. To respond helpfully to the challenges ahead it is necessary to summon the intellectual and political courage to face the depth and extent of the problem that faces humanity. It is of great relevance to manifest a will to become secure, realizing that the process of achieving security in this sense demands sacrifice, patience, the resources of the human imagination, commitment to the relief of insecurity in concrete circumstances, and a continuous dialogue which is sensitive to diversities of situation and perspective.

Attention needs to be called to the geopolitical character of commentary being disseminated by the global media network and by both the policy-making elites of states and the managers of the global economic order. Despite the ending of the Cold War, the evident misery of a large proportion of humanity, and the many signs of ecological emergency, the basic response of geopolitical security thinking can be summed up with a single word: *continuity*. Security continues to be calculated by the margin of destructive capacity possessed in relation to an expected enemy – the war-makers and weapons experts hold the keys that unlock the vaults that contain "security." And the achievement of security in a global setting is largely reduced to the management of boundaries of the territorial state – the degree of capacity to keep unwanted persons, ideas, things out, and to keep what is wanted within.

To the extent that security is globalized, it is associated with establishing the conditions that best enable the expansion of gross planetary product and stimulate the growth of world trade within a framework stabilized by policies that produce the triple indictment.[7]

What is remarkable about this geopolitical image of security is its durability, one that traverses the distinction drawn earlier between modern, state-centric geopolitics and postmodern market-geared geopolitics. Not even the horrors of continuous war shake this confidence, nor does the terror of weaponry of mass destruction, or the fiendish quality of electronic hyperwar, or the prospects of the militarization of space. The absence of critical self-reflection is appalling. What needs to be acknowledged here, among other challenging perspectives, is the timeliness and importance of feminist voices from around the world in fashioning other possible responses to this very real, often unacknowledged, presence of an unregulated Frankenstein in our midst.

The most currently dangerous of these militarist voices, but also the clearest, are being intoned in the United States, both at the level of public policy (nuclearism, the Gulf War) and at the level of popular culture (Rambo). *Wall Street Journal* editorials often articulate the mind of the White House regardless of which party is in control of government, as in a typical editorial entitled "Weapons for a Dangerous World." Its main concern is expressed as follows: "With weapons proliferating like rabbits, the US can only maintain military pre-eminence by investing in advanced systems of the sort that routed Baghdad . . . The Gulf crisis and victory changed the politics of defense, and rebutted the critics of the 1980s who said high-tech weapons would never work. Now's the time to send the critics running like the Iraqi army."[8] The militarist character of such opinions was heightened by the evidently "innocent" appearance of this editorial on the forty-sixth anniversary of the Hiroshima attack! Such a "coincidence" represents the acme of what Buddhists call "mindlessness." The regressive message poses a challenge: How can we go about encouraging mindfulness in relation to global civil security?

Conceptual Choices

The word "security" has acquired magnetism in recent years for both policy-makers and reformers concerned about the international scene. Security is, first of all, associated with strategic and military policy, with what has been called "national security" in Western countries. To focus on security is to seem serious about the well-being of the territorial state in relation to its foreign enemies. Peace activists during the Cold War challenged the militarist assumptions and content of national security by writing about "real security," arguing that economic restructuring, diplomatic reputation, arms control and disarmament, and stronger international institutions provided real security in the nuclear age, and that in contrast the constant preoccupation with better weapons systems, foreign bases, invulnerable deployments were obsessive and dangerously provocative to the other side – the results were, at best, an illusion of security, at worst, increased risks of a mutually disastrous war.

After the 1982 report of the Palme Commission (an independent commission of eminent persons convened to offer recommendations on "security" in the Cold War under the chairmanship of Olaf Palme, then between terms as Prime Minister of Sweden), the idea of "common security" gained some currency in political dialogue, establishing the idea that in the nuclear age even antagonistic states, and not just friendly states, needed to cooperate to reduce costs and take steps to avoid their mutual destruction. In effect, common security accepted the geopolitical framework, but stressed its adaptation to a technological and economic environment in which traditional notions of "superiority" and "advantage" had become dangerous delusions.[9] Common security induced a mood that could encourage demilitarization, but its initial effort was to reduce risks posed by the most dangerous forms and modalities of militarization.

Another closely related tendency has been for both elites and reformers to expand the scope of security to embrace all threats to human well-being, not just those in the war/peace setting. Such an impulse was closely aligned to another American tendency, that of declaring "war" on problems. Since no one could doubt that declaring war was the expression of a deep, all-out commitment, a war against poverty, a war against terrorism, a war against drugs were borrowing the credibility of real war to manifest dedication of purpose by leaders and politicians, including the willingness to allocate resources. Others in civil society and governmental circles have used "security" in the same spirit, to achieve credibility by showing that their concerns were not truly deviant and were the same as those of the political leaders of the superpowers. Under Gorbachev, Soviet officials advocated "comprehensive security" to express the idea that it was the security of the system, not of particular states or groups of allied states, that was now most important. In effect, this usage borrowed from the Palme Commission phrase "common security," which encouraged the realization that unless all were secure against the danger of war, none could be, and that it was war itself rather than an aggressive state that posed the greatest danger to security, however defined. The hawkish elites in the West never accepted this modification of the core understanding of security, insisting that the security of our side continued to depend mainly on having better weapons, a readiness to engage in warfare, and a willingness to fight without any limits on the instruments of violence if state interests were threatened – that is, true security rested as much as in the pre-nuclear era on being as militarily strong as possible relative to potential adversaries.[10] All other considerations were brushed aside as marginal or diversionary. This militarist, regressive view of security continues to prevail in the national security establishments of the North, among the analysts of world issues who work for the most influential "think tanks," and among most media specialists on war/peace issues.

In the aftermath of the Cold War this orientation has shifted directions, from East/West to North/South, but its essential character remains unchanged, even unchallenged. The transition to geogovernance is by stages and cumulatively shifting the orientation of geopolitics from modernist (balance of power) to postmodernist (world economic hegemony) preoccupations. Whether in time this will produce an "essential" change in the nature of security remains uncertain, and will be determined by whether or not postmodern stability turns out to be as dependent on war as modern stability. For the leadership of the G-7, security mainly means military supremacy in relation to actual and potential threats mounted in the South, while keeping in being thousands of nuclear warheads and strategic delivery systems in the event of a revival of tensions in the North.

At this point, the major uncertainty in the North concerns Russia, not its maintenance of "democracy" (which has already been substantially minimized as a goal), but its forced-draft commitment to marketization. If Russia's turmoil generates an ultranationalist, antimarket post-Yeltsin orientation, then strategic tensions *in the West* are likely to be revived. With Japan weakened and Europe bewildered, it is hard, as of the time of writing, to envision another scenario productive of such tensions.

If one is not captive of either modernist or postmodernist geopolitics, the challenge of security in the new era assumes a dramatically different form. A historical opportunity has been presented to promote demilitarization and to discredit the war system as a social institution implicit in human experience. The equity and ecological agendas of the planet reinforce this antiwar posture, and make an orientation of the whole (as opposed to part versus part) the only hope of humanity to meet its most serious challenges. In this regard, the refocusing of the geopolitics of hegemony on the South is not only generative of widespread suffering and deep injustice, but it is antiquarian in its attachment to the preoccupations of the past in a rapidly changing setting of the present. One expression of the strategy towards the South is to reshape the normative agenda to highlight the menace of nuclear proliferation, while leaving arms sales unregulated. Such a distinction again confirms the power of the market vis-à-vis the state in shaping geopolitical postures.

What is in question here is the tendency to take for granted the possession and further development and deployment of nuclear weapons by the countries in the North, as well as the implicit endorsement of the sovereign rights of arms producers to acquire weapons in whatever quantities, as well as to disseminate such weaponry to the South. A related and widespread distortion of political perception holds that the targets of military intervention pose a greater danger to global security than do the main perpetrators of military intervention. It is also the deformed statist normative vision that conceives of the North as more rationally responsible ("civilized") and less militarist and menacing than the South. There is a racist element present here that overlooks the history of warfare and abuse of humanitarian principles. Even in relatively progressive settings, policy discussion emphasizes the appropriateness of *targets* for benign intervention rather than questioning whether such *capabilities* should be funded and developed. In this regard, there are two suppressed considerations: virtually all intervention (aside from intraregional patterns) is North-to-South (never the reverse); the opportunity costs of funding interventionary capabilities may be the affordability of a welfare role for the state.

Having declared this outlook, it is necessary to include the whole gamut of concerns associated with global civil society in presenting an extended conception of security. It is plausible to argue that environmental decay, energy policy (oil, water, nuclear), demographic trends (including migrations), and economic restructuring in various settings should be treated as the main elements of a revitalized conception of security. This expansion of the scope of security moves in the right direction, but it still conceives of security largely from the heights of elite assessment, at best allowing the select advisor to deliver a more enlightened message to the ear of the prince.

In stark contrast, let us conceive of security first and foremost from the depths, from the experience of those most disadvantaged and vulnerable, from those consigned to wretched refugee camps for decades on end, for those without the necessities of life and denied the dignity of work and satisfaction, for those trapped in enclaves of local prejudice and more generalized oppression, for those peoples being forced to leave traditional habitats to make way for great modernizing undertakings, for those millions caught in the fearsome milieus of crime, corruption, and disease. On another level, many persons exist who are too humiliated by social oppression to disclose their true sexual preferences, especially if they are contrary to prevailing societal strictures. The sense of security advocated here is built in the first instance on the negation of insecurity as it is *specifically* experienced by individuals and groups in concrete situations. Security is not a static condition, but a process of value realization – it increases insofar as world order values are realized in particular circumstances. Such a reorientation should be a matter of emphasis. It remains an urgent priority to push a demilitarization agenda in all arenas of decision, but especially in state/society interaction within the lead geopolitical actors.

It is arguable that the redirection of resources required for a bottom-up approach is only feasible as part of "a peace dividend" achieved by way of statist demilitarization (reduced budgets, disarmament, political accommodation). As elsewhere, from this point of departure, this view emphasizes longer time horizons that relate to the conditions being created in the future in relation to health, safety, beauty, satisfaction and well-being. The future of global civil society can only be secured by acting to promote a global polity dedicated to the realization of world order values, the variant of geogovernance that is here termed humane governance. In this regard, the term *global civic security* is proposed to identify this insistence on tracking the priorities of security from the existential situation of individuals, groups, and of the human species as a whole, and of associating security, above all, with the valuations and understanding of social movements, activists, representatives of oppressed peoples, rather than with the assessments of experts, bureaucrats, politicians, media gurus.

The normative energy for security needs to emerge from the cauldron of perceptions, beliefs, myths, and values contained within global civil society. Elites, even if so inclined, cannot enact fundamental behavioral adjustments without being frustrated by deep resistance and depending on fascistic methods, and and even then they will be eventually cast aside. There are many examples in this century, perhaps none more poignant than the incredible bloodshed and oppressiveness associated with the collectivization of agriculture in Stalin's Soviet Union.

A major aspect of revitalizing security depends on parallel efforts to strengthen democratic relations between peoples and politics. The fundamental kinds of adjustment associated with reproductive behavior and lifestyle to enable viable, sustainable, and equitable development will have to emerge out of the informed responses of popular desire. If these assessments are correct, this can only happen if materialist and highly individualist ideas about human happiness are effectively challenged and replaced by the recovery of more spiritual and communal ideas of fulfillment. And if such a conjecture is more or less accurate, then some of the cultural orientations of the East seem more helpful than what has come to prevail throughout the West – in their different ways, Islam, Hinduism, Confucianism, Taoism, as well as many of the outlooks of premodern or indigenous societies offer their peoples traditions, in many variations, that emphasize spiritual and/or communal patterns of fulfillment. It is important to resist, as well, the temptation to romanticize the South and demonize the North. There are many aspects of these non-Western cultural heritages (and each is also rich in an array of countertraditions within itself) that are unacceptable from the perspective of world order values in relation to human rights and gender relations, including traditional practices involving physical cruelty and violence. At the same time, the West in its main Christian worldview, as well as in numerous countertraditions, offers many sources of inspiration that could support a nonmaterialist, communal civilizational mutation – perhaps none more potent than the life story of Jesus and his teachings, but also, in a more minor key, the Franciscan embrace of the entire created order as blessed. It is not necessary to abandon, let alone repudiate, these Western traditions to build support for an ecofeminist transition to humane governance.

In conceiving of these issues, there is more to "culture" than "religion," and more to religion than ecclesiastical doctrine and the formal role of churches and priesthoods. Modern society has through media and market, and associated propaganda of the state, built the foundations of a globalized culture that is secular, materialist, and conformist. There are, as well, countertrends, voices, and capabilities in this globalizing experience that seek to dissolve race and gender tensions, and call forth the spiritualizing energies of love, natural beauty, comic inversion. John Lennon was widely perceived as a voice on behalf of love and unity. Madonna, although often understood as an icon of materialist commercialism, can also be seen as an influential partisan in the struggle to break all chains of human bondage and to acknowledge the primacy of human solidarities that take precedence over differences and antagonisms based on race, gender, class. As emphasized throughout, human empowerment by way of microelectronics gives great potential, as yet only explored in the most preliminary ways, to democratizing initiatives that take account of the multiple arenas of action and decision in emergent postmodern contexts.[11]

In each instance, there are shadows as well as lights, but the message/

massage[12] is basically affirmative, although one might note that this cultural dimension of globalization has an elite bias and emanates mainly from the North, especially North America. In this regard there is a symbiosis between the regressive project to achieve "a sustainable hegemony" in this period of history, and cultural, market-driven globalization. This nexus is the generative basis for both postmodern geopolitics and a type of geogovernance that reinforces the triple indictment depicted in chapter 2.

Security, in dynamic correlation with sovereignty and democracy, requires change at the roots. Of course, we are dealing with a seamless web of societal practice and institutionalization, but it is in relation to security that one comes up most strongly against nonsustainable forms of development as a primary obstacle to the sort of redirection of policy that is here favored and considered necessary. In effect, it is being argued that security is not achievable within the matrix of modernism, or of geopolitical variants of postmodernism, involving as it does a continuation by way of adaptation and even an intensification of commercialism, materialism, and triumphalism. The consideration of these concerns re-emerges in the development chapter that follows, but it is impossible to deal appropriately with security as an aspect of humane governance without considering the relevance of culture and its receptivity to change, especially with respect to the glamorization of senseless, macho violence. The final chapter will take up a sustained consideration of human agency – that is, of programmatic initiatives that might exert influence on the directions taken by normative energy.

Such a repositioning of security exposes also the scandal of geopolitics in the history of the states system. In this context, it is not the statist outlook as such that is objectionable, but its absolute pretensions that seem most shocking.[13] First of all, the enormous destructive fury unleashed in the history of warfare has been neither truly defensive nor dedicated even for the benefit of the human community encompassed by territorial boundaries. The motivations for war throughout modern times were often an expression of the search for gold and glory on behalf of a small and selfish elite. Sometimes even a single individual has been able to produce collective carnage. Often wars were embarked on for the sake of strengthening and enriching the governmental regime in power at the time. By security was meant the persistence of the political status quo, or if expansionist, the satisfaction of statist and materialist ambitions, necessarily at the expense of others. Worse than this, especially with the steady advance of military technology, was the refusal to acknowledge and respect limits on the scale of destruction and suffering inflicted. This refusal was itself backed up by adopting a view of sovereign rights that included the conviction that the security of one's own state was an inherent right that could and should never be validly qualified, casting doubt on the meaningfulness of the international law of war as premised on ideas of mutuality and self-restraint. This evolution of absolute or total war is the supreme expression of one-sidedness, disregarding even the survival rights of the other. In the nuclear age, as has been frequently observed, war verges on genocide. In contrast, the stress here is on a Habermasian ethos that emphasizes the dialogic nature of all political relations, implying not only a concern for the other, but an acknowledgment that the viewpoint of the other is entitled to respect, a fair hearing, and a considered response.

With nuclear weapons, policies that boasted of the resolve to exterminate the civilian society of the opponent in the event of war reached a climax. Implicit also was the claim that it was acceptable in the course of war to inflict catastrophic damage on neutral countries and even to expose, without their assent, one's own people to annihilation, even to risk the survival of the whole species for the sake of defending a particular piece of geopolitical turf. In this regard, the insufficiencies of modernist notions of democracy seem dramatically clear. Neutral countries don't participate, and yet are placed at ultimate risk, making their claim of territorial sovereignty quite meaningless; at the same time the citizenry of a contemporary nuclear weapons state have almost no access to policies or decisions bearing on recourse to war, either directly or by way of representative institutions, given the secret protocols that guide executive policy.

The extraordinary scientific modeling studies showing a probable "nuclear winter" effect of any large-scale use of nuclear weapons have confirmed that, even if the other side never retaliated, recourse to large-scale nuclear war would likely be a disaster for friend and foe alike, as well as for the initiating side. Even before counterarguments were made that the effects of nuclear weapons might not be as serious for the climate as some studies argued, there was no indication of a willingness by government leaders to reconsider reliance on nuclear deterrence as the linchpin of strategy. Deterrence theorists merely insisted that the possibility of a nuclear winter showed how important it was to build even better, more fearsome nuclear weapons systems so that deterrence would be more likely to succeed, and thus catastrophe be averted. This rigid nuclearist mindset reminds us of an end-of-the-world cult that never abandons its steadfast confidence in its prophetic leader no matter how many dates pass on which the last judgment was supposed to occur. In religious thought such thinking is called millenarianism; in national security thinking it has been called deterrence theory. Such a system is as absurd as it is ethically depraved, and yet it is defended by an overwhelming majority of academic specialists who invoke "rationality," "realism," even "morality," with grim certitude to support their arguments on behalf of the continuities of security policy.[14] In this extreme instance of the tendency to think backwards, John Mearsheimer, an eminent contributor to the grand strategy debate in the West, actually argues that the worst possible future scenario for Europe in the aftermath of the Cold War would be one in which all nuclear weapons were eliminated from the region![15]

These militarist conceptions of security are so obviously outmoded that only geopolitical ideologues continue to endorse them. Indeed, within geopolitical circles such views are being challenged because of their modernist ties to a statist world. Postmodern geopolitics stresses trade and monetary regimes as the foundation of security. As the situation produced by technological innovation and human vulnerability becomes steadily more degraded and extreme, the war apologists become ever more steadfast and rigid, illustrating the dogmatizing behavior of a theology being overtaken by the onrush of events. Arguing with such adherents is generally futile, frustrating, and endless. The conventional wisdom that continues to guide most sovereign states in devising their national security doctrines poses a mortal threat to human well-being, and retains its hold on the political imagination in a manner analogous to an addictive drug.

The positions advocated here start from a different political and cognitive terrain. These conceive of military instruments as increasingly dysfunctional, being rarely helpful to the overall struggles for justice and joy in the world, and thus regard security as much more properly preoccupied with demilitarization in all dimensions of societal existence. The perspective of global civil society is that "war," however "just" from the perspective of defending territory, can never justify exterminist tactics, incidental devastation of other societies, deliberate attack on civilians, and serious harm to the global commons and the shared environment of the biosphere. These limits are fully applicable to uses of force and wars fought with a UN mandate or even under a UN command. The force used under the authority of the United Nations should be governed by stricter restraints than now pertain to state action as a result of the humanitarian laws of war (the Geneva Conventions of 1949 and the Geneva Protocols of 1977). There should be an absolute prohibition on tactics that risk any substantial civilian injury. A new legal code for UN operations is needed to develop the concrete implications of this position.

The collectivization of war or putting war in the hands of organized global community is not the end-point of the campaign to rid the world of war as a social institution. At most it is a step in the right direction if properly conditioned, but such a step is not necessarily abolitionist in character. It is possible that the security solution for postmodern geopolitics would be to concentrate most war-making roles in the United Nations, which would (or could) restabilize the role of war in the maintenance of the overall status quo, thereby entrenching patterns of privilege and exploitation. To revert to the now familiar, and not entirely satisfactory, analogy to slavery as a social institution, it would have seemed a feeble victory indeed if the end result of the antislavery movement was to have been the transfer of the slave trade to some supranational mechanism of regulation organized at the global level that was financed and dominated by the slave-trading states!

Collective security as compared to unilateral uses of force remains a preferable transitional means to organize the protection of territorial communities against aggressive uses of force, and it remains helpful to encourage an expanded UN role in this regard. But it is nonetheless undesirable to make collective security formats available to leading states and market forces for the pursuit of geopolitical strategies, nor should globalist inclinations lead us to pretend that this is a fulfillment of the UN role. The Gulf War is especially important to reflect upon because it delivers a series of mixed messages about this borderland between collective security and postmodern geopolitics. "Postmodern" here might be questioned insofar as it implies the predominance of market rather than statist factors. Their convergence was such, given US foreign policy at the time, that these types of motivation were deeply entwined with one another. The rationale, then, for labeling this an occasion of postmodern geopolitics is the belief that the UN would not have acted on Kuwait's behalf unless Gulf oil was at stake.

Kuwait was the victim of aggression and the UN was properly empowered to act effectively to ensure the full restoration of Kuwaiti sovereignty. But what the UN Security Council authorized was excessive. It was associated with actual war-making and geopolitical ambitions of both a statist and market character that tried to do more than get Iraq out of Kuwait and relied upon disruptive and excessive military force that produced severe civilian destruction and suffering, as well as large-scale environmental damage.[16]

One may derive from the Gulf experience both a reformist zeal and a degree of caution about making use of the Security Council to deal with the alleged aggressive behavior of specific political actors in the South. In the background it is disturbing that there is no availability of UN relief to victims of Northern aggression and intervention. During the Cold War this unavailability was explained by reference to the geopolitical stalemate that paralyzed the Organization. But since 1989 there are no excuses – yet the pattern persists. What recourse did Panama or Central America have in December 1989 when the US invaded, arrested Noriega, and installed a replacement leader, with the ceremony being conducted on an American military base? Or what help did the Sandinista government in Nicaragua receive from the UN after the US defied the World Court ruling of 1986, and continued to finance and supply the Contra efforts at military uprising and destabilization?

There is much value in the sort of incremental reforms of the United Nations that were proposed by the Stockholm Initiative of 1991. The Secretary General in a report to the Security Council of June 1992 entitled *An Agenda for Peace*, and other concerned observers, called for more independent financing, a more independent office of the Secretary General, standby forces, preventive diplomacy, and activation of UN Charter mechanisms for an expanded Security Council role in undertaking and overseeing UN peacekeeping and enforcement operations. Also to be welcomed is the idea of curtailing the use of the veto and a stronger arrangement for participation by the leading countries of the South in the Security Council, as well as a monitoring and participatory role for nongovernmental organizations and citizens associations in the form of a Second Assembly of the UN or a People's Chamber as a formal organ of the General Assembly. In addition, it is important to strengthen the procedures of accountability that relate actions of the UN to its own constitutional framework in the Charter. These would favor an easier and more habitual access to the World Court, especially in any setting where the UN Security Council has approved reliance on coercive measures, sanctions as well as war. Such considerations are mentioned here in relation to security, but merge with a presentation of the structural and constitutional aspects of humane governance that is the subject of the final chapter.

At the present time, the UN, especially the Security Council, often acts as if it were purely a creation of and creature of states and markets (expressive of its dual geopolitical character), at best promising to mitigate some of the most destructive aspects of unrestrained power politics, facilitating a level of interaction among perspectives that helps to shape a political consensus that is needed to address the global agenda. The UN generally does better in its operations outside of the war-prevention sphere. Reliance by the UN on world conferences to consider problematic aspects of international life, including environmental decay, poverty, population pressure, and resource shortages, is often a helpful contribution to the formation of global consciousness and discourse and is unwittingly also the occasion for democratic initiatives by way of counterconferences to push the development of global civil society. Ever since the Stockholm Conference on the Human Environment in 1972, UN conferences have been major organizing and networking settings for transnational social forces taking the shape of "counterconferences," "people's tribunals," and "alternate forums." Such a secondary set of events often overshadows the inconclusiveness of formal intergovernmental efforts. The notion of global civil security seeks to relate these developments to the circumstances of the peoples of the world, generating the will to reconstitute the UN as a civil institutional framework for governance that is responsive to transnational democratic procedures and priorities rather than expressive of the mixed motives of leading territorial states (this is, survivalist and hegemonic goals become intertwined in the operating structure and practices of the UN, and whether these allegiances can be realigned within existing frameworks generated by geopolitics is one of the hardest questions facing adherents of global civil security).[17]

The tendency to overrate governmental initiatives is a reflection of a statist outlook and leads to realist derivations from positivist thought of a century ago, seeking a data-based social science that offers objective and apolitical grounds for explanation and prediction, avoiding the subjectivism of values, emotions, and commitments. One ought to appreciate some of the critical contributions that this cognitive tradition has made in many of its investigations, including its critique of some variants of moralism and legalism that ignored the hard actualities of the global order, including the roles of violence, evil, and greed. But realism as the basis for explanation or prediction, or as the ground on which to build hope, has failed. Realist interpretations of history have been notoriously poor in anticipating the most cataclysmic changes of the era, including the great events of 1989–90 that caused the Soviet empire to splinter into many parts. The human mind is not strong enough to penetrate social and political reality in any scientifically convincing fashion, and any attempt to rest our grasp of the human situation on such a mental basis is bound to be a disappointment, as well as being insensitive to suffering. At the same time the human will is a factor that alters the play of forces by its existence. Since we can never know enough to be convincingly pessimistic or optimistic, there is no basis for either giving up or waiting for the future to happen.

Values, passions, commitments, empathy, and visions of an alternative future provide us with the only possible "cognitive" ground for our "realism" about the future. These issues are referred to here because "security studies" have under various labels been dominated by this positivist and militarist conception of reality. The coherence and usefulness of any approach to security depends on accepting the authority of normative conceptions of reality, however contested by social scientists and by government and corporate bureaucrats. Part of the damage done by geopolitics in either its modernist or postmodernist forms is to conceal the real bases of political behavior from the peoples of the world, confusedly claiming either a logic determined by the balance of power or a logic that is embodied in the market. This can lead to geogovernance in some form, but not to those positive variants of geogovernance called here "humane governance."

Transitions to Geogovernance

There are a series of situations in which choices are currently being debated that will make deeper sorts of repudiations of war and militarism either easier or more difficult. It is important to participate in these debates, and not necessarily with words and arguments alone. The strength of global civil society will be revealed through engagement in action, whether by way of demonstrations or in more sustained campaigns for reform and transformation, informed by independent and trustworthy news and commentary. It is necessary to reinvent effective instruments of political democracy. Since pressure on the governing institutions of territorial states is not likely to yield much change in the near future, it is crucial to devise more promising avenues for political activism in arenas that count in this early phase of a postmodern world. The leading issues of war and militarism are important for their own sake, but even more so as training grounds for participatory types of democratization that tend to bypass the state and reveal themselves in the crucibles of their concrete undertakings. Greenpeace in its various environmental campaigns is one variety of pedagogy. The struggle of the rubber tappers and the indigenous peoples of Amazonia to resist modernizing development by Brazilian entrepreneurs and developers is another variety of resistance. In each instance, violence was the response of the old order to the imaginative potency of nonviolence and massive grassroots resistance – the sinking of the Rainbow Warrior by French intelligence agents in the harbor of Auckland in reaction to the Greenpeace effort to obstruct French nuclear testing programs in the Pacific; the assassination by rich local ranchers of Chico Mendez, a rubber tapper in Brazil who had organized other workers to oppose the intrusion of modernizing projects, in a remote western corner of the Amazon basin.

It is natural to wonder whether such occurrences have anything much to do with war, militarism, security. Yet it is clear that they do. These encounters are symbolic meeting places, or kinds of battlefields, for the contest between old ways and new possibilities that will in the end decide whether global civil security is a serious political project for the early decades of the next century, or merely a rearguard fantasy of those unable to prevent the postmodern geopolitics becoming the defining current of history, however much they may dislike and fear it.

The postmodern reorientation and partial displacement of the state is happening. It is upon us for better and worse. The sequel to this modernist framework is what is being constructed and contested. Will it be primarily capital driven, guided by market efficiency, yielding a world order dominated by postmodern geopolitics? Or will it be more human oriented, shaped also by ideas of rights and a sense of the *human* interest, thereby giving rise to a geogovernance that incorporates the main tenets of humane governance? For the latter to occur, the transformative initiatives have to penetrate the sinews of social interaction at the personal level as well as reconstitute the basis of economic life and governmental function. Such a prospect does not envisage the dismantling of the world economy, but rather an equilibrium among global market, statist, and societal priorities.

Demilitarization: The Move to Historize the Dysfunction of War

The political order continues to be heavily shaped by militarist views of state-to-state, state–society, and global market relations. It is necessary to counter these views with other ideas about security in its primitive sense of providing protection against foreign enemies and domestic crime and violence, as well as against radical challengers of the economic status quo at the regional and global levels. A first step may be to try to domesticate the war system by support for certain prescriptive measures. This would involve prohibiting reliance on weaponry of mass destruction, including nuclear weapons. Hence a comprehensive treaty of prohibition would be an important milestone, especially if it encompassed the prohibition of threats of the sort made by reliance on deterrence theory and practice. It will be exceedingly difficult to persuade existing nuclear weapons states to renounce their nuclear option, and even harder to induce the complete destruction of their nuclear weapons arsenals. So long as some countries possess such weaponry and the means of its delivery, and others lack it altogether, there is a condition of acute vulnerability imposed on the non-nuclear societies of the world. Of course, the geopolitically preferred method to reduce such a sense of vulnerability was to extend a nuclear umbrella to friendly countries that perceived a threat from an adversary. But such an umbrella could be withdrawn, or withdrawal threatened, creating a severe sense of insecurity. Since the end of the Cold War the US government has emphasized its role as sole surviving superpower to oppose the right of *certain* additional countries to acquire nuclear weapons. As of 1994 the test cases seem to be North Korea, Iran, Iraq, and Pakistan.

There are two main modes of reaction to a nuclear threat directed at a country: for the country to acquire the capability, or to eliminate it elsewhere. The scale of destructive capability associated with retained nuclear weapons capability has been visually depicted by the chart in figure 5.1. The present nuclearist posture of leading states is to invert the problem by emphasizing nonacquisition of nuclear weapons by those states which do not currently possess the capability, implying that the danger to global security arises either because of the number of nuclear weapons states or because of the likely identity of the newly acquiring states. It tends not to regard the capability as such, or the current weapons states, as particularly problematic. The US government and Russia in their official stances, but also Britain, France, China, and Israel all seem utterly unwilling to give up their nuclear arsenals or to forego their continuous improvement. Such a posture is inconsistent with international law, with the ethics of the just war doctrine, and with a global security order based on some kind of sovereign equality of states.

One feature of the Gulf War in 1991 was the claim by the UN coalition forces, as set forth by the United States, that it was a legitimate war objective to destroy utterly Iraq's capacity to produce weapons of mass destruction, but especially to disempower Iraq from embarking on a program to acquire nuclear weapons in the future. This claim was partly hidden at the time behind the widely approved UN goal of restoring Kuwait's sovereignty. Its implementation is suggestive of an emergent doctrine in the North, as specified in Washington, to intervene coercively if necessary and possible to prevent the acquisition of nuclear weapons status by a country in the South without accepting any corresponding commitment at all to deprive itself of such a status.

What underpins this steadfastness of nuclearism in the West? Here is the rub. Nuclear weapons are perceived as positive instruments for maintaining "world order" on behalf of the status quo.[18] Partly, it is a matter of being in a strong position to deal with a militant challenger, such as Saddam's Iraq. Partly, it is a matter of seeking to reserve the option to threaten or use nuclear weapons in unforeseen future contingencies. In the background is the largely arbitrary view that some states

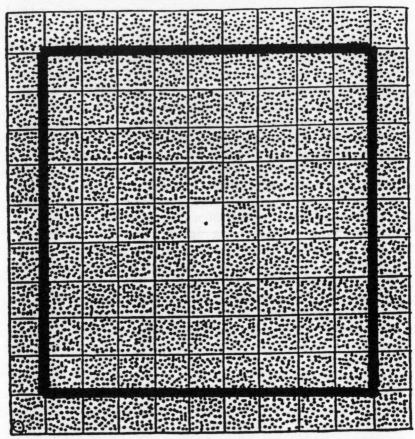

The dot in the center square represents the total firepower unleashed by all sides in World War II. The dots in all the rest of the squares show the firepower of the world's nuclear arsenal in 1982. The dots outside the thick line show how much has been eliminated; those inside the thick line represent all the firepower still deployed and stored at the end of 1992.

Figure 5.1   A representation of destructive capability (*Source*: Center for Defense Information, Washington, D.C., reproduced with permission)

are more suspect and inferior than others. It is not only the arbitrariness of this view that is being challenged, but the governance structure that it reveals: namely, the assumption of authority of the US and its friends to decide which states are "responsible" and which are not, is without any foundation in law or morality. There has never been a serious concern about the Israeli and earlier South African programs of acquisition. Why not? Both of these countries have frequently used force aggressively against their neighbors and are viewed with fear and suspicion within their respective regions. One has to conclude that the absence of concern is associated with an absence of a perceived threat from them in the North. But then what about China and India? There was concern, but the scale of these countries made it difficult to mount a challenge to acquisition directly. One realizes, then, that several factors bear on the perception that *some* instances of proliferation are intolerable, others bearable.

The character and scope of the problem is deepened when non-nuclear weapons of mass destruction are taken into account. Here the leading states in the North have been backing comprehensive regimes of prohibition, even if their own behavior is often ambiguous. This is especially true for biological weapons. The North has seemed to work hard to strengthen the Biological Weapons Convention by building confidence in its viability, although the very success of such a treaty admits the chasm separating states. Possession by weaker states of biological and chemical weaponry could be seen as a great equalizer in international relations, and so their banishment without doing the same for nuclear weapons is to choose to live with hierarchy and hegemony for the indefinite future, as well as with nuclear weapons capability.[19] Is it only a theoretical capability? With no Cold War, why fear the existence of such weaponry? And on the other side, why do the leading nuclear weapons states find it so difficult to get rid of the weapons?

Several positions need to be promoted by democratic social forces at the same time:

1 Weapons of mass destruction are illegitimate – no exceptions. The World Court Project is a civil society initiative, co-sponsored by IALANA (International Association of Lawyers Against Nuclear Arms), WOMP, and the International Peace Bureau, that persuaded the General Assembly in late 1994 to request an Advisory Opinion from the World Court on the question of the legality of the threat or use of nuclear weapons.[20]

2 It is necessary to expose the moral and political inadequacy of an exclusive emphasis on nonproliferation and on the prohibition of "poor man's atomic bombs' (that is, biological and chemical weaponry), and uphold the judgment that such a posture is a hypocritical expression of hegemonic approaches to global security.

3 Priority should be accorded to the importance of preventing a biological arms race and of rolling back the chemical weapons arms race.[21]

4 A process must be initiated that is based on the aim of total

denuclearization. Some would argue, of course, that in a world without nuclear weapons a political actor with one or a few bombs would be in control – such a nightmare scenario presupposes that there are no political resources to resist nuclear blackmail should it occur. But that it would occur is far from clear – despite vulnerable water and electricity systems around the world, such infrastructural vulnerabilities are rarely, if ever, threatened by terrorists. Are we to presuppose that terrorists are more responsible and restrained than political leaders of powerful states? Or more controllable?

Defensive Defense: A Demilitarizing Posture

Related to initiatives that scale back discretionary war-making and weaken hegemonic approaches to security are various ideas – hardware and software – that confine the military mission as unambiguously as possible to the defense of sovereign territory. These ideas would deny rights to keep foreign bases, forbid deep strike war plans, and would regard the regional and global projection of forces as illegitimate. To the extent that weak states require protection, the task would be entrusted to regional and global institutions operating under rigorous constitutional constraints and with the benefit of independent peace-keeping forces.

The essence of defensive defense is nonmilitary, premised on the avoidance of any aggressive diplomatic posture that would tend to antagonize and frighten possible target states. It would also mandate the pervasive training of the citizenry in the tactics and techniques of civilian resistance, with the objective of making it costly and frustrating for a potential aggressive state to encroach upon foreign territory. Depending on size, geography, and attitudes toward neighbors, military approaches to defense could be abandoned (Costa Rica) or radically scaled down, being adapted to land and temperament (Switzerland, Sweden).[22]

The benefits of defensive defense are immediate and significant: reduced costs, reduced influence of the military on the policy and governance process at the level of the state, reduced demand for weapons systems and arms imports, increased role of the citizenry in the maintenance and planning of security, reduced scope for war-making, increased appreciation of and reliance upon nonviolence as the foundation of durable security, repudiation of the militarist mindset and its attachment to weapons innovation, receptivity to innovative thinking about relations among territorial communities in the course of dismantling hegemonic structures and abandoning exploitative practices.

As with other dimensions of transitional reality, security can be reconfigured according either to the priorities of postmodern geopolitics or in relation to the project of humane governance. A mingling of these two vectors is likely to generate various new behavioral patterns at all levels of social interaction, with both encouraging and disappointing effects.

Of course, defensive defense is a process that can and needs to be continuously deepened and readjusted to changing perceptions and situations. One of its appeals is that its intelligent adoption does not depend on negotiating elaborate formal agreements. Defensive defense can be instituted by weak and by strong states acting in relation to very different perceived security requirements. Despite the militarist ortho-doxy, some initiatives of a defensive defense sort in relation to modernist geopolitics have been taken by various states: neutrality (Ireland, Austria, Sweden, Switzerland); nonalignment (most of the Third World); preventive diplomacy (China in relation to border disputes and Hong Kong); withdrawal (Soviet Union during Gorbachev era); unilateral disarmament (Eastern Europe since the end of the Cold War).

What specific measures are appropriate embodiments of defensive defense in the early stages of the postmodern era are a crucial object of inquiry. As suggested, a prime focus for adherents of defensive defense at this stage should be radical measures of denuclearization, including possibly the formal criminalization of nuclear deterrence. Another tack on postmodern defensive defense would be the creation of autonomous peacekeeping capabilities and financing at regional and global levels.

Collective Collective Security: A Demilitarizing Reorientation

The path toward demilitarization and nonviolence will be straighter if the real anxieties of the heterogeneous strands of civil society and the state are addressed. It is not enough to negate war and violence. It is plausible that aggressive, deeply aggrieved, and opportunistic leaders and movements might seek to exploit a demilitarizing setting, and that economic distress might make extremist politics appear to be the only corrective for a situation of societal desperation. For example, it is arguable that Hitlerism, fascism, World War II, and the atomic bomb all arose out of such a combination of circumstances created by Germany's humiliating defeat in World War I, an antiwar and appeasement ethos in the liberal democracies, the Great Depression, and the drift toward the economic strangulation of Japan.

There is little doubt that the deepening of collective security in the course of demilitarization could build public confidence and erode some arguments advanced in favor of retaining the war system. The initial public hopes aroused during the Gulf crisis favoring recourse to the UN Security Council confirmed the prospect for alternatives to interstate warfare. But since 1991 there has been a process of disillusionment with the capabilities of the UN for various reasons. These include the carnage inflicted upon Iraqi society and the failure of the UN to address the minimal security needs and the human rights of the peoples of the region. The mandate for the UN was confined to Iraq's aggression and war-making capability. As a result, the people of Kuwait were not "liberated" through the war from their antiquated royal autocracy, and the plight of Kurds, Shi'as, and Palestinians in both Iraq and Kuwait was subordinated to geopolitical maneuver. Adroit geopolitical bargains struck with Syria during the crisis weakened the sovereign rights of Lebanon still further. Israel was "rewarded" financially for staying out of the Gulf War, while Egypt and Turkey were paid to participate. After attention shifted in 1992–3 from Iraq to Bosnia, Somalia, and Haiti, the dynamic of disillusionment spread and deepened, engaging almost all segments of political opinion. In addition to the accusation that the UN Security Council was a geopolitical vehicle for US foreign policy, there were allegations that the Organization was inept and ineffectual, risking lives of UN forces needlessly and engaging in undertakings that were not justifiable in strategic terms or winnable in tactical terms.

This process of disillusionment with the first serious attempt at collective security by the UN since the Korean War was quite justified, but collective security nonetheless remains a necessary and desirable alternative to geopolitics provided it can be made more genuinely collective.[23] Peacekeeping forces are desirable, but the training of such forces should reflect the outlook of defensive defense and stress nonviolent tactics; their main purpose should be to avoid rather than wage war. Collective security must not involve the reinstitutionalization of war at the regional and global level, and if force is used it must conform to far stricter standards than those associated with the laws of war and even more so with the practice under these rules. It must also reshape the basic approach taken to the idea of defending territory and peoples against aggression – it needs to demilitarize our image of effective defense and to become more attentive to the social and cultural conditions that give rise to intense conflict and aggression in intergroup relations. In that latter regard, studying the experience of countries that have lived peacefully in close proximity over long stretches of time would be instructive, especially if their experience has led to the demilitarization of security policy and the widespread promotion of economic and social rights.

Latin America has avoided most of the deprivations connected with warfare, and yet its peoples have been acutely victimized by militarism, especially by militarist modes of governance and by exploitative collaborations between economic, political, and military elites. The dynamics of demilitarization needs to be conceived in multidimensional terms, extending to the global level as well. In the end collective security cannot, and perhaps should not, be effectively established unless accompanied by steady progress in the achievement of human rights, especially economic and social rights (but also on a foundation of dignity that rests on upholding civil and political rights, the *sine qua non* for the functioning and expansion of transnational democracy).

Civilianizing Governance: Demilitarization at Home

One of the immediately disturbing reactions to the battlefield results in the Gulf War was the American media treatment of the United States military commanders, Norman Schwarzkopf and Colin Powell, not only as war heroes, but as potential and strong candidates for the US Presidency. Such a confusion of the qualities required to lead a modern war with the qualities needed to govern a democratic society of a superpower revealed the extent to which war-making is given precedence over peacemaking in our imagery of political leadership. The idea that military specialists and war professionals should be democratically preferred to lead a government needs to be repudiated politically, but also at the level of popular culture.

Despite trends toward the criminalization of aggressive and illegal war-making, there remains a fascination with war as the ultimate test of personal and national character, especially if it results in one-sided victory. What seems to have been repudiated is warfare among major states in the North, where the balance of capabilities is such that both sides are likely to be devastated. In this regard, the experiences of World War I and World War II, including the atomic attacks against Japanese cities, produced a consensus that sought to prevent a third world war, no matter how antagonistic the strategic rivalry between the Soviet bloc and the West became. "Containment" was the mediating principle between the appeasement that failed in the 1930s and the war-fighting that was no longer a viable option. Whether containment was a tightrope or a fence is a matter of conjecture. Was the avoidance of a third world war mainly a reflection of reliable constraints or mostly a mixture of luck and a precarious balancing act (that brings excitement to a circus audience, but is the occasion for fear and trembling in geopolitics)?

Despite some regressions, as the questionable claims that the military commanders successful in the Gulf War would make excellent political leaders, it remains correct overall to discern a tendency that may yet be reversed and is not fully consistent – toward the repudiation of political rule by military officers. In this regard, the various experiences in Africa and South America are generally encouraging. First of all, military rule has turned out to be mainly inefficient and unpopular. Secondly, resistance to military rule has increasingly relied on techniques of nonviolent mass mobilization and civilian resistance, mounting challenges to the legitimacy of the governance pattern rather than seeking to disrupt governance by terrorist violence or even by building an armed opposition movement (typified by Maoism in its various guises, and most recently typified by the Shining Path movement in Peru).

The ordeal of Chile during the Pinochet dictatorship is exemplary, both discrediting the claims of the military to provide a successful alternative to civilian rule and building a movement of effective opposition that was simultaneously patient, persistent, and moderate in both choice of means and ends. Who could have imagined in the aftermath of Pinochet's bloody ascension to power in 1973 a peaceful transition to civilian, democratic government that included a continuing formal role for the displaced military leader?

The separate stories in Argentina, Brazil, Zaire, and Nigeria have reinforced the Chilean narrative, although the African instances as of the time of writing remain quite ambiguous. These are stories of struggle. They are not political fairy tales. The civilianization of governance may not be complete, as in Chile; the dynamics of democratization may zigzag back and forth, as in Argentina and Nigeria. Yet the realization that the military does not have the answer to the dilemmas of politics in the early postmodern era represents an evolving, and hopefully a durable, consensus. This consensus is supportive of the sort of political development animated by an envisioning of humane governance. A welcomed situation would be one in which the idea of proposing a military professional for high political office in the governance structure of a state or international organization would appear as inappropriate as the nomination of a known leader of organized crime!

Or better, where achievements in relation to the promotion of economic and social justice were seen as qualifying minority women for the highest political offices in the land! At least it is a step in this direction when Aung San Suu Kyi, the leader of the democracy movement in Burma, or Rigaberta Menchu, an activist among the Mayan people in Guatemala, receive the Nobel Peace Prize or Vandana Shiva, India's leading eco-feminist, is awarded the Right Livelihood Award. Even better would be the nomination of women of such calibre to be Secretary General of the United Nations or heads of leading states.

These comments are not meant to denigrate the military profession as such, but to insist that those who are specialists in violence are not the right people to govern. One might imagine a reorientation of the military sensibility that would make these concerns less relevant, but as matters now stand there remains a disposition in political culture to view victory in war as the best possible credential for success in peace. It is evident that the opposite proposition is closer to truth – that success in war is a warning sign for any civic order that is trying to diminish the role of violence in all aspects of its existence. This includes what Johan Galtung has so helpfully identified as "structural violence," those social and economic conditions that bring disease and death to the vulnerable underclasses of the world, creating shorter life expectancies and diminished life prospects.

To clarify this viewpoint still further it is necessary to express a committed opposition to the practice of capital punishment. The state should never have the right to deliberately kill an unarmed person. Someone who has engaged in sociopathic behavior that is dangerous should be confined, and to the extent possible helped to live redemptively; beneath almost every violent criminal profile is the tale of an abused childhood or a story of societal oppression. If we want to avoid violent crime we should do more about the protection and nurturing of children. Once the child has become an adult (criminal) it may be more difficult, or even impossible, to reliably accomplish rehabilitation. The democratization process requires the rejection of violence in all of its varied societal forms, including, for symbolic and intrinsic reasons, a rejection of the lethal option of killing those convicted of serious crimes.

What if capital punishment is democratically supported by the citizenry, even demanded by an overwhelming majority? As elsewhere, the postmodern ethical imperative is to evolve minimal universal criteria of acceptable behavior within the frame of global civil society. Democratic conviction in state/society relations needs to be superseded and conditioned in its practices by norms of human rights, including a prohibition on the imposition of corporal or capital punishment by any unit of governance. But suppose transnational democratic forces also favor such modes of punishment? The normative assumption being pursued here is that for the project of humane governance to succeed it must embody a pervasive ethos of nonviolence.

These concerns also bear on delicate matters at the core of many debates about social issues that are currently raging out of control in many settings throughout the world. The right-to-life contention in the abortion debate is that the deliberate killing of a foetus is a type of violence that should be opposed, yet it is also clear that the bearing of unwanted children, especially by those who are poor or emotionally disturbed, is a type of social violence as well as being a violation of woman's autonomy in relation to her body, a matter that does not depend on wealth or class factors. Much more discussion is required, with due account being given to particular cultural understandings of these profound matters of life and death. It is a setting in which both religious traditions and feminist perspectives need to explore alternatives, and remain sensitive to opposing outlooks. Socioeconomic lines should not be drawn that make abortion available to the rich, but a crime for the poor. Those who oppose abortion with violence – by bombing clinics – are plainly entrapped by a deformed sense of what is sacred about life.[24]

A further dimension to explore concerns ways to diminish the celebration of violence within the culture – from toys, games, and sports to TV soaps and movies intended for mass distribution, from the glorification of war and exploitative sex in history texts, advertising images, and public discourse to the refusal to take peace and nonviolence seriously in the education of the young and the socialization of citizens. Civilizing in these respects involves recasting our real sense of citizenship, loyalty, and patriotism – making world order values take the place of a preoccupation with victory, dominance, and even the benefits of affluence. Political life can never hope to attain a higher ethical plane of achievement than is affirmed by the practices, beliefs, and presiding myths of the supportive culture.

In this regard, the recovery of spirituality is essential to achieve transition to humane governance in the decades ahead. As of now, materialism and secularism are bonded with postmodern geopolitics, the globalization of the materialist, modern civilization of the West. The traditionalist/extremist backlashes associated with religious beliefs are a repudiation of the best features of modernism and a denial of the advent of a range of postmodern options. One expression of this anti-Western backlash has been the deliberate targeting of foreigners by religious extremist organization during the 1990s in Egypt and Algeria. Of course, the frequency of antiforeign and racist incidents in Europe, especially Germany, suggests that this backlash phenomenon is not just an Islamic pattern, or one linked to the non-Western world.

Existential Security for Humane Governance

Demilitarizing civil society also refers to the various sites of lived experience: home, workplace, school, and recreational spaces. It is in these primary human settings that the possibilities of displacing violence needs to be actualized if we are to have any real prospect of reshaping collective patterns of governance and intergroup relations on the basis of nonviolent approaches to mutual security. The complexity of this undertaking is as great as is its significance for our dedication to the challenges of humane governance. Variations of time, place, and cultural conditioning need to be taken into account even within societies, or else one risks imposing some new mutant form of puritanism or austerity in the name of world order values and humane governance. Dialogue and listening to the voices of the other are crucial.

One should take note and highlight patterns of child-rearing and female/male relations that have been generative of fear and anxiety, exhibiting a standard pattern of granting discretion to the stronger and inflicting pain and abuse on the weaker. The evidence is growing that physical violence against women and children is condoned in many distinct cultural and social settings in the world, and does not necessarily diminish with the modernization of the economy or with the emergence of postmodern consciousness.

Security is premised on the absence of fear in societal interaction, and this can only begin to happen if the threat and actuality of violence is diminished. The great prophets of nonviolence have understood the importance of aspiring after a kind of purity, a posture of unconditional nonresistance to evil, regardless of provocation or the possible efficacy of recourse to violence. There are complex questions of balance between creativity of expression and the discouragement of violence. Should pornography be banned? Hate literature? Violent sporting events? Hunting? If so, by what criteria? What procedures of administration? What due process?

Should the extension of security be related to animals and to nature generally? At issue here is not only the conservation of endangered species of plants and animals as part of reverence for the created order, but basic questions of animals' rights and the sanctity of nature.[25]

Violence toward animals and their abuse do tend to validate violence more generally in civil society. At a minimum, the cruel practices in the West associated with the production of veal and the raising of chickens should be prohibited.[26] While it is not clear there there is a link between meat-eating and political violence, in an environmental context questions of diet seem sufficiently related to sustainable and equitable development on a global scale to have some bearing on future human prospects. Without serious adjustments in lifestyle, not necessarily diet, the outlook for humane governance on a global scale is nothing more than the groping of the utopian imagination. Reflection, study, and dialogue on these matters would help strengthen the sort of global civil society that is being advocated here.

Ecological Dimensions of a Transition to Humane Governance

As has been argued, security involves something more than demilitarization. It is also increasingly a matter of establishing and maintaining the conditions of life that protect health, safety, beauty, renewable resources, climate, polar regions, oceans, rainforests, and river systems. Furthermore, an adequate ecological sensitivity would ensure that the burdens of adjustment were not transferred to future generations – for instance, by toxic disposal methods that are safe for 50 years but no more. The undertaking is formidable. Lester Brown, President of Worldwatch Institute, expresses the challenge in a manner that does not exaggerate its magnitude: "if we are to fashion a promising future for the next generation, then the enormous effort required to reverse the environmental degradation of the planet will dominate world affairs for decades to come."[27]

The ecological claim is that the global preoccupation with conflict among states and the militarized rivalries that constitute modern and postmodern geopolitics must give way in the years ahead to the cooperative and sustainable adjustments that will be needed if the peoples of the planet are to have minimal security in relation to food and water, and to pollution. Environmental protection must soon receive major allocations of attention and resources, as well as induce behavioral adjustments. Trends are not encouraging. Environmental concern has steadily risen all over the world, but its effects on public policy ebbs and flows, and is generally subordinated to the drive for growth, profits, and jobs. As a result, almost every indicator of environmental well-being has been recording continuing decay despite the deepening of environmental consciousness.[28] Moreover, background conditions are continuing to build pressures at geometric rates – more people, more consumption, greater acquisition of land for urbanization, continuing clearance of rainforests, rising numbers of cars, increasing energy use per capita and in the aggregate.

There is, to be sure, an important degree of acknowledgment that the ecological challenge is serious. The UN Conference on the Environment, the Earth Summit held in Rio de Janeiro in 1992, was a symbolic and substantive climax to this build-up of concern almost everywhere, but also an occasion of let-down and disappointment. It may have been particularly unfortunate that an anti-environmentalist like George Bush was the US President at the time. The lasting effect of the Rio Summit may be less evident at the intergovernmental and international institutional and norm-building levels than in fostering transnational linkages among environmental civil initiatives.

Given the relentless persistence of the varied factors contributing to ecological crises, it is evident that the concern is not nearly deep enough to generate any hope that environmental security can be provided in the decades ahead. Where the dynamics of adjustment do not enroach on lifestyle, mechanisms of state and market have demonstrated an impressive degree of environmental competence. There has been a response to ozone depletion: nondepleting substitutes for CFCs are being introduced rapidly (although with some distressing side effects) and by voluntary compliance with international standards by both states and corporate manufacturers, with adjustment costs to extend protection to activities in the South being borne by the North. There has been conservation of endangered species of whales (involving small economic burdens, and the eventual recovery of commercial stocks), and the quality of life on Antarctica is being upheld (the treaty regime is being strengthened, though this is partly because mineral development does not seem commercially viable for decades). These achievements have notably depended on transnational campaigns waged by citizens' associations, bringing pressures to bear on the economic and political powers that be. Yet optimism is hardly warranted. Contrary to enthusiastic earlier reports, recent evidence suggests that CFC substitutes have harmful environmental effects of their own. In addition, the behavioral impact of existing patterns of depletion may, at least for some areas, have gone beyond a point of no return. In Australia 75 percent of the people now alive are predicted to develop skin cancer during their natural lives even if precautions are taken.

But environmental security requires a willingness to make far more fundamental changes. Because so many factors contribute to environmental deterioration of different sorts, it is difficult to know where to begin. Amory Lovins and others have pointed out that technological innovations consistent with market activity can conserve enormous quantities of energy – weaker voltage electric bulbs, redesigned car engines, improved housing insulation and more efficient appliances. Certainly these avenues need to be explored and encouraged by civic action of many different varieties. But the political will required to make the market work in an ecologically sensible fashion is currently so absent as to be non-existent. Needed illustrative adjustments include fundamental changes in reproductive behavior (late marriage, birth control, shared parenting), diet (avoidance or drastic reductions in the meat content of diets), transport (elimination or drastic curtailment of routine reliance on the motor car, casual jet travel), shelter (restrictions on opting for private housing), energy (rationing or otherwise restricted use). These sorts of adjustments, no one of which is mandatory, will be most constructively made on the basis of a consensus shaped in global civil society, and enacted at first by affluent social classes in the more affluent countries. Without such encouragement, the period of inevitable adjustment is almost certain to produce societal trauma and likely to lead to ecofascist patterns of government, which in addition will likely be accompanied by a series of traumatizing ecocatastrophes. Elites administering states and markets can play constructive roles, especially in the North, by reinforcing the emergence of the necessary civil consensus, and by promoting policies that lessen, and even reverse, the most dangerous types of ecological decay. Enlightened leadership can extend the period available for adjustment, but it needs the political space to act that will depend upon populist pressures.

Conclusion: The Security Quest Continues

The quest for security must be evaluated relative to the historical situation, as well as related to a wide variety of specific settings. This report has taken a position in the security debate as it has unfolded within the existing framework dominated by realist perceptions, geopolitical ideas and ideals, and the pull of transition to geogovernance. What has been advocated has been a practice of critical engagement and alternative orientation, guided by the beacon of humane governance.

Here, in acknowledgement of the dangers of militarization and the associated globalization of an ethos of violence, the security priority has been a general effort to erode the emergent postmodern geopolitical consensus by proposing less destructive approaches to existing patterns of security policy. Part of such an effort involves the extension of the rule of law to the various domains of operative constitutionalism – making international law effective in relation to the use of force by large states and international institutions. Another part involves the resocialization of the peoples of the world by providing a critique of political violence and war, and by demonstrating the potency of popular mobilization and nonviolent strategies of political resistance and change. Merely formulating the broad characteristics of security appropriate for humane governance discloses a transformative outlook. Yet, even with the apparent continuity of realist reliance upon geopolitics, powerful countercurrents are evolving a variety of possible future constellations of ideas and structures suitable to this time of transition, moving security away from modernist state-centric geopolitics in the direction of market-driven postmodern geopolitics. In opposition to this stand are those countercurrents bearing on security in a world being partially transformed by the agency of global civil society. Such an alternative scenario is inspired by a vision of a realizable postmodern world order system that embodies humane governance.

The contours of that transformation become clearer in the next chapter devoted to development perspectives in a period of economic globalization, environmental constraint, and demographic pressures. The final chapter on governance stresses the instrumental role of law, constitutionalism, and institutions in the struggle over the shape and orientation of geogovernance, which is in large part a contest over whether the world order of the future continues to embody the inequities and dangers here condemned by reference to the triple indictment or whether geogovernance, democratization, and development can allow the varied peoples of the whole world to participate in the reflourishing of social, political, and cultural life in the century to come – which is what is meant by the label "humane governance."

To restate for purposes of clarity, humane governance is the preferred variant of geogovernance. Humane governance is not a structure to be blueprinted, but a process of engagement that is guided by an ethos of nonviolence. While ecumenical in spirit, humane governance is sensitive to and responsive to specific claims based on locale and difference. In this regard, a crucial early test of the clarity and integrity of adherents of humane governance is their attitude towards those who are vulnerable or in circumstances of acute distress.

6

The Struggle against
Globalization from Above

This chapter is devoted to the economic well-being of the peoples of the world, to assessing the main tendencies and countertendencies and affirming the normative project associated with the elimination of poverty and the creation of societal arrangements with the capacity and resolve to meet the basic needs of every person, including the need for self-esteem, health, a healthy environment, and meaningful and safe work for those of this and future generations.

Of course, economic and political factors cannot be entirely disentangled. As argued, globalization erodes self-determination at the level of the state with respect to economic policy choices, but it also induces some kind of homogenized political order. Such an expectation was part of the short-lived triumphalism centered in the West that arose at the end of the Cold War, expressed by the phrase "market-oriented constitutionalism" (a mixture of multiparty electoral rivalry, with political rights of speech and assembly, and a strong private sector that encourages property rights, foreign investment, and indigenous entrepreneurship). In the mid-1990s it is evident that market-oriented authoritarianism is rather firmly entrenched, in diverse forms, in the fast-growing states that comprise the Asian component of the Pacific Rim. Autocratic Singapore is illustrative of one type of regime, while market-oriented China is illustrative of its ideological opposite. What seems evident here, as elsewhere, is the diminishing significance of the ideological identity of a regime, which only a decade ago remained the organizing basis of global and regional security arrangements, and shaped alignments in war.

Although the commitment to democratization implicit in this report extends to all arenas of decision and social interaction, it does not imply an advocacy of intervention in state/society relations even under UN auspices – except in rare circumstances. The realization of economic well-being does imply the universal fulfillment of that portion of human rights devoted to economic rights, and in a manner that is mindful of environmental quality and limits, which necessarily and increasingly implies a commitment to family planning and constraints on lifestyle.

The Defining Role of Globalization

The discussion of "the new world order" prompted by the Gulf Crisis of 1990 was conceived at the time to be either a new emphasis on collective security under the aegis of the United Nations Security Council or, its polar opposite, a menacing cover for Pax Americana II, a post–Cold War posture spearheaded by the USA, seeking, above all, hegemonic control over the South to sustain the prosperity of the North. Both conceptions captured aspects of new realities in international life, especially in the setting of a radical challenge posed by a country in the South that threatened vital strategic interests of the North, as did Iraq's conquest of Kuwait, with its implications of threat to overall oil pricing and access to the Gulf oil reserves.[1] Perhaps, the most accurate view was some compromise between these two views: an enhancement of UN collective security roles, but under the control of the United States government, and with various side-benefits for a series of cooperating states.

But this line of interpretation focused on a crisis overlooked the unfolding structural drama of political life on a planetary scale: the globalization of the world economy. The dynamics of globalization, responding to the organization of capital investment, the play of financial and monetary forces, and market opportunity, and representing a fundamental transnationalizing trend in the organization of business and of financial resources, has been the subject of debate and speculation for several decades.[2] Its evolution and deepening proceeded throughout the period of East/West rivalry, and in many respects, overshadowed the ideological competition between capitalism and socialism. Yet globalization was also linked to the failure of state-led socialism. Undoubtedly, the discrediting and collapse of the Soviet bloc were accelerated by its perceived failure as an alternative economic order, and surely the early aftermath of state socialism was marked by an uncritical, wholesale embrace of the capitalist way by East Europe and the former Soviet Union, and even by China. As 1989 recedes, the post-Communist experience is more varied, with some unexpected electoral strength being shown by former Communist elites.

Significant expressions of democratic resistance to the forced-march character of the transition to capitalism have emerged in Russia and several East European countries. At this time of contradictory trends, it is difficult to tell whether this resistance will slow down or moderate transition to market-based systems, or whether it might even be supplanted by the type of ultranationalism represented by Vladimir Zhirinovsky's meteoric rise in the December 1993 Russian elections of a new parliament.

The "real" new world order is mainly a consequence of the internationalization or deterritorialization of the state in response to the various modalities of globalization.[3] Such a conception of globalization does not necessarily imply a highly centralized governance structure and coordinated market system. It suggests, however, two principal features: a significant, although uneven, loss of effective control by territorial states over the evolution of economic policy, including their own, combined with an economistic thrust in global policy formation that makes the goals of maximizing growth and profits almost unconditional, thereby temporarily consigning to the margins of the political process concerns about the ideological character of a political system and about adverse human and environmental effects.

In these respects, globalization is a world order challenge to statism, that is, the basic modern idea that sovereign states actually exert territorial supremacy on behalf of some conception of national interest, and that this territorial allocation of political authority provides the defining attribute of world order, giving sense to the label, "the state system." There are many ambiguities here since states are often multinational in composition. The governing elites of most states rarely represent the well-being of their citizenry as a whole.

One recent manifestation of globalization is the drive to organize regional trading and monetary systems in the North, and the various expressions of territorial resistances to this drive by traditionally rooted political forces. The struggles of the early 1990s that shaped up around the adoption of the Maastricht and NAFTA treaty frameworks disclose the main contours of debate, and the outlook of contending forces. Proponents were surprised by the degree of opposition, often involving populist and grassroots constituencies.

Another manifestation is the scaling back of the more advanced welfare programs – for instance, "the Swedish model" – under the pressure to achieve "international competitiveness," namely, the capacity to gain access to the European community and compete successfully in the world market. A further manifestation is a lack of concern in the North about those portions of the South which cannot be profitably integrated into the world economy, most especially, sub-Saharan Africa, a process accentuated by the partial substitution of the East for the South as the area most deserving of assistance, that is, most promising from the perspective of market development. This neglect of particularly distressed persons, social sectors, countries, even regions is an expression of "inhumane governance," overdetermined by historical, cultural, and ethnic affinities, geopolitical concerns about a new cycle of East/West antogonism, and the rating of potential market opportunities.

This pattern of globalization sharply challenges the North/South normative project that had been affirmed at an earlier stage of international history, and was a major premise of North/South relations during most of the Cold War. This premise was based on the primacy of a world of states, with a mixture of duty and incentive by the richer, ex-colonial states to assist the poorer states, and an overall societal commitment to take steps to ensure the elimination of poverty, to work toward the universal provision of basic human needs, to acknowledge and tangibly implement the right to development, and more recently, to protect and restore the environment. This agenda was widely endorsed by both capitalist and socialist centers of influence, although governments in the South, especially during the 1970s, were dissatisfied with the pace and depth of change in the world economy. These governments pressed hard for more drastic adjustments by the North under the mobilizing rubric of the creation of "a new international economic order": serious transfers of technologies and resources, major trade and investment concessions, a floor on commodity prices, and some acceptance of responsibility by way of the restructuring and redistribution of wealth for past "unjust enrichment." Although the North found such demands threatening and unwelcome, their credibility was definitely undermined, as well, by certain features of political life in the South, including evidence that many of the supposed economic benefits of assistance and adjustments from the North were being diverted for the personal benefit of elites and that several of the governments most loudly denouncing the inequities of the postcolonial world were themselves deeply implicated in repressive and corrupt practices in their own countries.

Highly relevant, also, was the experience of East and South Asia in which a series of states managed to achieve high rates of economic growth even in the face of global recession. Such a pattern revealed that confinement to the South was not by itself an explanation of persisting economic deprivation or exploitation. As the 1990s unfold it is evident that under certain conditions poor countries in the South can break into the world economy in a successful manner, and that vast opportunities for internal market expansion exist, as well. Limiting conditions appear to derive from population densities and prospects of population growth, generating serious short- and long-term environmental harm and impairing overall quality of life (for instance, the traffic and pollution problems that accompany the transition from bikes to motor scooters to cars in Asian cities). Singapore has responded in the manner of enlightened authoritarianism, requiring each car owner to have a certificate of entitlement, limiting the total number to 300,000, charging huge licensing fees, and providing one of the best subway systems in the world.

Yet the force of the contentions by leaders from parts of the South remains, and to some extent, has strengthened: the world economy still exhibits many features of the colonial era, and several types of unfairness have persisted in the postcolonial years. Beyond this, new inequities have emerged: patterns of indebtedness have produced a net outflow of capital from South (Asia, Africa, and Latin America) to North during the past decade or so of an estimated annual $50 billion, that is, servicing the debts of the South and the repatriation of profits exceed direct development assistance by about this amount each year.[4]

In fact, the normative project to promote equity in the operation of the world economy had been severely weakened by the 1980s: an ideological backlash successfully led by Reaganite and Thatcherite economic policies based on the glorification of the market and insistence on privatization had as its major consequence the encouragement and even subsidization of a kind of postmodern version of comprador capitalism, with greed transmuted into virtue. The movement for a new international economic order was discredited and abandoned. The application of this economistic approach to development by international financial institutions, especially the IMF and World Bank, led to the successful marginalization of UNCTAD and the Group of 77 (a caucus in the UN of more than 100 countries from the South which tries to develop common positions on policy questions) and their commitment to more effort by the North to help the South through reforms of trade and investment practices. The collapse of the Soviet bloc was treated as confirming claims about the overall economic superiority of capitalism, a view widely endorsed by now throughout the South.

The results, as already argued in chapter 2, involve a widening gap between rich countries and poor countries and between social classes within countries, as well as a diminished sense of public responsibility on the part of governing elites in most key states in the North for softening the social and environmental impacts of market forces. It is this overall picture of human distress and environmental deterioration, with its geographic, racial, and class boundaries, that makes it appropriate to describe the world economy as the embodiment of "global apartheid."

Placing this assessment in the setting of the wider argument of this report would associate these macroeconomic trends with the phenomenon of globalization from above. The world order outcomes are likely to accentuate the hierarchical character of class, race, and regional relations, with authority being shifted by stages from statist to market forces. The readjustment of state/society relations in the face of globalization is likely to take many forms, including especially turning the state increasingly into an agency for serving global economic priorities. To the extent that this happens, the Marxist conception of the state ironically takes on a new relevance, despite the collapse of Marxism. Of course, an appropriate theory of "economic determinism" for this period would need to be concretely rooted in the complexities, specific practices, and uneven impacts of globalization.

At present, many governments in the South feel globalization from above in two exceedingly intrusive forms. In the first place, there is the persistence of acute indebtedness in conjunction with market-oriented pressures to service their debt burdens by making structural adjustments at the expense of the most disadvantaged segments of society, along with the mandate to pursue such policies as privatization and receptivity to foreign investors by suppressing internal labor and wages. Secondly, the South is the target of the dissemination, through advertising and otherwise, of a consumerist ethos as a model for human happiness, conveying images of individual and societal fulfillment that would be environmentally disastrous locally and generally to the extent that they are even remotely realized on a global scale.[5]

This globalizing dynamic is only vaguely comprehended at present, and then usually in terms of specific manifestations, that is, as a global corporate presence on a local level or as a specific encounter between the IMF and a government in the South. What is less appreciated is the gradual emergence of financial and trade structures, a virtual system of global economic governance that is at once bypassing, superseding, and shaping statist geopolitics.

Resource Wars, Rogue Banking, and UN Impotence

The Gulf War and the BCCI (Bank of Credit and Commerce International) scandal disclose two types of linkages between geopolitical market forces and leading states. The United States government demonstrated its willingness and capacity to protect the global economic hierarchy against radical challenges from the South when it led the response in 1990–1 against Saddam Hussein's Iraq. The form of response was a significant reflection of the reality of the post–Cold War world, enabling the instrumental use of the United Nations and requiring richer states to contribute heavily to cover by collective action the cost of the military operation. The United States was able to forge a consensus among leading states (with only China hanging back in the form of an abstention in the Security Council), as well as several Arab countries, but was no longer a financial superpower willing to mount such a large-scale military operation out of its own budget. In addition, the democratic ethos in the United States is not currently prepared to risk the death of its young, a position reinforced by the prevalence of small-sized families in late twentieth-century America. Public opinion in the United States also resists the diversion of its energies over a long period for the sake of abstract market forces or to prevail in a resource war (although if the impacts of lengthy gas lines or of a reduced standard of living were sufficiently felt, a political will to wage even costly wars might well emerge).

This custodial role of geopolitical forces must be disguised. In the Gulf War the disguise was simplified by invoking Iraq's agression and Saddam's brutality and imminent access to nuclear weaponry as the reason for such a strong response. American elites, however, fully appreciated the relevance of strategic interests and were additionally pressured by Israeli concerns about the regional threat being posed by Iraq, although these factors were hardly mentioned in the public debate. In fact, the war was waged in a manner that both exceeded and underplayed its supposed objectives. Despite the claim that high-tech proficiency would limit devastation to military targets, the societal infrastructure of Iraq was substantially and deliberately destroyed, causing heavy civilian casualties, especially in the months after the ceasefire. At the same time, Saddam Hussein was allowed to remain in office as the Iraqi leader, and in the immediate aftermath of the war was even allowed to use Iraqi government military personnel and equipment to suppress Kurdish insurrectionary efforts in the north of Iraq and Shi'ia efforts in the south, despite these oppositional forces having been earlier encouraged by the UN alliance, and by Washington in particular, to revolt. The ambivalent relationship to Iraq as of the time of writing persists in the form of UN sanctions that impose their main burden on ordinary citizens of Iraq. In other words, the normative side of the Gulf War was partly a sham (collective security) and partly ignored (human rights, self-determination, and democracy for the peoples of Iraq).

These aspects of the Gulf War experience reflect its geopolitical essence, as opposed to George Bush's attempt at the time to portray the war as a world order test in the form of an exercise in collective security within the UN framework. Once the specifically Iraqi threats to Gulf oil reserves and prices and of nuclear weapons capabilities were removed, the geopolitical priorities in the region immediately shifted away from Iraq to the containment of Islamic fundamentalism and opposition to the multistate implications of support for Kurdish nationalism in Iraq. This new pattern of threat perception at a geopolitical level was not explicitly responsive to market pressures, but was consistent with the interests of economic globalization in regional stability, in deterring proliferation, and in opposing all types of radical nationalism, especially in the Middle East.

This appropriation of geopolitical capabilities to uphold economic interests is not new, nor should the unwillingness of ascendant states to act effectively to address humanitarian concerns be an occasion for surprise in light of international history. The calls for a more activist United Nations, taking on the burdens of "humanitarian intervention," is expressive of a certain compromise between normative responsiveness and geopolitical indifference, and will be discussed in the next chapter, which is devoted to governance. What can be observed at this point is the exceedingly limited willingness of leading states to take substantial risks or to commit resources on behalf of humanitarian ends, even in extreme cases of dire emergency or genocide. The response to genocidal challenges in both Bosnia and Rwanda reveals a reluctance to intervene even in such extreme settings, especially where strategic interests are perceived as marginal and inconsistent, and market concerns are virtually non-existent. The rivalry among European powers for influence in the Balkans also helps to explain the difficulty of achieving the kind of unified response there that might have exerted influence or even produced a solution at an early stage.

Only in delayed reaction to mobilized pressure from below, as occurred in late 1991, did the US government finally agree, with UN backing, to establish protective zones for the Kurds and Shi'as in Iraq. Similarly in late 1992, after heavy television coverage of the extent of human tragedy in Somalia, it agreed to mount a restricted intervention there to ensure that relief supplies could get through. Both of these instances suggest the partial receptivity of the global communications network to democratizing pressures in relation to humanitarian issues, but because market forces tend to be indifferent, the degree of response is likely to be half-hearted and belated, and generally not sufficient to rescue the victims or alter the basic relation of forces. The ordeals of Bosnia are tragically illustrative of this ambivalence, played out by counterproductive gestures such as the imposition of sanctions that have as their major effect the weakening of Serbian democratic (anti-Milosevic) social forces and the imposition of an arms embargo on Bosnia that accentuated the Serbian military advantage during the period of hostilities.[6] What is new is the globalized character of these challenges, the sense of impotence that now exists with respect to UN capacities and the degree of geopolitical indifference as to outcome.

The case of the Bank of Credit and Commerce International, which was also crushed in 1991, is a less obvious expression of geopolitics in the service of global economic forces than was the encounter with Saddam's Iraq, but no less significant. The breadth and depth of the banking scandal disclosed the extent to which transnational banking operations take place in a regulatory vacuum. One way to interpret the statist response, when it did come, was as an effort by G-7 forces to regain minimum control over banking to avoid a populist backlash that could reach far beyond BCCI and stimulate a long overdue challenge to the secretive, illicit, and exploitative character of "respectable" global banking. Several journalistic accounts of the downfall of BCCI make it clear that its operations resembled prevalent global banking practices more than they departed from them (for instance, heavy traffic in money laundering, reliance on secret accounts to hide dubious wealth and activities, and manipulative record-keeping and organizational structures to minimize regulation).[7]

What made BCCI different from powerful Western-owned international banks was the crudity of its operations and the high degree of internal fraud (that is, stealing from management and misappropriating deposits), but it also differed in its Islamic leadership and, ironically, its normative orientation. The bank was the only global bank with roots in and affinities to the Third World, and some of its practices exhibited what has been described in the media as its "visionary" character, such as loans to Asian small businesses in Britain and elsewhere which were unable to obtain credit elsewhere.[8] One wonders whether the resort to regulatory overkill in the United States and the United Kingdom was not designed, at least in part, to reassert Northern dominance of global banking – in effect, an approach analogous to nonproliferation claims in the setting of nuclear weapons.[9] It is acceptable for the North to retain and threaten the use of nuclear weaponry, but weapons of mass destruction should be forbidden to the extent possible in the South, even if military intervention must be threatened or even carried out. It is the same with global banking. Its dubious practices are acceptable if their control is vested in the North, but not if in the South, and certainly not in an undertaking dominated by Islamic capital.

What is implied here is complex, and not without ambiguity at the level of policy. At the very least, the BCCI case suggests a framework of financial institutions and operations that generally escapes statist control, and altogether eludes democratic accountability, often at great human cost. Extending democracy transnationally as part of the agenda of global civil society requires that far greater attention is devoted to the relevance of economic globalization and to the behavior of market forces. Unlike environmental and human rights concerns, these financial dimensions of policy remain at or beyond the margins of political consciousness of those dedicated to "a 'real' new world order," that is, a just world order based on equity, sustainability, nonviolence, and the realization of social and economic as well as political and civil rights.

The emergence of global civil society has so far been an uneven and uncertain process, and it has not been impressively relevant within the wider domain of globalization from above. In this regard, the existence of transnational social forces dedicated to environmental protection and human rights exhibits stronger lines of activity and influence, both challenging and empowering statist forces, creating a positive model. Underneath the analysis of globalization is the conviction that normative content can be introduced into global market operations only through the self-conscious and dedicated efforts of those social forces that have been associated in this report with globalization from below. Such a political process may be taking shape as a byproduct of transnational and grassroots resistance to NAFTA and other globalizing initiatives.[10]

Reviving and Extending the Normative Project: Humane Governance as a Legal Right

As suggested, the 1980s repudiated most major efforts of a global character to promote economic justice; the market-oriented view prevailed. Globalization had the further effect of reducing the political space for welfare/well-being policies in most state/society relations.[11] Stress is placed, instead, on increasing "competitiveness," that is, the capacity to penetrate the global market and to maintain internal market shares. Operationally, competitiveness assesses economic performance mainly by efficiency and stability criteria, and is preoccupied with market shares. Despite the great diversity of business conditions, such an orientation has further harmful human effects due to the increasing mobility of capital and financial capabilities, accompanied by the declining value-added provided by labor, and by the shift of emphasis in many countries to economic activities in which labor has been unable to organize effectively, alongside a cumulative decline in the leverage exerted by organized labor. Still, such a decline may not be permanent. New signs of labor strife are emerging in such countries as Indonesia, South Korea, and the Philippines, where recent spurts of economic growth owe a great deal to extremely low wage and salary scales, and labor discontent in the North is exerting some upward pressure on labor conditions in the South.

These emerging economic patterns register gains and losses for different geographic locales and for various sectors of economic activity. Distinctions between North and South are no longer sufficient to identify beneficiaries and victims. Homelessness and high levels of urban youth unemployment (especially, among minority and foreign youth) in the United States and Europe are suggestive of large pockets of poverty and human distress in rich countries. Spectacular rates of growth in the economic growth zones of southern China and Indonesia are illustrative of prosperity achieved in a setting previously treated as doomed forever to mass poverty. Aggregate figures of economic performance tend to hide regional, class, gender, and ethnic disparities in human circumstances, and to obscure the locus of acute suffering that afflicts those most vulnerable. Statistical averages, unless disaggregated, do not inform us about these specific circumstances, and suppress evidence of adversity. In contrast, a defining characteristic of compassionate geopolitics is to link economic policies and performance with the specificities of actual human circumstances, to regard the reduction of poverty and social distress through the provision of meaningful work as more indicative of economic progress than high rates of growth, positive information about average income, and rising share prices on stock exchanges.

A rights approach to human betterment is partially at odds with a market approach. The logic of the market is essentially deferential to money as an indicator of value and worth, and it is trustful of growth, productivity, and efficiency as providing the best material foundations of progress, expressed by Adam Smith through the metaphor of "the invisible hand." In contrast, the logic of rights (and duties) invokes substantive standards to assess the degree to which individuals and groups are protected against various forms of abuse, and are provided with opportunities to live lives of dignity. The extension of the rights approach to the domain of economic policy is a great achievement of the last half-century. It is mainly attributable to the influence of welfare thinking, but was given political potency at the global level by the socialist bloc under Soviet leadership, and was further reinforced by the nonaligned movement. While this statist emphasis was hypocritical, often grotesquely so, given internal patterns of discrimination and poverty in "socialist" countries, it nevertheless unintentionally validated demands for the fulfillment of minimum economic expectations.

A more impressive implementation of economic and social rights over the next decade will depend on a much stronger political process, both at the grassroots and transnationally. In achieving it, it would be important to engage the transnational social forces that constitute global civil society, especially since leading industrial governments and even human rights nongovernmental organizations have never treated economic and social rights as either capable of implementation or as nearly as important as political and civil rights. In effect, even the transnational effort on behalf of human rights needs to become more responsive to the circumstances of the economically abused in the years ahead.[12]

It should be recalled that the impressive implementation of civil and political rights was not anticipated when the foundational document, the Universal Declaration of Human Rights, was adopted by General Assembly vote in 1948. Governments subscribed formally to the rather far-reaching normative commitments embodied in the Universal Declaration but their intentions at the outset were not serious in the sense of undertaking to adapt their behavior to the requirements set forth. The Communist states, in particular, were cynical enthusiasts, presupposing that their strong insistence on territorial sovereignty would ensure the absence of real pressure to comply, and to the extent that such pressure was mounted it could be easily dismissed as capitalist, Western propaganda. The West had a somewhat analogous attitude, relying on the positivist idea that the Universal Declaration was not a binding document of a treaty sort, that liberal democracies conformed to human rights standards in any event, and that to the extent that other sorts of demands were mounted in the name of social or racial justice, these could be dealt with in terms of sovereignty or by claiming that the alleged grievances were mere expressions of alien ideologies or of hostile propaganda.

What was unexpected in 1948 was the potency of an evolving network of transnational human rights organizations able to use information about violations of human rights standards as a source of influence, and building public support for compliance. In addition, some governments, most notably the US government in the early years of the Carter Presidency, associated its foreign policy with the promotion of human rights. These developments, in turn, encouraged opposition groups in authoritarian settings to invoke human rights commitments as a way of putting repressive governments on the defensive, especially those governments which had formally obligated themselves to uphold human rights standards. The culmination of this dynamic was evident in the late 1980s in East Europe, reinforced by the process included in the Helsinki Accords of 1975 to monitor compliance with human rights commitments. In effect, the violation of international standards eroded the legitimacy of entrenched governments and stiffened the will of domestic oppositional forces, leading several elites in Eastern Europe to abandon power rather than resort to large-scale repressive violence that would have had to have been directed at the entire population. Another reinforcing factor was provided by the reversal of Soviet attitudes during the period of Gorbachev's leadership, making the governments of East Europe realize that their repressive policies no longer had the backing of Moscow. It is revealing that it was in Romania, a Communist country with a measure of independence from the Soviet Union during the Cold War, that the Communist leadership exhibited a will to power that manifested itself in violence against its own citizenry when it was challenged. China was another instance, certainly more independent than Romania, a country neither tied to the Soviet Union, nor part of the Helsinki process; China was governed by an elite not seriously inhibited by external pressures and operating in a region where authoritarian rule was not being seriously challenged even in such non-Communist countries as Indonesia and Singapore.

The relevance of this experience is twofold. First of all, standard setting by governments can provide an influential normative framework, but its existence may not bring about change by itself unless it is sufficiently reinforced by a suitable political process; in the case of human rights, these pressures were largely generated by voluntary associations of citizens in conjunction with domestic oppositional forces and some international support. Secondly, the implementation of human rights may not be possible where the resolve and unscrupulousness of the leadership in a given state manage to stifle dissent and muffle outside criticism, or where geopolitical factors insulate repressive states from strong pressures (for instance, the oilproducing, Western-oriented states in the Gulf). Asian countries provide the clearest illustration of this pattern; repressiveness is overlooked in deference to economic opportunities.

Still, the formal acknowledgment of economic and social rights is impressive, being already an integral dimension of the Universal Declaration. In addition to the articles of the Declaration affirming equality of all persons and the right to be protected against any form of discrimination and abuse, there are a series of provisions of this seminal 1948 document that bear explicitly on economic and social well-being, although the sexism embodied in the formal language dates the document as preceding the raising of consciousness on matters of gender equality. Article 22 affirms that every person enjoys "the right to social security and is entitled to realization, through national effort and international co-operation, and in accordance with the organization and resources of each State, of the economic, social and cultural rights indispensable for his dignity and the free development of his personality." Articles 23 and 24 establish work as a right, including "protection against unemployment," and mandate labor organizing as a legal right, as well as decreeing equal pay for equal work, sufficient compensation to enable a life of dignity for the person and the family, and levels of rest and leisure that include periodic paid holidays. Article 25 (1) is remarkably far-reaching, establishing the normative basis for an inclusive approach to economic well-being: "Everyone has the right to a standard of living adequate for the health and well-being of himself and his family, including food, clothing, housing and medical care and necessary social services, and the right of security in the event of unemployment, sickness, disability, widowhood, old age or other lack of livelihood in circumstances beyond his control." Education as a right is also confirmed in broad terms. The whole array of expectations is endorsed by a radical normative promise in Article 28: "Everyone is entitled to a social and international order in which the rights and freedoms set forth in this Declaration can be fully realized."

The normative promise of Article 28 is, to a substantial degree, a commitment to establish a just world order premised on humane governance, and can be viewed as the legal enactment of a utopian program, especially by reference to existing circumstances confronting most peoples. To make Article 28 into a political project of global civil society would seem to be an irresistible undertaking if economic well-being is to be promoted in the years ahead. A central feature of Article 28 is to acknowledge the relevance of the global setting to the capacity to realize economic and social rights, and to suggest that accommodation requires more than compliance by states or assistance efforts by rich sectors of international society – it may well imply restructuring of the political order in all of its dimensions if that is what is necessary.

The elaboration of normative standards has proceeded steadily since 1948, and only a few highlights can be noted here. A major step was the drafting and negotiation of the International Covenant on Economic, Social and Cultural Rights, completed in 1966, and entered into force as a treaty in 1976. A number of important countries have yet to ratify this Covenant, including the United States; in the past decade the US government in particular has attempted to denigrate economic and social rights as an inappropriate focus for the human rights community, although this attitude has weakened during the Clinton Presidency, and the US supported economic and social rights at the UN Conference of 1993 in Vienna. The Covenant specifies in greater detail the economic and social rights previously posited in the Universal Declaration, and does so as a matter of legal obligation.

A significant addition, given especial salience by being the subject of Article 1 in both Covenants, is the endorsement of the right of self-determination as belonging to all peoples; "By virtue of that right," the peoples of the world shall "freely determine their political status and freely pursue their economic, social and cultural development." The second Covenant also confirms and elaborates upon the economic and social rights conferred by the Universal Declaration, including in Article 11(1) the right of everyone to "an adequate standard of living for himself and his family," and in Article 11(2) "the right of everyone to be free from hunger." Article 16 calls for reports on steps taken and "progress achieved", ECOSOC (Economic and Social Council) is given a role in making recommendations to the General Assembly with respect to implementation, but in actuality, little effort has been made to regard the legal obligation to respect economic and social rights as enforceable, even to the extent of gathering information and identifying noncompliant behavior of parties. At most, some standards have been embodied in domestic legal systems, enjoy some status as "law," but have not been pushed hard transnationally from below, and so have remained behaviorally inert on a global level. The US has challenged even this soft law status during the 1980s, following on its own failure to ratify this Covenant. However, since the Universal Declaration has come to be regarded as binding customary international law, it is arguable that the US government is already bound to uphold the economic and social rights, in the sense of basic human needs, of its citizenry, an obligation that takes on added weight given the level of affluence and waste in the US lifestyle and the wildly skewed pattern of income distribution.

Many other normative standards pertaining to economic and social rights have been formulated and formalized in recent decades, including rights specifically designed to ensure equality to women, protection to children, and some measure of protection to stateless persons and refugees.[13] Also relevant have been the efforts through regional instruments to impose duties with respect to economic and social well-being.[14]

Accelerated efforts are also being made, after decades of neglect, to protect the distinctive economic and social circumstances pertaining to indigenous peoples.[15]

Perhaps, the culmination of standard-setting initiatives within the UN setting has been the Declaration on the Right of Development adopted in 1986 by the General Assembly. The Declaration sets forth a human-oriented conception of development as distinct from a commodity-oriented or money-oriented conception. Article 1(1) expresses this outlook: "The right of development is an inalienable human right by virtue of which every human person and all peoples are entitled to participate in, contribute to, and enjoy economic, social, cultural and political development, in which all human rights and fundamental freedoms can be fully realized." Article 1(2) incorporates the right of self-determination into the right of development, including the assurance that all peoples enjoy "their inalienable right to full sovereignty over all their natural wealth and resources." This perspective is specified in the Declaration, including Article 3(1) that asserts that "States have the primary responsibility for the creation of national and international conditions favourable to the realization of the right of development." The right to development is established as dependent upon observance of other human rights, including political rights, thereby invalidating claims that development priorities of poorer countries might justify an authoritarian and abusive neglect of other kinds of rights. Yet, as has been already noted, authoritarian structures and practices will be shielded from global pressure if economic expediency or geopolitical logic so dictates.

So far, the transnationalization of human rights has been successfully achieved only (and even then only partially and fitfully) in relation to civil and political rights, that is, the "first generation" of human rights. Economic and social rights, often called second-generation rights, have not fared nearly so well, despite being affirmed in formal and far-reaching respects in the Universal Declaration and in the 1966 Covenant on Social, Economic, and Cultural Rights, as well as in several regional instruments. And as for third-generation human rights, those of a collective character, most notably the right of development, these have generally been viewed as a purely aspirational statement of rhetorical value, not to be regarded in any serious sense as part of the rule of law in international political life. Why not? The political will to implement these standards is not yet manifest within global civil society, and even less so, at the level of states or international institutions. The most successful of the transnational human rights groups, Amnesty International and the various human rights watch groups, focus virtually all of their attention on gross violations of political and civil rights, abuses of the human person by means of direct state action.

How can one get economic and social rights taken seriously? A beginning is to assess the abridgment of these rights, and the degree to which market and state forces are jointly and severally responsible for the damage done to peoples by way of a failure to provide food, health care, education, shelter, work for their citizenry, and whatever additional ingredients of human dignity possess cultural resonance. Several preliminary efforts in this direction can be noted: some monitoring groups exist that focus on the economic dimensions of a just world order, as do undertakings to document the human consequences of current practices. These undertakings include newsletters, counter-conferences at important gatherings organized by statist and market forces, transnational "tribunals' composed of prominent citizens which issue "judgments" pertaining to the failures of world economic policy; these include sharp critiques of the IMF/World Bank approach to development and the priorities that control the agenda of the annual economic summit meetings of the G-7, (which, since 1994, with the addition of Russia, has become the G-8). Yet the overall impact of such initiatives remains trivial as compared to what has been achieved by globalization from below in the setting of political and civil rights and environmental policy.

There are at least two important deficiencies in a rights approach to economic well-being. First of all, a failure of mobilization of wider public concern both at the grassroots level and in relation to the part of the media which is receptive to material on avoidable human suffering and on explanations of why the current world economy has not directed more attention to overcoming poverty and other forms of economically grounded distress. Secondly, a failure of explanation, because economic policy issues are not linked convincingly to such matters as population growth, military spending, and environmental harm and because guidelines are not offered and an orientation not given for an alternative to comprador capitalism on a global scale. The absence of a theoretically plausible alternative is particularly serious since it makes the critique of existing economic arrangements and practices seem shrill and irrelevant, helping to explain the failures of mobilization and influence. This difficulty has, quite obviously, grown in magnitude given the complete failure of state socialism to uphold the economic and social rights of their own peoples despite resting their legitimacy and ideological superiority upon such a commitment. There has been a discreet abandonment of a socialist economic approach by remaining socialist governments, most prominently by China, but also by Vietnam and

North Korea, and even to an extent by Cuba. In Nicaragua the electoral repudiation of the Sandinistas in 1990, although a consequence of several factors, has also been generally interpreted as one more indication that socialism works worse with respect to meeting the material needs of people than does capitalism. Finally, the move to regionalize trade and monetary arrangements in the North is a further expression of the view that welfare arrangements are less important than trade expansion and international competitiveness, overall an indication of the ascendancy of a view of the future being shaped by globalization from above. To challenge this ascendancy is partly a cognitive task of setting forth a program that is likely to work and partly one of political education and mobilization. The normative landscape is currently far more supportive of economic and social rights than is the political and cognitive climate.[16] Changing the political and cognitive climate presents a major, indispensable challenge to those social forces associated with globalization from below, and its commitment to humane governance.

Reallocating Resources without a Cognitive Breakthrough

Much can be achieved by reallocations of priorities, essentially reversing what political systems do when confronted by a rising threat to their security. Such reallocations to improve the social quality of life and the realization of economic rights are possible on the basis of political will alone, and do not presuppose "a new socialism" or even a recommitment to welfare capitalism. The formation of such a political will would require grassroots and transnational challenges directed at overcoming the current mood of indulging *cruel* capitalism. Throughout its history, and with many variations through time and space, and in response to a stream of technological innovations, capitalism has oscillated between "a cruel" and "a compassionate" pole along a rather wide spectrum. The most plausible short-term goal of advocates of humane governance is to draw capitalism back toward its compassionate pole, thereby neutralizing the drift of globalization from above toward the cruel pole.

Closely linked to the affirmation of economic and social rights is the issue of financial feasibility. Lurking close to the political consciousness of the sceptical mainstream is the assumption that the resources needed to address the social agenda of world poverty would drag down the living standards of affluent sectors of the world economy.[17] Several significant efforts have been made to demonstrate that the scale of resource commitments needed to address the various dimensions of world poverty is well within reach without threatening either the lifestyle of the rich or the prevalence of market-driven economic policy.

The World Game Institute in Philadelphia has calculated that a rededication of 25 percent of 1991 military expenditures would have the capacity within a decade to meet the challenge of economic and social rights, *and* pay for the costs of a global environmental clean-up.[18]

UNICEF in its 1992 annual report on *The State of the World's Children* put forward a program in the form of ten propositions. Proposition 7 read as follows:

That a process of demilitarization should begin in the developing world and that, in step with that process, falling military expenditures in the industrialized nations should be linked to significant increases in international aid for development and for the resolution of common global problems.

This target is reinforced by the following statement:

The amount now spent on the world's military exceeds the combined annual incomes of the poorest half of humanity. The goals of the World Summit for Children – including drastic reductions in malnutrition and disease and a basic education for all children – could be met by reallocating 10 percent of military expenditure in the developing world and 1 percent in the industrialized world.[19]

In *The State of the World's Children* for 1993, UNICEF estimates that for an extra $25 billion per year spent over the course of a decade "it should be possible to bring to an end the age-old evils of child malnutrition, preventable disease, and widespread illiteracy."[20] This figure of $25 billion is compared to other expenditures being made in the public and private sectors:

. . . it is considerably less than the amount the Japanese government has allocated this year to the building of a new highway from Tokyo to Kobe; it is two or three times as much as the cost of the tunnel soon to be opened between the United Kingdom and France; it is less than the cost of the Ataturk Dam complex now being constructed in eastern Turkey; it is a little more than Hong Kong proposes to spend on a new airport; it is about the same as the support package that the Group of Seven has agreed on in 1992 for Russia alone; and it is significantly less than Europeans will spend this year for wine or Americans on beer.[21]

This UNICEF report goes on to argue that, at present, less than 10 percent of the budgets of governments in the South is devoted to meeting the basic needs of their peoples, and further, that less than 10 percent of the $40 billion given annually in bilateral aid is directed toward meeting human needs; in the language of the report, "this means the amount given for nutrition, primary health care, water and sanitation, primary education, and family planning, comes to about $4 billion a year."[22]

There are three obvious ways to generate sufficient additional resources to address these problems: from a peace dividend, from a major write-down of indebtedness, and from a world tax on energy consumption or transnational financial transactions in a context of attention to family planning, both to safeguard the benefical effects of positive economic performance and to alleviate burdens and pressures on the state. Several of these measures are discussed with some precision in the UNDP *Human Development Report 1992*. Considerable money can be raised and dedicated to meeting human needs simply by reducing military expenditure, and this should be a generally easy political undertaking, despite some hardships at a community level, given the small prospects of strategic warfare in the decade ahead. The *Human Development Report* formulates the following proposal: "All countries, industrial and developing, should commit themselves to reducing military expenditures during the 1990s by at least 3 percent a year. This would yield by the year 2000 a total peace dividend of around $1.5 trillion – $1.2 trillion in the industrial countries and $279 billion in the developing countries."[23] Because of special interest groups, reallocations are never truly "easy," but require leadership from above and pressure from below. Bureaucratic resistance to transfers from military to social goals is especially stubborn given the entrenchment of these interests and the dependence on such activities of portions of the workforce and of particular communities.

On debt, the South currently transfers annually more than $50 billion in net capital assets to banks and international financial institutions in the North; reducing this amount by 50 percent would seem both politically feasible and in the interest of world trade expansion, thereby relieving pressures on the indebted countries, and allowing their governments to expand the social content of their annual budgets.

Energy consumption taxes have generally been associated with environmental clean-up especially in the global commons, and are discussed in this context in the *Human Development Report*, but the financing potential of such a taxing authority could just as easily be directed in part to the elimination of poverty. The report sets forth the following as an example of what it calls "various promising ideas" on funding: "A consumption tax of a dollar per barrel of oil, collected at source, would yield around $24 billion a year (73 percent from industrial nations). An equivalent tax on coal would yield $16 billion a year."[24] Additional funds could be obtained from a comparable tax imposed on nuclear energy. Even larger amounts could be raised by placing a tiny transaction tax on transnational currency flows.

Aside from matters of political will, or possibly as an expression of its absence, doubts exist about whether the problem of avoidable suffering is fundamentally one of monetary resources. Bureaucratic ineptitude and structural obstacles seem to make the task of translating budgetary commitments into behavioral results difficult. UNICEF argues differently, contending that tangible results have been and can be achieved in proportion (roughly) to increases in financial commitment, especially if official policies are monitored and reinforced by vigilant individuals and groups in global civil society.[25] This sense of dependence by international humanitarian efforts on collaboration with positive social forces in civil society is definitely a new and hopeful motif in the 1990s, an indication that globalization from below is being acknowledged as a real force in international political life. The 1993 UNICEF report illustrates this collaborative perspective by reference to Bangladesh's success in "lifting its level of immunization from 2 percent in 1985 to 62 percent in 1990" despite being one of the poorest and most crowded countries in the world. The implication of the report is that if Bangladesh can make such dramatic progress, any country could do at least as much if properly motivated and mobilized. The process that made for success in Bangladesh is described in the following terms: "Never in the country's history," wrote a UNICEF officer in Dhaka, "had so many groups come together for a single social programme: the President, eight social sector ministers, parliamentarians, senior civil servants, journalists, TV and radio, hundreds of nongovernmental organizations, social and youth clubs, religious leaders, film and sports stars and local business leaders all worked successfully towards a common goal."[26]

UNICEF points to tangible achievements arising from inducing governments to make normative promises, first of all in the Convention on the Rights of the Child, which came into force in 1989 when it achieved the necessary 20 ratifications (by now, in record time, more than 120 countries have ratified), and secondly, through the influence of the goals set at the 1990 World Summit for Children attended by more than a hundred heads of state. UNICEF also points to its specific successes, as with the immunization of children against preventable disease; acknowledging that the convention and the goals of the summit are largely "promises on paper," the 1993 report insists that when "in the mid-1980s, over 100 of the world's political leaders accepted the goal of 80 percent immunization by 1990, that, too, was just a promise on paper. Today, it is a reality in the lives of tens of millions of families around the world."[27]

There are some other factors that seem helpful for efforts to revive the normative agenda through the commitment of additional resources. With the end of the cold war, the military establishments in leading countries, including the United States, are busy redefining security to encompass the humanitarian agenda; unlike Bosnia, where the US military leadership saw itself on the brink of a Vietnam-like quagmire, the *initial* limited relief of 1991 operation of ensuring the delivery of food to hungry people in Somalia seemed when first undertaken like a mission that could be successfully completed within a given time frame without incurring great losses.[28]

Much also depends on the perceptions of the public, and hence on the media presentation of successes and failures. If Cambodia eventually succeeds in establishing a constitutional democracy and El Salvador somehow restores reasonable stable governance, humanitarian action will again be seen as positive for both normative reasons (ending suffering) and strategic concerns (confining conflict, ending refugee flows). Public opinion is being shaped during the mid-1990s as to whether transnational humanitarian operations are essentially futile and a waste of money, or whether they are a sound investment in a more stable and equitable future.

But the obstacles should not be underestimated. There will be major failures, as in Bosnia, because leading states disagree on the proper response, because the most serious challenges require an interventionary response that may fail even if the political will and resources are available, and because public leaders or leaders of opinion cannot be sufficiently motivated in the absence of perceived strategic interests. These setbacks will be magnified by what *The Economist* has described as "compassion fatigue," a tendency, especially among cynics, conservatives, and the affluent, to feel overwhelmed and to dismiss appeals for help as sanctimonious and ineffectual gestures.

In the background, of course, is the still entrenched realist mindset and its current preoccupations with "competitiveness" as the key to success in the intense struggle for global market shares in the 1990s. Without a major shift in perception, such an outlook regards humanitarian concerns as a burden on market forces that will induce adverse economic consequences. Such a view is reinforced by a prevalent, if unfair, dismissal of welfare approaches to human betterment as breeders of inefficiency and builders of cumbersome bureaucracy.

How this debate will be resolved is uncertain, and may well depend on the degree to which civil society is mobilized, and for what ends. The Maastricht and NAFTA struggles to win public approval show that economic policy is becoming a matter of high politics, that citizens are recognizing that the globalization of capital can pose threats to their territorial standards of living even in affluent countries. Whether this defensive reflex will prevail over the effort at the further integration of capital is uncertain, but one possible outcome could be a kind of compromise in which integration is supported politically, but only if accompanied by suitable normative commitments of a supranational character.[29]

Much will also depend on the perceived feedback by various constituencies as to the impact of NAFTA, Maastricht, and GATT. If the experience of opposed constituencies is positive, then the drive toward regionalization and globalization is almost certain to accelerate. If negative, then resistance is likely to mount and the tensions between territoriality and globalization will grow more severe.

Finally, leadership will play a role. The emergence of a charismatic personality in civil society or as the head of an important state could ignite the popular imagination, giving the normative agenda a salience that it requires if it is to assert humanitarian priorities in the face of realist and economistic sources of resistance. Particular leaders in specific circumstances can shape the destiny of their peoples for better and worse. Imagine Indonesia without Sukarno (from 1949 to 1965) and Suharto subsequently. The postindependence giants forced by the surge of Afro-Asian nationalism confirm the significance of the leader: Nkrumah, Nehru, Nasser, Lee Kuan Yew, Zhou En Lai, Ho Chi Minh. In retrospect, their ideological affinities matter less than their capabilities to promote the goals of their peoples. There are, as well, dark geniuses who deform the destinies of their peoples: Pol Pot, Mobutu, Stalin, Khomeini. Leadership matters despite structure and shared destiny.

The Demographic Dimension

Improving the material conditions of humanity in a manner that does not deteriorate the environment is closely linked to matters of lifestyle and the control of demographic trends. Some disturbing factors need to be acknowledged: the continuing dynamics of urbanization, especially in the South, increase pressures to disseminate patterns of consumption that are difficult to reconcile with equity to future generations or with the overall commitment to maintain, if not improve, environmental quality. Mere statistics of population growth help us realize the magnitude of the problem and to focus our attention on the South. As cities "advance," the mobility of the population increases – as measured by the speed of locomotion, but not necessarily by the duration of time taken to reach normal work/home destinations. One imagines Shanghai traffic as the clouds of bicyles become motorized, or Saigon (Ho Chi Minh City) as the multitude of scooters and cycles are superseded by cars, or Bangkok, Manila, and Cairo as they increase even further "the benefits" of modernity.

It is generally agreed that more than 90 percent of the expected increase in population over the next decade is taking place in the South (that is, in Asia, Africa, and Latin America), and that the overall population of the South has increased from 1.7 billion people in 1950 to about 4.2 billion in 1991, and is expected to increase to almost 5 billion by the year 2000. Each year 92 million additional people are being added to the global population – something of the order of 10 cities the size of New York or London – an absolute increase that is greater than ever before in history, although the overall rate of world growth has fallen from its high of 2.1 in the 1960s to about 1.7 in recent years.

There is a reluctance to acknowledge the seriousness of demographic patterns and pressures at a global level because of religious and cultural sensitivities to issues such as birth control; this makes it more difficult to fashion appropriate policy responses. At most, the reports of international institutions are acknowledging the problem, but in muted and marginal forms, although the UN Conference on Population and Development held in Cairo (1994) did usefully focus demographic policy on improving the overall circumstances of women, especially young girls. In a summary of action to be taken in conjunction with the implementation of Agenda 21 as adopted in 1993 at the Rio Summit on Environment and Development one finds the following language:

> Rapidly increasing demands for natural resources, employment, education and social services will make it difficult to protect natural resources and improve living standards . . . All countries will have to improve their capacities to assess the environmental and developmental implications of their population patterns, and to formulate and implement appropriate programmes. These policies should be designed to cope with the inevitable increase in population numbers, while at the same time incorporating measures to bring about demographic transition.[30]

As it is stated in the Brundtland Commission report:

> Present rates of population growth cannot continue. They already compromise many governments' abilities to provide education, health care, and food security for people, much less their abilities to raise living standards . . . Yet the population issue is not solely about numbers . . . threats to the sustainable use of resources come as much from inequalities in people's access to resources and from the ways in which they use them as from the sheer number of people . . . Nor are population growth rates the challenge solely of those nations with high rates of increase. An additional person in an industrial country consumes far more and places far greater pressure on natural resources than an additional person in the Third World. Consumption patterns and preferences are as important as numbers of consumers in the conservation of resources.[31]

In a sophisticated neo-Malthusian argument to the effect that population growth is outstripping the carrying capacity of the earth, Paul Kennedy assesses demographic and lifestyle patterns, offering us this conclusion:

> It is inconceivable that the earth can sustain a population of 10 billion people devouring resources at the rate enjoyed by richer societies today – or even half that rate. Well before total world population reaches that level, irreparable damage to forests, water supplies, and animal and plant species will have occurred, and many environmental thresholds may have been breached.[32]

As Kennedy suggests, "a population explosion on one part of the globe and a technology explosion on the other is not a good recipe for a stable international order."[33]

Corrective actions in both domains are complex in their causal consequences and politically and ethically controversial, so much so that there is a strong disposition on the part of leaders to pretend such problems don't pose immediate policy and behavioral challenges. Normatively, as well, demographic policy remains a contested domain: the Catholic church continues to oppose family planning and various right-to-life groups deny women control over reproductive decisions. But evidence has been mounting that family planning programs achieve positive results in poor countries in rough proportion to the scale of the effort made.

The most humane and generally effective way to stabilize population levels is through economic growth, especially overcoming poverty, but such a path encourages the adoption of industrial consumptive patterns that are environmentally destructive. In terms of goals, it is necessary to encourage both humane restraints in population expansion and the introduction of more environmentally benign technologies, together with the phasing out of environmentally destructive technologies. As has been suggested earlier, market and statist forces can be enlisted in such adjustment efforts, but only if pushed hard by mobilized social forces, that is, from below, operating locally, nationally, transnationally, and with due regard for human rights. The failure to provide effective progressive political leadership in relation to these concerns is likely to strengthen civil pressures to respond coercively at the expense of those most vulnerable.

Indonesia provides an incentive structure by way of education and health care which is free for the first two children but not for additional offspring. Evident in such an approach is both a reliance on the self-interest of the citizen, and an imposition of an unjust punishment. The third or fourth child didn't choose to have "irresponsible" parents! Also, in certain cultural settings, as in parts of rural China, a state policy of one-child or two-child families has led to neglect of weak or sick female babies, and even to female infanticide.

Poverty is linked to rapid population growth as both cause and effect. High rates of population growth correlate with impoverishment, and a demographic transition to lower rates occurs as standards of living rise above subsistence levels. The comparison of Europe and Africa is instructive, as Paul Kennedy suggests; in the 1990s Europe's population is growing at 0.22 percent per year, compared to 3 percent for Africa, that is, Africa is growing 15 times faster than Europe! Or, as he also puts it, "in 1950 Africa's population was half of Europe's, by 1985 it had drawn level (at about 480 million each), and by 2025 it is expected to be three times Europe's (1.58 billion to 518 million)."[34] The strain of rapid population growth places additional pressures on already overburdened governments, inducing a poverty/population cycle that defeats the pursuit of human development goals, as well as testing or exceeding limits on available energy supplies and on fresh water.

Crowding generates tensions and conflict, especially amid massive poverty and a perception of deprivation. One effect is to induce migration, both to escape chaos and violence and in search of a livelihood. The steady growth of peoples internally displaced and of refugees seeking asylum and economic migrants is becoming a serious problem in several regions, including Europe and North America, and is a symptom of wider, deeper societal distress. Chauvinistic backlashes are taking place, along with efforts to deter these flows, especially in the face of high indigenous unemployment and prolonged recession in the richer countries. Germany for more than a decade has been the scene of the most vivid enactment of this drama it has recently abandoned its welcoming approach to asylum in the face of rising rightist attacks on foreigners and a general nationalist mood that is hostile, in general, to the claims of refugees and, especially, of economic migrants at a time when it is experiencing added strains from the costs and traumas of reunification.

Even more expressive are the tactics of Muslim extremists in Egypt and Algeria who are seeking to undermine secular states by directing lethal violence at foreign tourists and investors. It should be acknowledged that these tactics have been adopted, in part, as retaliation for alleged abuses of state power (violence against religious militants and a refusal to honor the electoral victory of the Islamic Salvation Front in Algeria).

The breakdown of governance structures in poor, crowded countries cannot be attributed directly to demographic pressures, but the presence of such pressures certainly seems relevant. Depending on the setting, ethnonationalist and fundamentalist tendencies may offer more immediately persuasive explanations of failed states, but these tendencies are themselves generally manifestations of popular despair induced by the inability of more moderate and modernizing elites to bring about real improvements in human well-being. This inability is underscored, especially in countries enduring chronic high unemployment and poor human development records, by a rapidly expanding population, with the largest increases concentrated among the poorest sections of the population, building up additional demands on the public sector and creating an ever-larger pool of acutely distressed persons with little to lose.

Although human development is the main answer, transnational and international efforts to diminish population growth are helpful, and perhaps indispensable. Education in family planning techniques, especially in poor rural districts, has been effective over time in encouraging smaller families. Providing services for family planning in safe, convenient, pleasant surroundings reinforces informational and educational efforts. Improved health care and nutrition for mothers and children would reduce infant mortality rates, creating less pressure to have large families to ensure the survival of some children. Public responsibility for the care of the aged would also be helpful. Increased allocations of funds for assistance in carrying out programs of population restraint and social security would seem beneficial.[35]

An Emergent Consensus: Sustainable Human Development

The dominant motif of globalization-from-above market logic with minimal attentiveness to adverse human and environmental side-effects is being contested in several distinct arenas. First of all, it is opposed by transnational social forces devoted to debt relief, local grassroots initiatives, as well as by the overall tendency of globalization from below to be a vehicle for human-centered and earth-sensitive values and approaches. Secondly, initiatives are arising from several sectors of the global community, including those arenas within the United Nations system not fully subordinated to the imperatives of geopolitics[36] and encompassing global commissions constituted by the more visionary wing of political establishments.[37]

The main impact of these efforts so far has been to preserve a hopeful and compassionate view of the human condition in the aftermath of the Cold War, with its seemingly uncritical endorsement of pure capitalism and its equally emphatic repudiation of all orientations tainted by Marxist or socialist influence. In effect, the struggle at this point is Hegelian in character, being about the weight of competing ideas. More progressive forces are on the defensive, seeking above all not to lose out in the war of ideas despite the market/media/statist collaboration that is embarked upon a project of inhumane governance for the planet. Such a characterization of the outcome of globalization from above is not meant to be an indictment of evil intent; at most, it is deliberate mindlessness, analogous to driving a car through a crowd of pedestrians at breakneck speeds, and not slowing down despite the many casualties en route. To the extent that these casualties are noticed at all, they are rationalized as a small cost to achieve the benefits of high speed modern travel or as inherent in any effort to reach the necessary destinations of increasing productivity.

The 1980s were notable for the excitement associated with new social movements animated by specific normative objectives and given political influence by transnational citizens' associations. These movements to varying degrees distanced themselves from market and statist forces, although their tactics did not aim at their destruction and nor did they rely on violence as an instrument to exert influence. Most notably, these movements worked transnationally and locally for environmental protection of various sorts and promoted human rights and democracy. Some participating perspectives achieved particular prominence, such as transnational networks created by women and indigenous peoples and giving birth to the image and possibility of global civil society. One side of this activity included the growing engagement of professionals, especially lawyers and doctors, acting in their professional capacities, but dedicated to promoting a more peaceful and equitable world.[38] Although the substantive agendas of these myriad undertakings were often shaped by local and regional challenges, the normative effects were more widespread and diverse, helping to recreate a political climate in which the advocacy of social and economic well-being for everyone on the planet regained a measure of renewed credibility – both critical of market/statist orientations and avoiding the impression of reproducing the slogans and mistakes of the traditional left. One of the exciting contributors to this creative process of political rediscovery in the 1980s was the green movement, especially the German Greens, with their innovative political call: "neither left, nor right, but in front."[39]

The global commissions were helpful to varying degrees in keeping a normative banner waving, reinforcing the conviction that the global community, as such, represented people and their well-being above all else. The Brundtland Commission was especially successful, both in relation to public and elite consciousness, and not only with respect to the need for coordinated action among states to address a series of severe environmental problems. Perhaps the most enduring influence of Brundtland, aside from giving the global process on environment a major boost, was to link environmental protection with human-centered development, a focus conceptualized as "sustainable development."[40] The definition given is indicative of intent, but too vague to offer guidance: "Sustainable development is development that meets the needs of the present without compromising the ability of future generations to meet their own needs."[41]

Such a conceptualization helped build a bridge between North and South, and enlarged the environmental dialogue in a manner that forged a new consensus on normative perspectives at the global level. The big breakthrough by Brundtland was its rejection of a physical or reductionist approach to sustainability, and its adoption of a planetary developmental and equity approach: "The satisfaction of human needs and aspirations is the major objective of development . . . A world in which poverty and inequity are endemic will always be prone to ecological and other crises. Sustainable development requires meeting the basic needs of all and extending to all the opportunity to satisfy their aspirations for a better life."[42] It is significant that the South Commission, under the chair of Julius Nyerere, in its report, *The Challenge to the South*, acknowledges the importance of environmental protection for the overall achievement of development objectives.[43]

The important framework document adopted at the 1992 Earth

Summit carries forward this theme with admirable normative clarity. The entire Rio Declaration "On Environment and Development," as implied by its name, is an expression of this outlook, but principles 1, 3, and 5 are of particular relevance:

Principle 1 – Human beings are at the centre of concerns for sustainable development. They are entitled to a healthy and productive life in harmony with nature.

Principle 3 – The right of development must be fulfilled so as to equitably meet developmental and environmental needs of present and future generations.

Principle 5 – All States and all peoples shall cooperate in the essential task of eradicating poverty as an indispensable requirement for sustainable development, in order to decrease the disparities in standards of living and better meet the needs of the majority of the people of the world.[44]

There are important shifts in the approach to development taken in the South that, while different in nuance from more globally oriented formulations, move in a far less confrontational direction:

In our view, development is a process which enables human beings to realize their potential, build self-confidence, and lead lives of dignity and fulfillment . . . It is a movement away from political, economic, or social oppression. And it is a process of growth, a movement essentially springing from within the society that is developing . . . Development is based on self-reliance and is self-directed."[45]

This formulation both locates primary responsibility for development within existing states, and indicates a resistance to all forms of interventionary instruments that encroach upon sovereign rights. But it also allows for "decentralization" and "privatization," as well as endorsing the view that positive development presupposes democracy on the ground, especially in the form of meaningful participation and governmental accountability to the citizenry.[46]

The acknowledgment of gender issues and perspectives is a further critical step in the process of clarifying the content of sustainable human development. The report of the South Commission is very explicit in its call to take strong corrective measures to enable "the mobilization of women as equal partners in development."[47] Among the policy steps advocated are progress toward providing women with equal pay for equal work and ensuring that women are fully and equitably represented in all organs of decision. Women also bring to the fore certain concerns that are either neglected or misunderstood, including the assertion and effective protection of reproductive rights, the identification of concealed and unpaid labor performed overwhelmingly by women, and the design of new frameworks for compensation and recognition of productive labor which are more sensitive to the distinctive contributions and talents of women. It is also important to include feminist critiques of patriarchy and alternative models of power and authority in all processes of inquiry into how to shape a global polity for the twenty-first century, and this will only happen if feminist women of diverse racial and cultural backgrounds participate prominently in all reform initiatives.

Perhaps the most notable contribution of the United Nations to the rebuilding of a normative consensus on economic well-being is being produced in the form of the annual *Human Development Report* issued by the United Nations Development Programme, combining sophisticated conceptualization and statistical data with policy recommendations that move beyond short-range conventional reformist steps. The orientation rests on the central idea of "human development," defined "as the process of enlarging the range of people's choices – increasing their opportunities for education, health care, income and employment, and covering the full range of human choices from a sound physical environment to economic and political freedoms." It endorses the Brundtland stress on the complementary character of working for the environment and against economic oppression: "Global poverty is one of the greatest threats to the sustainability of the physical environment and to the sustainability of human life."[48]

There is also an attempt to bring the issue of growth constructively into the dialogue on sustainability, but in a manner that privileges the position of the poorer countries – "For these societies, there is simply no choice between economic growth and environmental protection. Growth is not an option – it is an imperative. The issue is not only *how much* economic growth, but *what kind* of growth. The growth models of developing and industrial countries must become models of sustainable human development."[49] *Human Development Report 1993* correctly calls attention to "a new and disturbing phenomenon: *jobless growth.*"[50] In effect, there is economic expansion, but it does not improve employment opportunities, reflecting capital-intensive strategies of growth and corporate restructuring for the sake of greater competitiveness. This series of developments illustrates a tension between growth as conceived in aggregate GNP terms and as human development.

Institutional innovation may be needed if sustainable human development is to influence policy and behavioral patterns as well as the ideological discourse. *Human Development Report 1993* suggests in this spirit that to "contribute effectively to sustainable human development will probably require some form of Economic or Human Security Council within the UN, where all nations can participate on the basis of geographical representation – with none holding a veto – to provide a new decision-making forum."[51] Such a proposal exhibits, also, a new democratizing ethos extended to the UN system, and acknowledges the crucial role that is being placed by nongovernmental organizations and initiatives rooted in civil society.[52] As stressed earlier, enhancing the role of women in specifying the priorities and techniques of human development is of utmost relevance to ensure the normative success of such proposals.

Under the auspices of what the report labels as "international civil society," itself a meaningful indication of the political roles being played by transnational social forces, *Human Development Report 1992* proposes that serious consideration be given to what it calls "a new global compact." Note that the terminology of compact is different from "contract" or "covenant," with its implications of a legal document. The driving idea here is that the end of the Cold War establishes a new global situation in which the North and the South could strike a world order bargain that would be mutually beneficial and help the peoples of the world as a whole to realize the goals of sustainable human development. The shape of the bargain is set forth:

> Developing countries might want to see the compact help them achieve at least the following:
>
> *Essential human needs* – to be attained by the year 2000. These should include universal basic education for men and women, primary health care and safe water for all, the elimination of serious malnutrition and at least 80 percent access to family planning.
> *Employment* – to create sufficient job opportunities to absorb the new additions to the labour force and reduce absolute poverty by 50 percent.
> *GNP growth rate* – to be accelerated significantly to implement the foregoing objectives.[53]
>
> Industrial countries might want the compact to cover some of the shared global objectives that are of immediate priority concern to them:
>
> *Drug trafficking and pollution* – to be tackled by close cooperation among all countries in the world.

Immigration pressures – to be relieved through creating more job opportunities within poor nations.
Nuclear threats – to be eliminated as international tensions are defused and countries willingly accept reductions of nuclear weapons, including non-proliferation policies.

Certainly, developing and industrial countries would *jointly* agree that the foregoing goals can be successfully pursued only with firm policy commitments to the following:

Global peace and disarmament – besides strengthening global and regional peace arrangements, military spending to be reduced progressively in both industrial and developing countries.
Development security – to prevent the accumulation of unmanageable debt burdens, whether environmental, financial or social.[54]

The proposed elements of the new global compact need discussion and elaboration, and will certainly require reformulation, but the idea of coherent bases for reform is suggestive of a globalist approach that is centered in human well-being.

It is also important to mention the UN Summit for Social Development scheduled for the fiftieth anniversary year, 1995, representing another battleground in the struggle for the soul of the United Nations. This initiative, being carried forward by the energy and skill of Juan Somavia, Chile's ambassador to the UN, moves in the same direction as the UNDP reports, but adopts and proposes the language of social development, and assigns priority to certain goals: poverty, jobs, and societal cohesion. It is pre-eminently people oriented, and seeks to reinsert normative claims into the development process and to confer renewed and reinvigorated responsibility for their realization on states and international institutions. Again, it is a way to mitigate market-driven globalization without making a direct challenge, striking a compromise that ultimately seeks to reconcile well-being concerns with efficient market operations. Additionally, there is the search for reconciling political language and forms that avoid either suggestions of redistributive obligations in the North or rest their case on a plea for charity in the form of expanded economic assistance from the richer countries.

Sustainable human development is both a precondition for and a critical dimension of what is called "humane governance" in this report. The implementation at state/society and local levels will depend on political struggle, leadership quality, and on cultural style. Thus the universal language is meant to provide a forum for discussion and dissent, but not to imply a blueprint or a single line of solution. At most a spirit of likemindedness is implied relating to such matters as the avoidance of suffering and waste, the affirmation of individual and collective dignity, and the need for a multifaceted search for modes of existence that are satisfying and durable. At the core of humane governance is the conviction that the human experience needs to be spiritually nurtured in many ways if it is to flourish in the millennium to come.[55]

A Concluding Note

Prospects for improving the economic circumstances of the peoples of the world, especially the poorest, will depend largely on self-reliant action, but moves to assess economic performance by reference to criteria of sustainable human development can help guide policy at all levels of social action. Some form of global compact needs to be put into operation as a way to emphasize the mutual and complementary interests of North and South, and thus to inhibit abusive and antagonistic forms of interaction.

Also, economic well-being cannot be adequately promoted without simultaneously extending mechanisms for participation and accountability of peoples, thereby connecting the struggle for human rights and democracy in the political domain with the quest for economic rights in the social domain. Notions of accountability and participation have been more and more successfully asserted in state/society relations in many, but not all regional settings, but there is an increasing need to press parallel claims with respect to international institutions, including in relation to the various parts of the UN system and, even more urgently, in relation to the transnational flows of capital and money through the undertakings of banks, corporations, and speculators.[56]

The post–Cold War setting is weighted against the satisfaction of such claims. Globalization from above, with the collaboration of leading states and the mainstream media, resists any serious inhibition on market dynamics in the name of either equity or sustainability. Hopes for overcoming this resistance depends on the conjoined activity of those transnational social forces that comprise globalization from below with some marginal sectors of the organized international community (for example, UNDP and UNICEF in the UN and the Strasbourg institutions – European Parliament, European Commission of Human Rights, European Court of Human Rights) and with the backing of the more visionary voices drawn from among the global political elite as expressed through the reports of global commissions of eminent persons.

These issues, except as locally manifest, are generally removed from live public concerns. Educational efforts to clarify this encounter are essential at this time, as are mobilizing initiatives such as popular tribunals directed toward exposing the human consequences of IMF/ World Bank policies or of the G-7 role.[57]

7

In Pursuit of Humane Governance: Building Hope in the Coming Era of Geogovernance

Great visionary opportunities for the enhancement of the human condition are contained within the fluidity of circumstances that make this period of history turbulent and fraught with contradiction and surprise. Such opportunities coexist with the most appalling spectacles of human tragedy and mass suffering visually disseminated by television and on the information superhighway, and coupled with dire prophesies of even darker times ahead. As has been argued throughout this report, statist control of the political, economic, and cultural dimensions of globalization is failing to meet the challenge, while the virtually unregulated "management" of globalization by transnational market forces is fraught with failure. The need and opening exists for the rise of transnational democratic initiatives to contend with and complement statist and market forces by making increasingly self-conscious and long-range efforts to achieve humane governance at all levels of social interaction. It is this interplay of opposed tendencies, now contending to shape this post-Cold War phase of history, that lies at the core of the unfolding process that is the drama of this transitional period.

A part of the project of strengthening global civil society is to challenge prevailing managerial and calculative styles of policy justification based on economistic guidelines. Instead, it is sought to reconcile public policy with moral and legal considerations, adopting what has been broadly identified as a "normative" outlook. To be normative is not to ignore obstacles, constraints, and past failures. It is a posture toward choice and decision that seeks to clarify alternatives and their probable effects. To pursue transformative goals associated with governance requires an appropriate political language, as well as an explicit rejection of inappropriate political language. The alleged utopian character of humane governance cannot be allowed to diminish the visionary possibilities that genuinely exist yet lie largely latent, needing to be actualized in the years ahead if the twenty-first century is to become a time of realized hopes. As has been true throughout the experience of WOMP, normative horizons of opportunity, as defined by and for the peoples of the world, are the truest test of political possibility.

A major contention of this report is that historical forces associated with technological capabilities, increasing levels of complexity, interaction, and fragility are inevitably bringing into being some version of geogovernance. The idea of geogovernance is associated with comprehensive control, especially at macrolevels of interaction. Nothing is implied about the quality or structural character of control, except that there is some degree of guidance and regulation of a global scope. It will be some mix of the following elements: market driven (an extension of informal arrangements); state driven (G-7 enhanced); supranational (regionally or globally institutionalized with governmental powers); democratically derived (constitutionally based, with rule of law attributes, and procedures for broad participation and accountability); microcentric (dispersed at the level of local neighborhoods with more or less effectiveness and respect for human rights).

Geogovernance, then, does not as such presuppose central guidance mechanisms oriented around either market dynamics or global institutions. Geogovernance, at least in certain of its aspects relating to security of the person, might come to rest on the authority of clan, village, tribe, or family rather than on some type of governmental control. The emergence of "people's courts" in the federal state of Bihar (in India) is illustrative:

> There was no judge in black robes, no defense attorneys, no rules of evidence, and no right of appeal . . . Instead of turning bandits over to the police, local residents, egged on by members of a violent Communist farmers' group, took matters into their own hands . . . The people's courts are just one example of the collapse of government in this region of Bihar.[1]

Note that governance can exist at any level of social complexity without the existence of a formal bureaucratic mechanism in the shape of a government.

As matters now stand, preponderant efforts are being made by market and statist leadership in the North to shape the collaborative process by which geogovernance emerges. It is important to contest this prospect of control by globalization from above. The possibility of other types of geogovernance capable of achieving a condition of increasingly humane governance is the visionary unity that binds together the diverse adherents of global civil society. Whether focused on local enhancement of life circumstances and political structures or motivated by solidarity with all the peoples of the world, born and unborn, and dedicated to the sustainability of the biosphere of this planet earth, there is a common normative thread linking the concrete to the general. This positive outcome of the dynamics of globalization can only happen, however, if there occurs a massive upsurge in the years ahead of transnational democratic forces animated by loyalties to the species as well as to people's own race, gender, or class.

Diminishing Statist Capacities and the Growing Pains of Global Civil Society

The dominant mode of governance for the world as a whole during the last several centuries has been state-centric (including a variety of colonial arrangments) up to this point, but what will it be in the decades ahead? The modern era has been politically dominated by the territorial state as it evolved in Western Europe. The colonial subjugation of most of the non-Western world represented an effort to substitute imperial rule from without for the territorial authority of indigenous elites. The collapse of colonialism over the course of the last half century has spread the state system to all corners of the globe. States, and only states, acquire sovereign rights in global arenas, including rights of membership in international institutions.[2] States, and only states, confer nationality and the status that allows the legitimate use of the global commons for purposes of travel or communication. States, and only states, have the authority and capabilities to wage war beyond their borders, although peacekeeping operations of the United Nations and regional bodies appear to represent a distinct source of authority. And, of course, violent political movements wage war often with the objective of controlling or creating a state. The ethos of self-determination gives some legitimacy in oppressive circumstances to claims by nonstate actors to rely on the tactics of armed struggle.

Despite these defining circumstances of world order, statist forces are losing control, above all to elusive actors and activities associated with globalization from above and as a consequence of the dynamics of environmental deterioration by way of ozone depletion, climate change, and pollution of the global commons. Globalized television is also having profound deterritorializing impacts, whose effects are still uncertain, and generating experiences of news, music, and the imagery of "the good life" which are increasingly shared. Unwelcome intrusions on territorial domains by way of drugs, illegal immigrants, terrorists, organized crime, and Third World missionaries also reveal the permeability of boundaries and the tenuous quality of the territorial control being maintained even by strong states, that is, states with the military and police capabilities to guard their borders against concerted military encroachment and patrol their streets for the sake of "law and order." Even internally there is a cumulative tendency toward a loss of statist control. The market disperses control and influence, and generally is complemented by gray and black market operations, as well as by organized crime. The extent and depth of corruption and influence peddling, as well as media scrutiny, is sharply curtailing governmental capacity to project authority effectively. Beyond this, faxes and personal computers with modems are empowering individuals and groups within society, thereby reshaping the perception, exercise and locus of power through the rapid, cheap, and reliable exchange of information and plans. Tactics of resistance and opposition are discovering vulnerable pressure points, as in antiforeign terrorist campaigns in Egypt and Algeria, which have the goal of discouraging tourism and investment to the point of triggering a political collapse.

These unwelcome forms of territorial openness are structural, technological, and cognitive in character, indissolubly linked to the welcome forms of openness associated with trade, investment, entertainment, information, and human rights. The reality of the global village is encompassing and bewildering, and as such is subverting the state, as well as endowing it with a global reach. Withdrawal from global and regional participation is possible, but at a great cost economically and culturally, and with the probability of adverse human rights consequences, as in the case of Iran since the time of its Islamic revolution.

The eclipse of the state is also being attributed to the rise and renewed intensity of ethnonationalist and religious identities. Samuel Huntington, generally known in academic circles as a quintessential realist championing state power, has now argued that we are at the early stage of a civilizational sequel to the era of statism: "Westerners tend to think of nation-states as the principal actors in global affairs. They have been that for only a few centuries. The broader reaches of history have been the history of civilizations. It is to this pattern that the world returns."[3] Huntington sees the future being shaped in the crucible of intercivilizational encounter and rivalry, a pattern that he believes will challenge and likely displace the West from its position of ascendancy. In this view, globalization is secondary to civilizationism, or as Huntington argues, "for the relevant future, there will be no universal civilization but instead a world of different civilizations, each of which will have to learn to co-exist with others."[4] The Gulf War can be viewed as the first intercivilizational war of this century, and the victimization of Turkish Muslims in Germany and Bosnian Muslims in the former Yugoslavia are further indications of the centrality of civilizational factors. Nevertheless, civilizational entities, although highly significant, especially to the extent they are reinforced by economic regionalism, seem unlikely to offset the impact of more globalizing phenomena, especially given the intermixing of civilizations as a result of travel, migration, and a worldwide media net. Additionally, civilization-scale analysis misses some forms of turbulence associated with intense ethnonationalist, intracivilizational strife, as on the Indian subcontinent, in the Balkans, and in sub-Saharan Africa.

Another reading of the post-state circumstance identifies and considers crucial two seemingly divergent sets of tendencies: the relentless moves toward economic integration versus a variety of localist backlashes. As David Fromkin expresses it, "the central question in the politics of the twenty-first century everywhere in the world will be the tension between holding together and pulling apart: between the centripetal pull of a modern global economy that requires regional and planetary organization, and the centrifugal push of atavistic tribalisms." Fromkin construes this tension in modernist terms that privileges globalism, writing that it is "a conflict that pits rational interests against irrational feelings," and argues that whatever the outcome "this struggle, rather than a conflict between Great Powers, seems likely to be the overriding issue."[5] The linking of the market and technological innovation to "rationality," and rationality to human betterment, while considering religious and traditionalist rediscoveries as inherently "irrational," and hence destructive, is the basis of a new, emergent credo of Western superiority and hegemony. It is being complemented by the economic success of Asian market-oriented authoritarian states, evident in its most realized form in the prosperous city-state of Singapore. Such an outlook slides easily toward the re-embrace of colonialist pretensions, that is, saving the South or portions of the North from their own destructiveness; protectorates, the implication is, would contain these irrational tendencies precluding transition to the bliss of modernity.[6]

There are other deterritorializing energies, including those motivated by transnational solidarities, whether between women, lawyers, environmentalists, human rights activists, or other varieties of "citizen pilgrims' associated with globalization from below. They are committed more or less consciously to the construction of a compassionate global polity in the decades ahead, having already transferred their loyalties to the invisible political community of their hopes and dreams, one which could exist in future time but is nowhere currently embodied in the life-world of the planet. This dynamic of shifting political identities is fundamental, but also disguised and gradual, without any formal or even psychological ritual of disaffiliation. The citizen pilgrim, by and large, continues to pay taxes and travel on passports issued by a territorial government, but her dreams and projects are elsewhere, part of that journey to the future undertaken without restrictions based on race, class, nationality, age. To the extent that global civil society becomes a reality in the imagination and lives of its adherents, the reality of territorial states will often recede in significance even though it may never entirely disappear. In some settings, states under inspired leadership might engender strong loyalties precisely because the outlook is compassionate and globalized.

These "realities" are ideas or social constructs, not things, and their significance depends on how they influence feelings, beliefs, and actions, even possibly without our full conscious appreciation, as when someone is drawn toward vegetarianism or meditation at a given time. The commitment of activists to support the self-determination drives of various indigenous people seems unconsciously expressive of a wider ethical orientation, which might be described as compassionate globalism, a process and a vision animated by humane governance.

The Weight of Recent History: The Ascendancy of the Weak State

The tradition of geopolitics, with its accompanying realist mindset, has been preoccupied during recent decades with the containment of strong states, that is, states that if not contained might project their military power beyond their own sovereign territory and engage in armed aggression. World War I and World War II were interpreted as resulting from failures to contain an expansive strong state, namely Germany. World War II, in particular, has been interpreted as being encouraged by "appeasement," that is, by the refusal to meet strength with strength in peacetime. Learning "the lesson of Munich," governments seeking to promote stability during the Cold War years applied the Roman maxim "when at peace prepare for war." This approach has been praised by realists, being called "the long peace."[7] The ending of the Cold War, especially in its Eurocentric dimensions, during the Reagan/ Bush Presidencies, which relied upon militarist approaches, has added to a disastrous tendency to believe that the relative scale of military capabilities continues to be the key to global security.

There is a certain historical plausibility to a carefully circumscribed version of containment/deterrence thinking in the setting of rivalries among leading states, especially given a dependence on war-preventive strategies in conflicts between countries possessing nuclear weaponry.[8] But in the aftermath of the Cold War, especially in light of the collapse of the Soviet Union and the weakness of Russia as a state, the main challenges to stability derive from radically different sources. The main crises of the early 1990s, whether in the former Soviet Union, former Yugoslavia, Somalia, Sudan, or Liberia, reflect the new ascendancy of the weak state.[9] The weak state is challenging the governance resources of world order in radically different ways than did the menace posed by the external ambitions of the aggressive strong state.

The weak state offers the world a series of horrifying spectacles of death, destruction, cruelty, devastation, massive suffering. Often the collapse of domestic governance and the scale of political violence uproots a large proportion of the civilian population, leading to millions of people being displaced within their own country and to millions more entering the ranks of the world's refugees. The call for interventionary action for both humanitarian and security reasons is strong, but so is resistance to such calls, as the long ordeal of Bosnia during the early 1990s so well dramatizes. Leading governments are wary, partly with good reason, of becoming involved in large-scale military intervention, and tend to dump as many of the problems of weak states on the United Nations as is politically feasible. Countries in the South are also wary of authorizing interventionary responses for humanitarian goals even if the military operations are carried out with a mandate from the United Nations, partly from a genuine fear of revalidating Western hegemony, this time disguised by its UN auspices. Such opposition may also reflect unworthy motives in shielding abusive state/society relations from scrutiny and censure. Still, there is little evidence that military intervention will succeed in the face of determined territorial resistance, even if directed toward a good end, carried out with positive intentions, and based on appropriate capabilities.

As with strong states, the challenge of weak states can only be successfully met, if at all, through anticipatory activities. But unlike the militarist approach to strong states, only a developmental approach has any hope at all of "deterring" the collapse of weak states. In effect, there exists a strong incentive to prevent the collapse of governance at state and regional levels. This incentive is motivating Western passivity toward the revival of Russian militarism in its "near abroad" and in relation to minority peoples in Russia, as well as large transfers of resources and assistance to Russia and East Europe, but whether money and the acceptance of spheres of influence can prevent the breakdown of governance is doubtful. What is more credible as the basis for response is the longer-range case for an indirect approach to the challenges posed by weak states.[10]

There are two closely related ideas here that are exerting an influence on traditional patterns of governance in a still predominantly statist world. The first is the virtual futility of reactive approaches, including military intervention, once weak state crises have passed certain thresholds of intensity; the failure of governance in relation to Bosnia, Somalia, Rwanda, or earlier, Lebanon and Sudan are illustrative.[11] But the point about failure is broader – the secondary dangers of weak state collapse are also not containable, and are capable of generating disastrous shock waves that have severe effects at a distance: for instance, the connections between the violent implosion of the former Yugoslavia and the increasing numbers of refugees and asylum applicants in Europe, the rise of extreme right politics elsewhere in Europe, and the consequent destabilization of constitutional democracy at a regional level. Weak state collapse or ineptitude often leads to huge refugee flows; it can lead to the distribution of more sophisticated weaponry to terrorist groups, may be linked to the transnational drug trade, and can quickly overwhelm existing relief and humanitarian assistance capabilities.

Another potential series of adverse reverberations could arise from the demise of the multiethnic secular state of Bosnia, and its replacement, after numerous unpunished crimes against humanity, by ethnically cleansed successor mini-states. The precedent of territorial conquest by way of ethnic cleansing that has been created in Bosnia is a dreadful augury of the future, and is linked, as well, to the extremist politics of identity being practiced by the extremist Islamic groups which carry on their struggle against secularism by the deliberate targeting of innocent foreign tourists.[12]

The second broad effect is to help shift governance thinking away from militarist approaches (whether reactive approaches or preventive deterrence), inducing greater receptivity to indirect, long-range, nonviolent, and social reconstructivist approaches and thinking. To the extent that such a trend strengthens, there occurs a reconciliation between the self-interest of the North and the well-being of the South, at least in relation to matters of security, and since security is increasingly associated with avoiding weak state crises there is present a strong nonaltruistic motivation to overcome acute poverty.

The argument here is that the horrifying spectacle of weak state collapse, releasing ethnic passions and hatreds, contains within its whirlwind a contrary set of possibilities that are more hopeful in character: if hegemonic portions of the world economy are threatened, if military intervention is not a prudent or politically viable option, and if reconstructive approaches would be mutually beneficial, then the potential exists, if wisdom takes command, for the emergence of realism with a human face! How to activate this potential is the most immediate challenge. A deeper critique of conventional realist thinking, especially its implicit confidence in the efficacy of military approaches to security threats, would help create the right sort of policy atmosphere, but resistance will not be overcome by reason and argument alone. There are too many entrenched interests and bureaucratic structures committed to the old ways. Yet it is necessary to depict alternative lines of response that seem more promising from a problem-solving and global security perspective. There are elements of such a critique of militarism and the war system already in place, stimulated by the growing appreciation even among realists of the mutual destructiveness of warfare between strategic rivals, and not only, or even mainly, in view of nuclear weaponry.[13]

But realist self-criticism is superficial, constrained by its gloomy view of human nature and its pervasive skepticism about any commitment to alleviate suffering or inequity. The voices of global civil society need also to be heard, grounding hope on their conviction that freedom, democratic forms, and people-to-people initiatives can shape the future, including the extent to which human decency is perceived as expected, even "natural," almost entering into the anthropological definition of the person. One such voice from global civil society is the advocacy of nonviolence and the appreciation of its historical potency in relation to a wide variety of concrete circumstances. Still, progressive circles have been badly split in the post-Cold War period on whether and how to intervene militarily in the face of human disaster. What has yet to emerge on a sufficient scale to challenge militarist perspectives is something of the order of a transnational resistance effort, nonviolent, yet militant.

Seeking a Realist Realignment of Geopolitics after the Cold War: Emerging Shapes of Global Governance

It would be a serious mistake to suppose that political elites, whose members are often culled from the ranks of globalized economic elites, are hostile to the call for global governance. There is a growing elite appreciation that economic integration, the mobility of capital, the scale of technological innovation, areas of political instability, and the menace of certain forms of environmental and societal decay are posing challenges that states cannot handle on their own either by way of conflict (balances of power and hegemony) or through cooperation (regimes facilitating the enactment of reciprocal relations for mutual benefit). Yet the realist political imagination is so constrained by its own past, dominated by preoccupations with war and violence and by skepticism about fundamental change that it has not been able to design and implement schemes for global governance. These constraints are reinforced by the reluctance of national citizenries for emotive and self-interested reasons to endorse globalizing initiatives. The realist push toward global governance is being resisted, partly out of genuine concerns and partly for confused and inappropriate reasons, by territorially oriented democratic social forces.

There are three important settings which disclose realist thinking about global governance, thereby providing an "other" for the kinds of global governance favored by the progressive elements in global civil society. First of all, in relation to regional institutional forms that exist to consolidate markets, move money, protect the environment, defend human rights, and settle security policy, Europe is the main testing ground for this sort of regionalist effort to complement, and to an extent supplant statism. There are also various types of regional initiatives taking shape in Asia, Latin America, North America, and Africa. In the course of the struggle over the approval of the Maastricht Treaty in the early 1990s, it was evident that statist establishments in the main European coutries overwhelmingly supported the treaty as beneficial, despite the loss of sovereign rights, while populist and nationalist counterelites provided the core of opposition. Within each regionalism there was also an encounter about the extent of social content that should be built into the new framework, often centering on whether minimum wage and salary levels should be fixed or safety and environmental standards set.

A second and complementary view is to augment the frameworks associated with the leading industrial democracies, especially the Group of Seven, now expanded to take in Russia, (and which might – with the help of a normative blindfold – admit China as well). Such thinking is usually informed by a positive appreciation of the historic role of "the great powers" in providing for "international stability," a conceptualization antecedent to that of "global governance."[14] The driving idea here is essentially managerial in character, a recognition of the growing need for coordination of policy and behavior on a number of fronts, reinforced by a conviction that more participatory frameworks, even the UN Security Council, would be too cumbersome, not sufficiently likeminded, and not as ready to collaborate with global market forces as junior partners. The preference for G-7, or even G-3 (US, Japan, Germany), as against the UN Security Council also incorporates a judgment about political trends – namely, that within the decade deeper tensions of a nationalist character will place governments at greater odds with one another, possibly not at a war-threatening distance, but in a manner that would hamstring a more broadly representative intergovernmental body.

The arguments advanced in favor of an expanded G-7, which would meet more often and at different levels of authority, taking on a broader agenda, also arouse suspicion and opposition. The G-7 framework is widely perceived in the South as a vehicle for maintaining the hegemony of the North and as a rejection of broader participation by the South and of accountability of market forces to the global community, especially with respect to economic policy. As such, it is often viewed as neocolonial, tied to financial and trade arrangements that are discriminatory toward the South and unresponsive to the grievances and priorities of the South. This exclusion of the South is no longer even consistent with economic potency. The Pacific Basin countries of Asia are rapidly becoming major players in the world economy, growing at a far more rapid rate than European countries, Japan, and the United States. For Canada to have an ensured seat at the annual economic summit, but not India or China or Indonesia, is to disclose how stilted are the criteria for participation.

The G-7 path amounts to a strategy for stabilizing and insulating global apartheid in an era of rapid change. Another related line of criticism involves the nonrepresentative character of G-7 (by reference to geography, gender, race, and sheer numbers) from the perspective of the world, undermining claims of legitimacy as a source of global policy.

The weight of these criticisms has influenced some elements of political elites in the North to favor a focus on global governance in the form of an augmented Security Council, to function as the reconstituted core of the United Nations. Americans of liberal persuasion tend to prefer the UN as the linchpin of global governance, both because of the idealistic trappings and because the relevance of military strength is greater. Because of its origins, economic mandate, and set-up, G-7 is assured of embodying a more multipolar conception of global governance than the Security Council with its emphasis on security issues.

Even though the Security Council has five Permanent Members, each with a veto, it has fashioned a more unilateral conception of leadership in its crucial undertakings, partly out of logistical necessity related to mobilizing peacekeeping and peace enforcement capabilities. In a sense, the Gulf War was a dry run for global governance in this mode being nominally transferred from Washington to New York. It was supported by both political parties in the US, and in the end perhaps more ardently by the Democrats, who championed the UN auspices as heralding the reawakening of the sort of liberal internationalism which had been an ideological casualty of the Vietnam War.

Here the line of criticism is more tangled. Of course, as indicated earlier, progressive forces criticized the Security Council for allowing itself to be appropriated by hegemonic patterns before and during the Gulf War for the sake of US-driven geopolitics, and more broadly for being complicit in maintaining a framework of double standards with respect to implementing international obligations. At the same time, these forces, as agents of global civil society, regard the United Nations as an indispensable, and potentially promising, focal point in their visions of global governance.[15] Hence, the debate on UN reform is more about "substance," matters of representativeness in terms of authority structures, access for democratic social forces, independence in relation to geopolitical pressures, and respect for constitutionalism in mandating peacekeeping action, especially if that action entails forcible intervention in internal affairs in the absence of genuine host country consent.

These three paths to global governance are all being cleared to some degree; none precludes the other, although intra-elite disputes about appropriate emphasis are currently being carried on in the corridors of power. Two of these paths (regionalism, UN) are also being used, but in a different spirit and with differing normative horizons in view, by the agents and agencies of global civil society. As subsequent sections contend, ethical orientation and political will matter more than structural form when it comes to the design and assessment of different models of global governance. The historical prospect of global governance in some form, at some depth, is being widely welcomed and is regarded by globalists of all persuasions, and by many localists and communitarians as well, as a necessary and possibly inevitable alternative to ecological entropy and economic disintegration. The dividing questions concern the orientation, politics, and animating vision that are to shape this build-up of global capabilities. They contrast, on the one side, a collaborative relationship between statist protectors of order in the global marketplace and the most influential transnational financial/commercial operatives, and on the other, the ensemble of green, people-oriented transnational advocates of sustainable human development, the inchoate social forces that together are giving shape and weight to global civil society.

On the Unexpected, and as yet Undemonstrated and Uncertain, but Still Surprising and Notable Efficacy of Nonviolence

Let us first situate this inquiry into the relevance of nonviolence. The emphasis here is upon governance, especially the distinctive challenges being posed by the ascendancy of the weak state, but also the degree to which such valued ends as the protection of human rights, the establishment of constitutional democracy, the elimination of acute poverty and inequity, and the enhancement of cooperative interaction for a variety of widely shared goals can be effectively achieved. The social forces that compose the backbone of global civil society tend to be strong, although not necessarily unconditional, adherents of nonviolence. When the United Nations is mobilized to confront a demonic leader such as Saddam Hussein or Slobodan Milosevic, then opinions divide sharply among progressive activists and intellectuals around questions of the appropriateness and effectiveness of military responses. Nevertheless, much of the energy of globalization from below is directed against violence and militarism, and more fundamentally, refrains from tactics that rely on counterviolence. This is especially evident in relation to the tone and content of the most influential voices of women, of indigenous peoples, of environmental activists. It is also evident in the violent backlash that strikes back at nonviolent militancy, exhibiting the contrast between the violent dispositions of statist and market forces and the nonviolent vulnerability of transnational social forces – the apparent murder of Karen Silkwood by agents of the nuclear power industry, the detonation of bombs placed on the Greenpeace ship *Rainbow Warrior* by French intelligence agents while in port in Auckland, the assassination of Chico Mendez by Brazilian ranchers, the killing of Archbishop Oscar Romero by Salvadorean paramilitary units.

During the 1980s many of the most important, and then encouraging, political changes were brought about through nonviolent initiatives, and not only from below. Mikhail Gorbachev's reorientation of Soviet internal and foreign policy was a remarkable display of nonviolent statist leadership, even if its more far-reaching consequences were not intended. But Gorbachev's "new thinking," if it had been matched or adopted in the West, might have had an extraordinary demilitarizing impact: it might have moved close to the achievement of a world without nuclear weaponry, established in practice policies associated with "comprehensive security" or "common security," and set in motion a powerful demilitarizing dynamic that would have included strengthening the United Nations and enhancing respect for the World Court and the rule of law in international relations. If such a momentum had been reinforced by massive economic assistance, the whole set of problems flowing out of rapid Soviet disintegration might have been mitigated, or at least handled in a less dangerous way, avoiding some of the worst manifestations of the weak state syndrome. If the political imagination of critical leaders in the West had been more sensitive to this extraordinary historical opening, and instead of celebrating "victory" had taken the path toward demilitarization and the establishment of global governance on the basis of an ethos of nonviolence, the crisis of the weak state and the array of backlash experiences might have been avoided, or addressed in a far more constructive fashion.

The Soviet example is especially serious because it involves the break-up of a nuclear superpower, producing spontaneous nuclear proliferation at the strategic level and in a setting in which both severe civil strife and warfare between the units are distinct possibilities; the warfare that has attended the break-up of Yugoslavia is suggestive of the potential magnitude of the post-Soviet danger. There is also the correlative danger of the reactionary backlash in the form of ultra-nationalism and fascism as the early experience of market and constitutional order impacts negatively on the lives of the vast majority.

There are two distinct kinds of assessment. The first takes note of the largely nonviolent transition from Communism in the former Soviet Union and East Europe, a signal achievement given the scale and depth of the transformations. The second is critical of both elites and publics in the West for their failure to seize the opportunities presented to press the world toward demilitarization and institutionalized nonviolence at regional and global levels. The duration of these openings can never be ascertained, but surely with the break-up of the Soviet Union, the displacement of Gorbachev by Yeltsin, and the virtual return of autocratic rule to Russia that historic opening has disappeared, at least for now.

But the turn to nonviolence has been evident elsewhere, although without generally being acknowledged as such, and without achieving transformative results: in Iran during the struggle against the Shah; in the "people power" movement in the Philippines which swept the dictatorial Marcos regime from power in 1986; in China during the democracy movement, even though it was crushed and driven abroad and underground following the massacre in and surrounding Tiananmen Square in June of 1989; in the human rights and democracy struggles being waged by movements in Myanmar, Nepal, South Korea, and Taiwan during this same period; in the *intifada*, especially during its early phases in the late 1980s, pitting Palestinian stones against Israeli bullets; and in the negotiated transition to an inclusive democracy in South Africa, which included the repudiation of apartheid by the main section of the South African ruling white elites despite decades of ideological racism implemented by a brutal and persecuting regime, and which brought the ANC and Nelson Mandela constitutionally to power. Further, the efforts to resolve several long-festering internal wars through negotiation and by reliance on the good offices of the United Nations have made significant steps toward nonviolent conflict resolution in a number of difficult situations, including those of Namibia, Cambodia, and El Salvador. Although these undertakings may fail at some point, they reflect an increasing willingness to substitute nonviolent approaches for violent ones. In effect, the 1980s and early 1990s have seen an extraordinary turn by oppositional political movements toward reliance upon nonviolence for both pragmatic and principled reasons, even raising the possibility of a post-Leninist revolutionary politics that, in contrast to Leninism, is hopeful about the prospects for displacing or reconstructing, rather than smashing, the old state, and is committed to a high degree of reconciliation with former enemies.

There are rough edges, as in relation to controversial impunity practices in Latin America of exempting from legal scrutiny or governmental punishment those implicated in past practices of torture and abuse. Can one, should one overlook crimes against humanity in the Nuremberg sense for the sake of a politics of accommodation? Are there alternatives? How, in varying circumstances, should the outer limits of reconciliation be identified and an ethos of responsibility sustained given the way the world is structured? Is it enough to document crimes of the past, while exempting the criminals from apprehension and punishment? These questions cannot be answered in the abstract, but only on a case-by-case basis, given the alternatives concretely available.

Beyond this, it is not yet evident whether transformational goals can be reached by nonviolent means. The 1993 experience in Yeltsin's Russia is not encouraging, with the parliament suspended and its building shelled, autocratic powers claimed for the state, and an imperial foreign policy pursued against the former republics situated within "the near abroad" (a Russian version of regional supremacy that resembles the Monroe Doctrine).

Mahatma Gandhi and Martin Luther King waved the banners of nonviolence in an explicit and dramatic fashion. Their lives, struggle, and political language were dominated by such a commitment. The occurrences of the last decade were often not labeled "nonviolent" and nor were careful theoretical statements of position set forth. Some writers in East Europe leaned toward a redefinition of a politics of resistance that accepted the premise that tactical considerations of vulnerability to military repression and learning from the past disclosed the importance of confronting the government without attacking it head-on and violently – remembering earlier attempts, most notably in Hungary in 1956, and their disastrous results.[16] Feminist and green writings are generally underpinned by nonviolence, but again rarely is the effort made to articulate a fully coherent approach.[17]

In putting forward these proposals for transforming the United Nations, one line of recommendation will be to take steps to upgrade the relevance of nonviolence to all phases of UN activity and to reverse a recent tendency to conceive of responses to aggressions (Iraq against Kuwait, Serbia against Bosnia) in overly militarist or "realist" terms. The background point relevant here is to assert as a priority for adherents of global civil society – citizen pilgrims – the self-conscious promotion of nonviolent conflict-resolving in *all* arenas of decision, that is, in approaching domestic discord at the level of family and neighborhood, as well as in designing the framework within which the UN Security Council carries out its security roles. Feminists, in particular, have been influential in their exposure and discrediting of various forms of concealed and overlooked violence in personal spheres of interaction, but little concerted attention has been given to concealed and tolerated violence as practiced by international institutions. Given the extent of influence possessed by the strongest and richest states on UN activities, it is hardly surprising that the UN also associates effectiveness with military capabilities and outcomes, regarding diplomacy as the exclusive domain of governments even in situations in which the official leadership is oppressive and its opposition is democratic and peace-oriented. Why should UN operations be guided by military notions of "victory," and not by a search for "peace"? Why not also negotiate "peace" with representatives of peoples or of democratic movements rather than only with official leaders who are often themselves perpetrators of crimes against humanity on a massive scale? Bosnia and Cambodia are illustrative of both the problems and opportunities of such an approach.

Why should not religious leaders and moral authority figures "intervene" on behalf of nonviolent conflict resolution, not with threats of air strikes, sanctions, embargoes, but by bearing witness to the suffering and cruelty of the unresolved encounter? Such initiatives were being attempted in the former Yugoslavia during 1992–4, but the media averted its gaze. "Realism" also deforms journalistic portrayals of reality, reproducing the militarist imagination.

Nonviolence also implies an enhanced respect and role for just law (that is, incorporating a comprehensive set of human rights, political and civil, but also economic and social) at all levels of social interaction. The widest structures of interaction, which pertain to global governance, will only be compatible with humane governance if these rest on a normative foundation of international law, including the Nuremberg Principles, and a strong disposition toward nonviolence. The future is almost certain to be dictated by some coalition of market and statist forces, the latter being relegated to an increasingly subordinate role by the invisible leaders of the globalized world economy, who could become the real holders of ultimate power. One relevance, then, of nonviolent thought and initiatives is to demonstrate clearly that an alternative set of possibilities often exists in conflict situations of all varieties. It is a crucial part of the shared identity drawing together the various strands of feeling and perspective composing the rainbow of activities and aspirations that we have labeled globalization from below, the energy behind global civil society dedicated to the building of transnational or cosmopolitan democracy.

Institutionalizing Humane Governance at a Global Level: Reforming (Transforming) the United Nations

Undoubtedly, differing attitudes toward the future of the United Nations are at the core of controversy about fashioning institutional responses to economic and cultural globalization, and about how best to adjust and take advantage of the disappearance of conflict at the strategic level. The end of the Cold War, *tout court*, as has been earlier indicated, is a Eurocentric judgment, but the collapse of US/Soviet interbloc relations, changes in strategic weapon deployments and targeting plans, the disappearance of interventionary and ideological rivalry on a global scale have combined to establish a fundamentally different global setting, despite some remnants of the Cold War era, especially in East and South Asia.

The reformist perspective relating to the United Nations at the start of the 1990s has been influentially expressed in two reports, that of the

Secretary General, Boutros Boutros-Ghali, called *An Agenda for Peace*, and that of the Stockholm Initiative on Global Security and Governance, entitled *Common Responsibility in the 1990s*.[18] Both these documents reflect the post-1989 outlook, but were also conceived and written under the impact of the UN experience, for better and worse, in the Gulf War. Given the velocity of recent international history, especially the troublesome, unresolved debate about the viability and legitimacy of humanitarian interventions under UN auspices, it seems likely that these reports, if written in 1995, would rethink global governance in light of the susbequent UN efforts, still not resolved, in Cambodia, Bosnia, Somalia, Rwanda, and Haiti. The difficulties of sustaining intervention in a weak state have posed a series of constitutional and logistical questions about the extent of a beneficial and politically acceptable UN role. The Gulf War raised constitutional questions about adherence to the Charter in several key respects. In contrast, the weak state challenge, paradoxically, has once again raised concerns about UN effectiveness. Such a critical line argues that if the UN cannot stop genocide in Bosnia or Rwanda, then the Organization suffers from a critical failure of capabilities and/or will. The issues posed here are deeply troubling and urgent, yet resistant to being solved along traditional lines. Why? Even with a much more impressive array of capabilities and resources, and a strong political will, interventions mounted against determined opponents have rarely succeeded in recent decades. To find effective responses here may also involve nonviolent forms of intrusion and diplomacy, and a turn away from militarist responses – even in the face of violence and criminality.

To some extent *An Agenda for Peace* anticipates and addresses these new challenges by its emphasis on "preventive diplomacy," "peacemaking," and "post-conflict peace-building," each calling for an enhanced UN role that is more responsive to the main patterns of weak state challenges, such as have arisen in Cambodia, Somalia, Namibia, and Macedonia. Much more effort is needed by way of taking account of these UN frustrations, and learning from them. It is also evident that the priorities associated with economic globalization and its domestic impacts discourage any greatly expanded commitment of resources to the United Nations at this time.

Essentially, almost all reformist work on the UN is dedicated to "strengthening" within the framework of existing approaches, that is, making the Organization more effective in relation to the structure in place and the tasks assigned, but not raising underlying issues of statist control and anachronistic influence by leading member states.[19] *An Agenda for Peace* definitely moves sensibly in this direction, proposing more room for independent diplomatic initiatives by the Secretary General, more steps in the direction of establishing peacekeeping capabilities under UN control, and more direct access to financial resources on a scale sufficient to meet existing obligations and unexpected demands, often of an emergency character.

At the same time, and somewhat inconsistently given the peace and security agenda that presents itself as increasingly dealing with largely internal problems, Boutros Boutros-Ghali offers reassurance to prospective targets of UN operations: "In these situations of internal crisis the United Nations will need to respect the sovereignty of the State; to do otherwise would not be in accordance with the understanding of Member States in accepting the principles of the Charter."[20] To invoke sovereignty in such a setting is to pretend by rhetoric to deny patterns of UN practice that have been moving in the opposite direction in relation to diverse situations in such countries as Angola, Somalia, Iraq, and Cambodia.

In the end, *An Agenda for Peace* seeks more authority and more capabilities to get the job done in an era of weak state ascendancy. The Secretary General urges an expanded commitment of members by way of earmarking military forces for peacekeeping and peace enforcement, including a "prepositioned stock of basic peace-keeping equipment" and the provision of "air and sea-lift capacity" free or at less then commercial rates. The report also makes a series of relatively modest proposals to alleviate financial pressures that have dogged the Organization at the very time when expectations about its proper role have been expanding so rapidly. Specific proposals include a Humanitarian Revolving Fund of $50 million to be used for "humanitarian emergencies," and the establishment of a UN Peace Endowment Fund, with an initial funding of $1 billion, that would be available "to finance the initial costs of authorized peace-keeping operations, other conflict resolution measures and related activities."[21] Many other suggestions are put forward, of an incremental character, to enable the UN to be more effective as a political actor serving a membership constituted by sovereign states, yet dominated in its security operations by the United States and its closest allies.

More valuable reforms from the perspective of humane governance are the efforts of the *Agenda* to make the UN more autonomous. The most striking statement in the whole report is the veiled, yet surprisingly pointed criticism of the extent to which the UN was manipulated by Washington during the Gulf War: "Never again must the Security Council lose the collegiality that is essential to its proper functioning . . . a genuine sense of consensus deriving from shared interests must govern its work."[22] With the help of bad memories and with such an end in view, more independent capabilities would help give the Security Council greater composure to act collegially; in the Gulf crisis the UN was vulnerable to being bypassed altogether by the United States and its partners, and the Security Council lacked the means to challenge Iraq's aggression without the fullest backing from the United States.

As the US arguably needed the UN to legitimate its call to war, there existed the basis for a more balanced bargain that would have preserved a greater measure of collegiality within the UN while acquiring the necessary capabilities from the US-led coalition. Such speculation side-steps the other line of critique – namely, the willingness of the UN to mandate a rush to war, and then to define the military objectives by reference, in the end, to geopolitical concerns about regional balance and nuclear weapons concerns, rather than by reference to the animating consensus to restore Kuwaiti sovereignty and, as a next step, to promote human rights and democracy for all the people of Iraq. Leaving Saddam Hussein as Iraqi head of state helped to deter Kurdish nationalism in the region and to contain Iranian expansionist ambitions, but it also ratified oppressive Iraqi governance.

The establishment of a UN enforcement capability composed of specially trained volunteers rather than personnel belonging to the military services of particular countries has been suggested as a way to move toward a supranational (rather than international or geopolitical) model of peacekeeping; to diminish the war-fighting orientation of military operations, the idea of "a transnational police force" has also been recommended.[23] It is possible that the police orientation could also be made relevant to larger, unresolved crisis situations where military interposition may be unacceptable or impossible. Such an independent UN volunteer force, on the basis of special training for a variety of roles, could shape its identity as combining police and military features, but always mindful, more so than states in warfare, of an overriding duty to minimize any semblance of war-waging activity and with a sense of commitment to avoid, to the maximum extent possible, civilian damage. The UN should define its own conception of the use of force as a last resort and with a far higher level of self-imposed restraints than the level of legal guidelines for states.[24]

Another approach taken by the *Agenda for Peace* is to encourage wider recourse to the World Court in situations where Security Council initiatives seem to violate the Charter, or even other applicable international law standards. Such recourse in the setting of the Gulf crisis might have challenged the excessive delegation of operational and strategic discretion to the United States, or the abandonment of economic sanctions without a finding of their failure, or the essential abandonment of the Chapter VII framework for coordination of an enforcement action to ensure the collectivity of collective security. It is important for activist groups and for representative initiatives in global civil society, especially those composed of lawyers, to add their own independent weight to this call by the Secretary General for a stronger reliance on the rule of law as a framework for UN actitivies in the peace and security domain. One could imagine civil society projects that included the formation of a Security Council Watch and an overall capability for monitoring the UN, assessing from a constitutional perspective the activities of this most controversial of UN organs, issuing impartial and reliable reports. This would be an approach that builds on the very considerable success of the human rights watch groups. Other complementary initiatives might include an annual report from an NGO or Global Civil Society on UN successes and failures that was an alternative to the annual report of the Secretary General, being either modeled on that report, or a response to it. An additional possibility would be to satisfy informational needs on UN activities in the spirit of the Worldwatch Institute's series of annual volumes on "the state of the world."[25]

In most respects *Common Responsibility in the 1990s* reinforces *An Agenda for Peace*, calling for identical types of strengthening and regarding the Gulf War experience as pointing attention to the question of collectivity – that is, the need in future to ensure wider participation by member states and far greater deference to the Charter as an authoritative constitutional framework.[26] The Stockholm Initiative is broader in scope than the Secretary General's report, which was prepared in response to a Security Council request for recommendations on matters of peace and security. In addressing North/South issues, both development and population are treated as central concerns. The Stockholm Initiative departs somewhat from the wider accommodation that Boutros Boutros-Ghali seems to have made with the laissez-faire geopolitical mood. The Initiative proposes the adoption of specific antipoverty goals, recommends drastic debt relief, and encourages an expansion of development assistance up to 1 per cent of GNP by industrialized countries. Such positions undoubtedly reflect the influence of the South in the membership of the commission and thereby dramatizes its divergence from the Secretary General's approach, not only in the *Agenda* but in his overall UN leadership role. Either for reasons of conviction, or in the face of political realities, Dr Boutros-Ghali has consistently worked to marginalize development grievances, at least during his early years in office. He eliminated the

UN Center on Transnational Corporations at the very time when such efforts should have been dramatically expanded. Again, the global civil society perspective, reinforced by the BCCI revelations, should have mounted a huge public campaign to retain the Center.

The Stockholm Initiative is not nearly as responsive to the priorities and outlook of transnational market forces as is *Agenda for Peace*, but neither is it sufficiently concerned with the adverse human and environmental consequences of an unconditional capitalist approach to regulation and welfare. Somewhat incoherently, it ignores globalization from above altogether, while reiterating a social democratic reformist agenda. Its welcomed call for the renewal of a compassionate programmatic approach to global economic policy is hollow unless it is situated in the reality of the evolving world economy. In this regard, institutional reform at the global level must also approach the IMF and World Bank with a somewhat critical eye, as regards both their distance from global civil society and their closeness to the hierarchy of market forces which is giving structure to economic globalization.

As stressed in the preceding chapter, such sites of struggle to redefine the relationship between the human interest and market forces need to become democratized along two axes (more participation by countries from the South; more participation by representatives of global civil society) if sustainable human development is to become more than a pipe-dream and if global governance is to be made effective and humane.

The most important contribution of the Stockholm Initiative was to put "global governance" on the conceptual and policy map in an influential way. It was the first move after the Cold War, appropriately expressed as "in the spirit of San Francisco" by prominent world leaders, to call for a concerted effort at institutional renewal: this call was formalized as a proposal to hold "a World Summit on Global Governance . . . similar to the meetings in San Francisco and Bretton Woods in the 1940s."[27] It was reinforced by a proposal to form "an independent International Commission on Global Governance," and this has been carried out. The Commission was created in part to work out suggestions for what a world summit might accomplish. It would be important to ensure that representatives of global civil society participate as full members in the formal activities of the Commission, as well as in executing the plan of work. As now constituted the Commission has some members (although a tiny fraction) who might consider themselves to be citizen pilgrims, at least to some extent.[28]

An encouraging conceptualization of several aspects of global governance is to be found in the *Human Development Report* in recent years.

First of all, the political construction of the historical situation is similar: "For the first time in human history, the world is close to creating a single, unified global system. But an agreed and participatory system of global governance remains a distant dream."[29] This assertion is not reinforced by a critique of emergent patterns of control over globalization, except indirectly by way of a plaintive question posed as follows, "This [economic globalization] has left an urgent and disturbing question wandering round the corridors of power: In a period of rapid globalization, who will protect the interests of the world's poor?"[30] To quote from the famous Bob Dylan song that typified the disillusioned yearnings of the 1960s, "The answer, my friends, is blowin' in the wind." Not the wind, but in the quite deliberate market-oriented biases that mainly disavow the implications of a distinct effort to protect the poor aside from eventual trickle-down effects of market efficiency. A critique of economic globalization and how to moderate its adverse human consequences must be carried forward as an urgent intellectual task by economically literate and politically sophisticated citizen pilgrims.[31]

But what *Human Development Report 1992* does that is quite remarkable is to put forward some bold suggestions for institutional reform under the evocative heading "Global Institutions for the Twenty-first Century." These suggestions go quite far: a global central bank, including the creation of a common world currency, with a particular responsibility to service the needs of poorer countries; the establishment of "a system of progressive income tax" to be imposed on rich countries for the benefit of poorer countries and whose revenues would be transferred according to agreed procedures rather than by one-way practices associated with conditionality; an international trade organization that "would merge the functions of GATT and UNCTAD" to enable equality of access by all countries to the benefits of expanding trade; and a strengthened UN system that would include the establishment of a Development Security Council entrusted with evolving "the broad policy framework for all global development issues." It goes on to specify that "these issues range from food security to ecological security, from humanitarian assistance to development assistance, from debt relief to social development, from drug control to international migration."[32] Such a vision, if implemented by way of concrete reform initiatives, would move significantly in the direction of humane governance, helping to enable the UN system to meet the functional and ethical challenges of economic globalization.

The Global Civilization Project is the most recent effort by WOMP to encourage transnational scholarship on positive models of global governance.[33] This line of speculation, initiated under WOMP auspices in the late 1960s, was animated from the outset by fundamental normative concerns, the quest for a safer and more equitable world respectful of the rights of persons and of peoples, now and in the future, and dedicated to the delegitimation and eventual abolition of war as a social institution. There were, of course, many differences of viewpoint among WOMP participants on matters of priority and feasibility, but there was a high degree of consensus with respect to the relevance and orientation of giving priority to valued human ends, the reduction of suffering, and the avoidance of catastrophe. In the circumstances of the 1990s the application of this normative perspective finds a particularly fruitful time during which to stress the role of international institutions and of the rule of law at regional and global levels of interaction. The efforts noted earlier in this section, especially those associated with UNDP as expressed in recent Human Development Reports and with the Stockholm Initiative as carried forward by the Independent Commission on Global Governance, confirms the judgment that now is the best time since the founding of the UN to put forward bold and comprehensive ideas about institutional change at the regional and global levels. A mere decade ago such proposals would have seemed hopelessly out of touch with the prevailing geopolitical mood of preoccupation with the nuances of bipolarity.

As has been suggested, not all of these globalizing trends are to be uncritically affirmed. The G-7 orientation is essentially an alternative approach to global governance that needs to be redirected and challenged, or else the human and environmental consequences of continuing economic globalization are likely to be mainly detrimental. That is, the need for global governance is now so widely recognized that its realization is itself in danger of being appropriated by the last gasp of geopolitics. The emphasis here on the transition from geopolitics to humane governance is intended to foster a conception of global governance that is fashioned to a significant extent by the values and priorities of transnational democratic forces, that is, by civil initiatives associated with globalization from below, including the energetic influence of citizen pilgrims of widely different ethnic, cultural, religious and geographical backgrounds. Such a conception will inevitably be a vehicle for the expression of ethical concerns, but it will also provide a process of participation as well as a sharing and nurturing of ideas.[34]

Globalization from below also manifests its specific identity in current discussions of UN reform. Perhaps a short discussion of proposals to reform the Security Council can serve to illustrate this movement. As might be anticipated, the G-7 outlook generally favors the addition as permanent members of the two now unrepresented financial superpowers, Japan and Germany, making the Security Council more reflective of geopolitical reality during a time of preoccupation with global economic policy. Anticipating opposition from the South, and needing some sort of political consensus, there are hints that a bargain could be struck – Japan and Germany, but also some rotating mix of populous states in the South as quasiregional representatives, say, India, Indonesia, Nigeria, and Brazil, possibly given permanent seats, but not the veto.

There are discussions in less statist circles about a similar bargain, but one that reduces the European presence on the Security Council to one permanent seat, allowing Germany, France, and the United Kingdom to rotate. Some proposals are now circulating which rely on two and even three categories of permanent Security Council membership: first, the original five as veto powers; secondly, several regional representatives as new additions to the permanent membership but without a veto; and thirdly, states drawn from the rest of the general membership, elected for five-year terms and eligible for reelection. Any proposal that dilutes the existing status and entrenched rights of members of the Security Council, especially those that possess a veto, will confront virtually insurmountable resistance, given the need for their approval of any Charter amendments. Nevertheless, it is now agreed that the anachronistic structure of the Organization needs to be confronted in this dimension to avoid undermining the legitimacy of the UN.

Perhaps, a transnational campaign calling for a constitutional review conference on the fiftieth anniversary of the UN, coupled with the appointment of a preparatory commission with appropriate NGO participation, leading to a full-fledged world summit on constitutional issues in the year 1999, is the most practical way to acknowledge the obstacles to insitutional renewal at this time without succumbing to them.[35]

The perspectives of global civil society favor these kinds of reforms to take account of changes on the world scene and to create a body more broadly representative of and responsive to the peoples of the world. However, it would strongly endorse and promote the consideration of more radical innovations in the conception of permanent member status in two particular respects, that is, to take account of normative achievement (legal, ethical, humanitarian contributions) and of severe material deprivation (poverty, natural and social disasters, resource deficiencies, especially food and water), as well as redesigning the selection process itself.

Normative achievement could be encouraged by reserving a seat on the Security Council to reward "a moral superpower," and another would be set aside for a country falling within the group of the economically most disadvantaged (possibly as measured by UNDP yardsticks). As far as selection is concerned, these seats could be filled for five-year renewable terms after designation by a panel of winners of the Nobel Peace Prize for the moral superpower and by a panel of eminent persons and leaders of the ten most appropriate citizens' associations for the representative of the most disadvantaged. The central idea of this proposal is to challenge the conventional correlation of military and economic capacity with political stature and constitutional status.

Why should permanent membership be confined to the five declared nuclear weapons states (these states also being the five leading arms suppliers), or expanded to include the new financial superpowers? In the spirit of humane governance, should not moral qualifications, including adherence to international law and the promotion of human rights at home and abroad, be acknowledged by status and access? Beyond this symbolic statement is the conviction that the participation in the debate of states on behalf of the particular identities of a moral superpower or of the most severely disadvantaged states is substantively necessary if the Security Council is to achieve credibility and legitimacy in the eyes of the majority of the peoples of the world. In addition to these proposals for the selection of states with different bases of distinction would be the provision of seats for nonstate actors (representing religion, labor, the arts).

The UN Security Council is symbolically important, as well as a key actor, in the emerging world order. These proposals are meant to express the most distinctive claims of globalization from below: the emphasis on normative criteria of political stature, the significance of acknowledging claims to participate in security structures by those who represent the most insecure and deprived peoples of the world, and the pervasive relevance of the democratizing imperative when it comes to the redesign of global institutions.

Of course, membership is only one dimension of constitutional identity. Voting procedures, financial arrangements, judicial review, implementing limits on recourse to force, encouragement of nonviolent conflict resolution, and a pedagogy of humane governance are other dimensions that need to be developed from the perspective of global civil society. And, of course, the UN system cannot be reduced to the Security Council. Other parts of the system need to be examined critically from these perspectives and reconstituted to reflect the needs and hopes associated with humane governance.

Enhancing the role and influence of the World Court is a particularly high priority at this time for citizen pilgrims, both to provide a review of contested behavior by states which is oriented to law and peace, and to ensure that the various organs of the UN respect their procedural and substantive limits and do not become vehicles for geopolitical ambition. This concern applies especially in settings involving the use of force and to the imposition from without of policies (for instance, IMF programs of structural adjustment) that infringe on the political, economic, and social rights and prospects of the poor. At present, the emphasis should be on the unused potential of the World Court, including its relevance to the projects of global civil society. An illustrative initiative, involving a collaboration between transnational citizens associations, is the World Court Project, whose purpose is to induce the UN General Assembly to request an Advisory Opinion from the World Court on the general issue of the status of threats and uses of nuclear weapons under international law.[36] This is a transnational undertaking sponsored by the International Association of Lawyers Against Nuclear Arms, the International Peace Bureau, and the International Physicians for the Prevention of Nuclear War. These prominent organizations, active in the world peace movement, have never formally cooperated before, and thus this coming together of professional groupings of lawyers and doctors, as well as a more general peace group, is notable as a process. A dramatic complementary effort has resulted from a request by the General Assembly of the World Health Organization for an Advisory Opinion from the World Court on the legality of nuclear weapons in light of adverse health effects in the event of use. It is both discouraging and notable that the nuclear weapons states, especially the United States Government, have been making a furious effort to block or deflect a *legal* appraisal of their policies on nuclear weapons. This is discouraging because it exposes the intense attachment to nuclearism by the West even in the aftermath of the Cold War, and notable because the opposition to a World Court Advisory Opinion implicitly acknowledges the relevance of the legalist attack on this weaponry.

The immediate purpose of such an initiative is to push the majority of governments to move a step further in their calls for the prohibition of all threats or uses of nuclear weaponry.[37] It is also an effort by the forces of globalization from below to invoke international law for purposes of humane governance, which include the denuclearization of political conflict and the commitment to a nuclear-free world. To attempt such an appropriation of law is not a small undertaking, as international law has been typically, and often cynically, regarded as an instrument of statecraft and geopolitics, with only governments in relations with one another entitled to invoke its rules as the basis of claims or grievances, and only powerful governments in a position to act as enforcers. For citizen pilgrims to invoke international law and seek authoritative guidance from the World Court suggests many lines of possibility for democratic participation in the actualities of global governance. In fact, a further step favored here would be to give such transnational citizen associations their own right – separately from the General Assembly and assuming some process of authorizing credentials – to pose questions of international law for the World Court to resolve by way of an Advisory Opinion.[38] Alternatively, such competence could be linked to a second assembly within the UN system composed of representatives of such transnational groups rather than of governments.

But it is necessary to ask some difficult questions about the wisdom of such recourse to a judicial body composed of individuals nominated and elected by states: how can one be confident that the World Court will decide "our way"? And even if it does, will not the decision be merely "advisory"? Is it plausible to believe that the nuclear weapons states will heed such advice? The response offered here is based on a general belief that the struggle against nuclear weaponry must be waged on many different terrains, with no single one being decisive. There is evidence that the World Court, given the consensus on illegality among international law specialists and in view of prior pronouncements of illegality by the UN General Assembly, is most likely to reach a majority view on the legal issues supportive of the goals of the World Court Project. It is possible that the majority of the court would favor a compromise by way of evading the issue posed, challenging its "legal" nature, its appropriateness in an "advisory" setting, or even the competence of the UN organ to pose questions of such an hypothetical character. It is possible, but not likely. With the backing of such an Advisory Opinion there would be weight added to the pre-existing efforts by religious, legal, and health oriented groups to challenge all aspects of reliance on nuclear weaponry. If governments refused to respect such a decision, then new kinds of political pressure could be mounted. The whole process of seeking and implementing such an Advisory Opinion on this subject could have an enormous mobilizing impact upon world opinion, and would serve the pedagogical purpose of instructing citizens and leaders on the illegality of all weaponry of mass destruction. It could lead, as well, to the expansion of constitutional democracy on a domestic level to include the legal right of any citizen or organization to initiate action in a national court to obtain an order to the government to comply with the World Court decision, even if it is only an "Advisory Opinion," especially if the advice reinforces what was in any event an obligation under international law.[39]

But let us suppose that the World Court refuses to respond, or responds in an unexpected manner, let us say by insisting that legality or illegality can only be assessed in the context of actual use, or contending that, given the reliance for so long on this weaponry by several important states (indeed, the five declared nuclear weapons states are the five permanent members of the Security Council), the issue of legality can only be resolved at this late stage by a treaty. (Implicit here is the argument that if nuclear weaponry is so manifestly illegal, why has it taken half a century to formulate the challenge?) While such an outcome would be an immediate disappointment, it would not necessarily defeat the main purpose of the undertaking, namely, the delegitimation of nuclear weaponry. If well organized, such a reactionary response by the World Court could itself provoke a grassroots reaction and accelerate efforts elsewhere to establish the illegitimacy of nuclear weapons. Such an outcome might also prompt efforts to restructure the World Court to remove its inclination to serve geopolitical masters. As matters now stand, each nuclear power is represented by a judge and these judges are likely to have seniority and be persuasive with their brethren, the ethos of the Court being to avoid rendering decisions that are not likely to be observed. A shift from the Nicaragua case where the Court took on the US government back in 1986 to the Libya case where it backed off in 1992 can be discerned.

The experience of the World Court in relation to the status of Namibia is illustrative. Ethiopia and Liberia approached the Court in the mid-1960s to declare that South Africa's administration of the territory now called Namibia on the basis of apartheid violated its duty as the mandatory power and violated international law. To the shock of the world community, the World Court decided in 1966 that South Africa had the discretion to act in good faith as it saw fit.[40] In reaction, the General Assembly accelerated its call for the invalidation of South African rule and proclaimed the establishment of an independent Namibia. In addition, the outcome in The Hague made the South realize that it must pay closer attention to the outlook of the judges who are elected to the World Court. A few years later the General Assembly came to the Court with its own request for an Advisory Opinion, and was rewarded with a strong endorsement of its repudiation of South African mandatory claims. The World Court as institution and the specific claim against South Africa both benefited despite the short-run disappointment of "defeat" in 1966.[41]

Enhancing the Rule of Law, Democratization, Accountability, and Demilitarization

Global civil society also needs to be concerned about the internal adherence to international law and the role of citizens and their associations in pressing for adherence. Compliance with international law by states and market forces should become an entitlement of the peoples of the world, enforceable through their formal right of access for such purposes to national courts. Given the realities of the global village, the republican promise of limited and accountable government can only be upheld if citizens are entitled to a foreign policy that adheres to the constraints imposed by international law. This possibility is of great importance in relation to superpower or strong state action, that is, projecting military power beyond its territory. Often external checks are not available, and the only assurance of law-oriented behavior is through the existence and effective use of internal checks on abuse of state power. While such an extension of the rule of law to the domain of foreign policy is generally important, it is of critical relevance in the United States, given its role as global leader, its republican tradition of political legitimacy based on checks and balances,[42] and most of all, given its tendency to project its military power overseas with scant regard for international law constraints, and even for some procedural constitutional constraints (especially, the Congressional power to declare war).[43]

One tendency to induce compliance with international law by states has been by way of civil disobedience or civil resistance, the deliberate symbolic and nonviolent violation of domestic law as a way to challenge the refusal of the government to uphold the more paramount obligations of international law, especially in the area of war and peace. This posture of citizen action has been increasingly tied to notions of accountability and responsibility that are rooted in the Nuremberg judgment imposing individual criminal liability on the defeated leadership of Nazi Germany for its failure to uphold international law.[44] Since the Nuremberg Principles were officially formulated by the UN expert legal body, the International Law Commission, and then embodied in a unanimously endorsed General Assembly resolution, it is correct to conclude that the Nuremberg guidelines are now an authoritative part of modern international law. It is also correct to understand that leading states have often violated these restrictions on governmental conduct.[45] The role of grassroots activism is to challenge this gap between legal commitment and political behavior, seeking to expose it and, to the extent possible, to close it.

What, then, is caught up in this Nuremberg net of responsibility? The basic claims relating to official accountability are associated with the three categories of state crime:

> Crimes against the Peace, in essence, the planning, preparation, and engagement in aggressive war, that is, recourse to armed force in violation of the UN Charter prohibition in Article 2(4) and not falling within the self-defense exception of Article 51;

> Crimes of War, in essence, gross violations of the limits of the law of war imposed on the conduct of hostilities, especially as set forth in the Hague Conventions of 1899 and 1907, as well as the four Geneva Conventions of 1949 and the two Geneva Protocols of 1977;

> Crimes against Humanity, in essence, acts of cruelty and unjustified coercion against civilians, including severe denials of human rights, and reliance on genocidal means and rationale, "ethnic cleansing."

In effect, the Nuremberg Principles impose on leaders an unconditional legal responsibility for adhering to these guidelines. Excuses about sovereign rights, supreme national interests, military necessity, or superior orders are unacceptable. The duty to obey is unconditional. A person is bound to act on the basis of a complementary rationale: with knowledge that a government is planning aggressive war or is proposing to fight with indiscriminate and first-strike weaponry, a person has the duty to take all reasonable steps to prevent the consummation of such serious types of criminality. Furthermore, national courts should inquire into such allegations if they are supported by sufficient evidence to satisfy tests of reasonable belief. Disobedience by officials in relation to international law is a serious threat to the possibility of constitutional governance of the global village in relation to the most vital matters bearing on human well-being and survival, whereas compliance would diminish greatly the role of violence in state-to-state relations and of cruelty and grave danger in state-to-peoples situations. Implementing the Nuremberg Principles as a normal part of constitutional democracy would contribute to the demilitarization of political life throughout the planet and would help reconcile the state system – the legacy of Westphalia – with contemporary requirements of humane governance. Some closely related civil society initiatives can be mentioned, not to assess their specific merits, but to suggest the range of possibilities. One preliminary idea would be the establishment of a Nuremberg Watch, that is, a transnational networking effort by individuals to monitor state and market behavior to gain information about the commission of crimes of state, and the issuance of various kinds of reports designed to mobilize pressures for exposure, apprehension, and compliance. Market behavior is relevant in many respects, but most obviously in the context of arms sales of prohibited weaponry to states embarked upon aggressive warfare. The work of a Nuremberg Watch could be used to prepare indictments on behalf of victims by an international criminal judicial process that is itself a civil initiative. An additional possibility would be to prepare draft treaty instruments delimiting economic crimes of state, for instance, appropriation of public funds for private purposes, as has been done repeatedly by dicators in the South, taking advantage of secret banking practices in Geneva and elsewhere to hide "dirty money."

There are other democratizing initiatives that depend upon globalization from below. One example is the important effort to challenge essentially unregulated commerce in non-nuclear armaments. Both statist and market forces, to varying degrees, have strong incentives to maintain the status quo with respect to arms sales, such exchanges being treated as falling within sovereign discretion at both ends of a transaction. Only by bringing out into the open the relation between arms sales and the incidence, magnitude, and criminality of military and paramilitary violence can the issue be put on the political agenda of major states and of international insitutions. Furthermore, unless restraints on sales are correlated in some way with restraints on production, the effects of an exclusive focus on sales alone is likely to be perceived by countries in the South as one designed to ensure their subordination, thereby giving encouragement and justification to the proliferation of indigenous arms production capabilities. One mechanism for transnational consciousness-raising is the preparation by citizens groups, relying on experts, of draft conventions that provide a framework for a demilitarizing process. The International Association of Lawyers Against Nuclear Arms has sponsored international seminars in 1993 and 1994 to assess such a proposal in the form of a Draft Convention on the Monitoring, Reduction, and Abolition of the International Arms Trade. Vetting this proposal in an informal setting with representatives of governments and international institutions participating is creating sufficient credibility to encourage a range of lobbying efforts directed at governments and other policymakers throughout the world.

The voluntary registrar of arms sales through the United Nations is a modest acknowledgment that the subject is one of concern to the organized global community, and has the important implication of associating a modicum of transparency with global reform. At a time when access to information is such a formidable instrument of power, the extension of transparency to any domain of military operations creates an added possibility of a participatory role for citizen pilgrims and their associations. But it should be noted that transparency in relation to arms sales will not be achieved until disclosure is made mandatory and universal, and a capability exists to identify and respond to instances of nondisclosure. Transparency is the obverse of secrecy, and secrecy is the mantle that state and market forces throw over a range of activities which could not easily withstand the impact of moral, political, and legal scrutiny.[46]

The role of global civil society at this stage is to launch such projects and build transnational support for a political campaign that aims to achieve specific demilitarization objectives. Resistance will be formidable, but the process of struggle is itself part of the globalization of democracy that is integral to the possibility of humane governance.

Toward Humane Governance

The realities of humane governance need to be worked out in the life-world, partly in the encounter with the entrenched territorial forces of the state system, partly in reaction to the various manifestations of globalization from above, and partly in coalition with congenial strands of transnational initiatives arising from global civil society.

The programmatic goals associated with the establishment of humane governance are not unconditionally oppositional in relation to market and statist forces. Indeed, the best hope for the future consists of negotiated compromises that enable a robust market to be respectful of the logic of sustainability and a reoriented states system mindful of human rights, including the right to development, but also the right to be protected against arbitrary market behavior. The deepening and extension of democratic publicity is critical to this collaborative process. Without relevant knowledge, responsible citizen participation is impossible, and without such participation, democratic correctives to abuses of political and economic power will be virtually impossible.

Beyond this, a central preoccupation of citizen pilgrims is with demilitarization, including a strong bias in favor of nonviolent responses even in the face of violence. Such a normative orientation does not exclude police, and even military violence under the auspices of international institutions such as the United Nations, but it places a continuous existential burden on all political actors to find nonviolent solutions and overcome a strong presumption against recourse to violence. The difficulties of organizing humanitarian interventions that alleviate suffering in Bosnia, Somalia, Rwanda, and Haiti argue strongly for such an approach, as does the appreciation that preventive diplomacy is generally less costly and more likely to be effective.

In this chapter, there has also been an emphasis on global constitutionalism, bringing law and morality to bear as an integral part of a wider nonviolent ethos. A precondition for the effective application of law and morality is governability, a salient concern in an era when the international repercussions of the weak state are so prominent. A variety of flexible, context-sensitive approaches to governability will be needed, with the prospect of both success and failure. UN efforts in Cambodia, Namibia, El Salvador, and Somalia are illustrative of an emergent pattern of trial and error.

Following governability the next most important priority is the creation of an effective framework of regulatory authority in relation to market forces. Such a possibility will only arise in response to concerted pressures from below, possibly dramatized by scandals and revelations which raise civic consciousness about the adverse impacts on human well-being of a continued toleration of unregulated market forces. But such dramatic events must also be interpreted from the perspective of a humane governance, or else each manifestation of criminality will be treated as a special case, not as a systemic disorder. The BCCI scandal and collapse is suggestive of the problem and of the difficulty of shifting attention from symptom to cure.[47]

Humane governance presupposes overcoming the triple indictment, thereby implying movement toward a reasonably fair world economy, with a serious commitment to the elimination of avoidable suffering and waste, and an enlightened view of resource use and conservation, aiming to improve the life prospects of generations to come.

This vision of humane governance is attainable, and thus is not utopian in a technical sense. Its attainment will be incredibly difficult, and may well seem unlikely given the strength of contrary tendencies, especially the linkage between media, capital expansion, consumerism, military technology, and the geopolitical mindset. But historical outcomes have included many surprises, some exhilarating, others shocking. We have little to lose, much to gain, by walking the paths of the citizen pilgrim, dedicated to achieving the type of geogovernance that can also be said to embody the hopes and dreams of humane governance.

8

The Essential Vision:
A Normative Project to Achieve
Humane Governance

> What is most revealing in this world is not where we
> are, but where we are going.
> *Anonymous saying*

> Every child is born with the message that God is not
> yet discouraged with humanity.
> *Rabindranath Tagore*

This final short concluding chapter attempts a normative overview of
the quest for humane governance. As such, it summarizes and to an
extent overlaps with earlier discussion.

The contemporary quest for humane governance builds on kindred
efforts in the past, while being rooted in an unfolding present, and
above all aspiring to achieve an imagined future. The idea of humane
governance is itself a way of expressing this process that is sensitive to
the shortcomings, achievements, and gropings toward human betterment on this planet. What shapes the orientation and gives it substantive
content in diverse settings is this normative underpinning, a blend of
legal, moral, and spiritual perspectives.[1]

To endow this underpinning with greater concreteness and sense of
direction, this chapter briefly depicts ten dimensions of this world-
encompassing normative project, acknowledging its historical depth yet
also identifying its inspirational and prophetic assumptions about the
future. Such a depiction should not be regarded as a listing of attributes
or an inventory, and far less as a program. Each aspect that is rendered
as distinct touches and influences the others in countless ways. There is

no terminal point for this normative project to achieve humane governance, not even in the imagination, much less in history. Considering the self-transcending character of human nature, and the embedded challenge of mortality and impermanence, there is no legitimate way ever to declare that humane governance has been achieved and that hence the normative project is finished: process, criticism, and transcendence are inherent in the normative identity of the human species.

Apparently, some indigenous peoples with a cyclical idea of time and a coherent cosmology approximate a perfected outlook on human possibility, but their own experience is a record of responses to recurrent challenges, whether deriving from nature or from hostile external human forces. What is universal in features of the normative helps to situate the politics of humane governance in a manner that facilitates communication across civilizational, nationalist, ethnic, class, generational, cognitive, and gender divides, but there is also implicit respect and celebration of difference and an attitude of extreme skepticism toward exclusivist claims that deny space for expression and exploration to others, as well as toward variants of universalism that ignore the uneven circumstances and aspirations of peoples, classes, and regions.

The normative project in its essence is constantly identifying and re-establishing the various interfaces between the specific and the general in each and every context, yet also keeping its spatial and mental borders open for entry and exit, being wary of any version of truth-claim as the foundation of extremism and political violence.

One of the perpetual predicaments facing those who hold to such a contingent view of truth is the presence of those who claim in one way or another absolute sanction for their approach to reality. We associate such unconditionality with religious extremism, but it is embedded in the scientific rationalism of the modern secular order. Nothing expresses secular fundamentalism more stridently than recourse to war as policy, often decided upon according to secret protocols even in constitutional democracies, and including the ultimate option to use nuclear weaponry potentially capable of disrupting the life support of the planet. Such arrogance exists on an unprecendented scale, and is in certain ways more sinister than "traditional" fundamentalisms because it claims exclusively for itself guardianship over this absolutist capacity to destroy (the real meaning of the nonproliferation regime can only be grasped as an aspect of the ideology that arises from a fundamentalist outlook on nuclearism).

To gain perspective on the normative project it is necessary to enlarge our sense of time, of the relevant historical interval within which change can be assessed. In this chapter the century as measured by the past one hundred years is taken as the basis for conjecture. The nature of this conjecture, by its authorship and in view of the globalization of the West, needs to acknowledge, despite conscious efforts to the contrary, a set of inbuilt Eurocentric biases. Arguably, the normative project as a global undertaking is itself a byproduct of Eurocentricism, even if it conceives of itself as oppositional and guided by a commitment to those who have been most victimized by its exploitative and hegemonic features.

The normative project posits an imagined community for the whole of humanity which overcomes the most problematic aspects of the present world scene: the part (whether as individual, group, nation, religion, civilization) and the whole (species, world, universe) are connected; difference and uniformities across space and through time are subsumed beneath an overall commitment to world order values in the provisional shape of peace, economic well-being, social and political justice, and environmental sustainability. As such, the normative project partakes of shared values and aspirations, trends, fears and expectations about the future, rooted hopes, visions of the possible. The framing of this project acknowledges primarily the efforts of movements and peoples at the grassroots, but also takes note of the participation of prominent leaders, governments and other institutions, as well as the specificity of opportunities and challenges arising in the aftermath of the Cold War. The normative project has ten dimensions.

Taming war   The contemporary normative project has its roots in the reaction to the barbarity of warfare. It was Grotius's horrified response to the Thirty Years War in Europe that gave birth to international law in the seventeenth century and to the specific regulatory urge to put limits on what states could do in the midst of war. This impulse ripened through time, leading to the Hague Conferences of 1899 and 1907 which brought together the leaders of the dominant states of the day, purporting to be the managers of the global order. For the first time a series of international law treaties were drafted and adopted to regulate the tactics· and weaponry of warfare to some degree, incorporating some customary principles of behavior embodied at high levels of abstraction in religion and morality: the requirement that tactics and weaponry distinguish between civilian and military targets, sparing the former; that force be used in a proportionate manner; that cruelty be avoided, including unnecessary suffering for those wounded or captured, even if part of the opposing military forces.

This endeavor to tame the conduct of war has persisted to the present. After World War II the Geneva Conventions of 1949 placed great stress on specific duties to protect the victims of war, including civilians and those military personnel wounded or captured in battle. These protections were later extended to the circumstances of intervention and civil war by the Geneva Protocols of 1977. Much current attention at the grassroots and governmental levels is being devoted to regimes of prohibition associated with weaponry of mass destruction: nuclear, chemical, and biological. At present, with respect to nuclear weaponry, the governmental emphasis has been on maintaining a partial regime (nonproliferation) as opposed to the efforts of transnational democratic initiatives to achieve a comprehensive regime of prohibition (delegitimizing nuclear weapons as such and arranging for their phased elimination from arsenals, thereby treating these weapons as chemical and biological weapons have been treated).

Whether this enterprise has been successful, on balance, remains controversial. Advocates claim that the suffering of war has been mitigated for millions of participants. Skeptics believe that the law of war is a hypocritical and deceptive misnomer which deflects reformist energy from war itself. At the root of the difficulty is the subordination of the principle of restraint to the achievement of victory in war by whatever means it takes. The supremacy of "military necessity" has tended to overwhelm the normative pressures of law, morality, and religion. This supremacy has been abetted by continuous innovation in the weaponry of war, the search by states for military superiority, and the development, reliance, and use of ultimate weapons and tactics in the course of winning World War II. Evidence of civilian devastation rarely inhibits tactics or weaponry. The current movement to prohibit landmines is illustrative. Despite the evidence of overwhelming civilian injury, much of it long after hostilities have ceased, governments seem reluctant to ban landmines, partly because of their cost–benefit advantages compared to other weapons. The debate itself confirms that nothing significant will happen until civil initiatives mount strong pressures.

Although the results are disappointing, the struggle to tame war continues alongside the wider, more dramatic series of efforts to abolish war itself as a hideous and outmoded social institution.

Abolishing war   The more fundamental struggle, at the very center of the normative project, is to challenge war itself, the social and political process of mass, intentional killing in the name of the state, for the sake of wealth and power, in defense of ideology and a way of life, allegedly on behalf of security in self-defense, but also to satisfy expansionist ambitions. This challenge directed against war is often analogized to the struggle against slavery, the divine right of kings, colonialism, each a social institution that like war was once generally accepted, at least by elites, as necessary and inevitable. Arguably, all advances in the human condition have involved challenging institutions and practices treated as necessary and inevitable.

The real and imagined carnage of war has been the principal impetus to abolitionist efforts, as have certain pacifist traditions of religious and secular thought. After World War I, in particular, antiwar sentiments flourished, taking aim at the legality of so-called "aggressive war" and at "the merchants of death" (those who made profits from arms sales). Public pressures were so great that leading countries subscribed to the Kellogg-Briand Pact of 1928 (also known as the Pact of Paris) that renounced war as an instrument of national policy, authorizing war only as a response to aggression, in a posture of self-defense. This new ground rule was invoked after World War II as a principal basis for convicting German and Japanese leaders of crimes against the peace for their role in planning and waging aggressive warfare. This prohibition is reproduced in the UN Charter in the form of Article 2(4), which prohibits altogether the use of force, although it is qualified by Article 51 which preserves the "inherent right of self-defense." The Charter seeks to restrict the scope of self-defense by requiring that only in situations of "prior armed attack" is self-defense permitted, and even then the claimant state is required to seek immediate approval from the Security Council.

As with the efforts to tame war, those to abolish war remain controversial and are not implemented to any great extent. States interpret for themselves what self-defense means, and have ignored the requirement of armed attack. The mobilization of response against aggression has been inconsistent and often half-hearted. Preparation for war, the tactics, secrecy, and weaponry have made war an integral part of the global landscape, especially in the South where more than 125 wars have been fought in the last 50 years. In the North, fear of catastrophic war, reinforced by deterrence and containment, avoided direct war during the Cold War, but added to the frequency and intensity of warfare in the South.

With the Cold War over, there is at present no strategic rivalry of the sort likely to produce warfare, but the war system seems as rooted as ever in the operational code of statecraft, expressed by way of large military establishments, expensive weapons innovations, huge arms sales, and interventionary diplomacy. What is also discouraging, especially during this period of geopolitical moderation, is the absence of moves from above or below that challenge seriously the war system, or even move toward large reductions of spending and embark upon ambitious types of disarmament. Yet the abolition of war remains a centerpiece of the normative project, and its political relevance is embedded in each and every dimension.

The intractability of war as a social institution suggests that unlike slavery and the other analogies relied upon by the new abolitionists, war is different: it presupposes shifts in the structures of power and authority, or at least in their normative foundations. Those who argue on the basis of structure generally regard world government as the precondition for disarmament; those who emphasize normative foundations tend either to insist upon democratizing the world (on the presumption that democracies don't go to war against one another and hence that if the foundations of authority in all states become democratic, there will be no political will to engage in war and the war system will wither away) or to disseminate the ethos of nonviolence throughout the whole gamut of social relations so widely that it undermines support for military approaches to conflict, displacing the war system in time by pacifism.

Making individuals accountable   As discussed in more contextual terms in chapter 7, one dimension of the normative project has been to make those in authority accountable for their transgressions, especially with respect to war and in relation to severe abuses of human rights. The essence of this approach has been to criminalize *aggressive* war, while not challenging rights of self-defense or military preparations. The Nuremberg and Tokyo War Crimes Tribunals at the end of World War II were the foundation of this struggle to impose individual accountability, and the decisions reached rejected defenses based on reason of state or superior orders. It was also notable that secondary trials were held to assess the individual responsibility of doctors, judges, business leaders, local military commanders, and local officials, expanding the reach of accountability to encompass those who variously implemented the policies of the regime or carried out independent atrocities of their own.

This Nuremberg experience, now being widely reassessed during the fiftieth anniversary year of the main judgment, has been criticized as "victors' justice." The crimes of the victorious powers, most notably the use of atomic bombs and the excesses of strategic bombing, were exempted from any scrutiny. The prosecutors at Nuremberg did pledge that the principles being laid down to judge the defendants would become binding international law that would henceforth be made applicable to the whole world and its leaders. Indeed, the UN General Assembly by unanimous vote endorsed the Nuremberg principles, seeking their authoritative formulation by the International Law Commission, the expert body at the UN, which in 1950 provided the text of these principles that is relied upon to this day to identify the nature of individual accountability.

Governments have not implemented the Nuremberg Principles. Indeed, the victorious powers in World War II, the countries which provided the judges, have each engaged subsequently in aggressive war. Further, these leading states have opposed efforts to institutionalize Nuremberg through the creation of procedures and some sort of international criminal court. The Nuremberg idea has been kept alive by two major developments: first, by activists who relied on the Nuremberg idea to challenge the supremacy of the state in the war/ peace area, validating the emergence of civil resistance as a step beyond what Thoreau and others had in mind by "civil disobedience"; secondly, after the Cold War, by moves toward convening war crimes tribunals to address allegations of genocidal behavior in Bosnia and Rwanda (even prior to this, issues of accountability emerged in various countries in South America as the transitions were made from the authoritarian rule of the 1960s to some sort of constitutional governance).

The importance of individual accountability to the establishment of global governance is evident. Crimes of states need to be deterred and, once committed, dealt with effectively if confidence in the emergence of wider regional communities of participation is to arise and if the formation of an eventual global community is to be encouraged. At this point, all the contradictions of world order are present: powerful states enjoy the full prerogatives of territorial supremacy and sovereignty, exempting leaders from accountability, especially if an authoritarian political order prevails; further, the diplomacy of reconciliation and peace often sharply conflicts with the impulse to impose individual responsibility – without surrender or defeat, the accused leadership is elusive and may well prolong its period of rule, fearing what the Argentinean human rights activist Jacopo Timmermann referred to in the 1970s as "the ghosts of Nuremberg."

Collective security   As has been indicated, especially in relation to security in chapter 5, one important strand of the normative project for a reformed world was to replace balance-of-power geopolitics with a rule-governed global security system that protected states threatened by aggressive war. Woodrow Wilson championed such an approach and advocated the creation of the League of Nations to achieve collective security. These efforts have persisted in various forms. The League was created but the United States refused to join, and when aggressive war occurred in Asia and Europe the response was ineffectual. Yet the idea of collective security persisted, and was embodied in a more detailed form in Chapter VII of the UN Charter. Again the experience of the Cold War confirmed the inadequacy of existing mechanisms of collective security, highlighted by the bipolarity of the period and the inability of the opposed blocs of states to agree upon the identity of an aggressor in most situations involving the outbreak of war. The defense of South Korea in 1950 was nominally a UN operation, but was substantively controlled by the United States, receiving a UN mandate only because the Soviet Union deprived itself of its veto by temporarily boycotting the Security Council in protest against the unrelated failure to seat representatives from the People's Republic of China.

As earlier argued, the Gulf crisis of 1990 presented a renewed, neo-Wilsonian opportunity to establish collective security. The conditions were finally right: clear aggression against a UN member; a political consensus of the permanent members of the Security Council; a threat to the strategic interests of leading countries; and the political will to provide the capabilities to perform effectively. The Gulf War that resulted in 1991 has had an ambiguous impact. It certainly established the possibility of UN effectiveness since Kuwait's sovereignty was restored and aggression was reversed. Yet the undertaking was again essentially geopolitical in motivation and character, the decisions being made in Washington, not at the Security Council in New York. When the challenge of Serbian aggression and ethnic cleansing in Bosnia arose a year later, the old circumstance of ineffectuality was again evident. Without both political consensus and a strategic stake of magnitude, leading states are not willing to pay the price for maintaining collective security. It was clear that countries without strategic relevance were on their own; the case of East Timor is exemplary, with Indonesia's aggression and crimes against humanity being neglected almost totally in the setting of collective security.

Not only is geopolitical practice discouraging, but leading states oppose the creation of independent UN capabilities by way of a peace force of volunteers and a reliable means to finance collective security. Perhaps collective security will take hold on a regional level during the decade ahead. In any event, the time has come to rethink collective security within the UN setting, associating UN uses of force with ideas of policing and reconciliation, not as a species of war-making. Such a reorientation would also greatly constrain uses of force that could not be focused on the elite responsible for aggression or genocide. The

Wilsonian impulse survives. Without collective security as an interim mechanism to deter and resist aggression, the prospects of abolishing war in the near future seem severely diminished.

Rule of law   The legal mindset has exerted considerable influence on shaping the priorities of the normative project for a reformed world order. In particular, US reformist energies since the Wilsonian era have stressed the importance of judicial procedures for the settlement of disputes. The establishment of a World Court in The Hague, initially in 1920, has epitomized this logic of world peace through law, although isolationist tendencies within the United States have polarized opinion on the desirability of enhancing the role and prestige of the judicial arm of the UN.

This manifested itself strongly during the controversy with the Sandinista government in Nicaragua in the 1980s. The Court decided in favor of Nicaragua with respect to the basic contention as to whether the US was illegally sponsoring Contra violence against an established state. This outcome so angered the White House that it withdrew the US from full participation, limiting its role to ad hoc arrangements to appear before the Court if it specifically agreed to do so. Additionally, the US government refused to abide by the 1986 decision, and the Security Council did not fulfill its Charter responsibility to implement World Court decisions. Surprisingly perhaps, the Non-Aligned Movement picked up the dropped baton, impressed by the objectivity of the World Court and its willingness to decide in favor of Nicaragua. It is highlighting the importance of obliging all countries to resolve their disputes by recourse to the World Court if diplomacy fails, and setting as a goal the year 1999, the hundredth anniversary of the initial Hague peace conference.

So far the reliance on judicial solutions has not been very successful in relation to fundamental conflicts involving core interests of states. The World Court has effectively resolved potentially troubling, long-festering, marginal disputes, especially involving disputed frontiers and maritime boundaries, as well as other technical matters. The regional role of judicial institutions in Europe is suggestive of how far the rule of law can be carried in crucial matters of economic policy and the protection of human rights, according precedence to supranational authority and subordinating in the event of conflict the highest expressions of judicial and legislative authority at the level of the sovereign state. The structuring of global governance on the basis of enhanced judicial roles within the various regional settings and for the world as a whole would be a major step in averting both civil and international warfare, being expressive of the disposition of well-governed political communities to entrust even the most serious disputes to third party procedures.

Nonviolent revolutionary politics   Earlier chapters have disclosed the dependence of humane governance on the emergence of a nonviolent ethos at all levels of social interaction, including the dynamics of intimate interaction within the family. The thrust of Mahatma Gandhi's courageous and brilliantly managed nonviolent anticolonial struggle against British rule in India introduced a radical new dimension into many subsequent political struggles for freedom, dignity, independence, and well-being that have been at the center of numerous historical narratives of the last half century. Martin Luther King imaginatively and powerfully carried a nonviolent orientation into the domain of race relations, specifically on behalf of civil rights for black Americans. Such victories were until recently viewed as special cases, and nonviolence was not widely regarded as capable of challenging major structures of oppression around the world. Then came a series of developments in the 1980s that gave a great potency to nonviolent political strategies, although with outcomes that were sometimes disappointing in various ways: the Khomeini-led revolutionary movement against the Shah in Iran; the People Power movement of Corazon Aquino in the Philippines; the various emancipatory struggles in East Europe against Communist rule; the *intifada* in occupied Palestine; the pro-democracy movement in China and other Asian countries, including Burma, Nepal, and South Korea; the negotiated settlements of long-lasting and seemingly perpetual armed struggles in South Africa, El Salvador, possibly Cambodia – and most recently even the struggle in Northern Ireland appears to be moving on to a political plane. (It has to be realized that these and other manifestations of nonviolence were never pure, and that recourse to nonviolent tactics often seemed to be for opportunistic and temporary reasons, and sometimes merely done as a clever adjustment to the lack of weaponry.)

This sense that nonviolence can challenge formidable power systems is indispensable in relation to the central struggles against war, militarism, and civic abuse of all types. It represents the countertradition to the persisting dominance of violence at all levels of social organization, and underpins the various approaches to the construction of a global civil society that both constitutes and is constituted by cosmopolitan democracy. Yet to achieve enduring results in relation to governance the commitment to nonviolence must be constantly deepened and extended to the most private spheres of human existence, including the socializing of the young, the reconceiving of "manhood," the aims of education, and the "pleasures" nurtured in the marketplace. The theory and practice of nonviolence involves the reconstruction of society, culture, and even consciousness, challenging many current practices, beliefs, and world-views in various civilizational spaces. Yet without the substantial displacement of violence in all its forms, humane governance is not attainable, especially given the global character of interaction that is becoming standard. Rwanda and Bosnia are neighborhood events for the entire world, and as such are not capable of being cordoned off even in a physical sense: refugees and disease flow across borders and reach distant shores by boat and plane.

Human rights As discussed in chapters 3 and 4, sovereignty and democracy are profoundly affected by the realization of human rights. The European idea of past centuries that the governing authority of a territorial state is supreme and unaccountable is challenged to the extent that the standards of human rights are effectively superimposed by either citizen initiative or external invervention. Sovereignty is subverted from without and diluted from within, giving rise to interventionary and resistance claims and prerogatives on behalf of the victims of abuse. In particular, the citizenry is morally and legally empowered to the extent it appreciates that its leaders can be challenged when they transgress the restraints on power as contained in the international law of human rights. In these regards, the protection of human rights represents a radical tendency in our historical period, but the potency of this effort depends on education (human rights need to be far better understood as empowering by those most victimized if they are to function even more widely as a political instrument of resistance and transformation) and a focus of conviction (human rights must appear consistent with cultural values, or at least these values must themselves be reassessed from within).

Recourse to genocidal practice by any government is increasingly regarded as a forfeiture of its claim to sovereign authority within territoiy. Other breakdowns of authority in terms of minimal provision of food, shelter, and medicine are being perceived as calling for a response by the wider regional and global communities. The extension of human rights from their civil and political character in liberal democracies to the economic and social concerns of the poor is a crucial transition in thought. The socialist challenge to capitalism and the individualist ethic were responsible for the broad, earlier acceptance that every person has the material entitlement to the necessities of life, a ground rule for humane governance already present in the seminal document, the Universal Declaration of Human Rights in 1948. With the market ascendant since the late 1980s, international competitiveness has been elevated as a criterion for policy choice and socialist concerns have been discredited. As matters now stand, the unmet challenge of economic and social rights is greater than ever. Ground has been lost in recent years. The only hope now is that globalization from below, with the many initiatives of transnational democracy and the emergence of global civil society, will rearticulate human solidarity in a manner that gives political weight to a renewed movement to achieve social and economic rights.

In the end, the struggle for human rights is the struggle against all forms of abuse, neglect, humiliation, and vulnerability. As Upendra Baxi has so eloquently argued in the setting of India, human rights in the end is a matter of taking suffering seriously. Looking back on this century of world wars and weaponry of mass destruction, it may well be that the gradual development of a human rights framework will be the centerpiece of a more hopeful narration of the experience of the period. Of course, the evolution of human rights is itself a source of suspicion, emanating from the West, reeking of hypocrisy, selective application, and contradictory implications. A wider process of creation and application is unfolding, and is essential, bringing into the domain of human rights the interplay of diverse tendencies within and between cultures, combining the educative imperative to know with the religious imperative to listen, to be humble in the face of the claims of the other, and above all, to refrain from linking the right of self-determination to claims of ethnic exclusivity.

Stewardship of nature   A recent addition to the normative agenda has been the rediscovery of human dependence on natural surroundings. Ancient peoples, of course, were acutely sensitive to their vulnerability to the severities of nature, especially cycles of drought and flooding. The modern scientific illusion supposed that technological ingenuity could enable human society to master nature, ignore limitations on resource availability, and expand indefinitely both resource-consuming lifestyles and the population of the planet. An emergent environmental consciousness over the last several decades, while still subordinate to market pressures and an ideology of growth, is emphasizing anew ideas of sustainability and limits. What these limits should be is a matter of fundamental political controversy, raising issues of conditions of survival at one end of the debate and matters of the conditions of human happiness and relations to the animal kingdom at the other end.

The distinctive challenge in the establishment of humane governance is to connect development with the stewardship of nature in a manner that realizes economic and social rights for all peoples, adjusting for unevenness of circumstance (correcting what has been identified in this report as "global apartheid"). At the same time, the enjoyment of the beauty of nature is the foundation of spirituality and creativity, and thus stewardship cannot be conceived of merely in materialist terms.

Positive citizenship   The foundations of community reflect the contours of individual and group identity, and more specifically in relation to governance, the quality of participation. In the West, positive participation has been associated with the shift from the status of "subject" (slave, vassal, serf) to "citizen." The modern media-shaped political life threatens individuals with a new type of postmodern serfdom, in which elections, political campaigns, and political parties provide rituals without substance, a politics of sound bytes and manipulative images, reducing the citizen to a mechanical object to be controlled, rather than being the legitimating source of legitimate authority.

What forms of political participation can combine rootedness in the circumstances of a given place (the grassroots test of integrity and relevance) with the connections and aspirations of an emergent global civil society is an essential, variable challenge. Empowerment from below as an alternative to the ritualization of politics at the level of the state and to subordination to those types of globalization that express market priorities is at the core of the evolving normative project. The projection of a global identity, without the conditions of community, and the claim now to be "world citizens" express striving for humane governance, but they also arouse serious suspicions that the necessary struggles associated with transformation are being evaded by the sentimental, New Age pretense that a reorientation of personal energy will suffice.

Positive citizenship, stressing this interplay between the concreteness of situation and the imagined community that represents humane governance, will mean various things in different societies. The idea of citizenship is being promoted, also, as extending beyond state/society relations and involving all relationships of a participatory nature, that is, institutions and practices that invoke authority. Positive citizenship also draws on nonviolence and human rights as inspirational sources. The greatest challenge, at present, is to reconcile the territorial dimensions of citizenship with the temporal dimensions: acting in the present for the sake of the future, establishing zones of humane governance as building blocks.

Cosmopolitan democracy This is the binding idea of democracy encompassing all relationships, providing the grounds of institutional legitimacy, and establishing the basis for procedures and practices linking individuals and groups with institutions. It is becoming the pervasive underpinning that has been evolving along several tracks for several centuries, and now, in tandem with technology and high finance, is necessarily operative across statist boundaries as well as within them. Of course, leadership styles based on hierarchy and soft authoritarianism remain potent realities, especially in the Asian/Pacific region and in Islamic countries; elsewhere, a democratic facade is fashioned to hide the persistence of authoritarian institutional controls. But what gives promise to the vision of cosmopolitan democracy is the legitimation of democratic ideas of governance on a universal basis, the embodiment of these ideas in human rights as specified in global instruments, the democratic implications of nonviolent approaches to resistance and reform, and most of all, the deeply democratic convictions of transnational initiatives that have begun to construct the alternative paradigm of a global civil society.

We can expect many ebbs and flows, many relapses and pitfalls, endless discussion about the failure and character of democracy, and yet the cumulative drift of the normative project has been and remains dedicated to the deepening and the expansion of democracy in relation to all fields of human endeavor. It is virtually impossible to imagine humane governance as a global phenomenon without presupposing the increasing influence and acceptance of participatory politics, whether or not called "democracy," resting on the dignity and worth of the individual, but also of the group. Democracy, in these senses, provides the indispensable organizing principle, with the aim that it can be eventually presupposed, possibly to such an extent that the label can and will be dropped.

These ten dimensions of the normative project, some of recent origin, but all with many antecedents throughout the world, suggest the contours of humane governance. Their emergence remains, as stressed throughout the report, generally subordinate to globalization from above, acutely uneven, provisional, precarious, at the margins, but yet undeniable. Whether the dynamics of emergence will create a toppling of "the Berlin wall" of militarist, market-driven, materialist globalism is far from assured. At the same time, such a shift in fundamental prospects for governance is a sufficiently plausible outcome as to make the struggle to achieve it the only responsible basis for positive citizenship at this stage of history. Whether ours is an axial moment of

5 The G-7 is the designation given to the seven leading industrial countries (Canada, Italy, France, Germany, Japan, Britain, and the United States), whose heads of state meet annually to discuss *world* economic policy and other shared concerns.

6 The IMF helps governments with weak currencies deal with falling exchange rates and payments on foreign debt, whereas the World Bank finances project support on the basis of loans at favorable rates. The IMF, in particular, also provides commercial banks with crucial guidance as to creditworthiness. If a country gains certification by the IMF, it can obtain capital for development and other purposes more easily, and at favorable rates, otherwise not.

7 Not all normative effects from liberationist political victories are positive. The status of women and ethnic minorities may regress despite (and because of) the overall dynamic of liberation, as in Eastern Europe in the 1990s.

8 The Trilateral Commission is a private elite policy group drawn from leaders in business, banking and academic life in Japan, Europe and North America. It meets periodically and issues reports on controversial matters.

9 Job loss is structural when it is based on unavailability which persists whether the economy as a whole is doing well or not from the perspective of growth. It is cyclical if job loss is a byproduct of rises and falls in market performance.

10 See Huntington, "A Clash of Civilizations?" for an influential assertion of this thesis.

11 The constitutional status of UN mandates seems to depend centrally on the compatibility between what is undertaken and Charter provisions. In the background, of course, is respect for the sovereign rights of Members, safeguarded by the prohibition in Article 2(7) on UN intervention in domestic jurisdiction unless it is a part of a Chapter VII enforcement operation. Here it could be argued that Iraq's repressive regime was linked with its recurrent recourse to peace-threatening uses of force.

12 See Alberto Ascherio and others, "Effect of the Gulf War on Infant and Child Mortality in Iraq," *New England Journal of Medicine* 327 (Sept. 24, 1992): 931–6; Harvard Study Team, "The Effect of the Gulf Crisis on the Children of Iraq," *New England Journal of Medicine* 325 (1991): 977–80.

13 This realist image of the UN competes with the idealist view of the UN as a political actor transcending geopolitics, or providing an alternative to statism. The position taken here is that the forces in international society confront one another within the UN to varying degrees. The UN was conceived to serve states as the subjects of world order, but has been increasingly penetrated by transnational social forces with democratizing styles and demands.

14 At the same time, like a formidable virus that adapts and resists agents for its suppression, nuclearism assumes new shapes and forms in the world of the 1990s, and beyond. Pre-emptive claims are asserted in relation to such unwanted nuclear contenders as Iraq, Iran, and North Korea, while the United States enjoys the freedom to contemplate the use of nuclear weapons

in the South with no risk of serious escalation attached, what might be labeled the re-emergence of "the Hiroshima temptation" (the rationalization of saving lives, among others, challenging the absoluteness of the so-called "tradition of non-use" that supposedly governed behavior during the era of mutual deterrence).

15 The immediate casualties of the Gulf War were estimated at 200 for the coalition side, 200,000 for the Iraqi side or 1000:1, approximately the ratio reported by the Spanish conquistadors who "discovered" the New World in the late fifteenth and sixteenth centuries. If subsequent civilian losses on the Iraqi side are added in, the outcome of the violence deployed is even more one-sided, more a massacre than a war.

16 Cf. Robert Jay Lifton and Richard Falk, *Indefensible Weapons: The Political and Psychological Case against Nuclearism*, 2nd expanded edn (New York: Basic Books, 1992).

17 The favorable trends here are provisional, and seem quite precarious. There is recent evidence that authoritarian alternatives to market-oriented constitutionalism can produce superior economic performance. Fujimora's Peru and Deng's China are outstanding examples, but Singapore, South Korea, Taiwan, Malaysia, Indonesia are often mentioned in this context.

18 The state remains salient, but may be finding its identity blurred by the opposed pulls of globalizing and territorial forces, as in the 1990s controversies about the treaty regimes of Maastricht, NAFTA, and GATT. There is also a concern about whether the state's formal status in world policy is not being ritualized, with real power being exerted off-stage by unseen and unaccountable forces aligned with the market, or more accurately, with emergent structures of economic privilege in a globalized economy.

19 The regional dimension of governance is also of great relevance, although regions, like states, embody the unevenness of human conditions. See papers by Björn Hettne and András Inotai published under the title *The New Regionalism: Implications for Global Development and International Security* (Helsinki: UNU/World Institute for Development Economics Research, 1994).

20 Although if the UN can be reduced to an instrumental role in relation to geopolitical priorities then its existence can be absorbed into realist designs for world order.

21 An endorsement of the politics of bounded conviction as an alternative to realism is not meant to open the door to religious and political fanaticism, or to be understood as an appeal to the irrational. This conception of "conviction" is *bounded* by an overriding duty to uphold international law, especially its prohibitions on nondefensive force and its embodiment of human rights; hence, the phrase "bounded conviction." There is no intention here to subordinate politics and law to the realization of higher, unconditional, transcendent "truths," or any implication that such a higher order of being can be usefully established to guide human endeavors. Rather these boundaries imposed are socially and politically *constructed*, and continuously *evolved*.

Chapter 2 A Triple Indictment of Inhumane Governance

1 Although not uniformly. The variations are partly a matter of economic competence in relation to job creation and profit margins and partly a matter of cultural orientation toward wealth creation. For insightful discussion see Charles Hamden-Turner and Alfons Trompenaars, *The Seven Cultures of Capitalism* (New York: Doubleday, 1993); see also Robert B. Reich, *The Work of Nations: Preparing Ourselves for the Twenty-First Century Capitalism* (New York: Knopf, 1991).

2 Such a perspective was especially pronounced in the immediate aftermath of the Gulf War. Since then, the failures of US leadership, including financial vulnerability, domestic gridlock, inept foreign policy assessments, and a tendency to wobble in relation to such challenges as Bosnia, Somalia, Haiti, and Rwanda have superseded the earlier grandiose conceptions of the US role in the post–Cold War world associated with the George Bush call for "a new world order."

3 The South Commission, *The Challenge to the South* (Oxford: Oxford University Press, 1990), p. 2.

4 Gernot Kohler, "Global Apartheid," in Richard Falk, Samuel S. Kim, and Saul H. Mendlovitz, eds, *Toward a Just World Order* (Boulder, Colo.: Westview, 1982), pp. 315–25.

5 Arjun Makhijani, *From Global Capitalism to Economic Justice* (New York: Apex, 1992), p. x; Susan George in discussing Third World indebtedness and Ali Mazrui in discussing the post–Cold War reality both relied on the global apartheid metaphor, apparently independently of one another and without reference to Kohler's earlier essay, in a volume of essays based on a Nobel jubilee symposium in Oslo, Norway. See Geir Lundestad and Odd Arne Westad, ed, *Beyond the Cold War: New Dimensions in International Relations* (Oslo: Scandinavian University Press, 1993), pp. 85–98 (Mazrui), pp. 171–88 (George).

6 T. C. Schelling, "The Global Dimension," in Graham Allison and Gregory F. Treverton, eds, *Rethinking America's Security* (New York: Norton, 1992), pp. 196–210, at p. 200.

7 Such a conclusion is not self-evident; Schelling in his essay on security interests concludes that the United States must safeguard "what we *possess* as well as what we appreciate," that is, the material standard of living, cf. p. 200.

8 For persuasive analysis along these lines see Timothy Garton Ash, *The Uses of Adversity: Essays on the Fate of Central Europe* (Cambridge: Granta, 1989). Other factors also relevant were the Gorbachev leadership and its "new thinking" as applied to Soviet–East European relations, and the severe economic failure throughout the entire Soviet bloc.

9 Document E/ICEF/1990/h.5, p.6: see *The State of the World's Children 1990* (New York: Oxford University Press, 1990).

10 Quotations from *The State of World's Children 1990*, p. 13.

11 UNDP, *Human Development Report 1991* (New York: Oxford University Press, 1991), p. 23.

12 One notable discussion along these lines is Paul Kennedy, *Preparing for the Twenty-First Century* (New York: Random House, 1992). This mood has been focused by the 1994 UN Conference on Population and Development held in Cairo.

13 Based on an account in the *Guardian Weekly*, May 7, 1991, p. 7.

14 For further on this, especially in an Indian setting, see Smitu Kothari and Harsh Sethi, eds, *Rethinking Human Rights: Challenges for Theory and Action* (New York: Horizons, 1989).

15 Abdullahi Ahmed An-Na'im, ed., *Human Rights in Cross-Cultural Perspectives: A Quest for Consensus* (Philadelphia: University of Pennsylvania Press, 1992).

16 Increasingly since 1992 Rushdie has made occasional public appearances, insisting that his identity as a creative writer depends on social engagement. There is no sign that Iranian authorities are moving toward a suspension of the death threat or even a termination of the reward. Other writers and intellectuals in the Islamic world have been threatened, injured, and killed for their allegedly anti-Islamic, or even for their secular, orientation. The Bangla Deshi writer Taslima Nasrin has been under such a threat from fundamentalist groups who intimidate the government. See her moving account of this ordeal in her "Sentenced to Death," *New York Times*, Nov. 30, 1993.

17 See "Comment," *Guardian*, July 22, 1991.

18 Ibid.

19 Such an imperative is the direct opposite of Samuel Huntington's suggestion that the United States augment intercivilizational rivalry between Islamic and Confucian societies as a way of diverting hostile energy from the West. See Samuel P. Huntington, "The Clash of Civilizations," *Foreign Affairs* 72 (1993): 22–49.

20 The assessment of recourse to violence by a state or international institution is dependent on the specific circumstances of the case. It is context dependent. What is being argued, however, is that given the difficulties of effective uses of political violence for purposes of global security and the immense human suffering that follows from large-scale warfare, there are strong reasons to explore all avenues of nonviolent conflict resolution with renewed vigor. Also, that media and educational efforts should be made to de-glorify war, and to resist the temptation to associate patriotism with a celebration of the sufferings of opponents, especially civilians, but also conscripted soldiers, and indeed all those exposed to the ravages of war.

21 For instance, Pierre Lellouche, "The Death of a Dinosaur," *Newsweek*, Aug. 5, 1991, p. 4.

22 The book edited by Charles W. Kegley, Jr bearing this title and collecting writing on the theme centers around a contribution by John Lewis Gaddis, who is responsible for labeling the cold war era as "the long peace," see Kegley Jr, *The Long Postwar Peace: Contending Explanations and Projections* (New York: HarperCollins, 1991).

pados [illegible]

socr.

1. intern concn of devices
If agt ch. a/s → abbs it as f. in same sense.

— o —

u

NPR

David Welna
NPR Foreign Desk
635 Massachussets Ave NW
Washington, DC 20001

23 A parallel question is raised by the electoral victory of an Islamic extremist movement that seemed dedicated to the destruction of democratic political forms, as was alleged to be the case in Algeria as of 1991. The problem is not, of course, new. The ascent to power by Hitler and the National Socialist Party took place in 1933 by constitutional means.

24 Cf. Lester Brown, "A New World Order," in *State of the World 1991* (New York: Norton, 1991).

25 For an example of the former see James N. Rosenau, *Turbulence in World Politics* (Princeton: Princeton University Press, 1990), and of the latter see John Mearsheimer, "Back to the Future: Instability in Europe after the Cold War," *International Security* 15 (1990): 5–56.

26 Published in the *Economist*, Feb. 7–14, 1992, p. 66; see their mildly critical editorial, "Pollution and the Poor," Feb. 15–22, 1992, pp. 18–19.

27 There is a more general failure of global leadership to be discerned in the early 1990s that includes the US. See, for instance, the *Time* cover story preceding the 1993 G-7 meeting in Tokyo with the title "What's Happened to Leadership?" *Time*, July 12, 1993. As of late 1994 every large democratic state was governed by a leader unpopular at home.

Chapter 3 Sovereignty: A Twisting Path from Modernism

1 J. Ann Tickner, *Gender in International Relations: Feminist Perspectives on Achieving Global Security* (New York: Columbia University Press, 1992); see also Adrienne Harris and Ynestra King, eds, *Rocking the Ship of State! Toward a Feminist Peace Politics* (Boulder, Colo.: Westview, 1989).

2 Alexander Wendt, "Collective Identity Formation and the International State," mimeo. paper, 1993.

3 Such representation may not be perceived as adequate by internal political communities, including cities, regions, or groups. There has emerged a movement at the grassroots to decenter the state as international actor. One expression of this is "municipal foreign policy," another is "citizen diplomacy."

4 Robert B. Reich, *The Work of Nations: Preparing Ourselves for the Twenty-First Century* (New York: Knopf, 1992).

5 See Tickner, *Gender in International Relations*.

6 For a range of relevant perspectives see Bart van Steebergen, ed., *The Condition of Citizenship* (London: Sage, 1994).

Chapter 4 The Democratizing Imperative

1 See David Held and Daniele Archibugi, eds, *Cosmopolitan Democracy: An Agenda for a New World Order*, (Cambridge: Polity Press, 1995).

2 For instance, where strong states operate behind the façade of a democratic government; the elected leaders lack the effective authority to control the

national security bureaucracy, enabling abuses to occur on a widespread scale. Many countries exhibit this pattern, outwardly conforming to the call for democratic governance, but lacking the real capabilities to protect the vulnerable enemies of the state from abuse and possessing a political culture that is accustomed to a militarist style (for instance, Turkey). Cf. Falk, "Democratic Disguise: Post–Cold War Authoritarianism," in Phyllis Bennis and Michel Moushabeck, eds, *Altered States* (New York: Olive Branch Press, 1993), pp. 17–27.

3 See Victoria Brittain, *Hidden Lives, Hidden Deaths: South Africa's Crippling of a Continent* (London: Faber and Faber, 1988).

4 David Held, "Democracy: Past, Present, and Possible Futures," *Alternatives* 18 (1993): 259–72, at 264.

5 For a compelling discourse see R. B. J. Walker, *Inside/Outside: International Relations as Political Theory* (Cambridge: Cambridge University Press, 1993).

6 For general discussions see M. Cherif Bassiouni, *A Draft International Law Criminal Code and Draft Statute for an International Criminal Tribunal* (1987); Christopher L. Blakesley, "The Need for an International Criminal Court in the New International World Order," *Vanderbilt Journal of Transnational Law* 25 (1992) 151: Jordan J. Paust, "Applicability of International Criminal Laws to Events in the Former Yugoslavia," *American University Journal of International Law and Policy* 9 (1994): 499–523.

7 Democratization as used in this report is not merely the substitution of elite orientations by populist or majoritarian orientations. Normative constraints by way of impartially interpreted international law, including human rights and the protection of democratic processes, impose boundaries on preference as the basis of policy. In addition, ecological constraints need to be integrated into the functioning outlook of those responsible for decisions, either by way of an extension of human rights and international law, or through appropriate institutional innovations (for example, an environmental security council or through a network of institutions with authority to enact necessary modes of environmental governance). Also, as earlier discussed – see chapter I – the empowerment of civil society is not unproblematic, possibly engendering regressive forces during a period of social fluidity and reproducing class, gender, and race hierarchies and patterns of deformation. For democratization to instill confidence that it will advance the cause of humane governance it must evolve in conjunction with progressive modes of social reconstruction within all settings of policy formation and implementation.

8 It must be observed that most transnational initiatives, including human rights organizations, remain exclusively concerned with state/society relations, and pay no attention to globalization. Some exceptions can be noted: The Other Economic Summit (TOES) and International Peoples Tribunal to Judge the G-7, Tokyo, July 1993.

Chapter 5 Security for Humane Governance

1 Part of this process is to redefine the domestic constitutional order. It has involved the marginalization of Congress in reaching decisions, leaving the locus of authority in the executive and the unelected national security bureaucracy (Pentagon, CIA). See John Hart Ely, *War and Responsibility* (Princeton: Princeton University Press, 1993).

2 Such a preoccupation does not mean that if strategic interests had been present that a successful interventionary operation could have been organized. Interventionary diplomacy has rarely succeeded in recent decades, even when backed by overwhelming military superiority (Vietnam, Afghanistan), in the face of determined resistance.

3 Robin Morgan, *The Demon Lover: On the Sexuality of Terrorism* (New York: Norton, 1989); I owe the phrase "transformative feminism" to Elisabeth Gerle.

4 K. Subrahmanyam, "Alternative Security Doctrines," *Bulletin of Peace Proposals* 21 (1990): 77–85.

5 Yoshikazu Sakamoto, "People's Security in Global Perspective," paper, Notre Dame WOMP Security Workshop, April 1991.

6 Ibid., p. 85.

7 In addition, the frame for this stability is seen to be continued hegemony by the North anchored in the United States. See Daniel Deudney and G. John Ikenberry, "The Logic of the West," *World Policy Journal* (Winter 1993–4). The nonproliferation issue is so important in the post–Cold War era as it seems to pose the only direct threat to this hegemony.

8 *Wall Street Journal*, Aug. 6, 1991, p. 6.

9 For text see Independent Commission on Disarmament and Security Issues, *Common Security: A Blueprint for Survival* (New York: Simon and Schuster, 1982).

10 The notable exception, of course, was a realist emphasis on the avoidance of actual strategic war in the North due to the realization that even "victory" would be "self-destructive." For this line of thinking see John Mueller, *Retreat from Doomsday: The Obsolescence of Major War* (New York: Basic Books, 1989). Mueller's argument unconvincingly minimizes the impact of nuclear weaponry on his central thesis that major war, as a consequence of mutual destructiveness and cost/benefit analysis, had become virtually obsolete as a conflict-resolving mechanism.

11 As was argued in chapter 4, modern modes of democratization were state-centric, emphasizing respresentation of the citizenry via periodic elections and multiparty campaigns. Premodern modes, as in the classical Athenian form, rested on direct participation, as do postmodern forms.

12 Cf. Marshall McLuhan, *The Global Village: Transformations in World Life and Media in the Twenty-First Century* (New York: Oxford, 1989).

13 As the sovereignty chapter makes clear, the early role of the modern European state in bringing internal security in the aftermath of feudalism

was in many respects positive, as was the struggle to modify, if not overcome, the pretensions of monarchy (such as the "divine right of kings") through struggle from below.

14 For an extreme, widely commented upon, version of such a position see John Mearsheimer, "Back to the Future: Instability in Europe after the Cold War," *International Security* 15 (1990): 5–56.

15 In Mearsheimer's words, "The worst order would be a non-nuclear Europe in which power inequities emerge between the principal poles of power," at 31.

16 Much of the civilian suffering came after the ceasefire, a deferred effect of the deliberate destruction of Iraq's water treatment system. Without potable water, disease, often fatal, spread widely among the population, with children under five years of age being particularly victimized. An aspect of this pattern of effects, in what was presented to the world as a UN undertaking, was the US approach to war-making, which is to rely on tactics that shift the suffering associated with war to the target society *as a whole*. In 1993 this approach was again evident during the UN presence in Somalia, especially during the phase in which the US tried to capture and/or kill Mohammed Farah Aideed, relying on helicopter gunships to minimize US casualties, but inflicting heavy losses on the Somali civilian population, thereby alienating the people in south Mogadishu, Aideed's stronghold, from the UN operation. Such an experience reinforces the argument that the UN must impose higher standards than those of the humanitarian law of war – with its virtually unrestricted deference to "military necessity" – on forces operating under its mandate.

17 Note the reliance on "transnational" to describe what David Held has influentially designated as "cosmopolitan democracy." There is no difference in substance. See among Held's extensive writings on the globalizing domain of democracy the collection edited by Daniele Archibugi and David Held, *Cosmopolitan Democracy* (Cambridge: Polity Press, 1994).

18 The attachment to nuclear weapons may also express modernist resistance to postmodern priorities and hierarchies. Control over nuclear weapons gives leading states a lingering zone of autonomy in relation to global market forces, as well as justifiably imparting a sense of self-importance for political leaders. If postmodern geopolitics threatens to turn elected leaders of powerful states into the constitutional monarchs of the twenty-first century – that is, virtual figureheads – then nuclear weapons policy is a way of retaining power at the state level. Of course, my point is partly rhetorical. Elected leaders have differing sources of legitimacy than hereditary leaders, and are likely for a long time to have an important substantive impact on policy.

19 Of course, the contention is made that nuclear weaponry cannot be "abolished" because knowledge cannot be disinvented or because the prospect of cheating in a disarmed world is too attractive. But then by such reasoning how can biological and chemical weapons be abolished?! The attachment to nuclear weapons is deeper than geopolitics, but it is also

sustained by geopolitics. See Robert Jay Lifton and Eric Markusen, *The Genocidal Mentality: Nazi Holocaust and Nuclear Threat* (New York: Basic Books, 1990).

20 An earlier request in partial form is being presented in 1994 to the World Court for an Advisory Opinion by way of the World Health Organization. The basic legal rationale is contained in a published legal memorandum. Nicholas Grief, *The World Court Project on Nuclear Weapons and International Law* (Northampton, Mass. Aletheia, 1992). The General Assembly request is broader, dealing with threat as well as use, and is more difficult to disregard on the ground of relevance. Opposition to the WHO was mounted by nuclear weapons states partly by claiming that use of weaponry was not a health issue.

21 On biological weaponry and warfare see Susan Wright, ed., *Preventing a Biological Weapons Arms Race* (Cambridge: MIT Press, 1990).

22 The idea of neutrality needs to be reconsidered in light of transition to geogovernance. Can states be allowed to opt out of shared financial and personpower responsibility for peacekeeping at regional and global levels?

23 The role of collective security is here restricted to self-defense situations within the compass of a strict reading of Article 51 of the Charter. Claims to intervene for humanitarian reasons do not fall within the mandate of collective security; such claims violate the social contract between states and the UN to respect domestic jurisdiction and sovereign rights, although there is a gray zone in the face of genocide or severe abuse of human rights, with a widely shared view that severe denials of human rights pose over time threats to international peace and security.

24 There are many dimensions here that often involve delicate intercultural moral judgments – for example, female genital mutilation, Hindu dowry and caste practices, Islamic divorce codes, repudiation of sexual deviance.

25 See Peter Singer, *Animal Rights and Human Obligations* (Englewood Cliffs, N.J.: Prentice Hall, 1989); Christopher D. Stone, *The Gnat is Older than Man: Global Environment and the Human Agenda* (Princeton, N. J.: Princeton University Press, 1993).

26 In the background are complex issues about violence as a component of civic culture, and how to minimize its impact. Not only the treatment of animals is at issue, but hunting and contact sports.

27 *State of the World 1991* (New York: Norton, 1991), p. 3.

28 As the noted ecological writer Norman Myers puts it: "We face environmental decline on every side. In just the past year we have lost 26 billion tons of topsoil, enough to grow 9 million tons of food and to make up the diets of more than 200 million starving people. We have lost almost 60,000 square miles, equivalent in area to New England, of tropical forest, which has cost us dearly in terms of timber harvests, watershed services, species habitats, and climate stability. Another 25,000 square miles, the same size as Ireland, have been desertified to the extent they won't be able to grow food again for decades at best. Tens of thousands of our fellow species have been denied living space on One Earth." Norman Myers,

Ultimate Security: The Environmental Basis of Political Stability (New York: Norton, 1993), p.6.

Chapter 6   The Struggle against Globalization from Above

1 Noam Chomsky, *World Orders Old and New* (New York: Columbia University Press, 1995) ch.6.
2 See Raymond Vernon, *Sovereignty at Bay* (New York: Basic Books, 1971); Robert Gilpin, *US Power and the Multinational Corporation: The Political Economy of Direct Foreign Investment* (New York: Basic Books, 1975); Richard J. Barnet and John Cavanagh, *Global Dreams: Imperial Corporations and the New World Order* (New York: Simon and Schuster, 1994).
3 Of course, the end of the East/West confrontation and the Soviet collapse has a series of world order consequences: an altered power configuration; diminished prospect of a major nuclear war; absence of strategic conflict among major states. Yet, as influential realist scholarship since 1989 demonstrates, the Westphalian/Machiavellian world-view remains essentially intact; for a partial exception to this view see James Rosenau, *Turbulence in World Politics: A Theory of Change and continuity* (Princeton: Princeton University Press, 1990).
4 *UNDP, Human Development Report 1992* (New York: Oxford, 1992), p. 89.
5 For a devastating account of the effects and scale of global advertising see Alan Durning, "Can't Live Without It," *World-Watch* 6.3, (May–June 1993): 10–18. The trend is alarming: "Total global advertising expenditures multiplied sevenfold from 1950 to 1990; they grew one-third faster than the world economy and three times faster than world population" (p.13).
6 It must also be noted that certain forms of intervention are much more difficult than others; humanitarian intervention in Serbia that is more than a feel-good holding operation might involve hundreds of thousands of troops, heavy casualties, and a prolonged, expensive, and politically unpopular presence in an occupying role.
7 Peter Truell and Larry Gurwin, *False Profits: The Inside Story of BCCI, the World's Most Corrupt Financial Empire* (Boston: Houghton, Mifflin, 1992); Jonathon Beaty and S. C. Gwynne, *The Outlaw Bank: A Wild Ride into the Secret Heart of BCCI* (New York: Random House, 1993).
8 See ibid.
9 Such an impression is further strengthened by comparing the regulatory severity used against BCCI with the rescue operation taken on in the USA in the aftermath of the savings and loan scandal, as well as with other instances of dubious global banking practices. Kathleen Day, *S & L Hell: The People and the Politics Behind the $1 Trillion Savings and Loan Scandal* (New York: Norton, 1993).
10 See Robin Broad with John Cavanagh, *Plundering Paradise: The Struggle for the Environment in the Philippines* (Berkeley: University of California,

1993); more generally see Jeremy Brecher, John Brown Childs and Jill Cutler, eds, *Global Visions: Beyond the New World Order* (Boston: South End Presss, 1993).

11 Arguably, some countries in the South have improved welfare/well-being policies as a result of globalization, raising slightly the low floor on wages, improving safety and environmental standards, widening employment opportunities, expanding the middle class. For instance, NAFTA is supposed to produce such effects in Mexico. For critiques of the NAFTA/GATT framework see Ralph Nader et al., *The Case against Free Trade: GATT, NAFTA, and the Globalization of Corporate Power* (San Francisco: Earth Island Press, 1993); Kevin Watkins, *Fixing the Rules: North–South Issues in International Trade and the GATT Uruguay Round* (London: Catholic Institute for International Relations, 1992).

12 As a beginning, it would be useful if all annual reports by human rights organizations included a section on economic and social rights. The annual *Human Development Report* of UNDP and the 1995 UN Summit on Social Development are moves in this direction, although neither grounds assessments in a right/duties matrix.

13 Among the relevant documents are the Convention on the Political Rights of Women; Convention on the Elimination of All Forms of Discrimination Against Women; Convention on the Rights of the Child; Convention on the Status of Refugees; Protocol Relating to the Status of Refugees; and the Convention Relating to the Status of Stateless Persons. For convenient texts of these documents, as well as those in the notes below, see Burns H. Weston et al., eds, *Basic Documents in International Law and World Order*, 2nd edn (St Paul, Minn.: West, 1990).

14 European Social Charter; African Charter on Human and Peoples' Rights.

15 Especially, the preparation of a Universal Declaration of the Rights of Indigenous Peoples undertaken under UN auspices by the Informal Working Group established by a subcommission of the Human Rights Commission; see also ILO Convention 169, adopted in 1989, which moved away from the earlier unacceptable stress on assimilation to an acknowledgment of basic rights to safeguard the distinctive way of life of indigenous peoples in the face of various forms of modernizing encroachment, but stopped short of an outright endorsement of a right of self-determination available to indigenous peoples. Such a right is claimed, however, in the UN Draft Declaration on the Rights of Indigenous Peoples under consideration.

16 By cognitive climate reference is made to a coherent approach to economic policy and the aim is to put forward one that modifies the current degree of deference to market logic and yet manages to sustain output and services at satisfactory levels.

17 Another strain of skepticism insists that governmental corruption and incompetence is so endemic at this point that resource transfers cannot be translated into the sorts of results that could induce human betterment.

18 Cf. *1991–1992 State of the World Conflict Report* (Atlanta, G.: International Negotiation Network, Carter Center of Emory University, 1992), pp. 24–5.

Ruth Sivard has been demonstrating for years that trivial reallocations of resources could achieve wonders with respect to alleviating human distress. See e.g. Ruth Leger Sivard, *World Military and Social Expenditures 1993* (Washington, DC: World Priorities, 1993).

19 There is a fuller rationale on pp. 45–8 of the report.

20 UNICEF, *The State of the World's Children 1993* (New York: Oxford University Press, 1993), p.1.

21 Ibid., pp. 1–2.

22 Ibid., 2.

23 UNDP, *Human Development Report 1992* (New York: Oxford University Press, 1992), p.89.

24 Ibid.,90.

25 The report also explicitly acknowledges and encourages the role of "international civil society" in making effective its recommendations for the promotion of human development.

26 UNICEF, *The State of the World's Children 1993*, 5.

27 Ibid., 4.

28 In 1994, humanitarian undertakings under UN auspices again seem to be less promising, since it is exceedingly difficult to keep them distinct from interference with ongoing political struggles, and from being nullified by determined forms of resistance. For general perspectives on humanitarian diplomacy see Kevin M. Cahill, ed., *A Framework for Survival* (New York: Basic Books, 1993). The growing reluctance of countries to give the UN adequate financial support in these settings is also a demoralizing factor that is undermining the credibility of both relief and peacekeeping roles.

29 Jorge G. Castaneda, "Beyond the Terms of Trade: The Broader Social and Political Supranationality and Grass Roots Coalitions," paper, on file, Princeton University, 1993; see also Castaneda, "Can NAFTA Change Mexico?" *Foreign Affairs* 72 (1993): 66–80.

30 *The Global Partnership for Environment and Development: A guide to Agenda 21* (New York: UN, 1993), p. 68.

31 *Our Common Future* (New York: Oxford University Press, 1987), p. 95.

32 Paul Kennedy, *Preparing for the Twenty-First Century* (New York: Random House, 1993), p. 331.

33 Ibid.

34 Ibid., p.24.

35 According to *Our Common Future*, the Brundtland Commission report of 1987, only 1.5 percent of official development aid was then being used for population restraint, and some countries had cut back or eliminated their contributions because of ideological issues; the report simply says that "this must be reversed" (p. 107); this reversal has started to occur, most notably in the United States, where the Clinton Presidency has restored support for UN efforts to promote family planning after more than a decade of opposition during the Reagan and Bush Presidencies. One of the adverse effects of the fall of Communism in Eastern Europe has been to increase the influence of the Catholic Church in several countries, leading to anti-

abortion laws, and other socially regressive steps, especially on the status and role of women.

36 The Security Council and World Bank/IMF are mainly subordinated; the UNDP, ECOSOC, UNICEF are more driven by normative mandates.

37 Examples are those bearing the names of Brandt, Palme and Brundtland along with the South Commission and the Commission on Human Governance. Also reflecting such visionary perspectives are global conferences on major world order issues under UN auspices. Although these conferences restrict non-state actors to the margins, transnational democratic forces have been increasingly influencing the formal, statist proceedings and asserting a media presence.

38 Both lawyers and doctors have been active in challenging nuclear weapons policy in a variety of settings.

39 At stake, centrally, as argued in chapter 4, was the reinvention of democracy, the empowering of civil initiatives, and a revisioning of reliance on political parties, elections, parliamentary and judicial institutions.

40 *Our Common Future*, pp.43–65.

41 Ibid., 43.

42 Ibid., p. 43–4.

43 The South Commission, *The Challenge to the South* (Oxford: Oxford University Press, 1990), pp.134–41.

44 Text of Rio Declaration in *The Global Partnership*, pp.3–9, principles quoted on pp.3–4; compare the Stockholm Declaration of the United Nations Conference on Human Environment with the Rio Declaration for a sense of the degree to which a normative consensus is being forged by North/South interaction at the global level. For the text of the Stockholm Declaration, see the Report of UN Conference on The Human Environment, June 5–16, 1972, UN Doc. A(Conf. 48114 (1972).

45 *The Global Partnership*, p.10–11. Ibid., pp.12–13.

46 Of course, there are some exceptions. Authoritarian Singapore is pioneering a paternalistic approach to environment protection, imposed from above and generally effective.

47 *The Challenge to the South*, p.129.

48 *Human Development Report 1992*, p.2.

49 Ibid., p.2; elaborated on in the 1993 report, pp.3–4.

50 *Human Development Report 1993*, p.3.

51 Ibid., p.7.

52 Cf.ibid., pp. 65–99.

53 There is some insensitivity expressed here to environmental constraints unless the idea of sustainability is also brought to bear; the early meetings of the Commission on Global Sustainability set up within the UN at the Earth Summit has suggested that the advocacy of growth has so far overwhelmed the supposed parity of concern for environmental protection; normative goals become pacifying diversions unless they are taken seriously in practice.

54 *Human Development Report 1992*, pp.88–9.

55 The calendar of the "world" is not uniform – Western hegemony should not be mistaken for an authentic universalism. On the island of Bali, for instance, the date is 78 years earlier, meaning that the new millennium will not begin until 2078.

56 It is important here to acknowledge the counter-example of the Singapore city-state, and more generally, the performance and apparent stability of market-oriented authoritarianism in Southeast and East Asia.

57 For an imaginative initiative generated by progressive social forces in global civil society see the Indictment of the International Peoples' Tribunal to Judge the G7, convened in Tokyo, Japan, July 3–4, 1993 (timed to precede the opening of the formal economic summit).

Chapter 7   In Pursuit of Humane Governance: Building Hope in the Coming Era of Geogovernance

1 *International Herald Tribune,* Feb. 3, 1994.

2 But as argued in chapter 3, sovereignty as a descriptive attribute of the territorial state, while still significant, is being steadily eroded by the various processes of globalization.

3 Samuel Huntington, "The Coming Clash of Civilizations – Or, the West Against the Rest," *New York Times,* June 6, 1993; longer version, "The Clash of Civilizations?" *Foreign Affairs* 72 (1993): 22–49.

4 Ibid.

5 David Fromkin, "The Coming Millennium: World Politics in the Twenty-First Century," *World Policy Journal* 10 (Spring 1993): 1–7, at 4.

6 See Paul Johnson, "Colonialism's Back – And Not a Moment Too Soon," *New York Times,* Magazine, April 18, 1993. In contrast, see Noam Chomsky, *World Orders Old and New* (New York: Columbia University Press, 1994); Edward Said, *Culture and Imperialism* (New York: Knopf, 1993).

7 John Lewis Gaddis, *The United States and the End of the Cold War: Implications, Reconsiderations, Provocations* (New York: Oxford, 1992), esp. pp. 168–92. This era of the past 50 years would more accurately be characterized as "the long war" if the history of the period were seen from the vantage point of the South.

8 The limited and contingent tolerance of nuclear weaponry based on their deterrent role was a major theme of the famous pastoral letter of the Catholic Bishops of North America issued in 1983.

9 There are also some interpretations of this period that highlight the dangers of a reconstituted ultra-nationalist Russian empire and of the so-called "backlash" states (in Western circles, Iraq, Iran, North Korea, Libya). See article by President Bill Clinton's National Security Advisor, Anthony Lake, "Confronting Backlash States," *Foreign Affairs* 73 (1994); 45–55.

10 Cf. the policy argument of Gilbert Loescher, *Beyond Charity* (New York: Oxford, 1993) in the context of refugees, especially the final chapter, pp. 180–205. See also the perspective set forth in the introductory essay to the

UNDP *Human Development Report* for the years 1992–4 (New York: Oxford University Press, 1992–4).

11 These failures need not be total or irreversible; successful restorative efforts can be undertaken after periods of chaos with varying prospects of success, as in Cambodia and El Salvador during the early 1990s.

12 It is, of course, ironic that Muslims are the principal victims in Bosnia, and the perpetrators elsewhere, as in Algeria and Egypt.

13 For an influential example see John Mueller, *Retreat from Doomsday: The Obsolescence of Major War* (New York: Basic Books, 1989).

14 This is often given the specific shape of a globalized Concert of Europe, see Charles A. Kupchan and Clifford A. Kupchan, "A New Concert for Europe," in Graham Allison and Gregory F. Treverton, eds, *Rethinking America's Security: Beyond Cold War to New World Order* (New York: Norton, 1992), pp. 249–66.

15 Such internationally minded perspectives are also appreciative of the present good work of such UN arenas as UNICEF, UNDP, and the UN Human Rights Commission.

16 George Konrad, *Antipolitics* (New York: Harcourt, Brace, 1984); Vaclav Havel, *Disturbing the Peace* (New York: Knopf, 1990); Adam Michnik, *Letters from Prison* (Berkeley: University of California, 1985).

17 Some excellent writing from these standpoints has appeared, including Petra Kelly's *Fighting for Hope* (Boston: South End Press, 1984), and James Douglass's books, especially *The Nonviolent Coming of God* (Maryknoll, N.Y.: Orbis, 1991), involving reliance on militant nonviolence as articulated in a series of practices associated with resistance to nuclearism and abusive government, often guided and inspired by the Nuremberg Principles; see also the comprehensive and valuable scholarship and advocacy by Gene Sharp, *Civilian-based Defense: A Post-Military Weapons System* (Princeton: Princeton University Press, 1990), and also Sharp, *Making Europe Unconquerable: The Potential of Civilian-based Deterrence and Defense* (London: Taylor and Francis, 1985).

18 The latter has generated an independent commission on global governance with a small secretariat in Geneva, while the former has formed the background for virtually all discussions of the future of UN peacekeeping in the early 1990s. See also Erskine Childers and Brian Urquhart, "Toward a More Effective United Nations," *Development Dialogue* 1–2 (1991): 1–96, and "Renewing the United Nations System," *Development Dialogue* 1 (1994): 7–213.

19 These issues are likely to surface in the form of criticism during 1995, the fiftieth birthday of the UN, especially the degree to which the Organization as established in 1945, and conceived of even earlier, reflected the then overriding reality of a victorious wartime alliance against fascism.

20 *An Agenda for Peace* (New York: UN, 1992), 17.

21 Ibid., 42.

22 Ibid., 45.

23 These ideas were put forward by Robert C. Johansen and Saul H. Mendlov-

itz, "The Role of Enforcement of Law in the Establishment of a New International Order: A Proposal for a Transnational Police Force," *Alternatives* 6 (1980): 307–37; compare Brian Urquhart, "For a UN Volunteer Military Force," *New York Review of Books*, June 10, 1993.

24 There is, here, the need for a fifth Geneva Convention on the Law of War, prescribing the conditions governing uses of force by the UN, possibly drafted under the auspices of the International Committee of the Red Cross, but with a distinct bias toward the narrowest possible conception of "military necessity."

25 The United Nations Association's series of volumes devoted to discussions of issues before the UN already performs this role to some extent.

26 Of course, collective implementation might again preclude the formation of a consensus, leading once more to accusations of irrelevance. Tosome extent, this has happened in relation to Bosnia. If more weighty strategic interests had been present, as might have been the case had the Serbs been seen as having nuclear weapons ambitions, this could have prompted a revival of unilateralism, that is, action outside of the UN – because no acceptable way can be found to uphold the geopoliticalinterest in preventing unacceptable forms of proliferation by acting within the UN.

27 *Common Responsibility in the 1990s* "The Stockholm Initiative" (Stockholm: Prime Minister's Office, 1992), p.41.

28 For instance, Wangari Maathai, the feminist and environmental activist from Kenya.

29 *Human Development Report*, p. 74.

30 Ibid.

31 The UNDP report is keenly conscious of the problem, but it does not offer a systematic critique that exposes the human costs of economic globalization, or set forth regulatory and policy instruments that might lead to better human results.

32 *Human Development Report 1992*, p. 78–9.

33 Among the publications that have shaped visionary thinking are the following: Grenville Clark and Louis B. Sohn, *World Peace through World Order*, 3rd edn (Cambridge: Harvard University Press, 1966); the four-volume series edited by Richard Falk and Saul H. Mendlovitz in the late 1960s, published by the World Law Fund under the series title *The Strategy of World Order*; the series sponsored by the World Order Models Project and published in the late 1970s by the Free Press under the series title *Preferred Worlds for the 1990s*; Saul H. Mendlovitz and R. B. J. Walker, eds, *Towards a Just World Peace* (London: Butterworths, 1987); R. B. J. Walker, *One World, Many Worlds: Struggles for a Just World Peace* (Boulder, Colo: Lynne Rienner, 1988); Richard Falk, Robert C. Johansen, and Samuel S. Kim, eds, *The Constitutional Foundations of World Peace* (Albany: State University of New York Press, 1993).

34 This latter form of grassroots transnational influence is being more and more directly acknowledged and encouraged by the more South-oriented activities in the UN system. David Korten, *Getting to the Twenty-first*

Century: Voluntary Action and the Global Agenda (West Hartford, Conn.: Kumarian Press, 1990).

35 The year chosen is 1999 rather than 2000 to avoid being swamped by millennial events, and to prepare for the new millennium with a program for constitutional reform that at least meets the minimal ethical and functional requirements of global governance. For suggestive perspectives on reform see Maurice Bertrand, *The Third Generation World Organization* (Dordrecht: Nijhoff, 1989).

36 The political and legal rationale is set forth in a legal memorandum by Nicholas Grief, *The World Court Project on Nuclear Weapons and International Law* (Northampton, Mass.: Aletheia Press, 1992).

37 These calls have been formalized over the years in a series of UN General Assembly resolutions, starting with UN General Assembly Resolution 1653 (XVI) in 1961.

38 An administrative commission could screen requests in a manner comparable to the procedures used to avoid frivolous claims being made in the European Court of Human Rights.

39 For comprehensive argument to this effect see Elliot L. Meyrowitz, *Prohibition of Nuclear Weapons: The Relevance of International Law* (Dobbs Ferry, N.Y.: Transnational, 1989).

40 The judges on the Court were evenly divided for and against the decision, but to break the tie the President of the Court, Sir Percy Spender of Australia, was given a second vote.

41 The same logic may apply to the refusal by the US to comply with the Nicaragua decision: nevertheless, the decision substantially reshaped the diplomatic process. For persuasive argument to this effect see Joaquín Tacsan, *The Dynamics of International Law in Conflict Resolution* (Dordrecht: Nijhoff, 1992).

42 Also relevant is the prominent role that judicial review plays in the US constitutional system, and the prestige and influence of the US Supreme Court.

43 Cf. John Hart Ely, *War and Responsibility* (Princeton: Princeton University Press, 1993).

44 A parallel process of indictment, adjudication, and punishment was initiated against surviving Japanese war leaders in trials held in Tokyo. For assessments see Robert H. Minear, *Victors' Justice: The Tokyo War Crimes Trial* (Princeton: Princeton University Press, 1971); C. Hasoya et al., eds, *The Tokyo War Crimes Trial* (Tokyo: Kodansha International, 1986).

45 It is important to realize in this context that violating a law does not invalidate it. If public policy is important it calls for more effective means to obtain compliance, including enforcement in some form.

46 Banking operations in relation to dirty money and covert operations by intelligence agencies are two other areas in which demilitarization and democratization goals cannot advance very far until secrecy prerogatives are effectively challenged and curtailed.

47 Three ways in which market forces respond in the face of disclosed scandal

are discernible: scapegoating of a vulnerable actor to take the heat off the wider pattern of practices; a cover-up that doesn't expose the deep roots of the scandal; compensating the victims with public funds so as to avoid a populist backlash (e.g. savings and loan collapse in the United States in the late 1980s).

Chapter 8   The Essential Vision:
A Normative Project to Achieve Humane Governance

1 More than the rest of the report, this chapter owes a considerable debt to Saul Mendlovitz who has been steadfast in his own endeavors to develop a normative macrohistory that narrates human experience in such a way as to enhance future prospects for the planet. It also owes a great deal to R. B. J. Walker, Yoshikazu Sakamoto, and Radmila Nakarada, especially their critical and cautionary approach to any kind of facile universalist embrace, and to David Held for his ceaseless exploration of the new frontiers of democratic thought and practice, especially the emergence of what he has called "cosmopolitan democracy." And finally, there are present here the strong and diverse influences of Lester Ruiz, Mohamed sid Ahmed, Dhirabai Sheth, Elisabeth Gerle, and Vandana Shiva, both as neutralizers of Eurocentricism and as vivid spokespersons of various "others" who have often been silenced in past inquiries into human betterment.

Select Bibliography

This bibliography lists books of particular relevance to the normative project depicted in chapter 8, and does not attempt to list books useful to the overall inquiry of the report.

An-Na'im, Abdullahi Ahmed, ed., *Human Rights in Cross-Cultural Perspectives: A Quest for Consensus*. Philadelphia: University of Pennsylvania Press, 1992.

Archibugi, Daniele et al., *Cosmopolis*. Rome: Manifestolibri, 1993.

Bedjaoui, Mohammed, *Towards a New International Economic Order*. New York and London: Holmes and Meier, 1979.

Bennis, Phyllis and Michel Moushabeck, eds, *Altered States: A Reader in the New World Order*. New York: Olive Branch Press, 1993.

Boggs, Grace et al., *Conditions of Peace: An Inquiry*. Washington, D.C.: Expro Press, 1991.

Brecher, Jeremy, John Brown Childs, and Jill Cutler, eds, *Global Visions: Beyond the New World Order*. Boston: South End Press, 1993.

Cahill, Kevin M., ed., *A Framework for Survival: Health, Human Rights, and Humanitarian Assistance in Conflicts and Disasters*. New York: Basic Books, 1992.

Camilleri, Joseph A. and Jim Falk, *The End of Sovereignty? The Politics of a Shrinking and Fragmenting World*. Aldershot: Edward Elgar, 1992.

The Challenge to the South, Report of the South Commission. Oxford: Oxford University Press, 1990.

Chimni, B. S., *International Law and World Order: A Critique of Contemporary Approaches*. Delhi: Sage, 1993.

Chomsky, Noam, *World Orders Old and New*. New York: Columbia University Press, 1994.

Clark, Grenville and Louis B. Sohn, *World Peace through Law*, 3rd edn. Cambridge: Harvard University Press, 1966.

Cohen, Jean L. and Andrew Arato, *Civil Society and Political Theory*. Cambridge: MIT Press, 1990.

Elias, Robert and Jennifer Turpin, eds, *Rethinking Peace*. Boulder, Colo. and London: Lynne Rienner, 1994.

Falk, Richard A., *A Study of Future Worlds*. New York: Free Press, 1975.

Falk, Richard A., *Explorations at the Edge of Time: Prospects for World Order*. Philadelphia: Temple University Press, 1992.

Falk, Richard A., Robert C. Johansen, and Samuel S. Kim, eds, *The Constitutional Foundations of World Peace*. Albany, N.Y.: State University of New York Press, 1993.

Galtung, Johan, *There are Alternatives! Four Roads to Peace and Security*. Nottingham: Spokesman, 1984.

Held, David, *Models of Democracy*. Cambridge: Polity Press, 1987.

Held, David, ed., *Political Theory Today*. Cambridge: Polity Press, 1991.

Held, David, "Democracy: From City-states to a Cosmopolitan Order?" *Political Studies* 40 (1992), special issue: 10–39.

Human Development Report, United Nations Development Program. New York: Oxford, annual vols since 1990.

Inglehard, Ronald, *The Silent Revolution: Changing Values and Political Styles Among Western Publics*. Princeton: Princeton University Press, 1977.

Kelly, Petra K., *Nonviolence Speaks to Power*. Honolulu: University of Hawaii, 1992.

Kim, Samuel S., *The Quest for a Just World Order*. Boulder, Colo.: Westview, 1984.

Kolko, Gabriel, *Century of Total War: Politics, Conflict, and Society since 1914*. New York: New Press, 1994.

Kothari, Rajni, *Footsteps into the Future*. New York: Free Press, 1974.

Kothari, Rajni, "On Humane Governance," *Alternatives* 12 (July 1987): 277–90.

Kothari, Rajni, *Growing Amnesia*. Delhi: Viking, 1993.

Kothari, Smitu and Harsh Sethi, eds, *Rethinking Human Rights: Challenges for Theory and Action*. New York: New Horizons; Delhi: Lokayan, 1989.

Kumar, Krishan, *Utopia and Anti-Utopia in Modern Times*. Oxford: Blackwell, 1987.

Kumar, Krishan and Stephen Bonn, eds, *Utopias and the Millennium*. London: Reaktion Books, 1993.

Makhijani, Arjunl, *From Global Capitalism to Economic Justice: An Inquiry into the Elimination of Systemic Poverty, Violence and Environmental Destruction in the World Economy*. New York and London: Apex Press, 1992.

Masini, Eleonora, ed., *Visions of Desirable Societies*. Oxford: Pergamon, 1983.

Mazrui, Ali A., *A World Federation of Cultures: An African Perspective*. New York: Free Press, 1976.

Mendlovitz, Saul H., ed., *On the Creation of a Just World Order*. New York: Free Press, 1975.

Mendlovitz, Saul H. and R. B. J. Walker, eds, *Towards a Just World Peace: Perspectives of Social Movements*. London: Butterworths, 1987.

Miller, Lynn H., *Global Order: Values and Politics in International Politics*, 3rd edn. Boulder, Colo.: Westview, 1994.

Minh-ha, Trinh T., *Women, Native, Other: Writing Postcoloniality and Feminism*. Bloomington: Indiana University Press, 1989.

Muzaffar, Chandra, *Human Rights and the New World Order*. Penang: Just World Trust, 1993.

Our Common Future: The World Commission on Environment and Development. Oxford: Oxford University Press, 1987.

Peterson, V. Spike and Anne Sisson Runyan, *Global Gender Issues*. Boulder, Colo.: Westview, 1993.

Rhinesmith, Stephen H., *A Manager's Guide to Globalization: Six Keys to Success in a Changing World*. Alexandria, Va.: American Society for Training and Development, 1993.

Röling, B. V. A. and Antonio Cassese, *The Tokyo Trial and Beyond*. Cambridge: Polity Press, 1993.

Said, Edward W., *Culture and Imperialism*. New York: Knopf, 1993.

Sharp, Gene, *The Politics of Non-violent Action*, 3 vols. Boston: Porter, 1973.

Sivard, Ruth Leger, *World Military and Social Expenditures*, 15th edn. Washington, D.C.: World Priorities, 1993.

State of the World, Worldwatch Institute. New York: W. W. Norton, annual vols since 1984.

Steenbergen, Bart van, ed., *The Conditions of Citizenship*. London: Sage, 1994.

Tickner, J. Ann, *Gender in International Relations: Feminist Perspectives on Achieving Global Security*. New York: Columbia University Press, 1992.

Toulmin, Stephen C., *Cosmopolis: The Hidden Agenda of Modernity*. New York: Free Press, 1990.

Wagar, W. Warren, *A Short History of the Future*, 2nd edn. Chicago: University of Chicago Press, 1992.

Walker, R. B. J. *One World, Many Worlds: Struggles for a Just World Peace*. Boulder, Colo.: Lynne Rienner; London: Zed, 1988.

Walker, R. B. J. and Saul H. Mendlovitz, *Contending Sovereignties: Redefining Political Community*. Boulder, Colo.: Lynne Rienner, 1990.

Williams, Raymond, *The Year 2000*. New York: Pantheon, 1983.

Index

accountability: of individuals 236–9, 246–7
Acheson, Dean 39
Afghanistan: military intervention in 15, 23
Africa: declining standard of living 29;
  Islam in 105; poverty in 57; *see
  also* Kenya; Nigeria; Rwanda; South
  Africa; sub-Saharan Africa
African National Congress (ANC) 127,
  129, 221
Agenda 21 195
Aideed, Mohammed Farah 264n
AIDS: homosexuality and 64
Algeria: religious fundamentalism in 105,
  106, 198; terrorism in 72, 210
Algonquin nation: sovereignty and 94
Allison, Graham 259n, 271n
Amazonia: tropical rainforests in 63
Amin, Samir 3
Amnesty International 187–8
Angola 30, 115
animal rights 167–8
An-Na'im, Abdullah Ahmed 260n
Antarctica 169
anticolonial struggles 250
apartheid: global 45, 49–55, 74, 112, 138; in
  South Africa 14, 30, 50–2, 127; *see
  also* racism
appeasement policies 39, 41, 161–2, 163
Aquino, Corazon 29, 250
Archibugi, Daniele 261n, 264n
Argentina 30, 164
arms trade 15, 70, 72–3, 139, 146, 238–9,
  245
Arne Westad, Odd 259n
artistic expression, freedom of *see* freedom
  of artistic expression
Ascherio, Alberto 257n

Asia-Pacific Economic Cooperation (APEC)
  81–2
asylum-seekers 197; in Germany 61, 130,
  198, 211; *see also* migration; refugees
authoritarian rule 109
autogenocide 97
avoidable harm 55–74; children 56–7;
  militarism 70–4; oppression 63–70;
  poverty 57–63
Ayodhya temple riots 130

Bangkok Declaration 26
Bangladesh 192
Bank of Credit and Commerce International
  (BCCI) 177–8, 180–1, 228, 240
Barnet, Richard J. 266n
Bassioumi, M. Cherif 262n
Baxi, Upendra 252
Bennis, Phyllis 262n
Bertrand, Maurice 273n
Bihar: people's courts in 208
biodiversity 91
biological weapons 159
bipolarity: collapse of 44, 49, 137
birth control 195; *see also* family
  planning; population growth
Blakesley, Christopher L. 262n
blasphemy: Christian beliefs 68; *The
  Satanic Verses* 65–6, 67, 68
'boat people' 97
Bodin, Jean 88, 98
Bolivia 29
Bose, Ajoy 64
Bosnia 20, 83–4, 162, 180, 193, 214, 240,
  251; anti-Muslim aggression 67, 211;
  'ethnic cleansing' 84, 123, 139;
  genocide in 20, 106, 179, 247; religious
  fundamentalism in 105; UN and 224;

war crimes 67, 99; war crimes tribunal 123, 247; as weak state 213
bounded conviction: politics of 41–4, 45–6
Boutros-Gahli, Boutros 22, 224, 225, 227–8
Brazil 164
Brecher, Jeremy 267n
Brittain, Victoria 262n
Broad, Robin 266n
Brown, Lester 168, 261n
Brown Childs, John 267n
Brundtland, Gro Harlem 33
Brundtland Commission 196, 200
Burma: oppression in 64, 128; pro-democracy movement 30, 165, 250; State Law and Order Restoration Campaign (SLORC) 128
Bush, George 32, 70, 117, 137, 169, 179, 212, 259n

Cahill, Kevin M. 268n
Cambodia 94, 193, 250; genocide in 97; Khmer Rouge 97, 128; UN intervention 128, 221, 224, 240; as weak state 224
capital: transnational 13
capital punishment 165–6; popular support for 6, 117, 165
capitalism: in 1980s 58; center/periphery patterns 48; class relations and 48, 58; cruelty of 47, 48–9; democratization and 115–16; franchise 36, 86; human consequences of 47–8; ideologically uncontested 48; restructuring phase 54; in Sweden 60; welfare 19, 96, 110
carrying capacity 196
Carter, Jimmy 183
Castaneda, Jorge G. 268n
caste: in India 5, 64–5
Catholic church: in Eastern Europe 117; family planning and 196
Cavanagh, John 266n
censorship *see* freedom of artistic expression
centralism 36
CFCs 169
chaos theory 43
chemical weapons 159
Chiapas Indians 13
Childers, Erskine 271n
children: avoidable harm 56–7; Convention on the Rights of the Child 192; mortality 56–7; poverty and 56; *The State of the World's Children* (UNICEF) 190–3; in sub-Saharan Africa 56; World Summit for Children 1990 192
Chile 29, 30, 129; Pinochet dictatorship 164
China: Bangkok Declaration 26;

demographic adjustments 62, 63, 197; economic growth 182; G–7 and 216; market economics 107, 172, 173; new world order and 107; nuclear weapons 159; oppression in 64, 184; preventive diplomacy 161; pro-democracy movement 30, 220–1, 250; resistance to UN 26; socialist economics, abandonment of 188
Chomsky, Noam 266n, 270n
Christian world-view 148
Churchill, Winston 39
citizen pilgrims 95, 211–12, 233, 234, 239
citizens' associations 87, 106, 199–200
citizenship: positive 253; sovereignty and 93–6
civil disobedience 97, 247
civilizationism 211; intracivilizational strife 211
Clark, Grenville 256n, 272n
class relations: capitalism and 48, 58
Clausewitz, Karl Marie von 39
climate change 209
Clinton, Bill 54, 61, 70, 186, 270n
Cold War 10, 24–5; costs of 24; democracy after 114–19; end of 2, 18, 30
collective security 152, 161–3, 173, 178, 247–9
Collor de Mello, Fernando 62
colonialism 209; anticolonial struggles 250; decolonization 25, 29
comity 38
commodification of women 68
"common security" 144
communications 13, 179, 210; information superhighway 13
compassion fatigue 193; *see also* disaster fatigue
competitiveness 6, 48, 104, 116, 181, 193; poverty and 104; social cohesion and 54; *see also* market
Conference of Security and Cooperation in Europe (CSCE) 102
Confucianism 148
constitutionalism 114; market-oriented 172
consumerism 19, 75, 118, 126
contraception *see* birth control
Contras *see* Nicaragua
Convention on the Rights of the Child 192
corporal punishment 166
cosmopolitan democracy 106, 254
Cree nation: sovereignty and 94
crime: rise in 98
Croatia 83–4, 139
Cuba 115, 188
cultural homogenization 36
culture: popular 13, 86

Cutler, Jill 267n
Czech Republic 5
Czechoslovakia 54

Day, Kathleen 266n
debt burden 23, 57, 177; *see also* indebtedness
debt cancellation 34, 191
decentralism 36
decentralization 10, 16, 201
Declaration on the Right of Development 1986 187
decolonization 25, 29
defensive defense 160–1; neutrality 161; nonalignment 161; preventive diplomacy 161; unilateral disarmament 161; withdrawal 161
demilitarization 31, 156–67, 236–9; based on hegemony and coercion 72; collective security 161–3; defensive defense 160–1; global civil society and 239; peacekeeping forces 162; statist 147; *see also* militarism
democracy 30, 138; after Cold War 114–19; constitutional 114; cosmopolitan 106, 254; geopolitical appropriation of 115; human rights and 111, 251; humane governance and 104–7; incorporating unrestricted capitalism 110; international law and 111; market 107; militarism and 24; military intervention and 115; pro-democracy movements *see* pro-democracy movements; promotion of 16; racism and 24; republican view of 111; rule of law and 111; traditional 106–7, 108–14; transnational 2, 17, 36, 85
democratization 28, 35, 71, 104–33, 236–9; agenda for 113; capitalism and 115–16; globalization and 89, 119; human rights and 126; market economics and 115, 120; militarism and 116, 117, 118; paradox of 126–7; of political behaviour 110; as process 110–11; of process of interpretation 113; pro-democracy movements *see* pro-democracy movements; state/society relations 111, 120
denuclearization 160
Deudney, Daniel 263n
development: Declaration on the Right of Development 1986 187; Human Development Reports 26, 56, 202–3, 228–9, 230, 232; human-oriented 187; IMF and 176; purist market approaches to 110; right of 187, 201, 239; sustainable 16, 63, 199–205;

United Nations Development Programme 202; women and 201–2
developmental policy 27–8
diet 168, 170
diplomacy: of Gulf War 23; interventionary 26, 42, 99, 115; preventive 161; realism and 39
disarmament 34; unilateral 161
disaster fatigue 76; *see also* compassion fatigue
displacement: politics of 79
dumping of toxic waste 75, 77, 133, 168
Durning, Alan 266n
Dylan, Bob 229

Earth Summit 1992 26, 32, 75, 169
Eastern Europe: capitalism and 173; Catholicism in 117; emancipation of 14, 30; NATO and 34; unilateral disarmament 161
eco-authoritarianism/fascism 118, 133
eco-imperialism 74–8
economic migrants 197, 198
ECOSOC (Economic and Social Council) 186
education: right to 185
Egypt 105, 114; Gulf War and 162; terrorism in 210
El Salvador 30, 193, 221, 240, 250
energy conservation 170
energy consumption taxes 191–2
environment: carrying capacity 196; CFCs 169; climate change 209; energy conservation 170; geopolitical leadership and 32–3, 135; grassroots concerns 7; greenhouse gases 63; overloading 16, 33, 62; ozone depletion 169, 209; pollution of global commons 33, 209; population growth and 196–7; pressures on 61; protecting 16, 200; security of 146, 168–70; sustainable development 16, 63, 199–205; toxic waste dumping 75, 77, 133, 168; tropical rainforests 63
Ethiopia 235
"ethnic cleansing" 84, 105, 123, 139; *see also* genocide
ethnic conflict 5, 7, 41, 98, 215
Eurofederalism 7
Europe: realism and 42; rise of 49; social cohesion 54
European Community 132; Maastricht Treaty 61, 93, 124, 131, 136, 174, 194, 216
European Nuclear Disarmament (END) 53

Fajgenbaum, José 62
Falk, Richard A. 258n, 259n, 262n, 272n
Falklands War 117

family planning 196, 198; *see also* birth control; population growth
feminism: commodification of women 68; international relations and 93; non-hierarchical relationships 93; nonviolence and 222; security studies 139–40
financial markets: globalization of 48
fiscal policies: globalization of 48
foreign aid/assistance 49, 57, 97; *see also* humanitarian intervention
foreign policy: human rights and 183–4; international law and 7; market factors priority in 109; realism and 42
fragmentation 11, 12, 13
France: multiculturalism and 98, 105
franchise capitalism 36, 86
freedom of artistic expression 68; pornography and 68; *The Satanic Verses* 65–6, 67, 68
Fromkin, David 12, 211
Fujimora, Alberto 107, 109, 139
fundamentalism 112, 126; Islamic 22, 105, 117, 179, 198; market dynamics, unconditional dedication to 112; secular 112

Gaddis, John Lewis 260n, 270n
Galtung, Johan 73, 165
Gandhi, Indira 62
Gandhi, M. K. 222, 250
Garton Ash, Timothy 259n
General Agreement on Tariffs and Trade (GATT) 120, 131, 194, 229
Geneva Conventions 1949 151, 244
Geneva Protocols 1977 151, 244
genocide 106, 139, 179, 251; in Bosnia 20, 106, 179, 247; in Cambodia 97; 'ethnic cleansing' 84, 105, 123, 139; in Rwanda 179
geogovernance viii-ix, 1, 4, 6, 11; capital-driven 135; forms of 9; G–7 *see* Group of Seven; Gulf War and 23, 138; human rights and 138; impact of 13; prospect of 12–14; and *see* sovereignty; transition to 79–82, 85, 91, 135, 155–6
geopolitics 1, 9, 101; leadership 31–2; market geopolitics 18; statism and 18, 85
Georgia: religious fundamentalism in 105
Gerle, Elisabeth 263n, 274n
Germany: former East Germany and 129–30; G–7 and 231; Nazism 5, 236; neo-Nazi groups 64, 130; refugees/asylum-seekers in 61, 130, 198, 211; rise of 49
Gilpin, Robert 266n
global civil security 147

global civil society 17, 35, 44, 69, 74, 113, 181; citizens' associations and 87; demilitarization and 239; international law and 236; sovereignty and 100, 101; transnational networks and 199–200
Global Civilization Project vii, viii, 229
global commons: pollution of 33, 209
global governance: emergence of 215–19
global market *see* market
global village 10, 11, 119, 210, 236
globalism 6, 24, 75, 89; democratizing 89; rejection of 94
globalization 10, 11, 12, 13, 47, 138; baleful effects of 36; as challenge to statism 174; defining role of 173–7; democratization and 89, 119; of financial markets 48; of fiscal policies 48; from above 86, 88–9, 105, 112, 114, 123, 139, 172–205; from below 87, 106, 112, 119, 125, 192, 199, 211, 230; popular resistance to 136; sovereignty and 98, 134; of trade relations 48
Gorbachev, Mikhail vii, 18, 27, 33, 34, 144, 184, 219, 220, 259n
green movement 200; nonviolence and 222
greenhouse gases 63
Greenpeace 155, 219
Grenada 115
Grief, Nicholas 265n, 273n
Grotius, Hugo 243
Group of 77 176
Group of Eight (G–8) 188
Group of Seven (G–7) 14, 15, 16, 132, 188, 206, 208; BCCI and 180; China and 216; exclusion from 50, 81; expansion of 216–17; Germany and 231; Japan and 231; Russia and 216; security 145
Gulf War 15, 137; collective security and 152, 248; diplomacy of 23; Egypt and 162; geogovernance and 23, 138; geopolitical character of 20–3, 177–9; as intercivilizational war 211; Israel and 40, 162; militarism and 70, 117; military commanders, media treatment of 163, 164; new world order and 173; objectives of 157; post-ceasefire inspections of Iraq 32; postmodern geopolitics and 152; realism and 40; as resource war 177–9; Syria and 162; television and 23, 163; Turkey and 162; UN and 21, 162, 224, 226; US and 21, 117, 226; *see also* Hussein, Saddam; Iraq
Gurwin, Larry 266n
gypsies: in Czech Republic 5

Hague peace conferences 1899 and 1907 86, 243
Haiti 162, 224, 240
Hamden-Turner, Charles 259n
Harris, Adrienne 261n
Hart Ely, John 263n, 273n
Hasoya, C. 273n
Havel, Vaclav 5, 33, 271n
Hegel, G. W. F. 88
Held, David 106, 119, 264n, 274n
Helsinki Accords 53, 102, 184
Herzegovina 83–4
Hettne, Björn 258n
Hinduism 148; extremism 65, 130; populism 117–18
Hitler, Adolf 39, 41, 261n
Ho Chi Minh 194
Hobbes, Thomas 39, 88, 98
homelessness 5, 182; competitiveness and 104; in US 54
homophobia 64
homosexuality: AIDS and 64; "outing" 69; rights of privacy and 69
Human Development Index 52, 56
human migration *see* migration
human rights 11, 16, 239, 251–2; accountability for compliance with 35–6; cultural aspects 105; democracy and 109, 111, 251; democratization and 126; foreign policy and 183–4; geogovernance and 138; Helsinki Accords 53, 102, 184; International Covenant on Economic, Social and Cultural Rights (1966) 52, 108, 185–6, 187; international standards of 67; in Latin America 221; organizations 183; right to work 52; sovereignty and 67, 102, 114, 251; traditional democracy and 109; transnationalization of 187; violation of as pretext for interventionary diplomacy 26, 42; watch groups 187–8
human solidarity 12, 99
humane governance 9, 17, 207 *et seq.*; contending images of 11–12; democracy and 17, 104–7; democratic obstacles to 6; language of 46; as a legal right 181–9; people-centered criteria of success 14; the personal, inclusion of 17; prospect of 14–16; security for 134–71; transition to, ecological dimensions 168–70; UN, role in 27; unborn, claims of 17; use of term ix
humanitarian intervention 97, 99, 127–8; by UN 42, 179; *see also* foreign aid/ assistance
Huntington, Samuel 10, 210–11, 257n, 260n
Hussein, Saddam 20, 21, 32, 40, 73, 138, 178, 180, 219, 226; *see also* Gulf War; Iraq

identity politics 11, 106
Ikenberry, G. John 263n
imperialism 209
income distribution 58–9; racism and 59; in US 58–9
indebtedness 61, 114, 176, 177, 191; IMF and 23, 61, 114; World Bank and 114; *see also* debt burden
Independent Commission on Global Governance 230
India: anti-Muslim riots 67, 130; Ayodhya temple riots 130; caste in 5, 64–5, 130; demographic adjustments 62, 130; Hinduism in *see* Hinduism; nuclear weapons and 32, 159; people's courts in Bihar 208; religious fundamentalism 65, 67, 105, 117–18, 130; untouchability 5
indigenous peoples 50, 199, 242
Indonesia 182, 184; demographic policy 197
information *see* media
information superhighway 13
inhumane governance 1, 2, 6, 175; triple indictment of 47–78
Inotai, András 258n
insecurity 139; *see also* security
International Association of Lawyers Against Nuclear Arms (IALANA) 159, 233
International Covenant on Civil and Political Rights (1966) 108
International Covenant on Economic, Social and Cultural Rights (1966) 52, 108, 185–6, 187
international law 103, 118–19, 123, 138; economic, social and cultural rights and 108; foreign policy and 7; inability to generate metacultural forms 68; new world order and 137; sovereignty and 102; war and 135
International Law Commission 236
International Monetary Fund (IMF) 14, 92, 132, 188, 206; controls 62; development and 176; indebtedness and 23, 61, 114; influence of 49; reform of 228; Structural Adjustment Programs (SAPs) 29, 49, 104, 135
International Peace Bureau 159, 233
International Physicians for the Prevention of Nuclear War 233
internationalism 39
intracivilizational strife 211
Iran 22; Islamic revolution 133, 210, 220; nuclear weapons and 31, 157; political oppression in 117; religious fundamentalism in 105; terrorism

118; war with Iraq 137–8; weakening of state sovereignty 94; women in 117; *see also* Khomeini

Iraq 134, 157; global oil price structure and 134; Kurdish nationalism 94, 162, 178, 179, 226; nuclear weapons and 31, 32, 157; Palestinians in 162; sanctions against 32, 178; Shi'as in 162, 178, 179; UN inspections of 32; war with Iran 137–8; weakening of state sovereignty 94; *see also* Gulf War; Hussein

Islam 148; censorship and 68; fundamentalism 22, 105, 117, 179, 198; Hindus and 65; in North Africa 105; revolution in Iran 133, 210, 220; stereotyping of 65; terrorism 67, 76; *The Satanic Verses* 65–6, 67, 68; *see also* Rushdie; victimization of Muslims 65, 211

Islamic revolution 80, 133, 210, 220
isolationism 39, 40
Israel: attacks outside borders 118; Gulf War and 40, 162; military actions 15, 118; non-Jews in 68; nuclear weapons 31, 158; PLO and 14

Japan: G–7 and 231; realism and 42; rise of 49, 60; social cohesion 54; "untouchability" in 64
Jesus 148
jobless growth 202
Johansen, Robert C. 271n, 272n
Johnson, Paul 270n
just war doctrine 157

Kegley, Charles W., Jr. 260n
Kellogg-Briand Pact 1928 245
Kelly, Petra K. 271n
Kennan, George 39
Kennedy, Paul 196, 197, 260n
Kenya 129
Khomeini, Ayatollah Ruhollah 65, 66, 67, 68, 117, 138, 194, 250; *see also* Iran
Kim, Samuel S. 259n, 272n
King, Martin Luther 222, 250
King, Ynestra 261n
Klerk, F. W. de 18
Kohler, Gernot 50–1
Konrad, George 271n
Korea: prodemocracy movement 30; *see also* North Korea; South Korea
Korean War 23, 162
Korten, David 272n
Kothari, Rajni 3
Kothari, Smitu 260n
Kupchan, Charles A. 271n
Kupchan, Clifford A. 271n
Kurdish nationalism 94, 162, 178, 179, 226

Kuwait: Gulf War *see* Gulf War; Kurds, Shi'as and Palestinians in 162

Lake, Anthony 270n
Latin America: declining living standards 29; human rights abuses 221; militarism 163
League of Nations 21, 39, 247–8
Lebanon 94, 118, 162
Lee Kuan Yew 194
legalism 39, 41
Lellouche, Pierre 260n
Lenin, V. I. 41
Leninism 221; *see also* Marxist-Leninism
Lennon, John 148
Liberia 235; as weak state 213
Libya 31, 235
Lifton, Robert Jay 31, 265n
Loescher, Gilbert 270n
Los Angeles riots 1992 20, 59, 95
Lovins, Amory 170
Lundestad, Geir 259n

Maastricht Treaty 61, 93, 124, 131, 136, 174, 194, 216
Macedonia 224
Machiavelli, Niccoló 39, 88
McLuhan, Marshall 263n
Madonna (Ciccone) 148
Makhijani, Arjun 51
Malaysia: Third World Network 94
Mandela, Nelson 221
Maoism 164
Marcos, Ferdinand 109
market 1, 36, 85, 95, 96, 134; technological innovation and 211; *see also* competitiveness
market democracy 107
market forces 6, 10, 16, 38, 135, 207; democratization and 115, 120; human and environmental costs of 138, 228; poverty and 58; realism and 41; sovereignty and 114
market geopolitics 18
market-oriented constitutionalism 172
Markusen, Eric 265n
Marx, Karl 41, 47
Marxist-Leninism: failure of 40–1, 43–4
Mattai 272n
Mazrui, Ali A. 66, 259n
Mearsheimer, John 151, 261n
meat-eating 168, 170
media 193; globalization of 36, 88–9; information superhighway 13; television *see* television; violence in 166; war, treatment of 163
Menchu, Rigaberta 165
Mendez, Chico 155, 219

Mendlovitz, Saul H. viii, 256n, 259n, 271n, 272n, 274n
Mexico 29; nuclear weapons and 32
Meyrowitz, Elliot L. 273n
Michnik, Adam 271n
microelectronic developments 10, 148
Middle East 25
migration: human 77, 197–8; *see also* asylum-seekers; refugees
militarism 18, 24, 55, 70–4, 80, 214; democracy and 24; democratization and 116, 117, 118; Gulf War and 70, 117; interventionary 15, 115; in Latin America 163; United States 143; *see also* demilitarization; war
military assistance programs 15
military leaders: as political leaders 163–4
military rule 164
military technology 23
military-industrial elites 21
Milosevic, Slobodan 219
Minear, Robert H. 273n
Mobutu Sese Seko (Joseph Désiré Mobuto) 194
modernization: cult of 112
moralism 39, 41
Morgan, Robin 140
Morgenthau, Hans 39
Moushabeck, Michel 262n
Mozambique 30, 115
Mueller, John 263n, 271n
multiculturalism 98, 104
Muslims *see* Islam
Mussolini, Benito 41
Myanmar 221
Myers, Norman 265n

Nader, Ralph 267n
Nakarada, Radmila viii, 274n
Namibia 221, 224, 235
Nasrin, Taslima 260n
Nasser, Gamal Abdel 194
national interests 20
national security 143–4
nationalism 24, 95; economic 34; fragmentation and 11; military power and 15; radical 179; in Russia 174; sovereignty and 80, 87, 89; statism and 87
NATO: East European countries and 34
nature: sanctity of 167; security and 167–8; stewardship of 252–3
Nazism 5, 236
Nehru, Jawaharlal 194
Nepal: pro-democracy movement 30, 221, 250
neutrality 161
New International Economic Order (NIEO) 27–8

new world order 18, 51, 96, 136, 137, 173–4; China and 107; Gulf Crisis and 173; international law and 137
newly industrialized countries (NICs) 28
Nicaragua: Contras 91, 115, 153, 249; Sandinista government 90, 153, 189, 249; United States and 33, 90, 91, 115, 153
Nietzsche, Friedrich 41
Nigeria 64, 164
Nkrumah, Kwame 194
nonalignment 161
nongovernmental organizations (NGOs) 56
Non-proliferation Treaty 31
nonviolence 70, 166, 219–23, 250–1; collapse of Communism and 43; democratization movements 30, 133; *see also* pro-democracy movements; effectiveness of 15; feminism and 222; green movement and 222; hegemony, control of 127; people power movement, Philippines 30, 220, 250; Russia and 133
Noriega, General Manuel 153
North American Worker-to-Worker Network 94
North Atlantic Free Trade Area (NAFTA) 61, 93, 124, 131, 136, 174, 194
North Korea 31, 134, 157, 188, 189
Northern Ireland 72, 250
nuclear war: obsolescence of 15, 30
nuclear weapons 16, 31, 150; acquisition of 157; China and 159; denuclearization 160; deterrence theory 150–1, 156; Eastern Europe 161; European Nuclear Disarmament (END) 53; India and 32, 159; Iran and 31, 157; Iraq and 31, 32, 157; Israel and 31, 158; Mexico and 32; neutral countries and 150; no first use 31; non-proliferation regime 31, 139; Non-proliferation Treaty 31; prohibiting 233; proliferation of 20, 157; retention of 32; Russia and 31; South Africa and 158; Strategic Arms Reduction Treaty (START) 71; testing 31, 75; unilateral disarmament 161; US and 31; Zimbabwe and 32; *see also* weapons
"nuclear winter" 150
nuclearism 31, 157
Nuremberg Principles 103, 123, 236–7, 246–7; Crimes against Humanity 237; Crimes against the Peace 237; Crimes of War 237
Nyerere, Julius 200

oppression 63–70; of artistic expression 68; in Burma 64, 128; in China 64,

184; of homosexuals 69; in Iran 117; political 117; pornography 68; by religious/cultural practices 64; revolutionary movements 69–70; state 63–4; *The Satanic Verses* 65–6, 67, 68; of women 64
Organization of Petroleum Exporting Countries (OPEC) 28
organized crime 210
organized labor: weakening of 48, 182
"the other": demonizing 40; populism and 41; sovereignty and 80; war and 73
ozone depletion 169, 209

Pacific Basin 29, 217
Pacific Rim 172
Pact of Paris 245
Pakistan 31, 134, 157
Palestine: *intifada* in 30, 127, 250
Palestine Liberation Organization (PLO): Israel and 14
Palestinians: in Iraq and Kuwait 162
Palme, Olaf 144
Palme Commission report 1982 144
Panama: US military intervention 34, 115, 153
patriarchy: constructions of political order 80; hierarchy structures 92, 93; populism and 41; security and 140; sovereignty and 92–3; statism and 92
patriotism 80
Paust, Jordan J. 262n
peace dividends 36, 191
peacekeeping forces 162
People's Plan 21 94
"the personal" 17
personal relations: reconstruction of 36
Peru 107, 109, 139; Shining Path 164
Philippines: labor strife in 182; people power movement 30, 220, 250
Pinochet Ugarte, Augusto 164
Pol Pot 194
Poland: resistance movements 53
polarization 12
political leadership 19–20, 194; geopolitical 31–2; military leaders and 163–5
political prisoners: torture and abuse of 63–4
popular culture 13, 86
population growth 62, 75, 194–8; birth control 195; Brundtland Commission 196; China 62, 63, 197; demographic management 62; demographic transition 195; environment and 196–7; family planning 196, 198; India 62, 130; Indonesia 197; poverty and 197; reproductive behavior 170
populism 41; Hindu 117–18; "the other"

and 41; patriarchy and 41; regressive 119
pornography 68
post-Communist societies 5
postmodernism 126, 150–1, 156
poverty 17; absolute 55; acute 16; aid levels 57; children and 56; competitiveness and 104; debt and interest payments 57; in Latin America 57; market forces and 58; population growth and 197; in sub-Saharan Africa 57; in US 130
Powell, Colin 163
preventive diplomacy 161
privacy: rights of 69
privatization 59, 201
pro-democracy movements: Burma 30, 165, 250; China 30, 220–1, 250; Nepal 30, 221, 250; Philippines 30, 220, 250; *see also* democratization; nonviolence
public opinion 193

racism: democracy and 24; income distribution and 58–9; *see also* apartheid
Rainbow Warrior 155, 219
rape 140; marital 64
Reagan, Ronald 115, 212
Reagan Doctrine 115
"real security" 144
realism 37–41, 75, 154, 212, 215, 216; comity 38; diplomacy and 39; Europe and 42; foreign policy and 42; Gulf War and 40; hegemonic roles 80; Japan and 42; legalism and 39, 41; market forces and 41; moralism and 39, 41; morality of 38; peace and 42; realist consensus 37; realist mindset 38, 41, 47; science and 38; security and 136; states and 80–1; US and 39, 42; war and 42
refugees 77, 97, 104–5, 146–7, 197; "boat people" 97; in Germany 61, 130, 198, 211; war and 139; *see also* asylum-seekers; migration
Reich, Robert B. 261n
religion: Eastern 148; extremism 13, 65, 98, 130; fragmentation and 11; fundamentalism *see* fundamentalism; sovereign authority based on 68; *see also* Catholic church; Hinduism; Islam; spirituality
reproductive behavior 170
reproductive rights 5, 62, 117, 196
revolutionary movements: Islamic revolution 133, 210, 220; oppression of 69–70
rights: economic policy and 182–3; economic and social 183, 186–8;

equality of 113–14; human *see* human rights; logic of 182
Rio Earth Summit 1992 26, 32, 75, 200–1; Agenda 21 195
Rockefeller, David 28
Romania 184
Romero, Archbishop Oscar 219
Rosenau, James N. 261n, 266n
Ruiz, Lester 274n
rule of law 236–9, 249–50; democracy and 111
Rushdie, Salman 65–6, 67, 68, 105
Russia 55, 139, 221–2; G–7 and 216; marketization 145; nuclear weapons 31; ultranationalism 174; as weak state 213–14
Rwanda 251; genocide in 179, 247; humanitarian intervention in 97, 224, 240

Sakamoto, Yoshikazu viii, 141, 274n
Sandinistas *see* Nicaragua
The Satanic Verses 65–6, 67, 68; *see also* Rushdie
Scandinavia: social services in 60, 96; *see also* Sweden
Schelling, Thomas 51–2
Schwarzkopf, Norman 163
science: realism and 38
secularism 68, 106
security: animals and 167–8; collective 152, 161–3, 173, 178, 247–9; "common security" 144; "comprehensive security" 144; continuity and 142; doctrines vii; environmental 146, 168–70; existential 167–8; feminism and 139–40; G–7 and 145; global civil security 147; for humane governance 134–71; insecurity 139; military 141; national security 143–4; nature and 167–8; patriarchy and 140; "real security" 144; realism and 136; reorienting 136–43; trade and monetary regimes as foundation of 151; war and 137
self-defense: right of 245
self-determination: right of 30, 186, 187
self-interest: maximization of 37
Sethi, Harsh 260n
Shah of Iran 109, 133, 220, 250
Shakhnazarov, Georgi vii
Shamir, Yitzhak 118
Sharp, Gene 271n
Sheth, Dhirabai 274n
Shi'as: in Iraq 162, 178, 179; in Kuwait 162
Shining Path 164
Shiva, Vandana 165, 274n
sid Ahmed, Mohamed 274n

Siddiqui, Kalim 66
Silkwood, Karen 219
Singapore 172, 176, 184
Singer, Peter 265n
Sivard, Ruth Leger 268n
skin cancer 169
Slovenia 83–4
Smith, Adam 38, 182
social cohesion: competitiveness and 54; in Japan 54
social movements: citizens' associations 87, 106, 199–200; transnational 86–7, 199–200
social services: privatization of 59; in Scandinavia 60, 96
social violence 73–4
socialism 26, 135; abandonment of 188–9; failure of 19, 173; *see also* Leninism; Marxist-Leninism
Sohn, Louis B. 256n, 272n
Somalia 94, 162; television coverage 179; UN and 15, 20, 127–8, 224, 240; US and 20, 127–8, 193; as weak state 213, 224
Somavia, Juan 204
South Africa: ANC 127, 129, 221; apartheid in 14, 30, 50–2, 127; democratization in 129; Namibia and 235; nuclear weapons 158
South Commission 50, 200, 201–2
South Korea 182, 221, 250
sovereign authority: religious 68; secular 68
sovereign state 1, 16; challenging 79–82; human rights and 67; strengthening 34
sovereignty 68, 79–103; as bonded with statism 82; for captive nations 81; and citizenship 93–6; defensive roles of 81; globalization and 98, 134; historical dimension 87–8; human rights and 67, 102, 114, 251; international law and 102; locating 83–93; market forces and 114; military defeat and 84–5; nationalism and 80, 87, 89; "the other" and 80; patriarchy and 92–3; persisting relevance of 90; "pooling" of 84; popular 101; "self" and "other" 80; sense of 90; state-centrism and 99, 209; statehood and 85; as status 90; symbols of 84; theology and 88; Yugoslavia and 83–4
Soviet Union: bipolarity, collapse of 44, 49, 137; collapse of 2, 14, 19, 30, 71; "comprehensive security" 144
Spender, Sir Percy 273n
spirituality 12, 166–7; *see also* religion
Stalin, Joseph 147, 194

State of the World's Children, The (UNICEF)
190–3
stateless people 97
states 10, 79, 209; nation-states 210;
realism and 80–1; system 68, 79,
149; weak *see* weak states; *see also*
sovereign state
statism 36; economic reform 28;
geopolitics and 18, 49, 85;
globalization as challenge to 174;
nationalism and 87; patriarchy and
92; sovereignty as bonded with 82
Steenbergen, Bart van 261n
Stockholm Conference on the Human
Environment 1972 154
Stockholm Initiative on Global Security and
Governance 1991 153, 224, 227, 228,
230
Stone, Christopher D. 265n
Strategic Arms Reduction Treaty (START)
71
structural adjustment programs *see*
International Monetary Fund; World
Bank
structural violence 73, 165
Subrahmanyam, K. 141–2
sub-Saharan Africa 6, 25, 29, 54, 175;
children in 56; poverty in 57
Sudan 94, 97; religious fundamentalism in
105; terrorism 118; as weak state 213
Suharto, Thojib N.J. 194
Sukarno, Achmad 194
sustainable development 16, 63, 199–205,
239
Suu Kyi, Daw Aung San 128, 165
Sweden: capitalism in 60; *see also*
Scandinavia
Syria: Gulf War and 162; weakening of
state sovereignty 94

Tacsan, Joaquín 273n
Tagore, Rabindranath 241
Taiwan 221
Taoism 148
technological capabilities 208
technological innovation 10, 13, 170, 211;
microelectronic developments 10, 148
technologies: emerging 11; military 23
television: globalized 209–10; Gulf War
and 23, 163; Somalia and 179;
violence on 166; *see also* media
territorial sovereign state *see* sovereign
state; sovereignty
terrorism 13, 72, 76–7, 117, 140, 164, 210;
Iran 118; Islamic 67, 76; Sudan 118
Thatcher, M. 117
Third World Network 94
Thoreau, Henry David 247
Thucydides 39, 111

Tibet 30
Tickner, J. Ann 93, 261n
Timmermann, Jacopo 247
torture: of political prisoners 63–4
toxic waste dumping 75, 77, 133, 168
trade relations: globalization of 48
transport 170
Treverton, Gregory F. 259n, 271n
Trilateral Commission 18, 28
Trompenaars, Alfons 259n
tropical rainforests 63
Truell, Peter 266n
Turkey 94, 114, 162

unemployment 47, 94, 182; competitiveness
and 104; in US 130
unilateral disarmament 161
United Nations 6, 10, 20, 25–9, 102, 126,
132, 138; *An Agenda for Peace* 224–8;
backlash against 26; Cambodia and
128, 221, 224, 240; demystifying 27;
General Assembly 26; Gulf War and
21, 162, 224, 226; "humanitarian
intervention" 42, 179; instrumental use
of 178; new world order and 137;
peace forces of 7; reforming/
transforming 223–35; Security Council
25, 50, 86, 92, 173, 217, 230–1, 232, 245;
Somalia and 15, 20, 127–8, 193; US
manipulation of 22, 85–6, 123
United Nations Center on Transnational
Corporations 26, 228
United Nations Charter 15, 21, 22, 27,
89–90, 102, 123, 153, 224, 226, 227, 245,
248
United Nations Conference on the
Environment *see* Earth Summit
1992
United Nations Conference on Population
and Development (1994) 195
United Nations Conference on Trade and
Development (UNCTAD) 26, 176,
229
United Nations Development Program
(UNDP) 52, 202; Human
Development Reports 26, 56, 202–3,
228–9, 230, 232
United Nations Educational, Scientific and
Cultural Organization (UNESCO) 26
United Nations Summit for Social
Development 204
United States: bipolarity, collapse of 44,
49, 137; capital punishment in 117;
economic decline of 49; as global
leader 21; Gulf War and 21, 117,
226; *see also* Gulf War; homelessness
in 54; income distribution in 58–9;
isolationism 39, 40; Los Angeles riots
1992 20, 59, 95; militarism 143;

Nicaragua and   33, 90, 91, 115, 153;
   North American Worker-to-Worker
   Network   94; nuclear weapons   31;
   Panama, intervention in   34, 115, 153;
   poverty in   130; realism and   39, 42;
   security and   135; as sole surviving
   superpower   49; Somalia and   20,
   127–8, 193; UN, manipulation of   22,
   85–6, 123; unemployment in   130;
   violence in   73
Universal Declaration of Human Rights
   (1948)   108, 126, 183, 184–5, 186, 187,
   252
untouchability: in India   5; in Japan   64
urbanization   62, 194–5
Urquhart, Brian   271n, 272n

Vattel, Emmerich de   88
Vernon, Raymond   266n
Vietnam   188
Vietnam War   15, 23, 51
violence: against women   140; civil   97;
   cultural celebration of   166; defensive
   127; social   73–4; structural   73, 165;
   in television and film   166; territorial
   security and   99–100; towards animals
   168; transformative   127; in US   73

Walker, R.B.J. viii, 262n, 272n, 274n
war   16, 17, 18, 55, 139; abolishing   244–6;
   aggressive, criminalization of   246;
   collectivization of   151–2; containment
   163–4; fascination with   163; Gulf War
   see Gulf War; individual accountability
   246–7; international law and   135; just
   war doctrine   157; media treatment of
   163; nuclear, obsolescence of   15, 30;
   "the other" and   73; realism and   42,
   80; role in maintaining status quo   11,
   152; security and   11, 137; taming of
   243–4; war system   9, 70;   see also
   militarism
war crimes: in Bosnia   67, 99; individual
   accountability   246–7; Nuremberg
   Principles   103, 123, 236–7, 246–7;
   tribunals   123, 246, 247
Watkins, Kevin   267n
weak states   212–15, 224

weapons: biological/chemical   159; high
   technology   21, 23; of mass destruction
   156, 159; nuclear   see nuclear weapons
Weldon, Fay   66
welfare capitalism   19, 96, 110
Wendt, Alexander   261n
Weston, Burns H.   267n
whales: conservation of   169
Wilson, Woodrow   39, 247
women: abuse within marriage   64;
   commodification of   68; death in
   childbirth   56; development and
   201–2; international relations and   93;
   in Iran   117; marital rape   64;
   maternal well-being   56; patriarchy and
   see patriarchy; pregnancy   56; pressures
   on   5; rape   64, 140; reproductive
   rights   5, 62, 117, 196; South
   Commission and   201–2; transnational
   networks   199; violence against   140
work: right to   52, 185
World Bank   14, 77, 92, 188, 206, 228;
   development and   176; indebtedness
   and   114; structural adjustment
   programs   104
World Court   32, 220, 226, 233–5, 249;
   Advisory Opinions   233, 234; authority
   of   7; independence of   33; US anti-
   Sandinista policies   33, 235
World Court Project   159, 234
World Game Institute   190
world government   6–8
world market   see market
World Order Models Project (WOMP) vii,
   viii, ix, 3, 159, 208, 229–30
World Summit for Children   1990   192
Wright, Susan   265n

Yalta system   53
Yeltsin, Boris   27, 107, 109, 139, 220, 221
Yugoslavia   30, 97; break-up of   20, 71–2,
   138; sovereignty and   83–4; as weak
   state   213;   see also Bosnia; Croatia;
   Herzegovina; Slovenia

Zaire   129, 164
Zhirinovsky, Vladimir   174
Zhou En Lai   194
Zimbabwe: nuclear weapons and   32